Heart of Fire: A Novel of the Ancient Olympics

Copyright © 2016 by Adam Alexander Haviaras

Eagles and Dragons Publishing, Stratford, Ontario, Canada

All Rights Reserved.

The use of any part of this publication, with the exception of short excerpts for the purposes of book reviews, without the written consent of the author is an infringement of copyright law.

ISBN: 978-1-988309-03-3

Paperback Edition

Cover design by Eagles and Dragons Publishing

*Please note: To enhance the reader's experience, there is a glossary of Greek words at the back of this book.

Praise for Eagles and Dragons Publishing and author, Adam Alexander Haviaras...

Historic Novel Society:

"...Haviaras handles it all with smooth skill. The world of third-century Rome—both the city and its African outposts—is colourfully vivid here, and Haviaras manages to invest even his secondary and tertiary characters with believable, three-dimensional humanity."

Amazon Readers:

"Graphic, uncompromising and honest... A novel of heroic men and the truth of the uncompromising horror of close combat total war..."

"Raw and unswerving in war and peace... New author to me but ranks along side Ben Kane and Simon Scarrow. The attention to detail and all the gory details are inspiring and the author doesn't invite you into the book he drags you by the nasal hairs into the world of Roman life sweat, tears, blood, guts and sheer heroism. Well worth a night's reading because once started it's hard to put down."

"Historical fiction at its best! ... if you like your historical fiction to be an education as well as a fun read, this is the book for you!"

"Loved this book! I'm an avid fan of Ancient Rome and this story is, perhaps, one of the best I've ever read."

"An outstanding and compelling novel!"

"I would add this author to some of the great historical writers such as Conn Iggulden, Simon Scarrow and David

Gemmell. The characters were described in such a way that it was easy to picture them as if they were real and have lived in the past, the book flowed with an ease that any reader, novice to advanced can enjoy and become fully immersed..."

"One in a series of tales which would rank them alongside Bernard Cornwell, Simon Scarrow, Robert Ludlum, James Boschert and others of their ilk. The story and character development and the pacing of the exciting military actions frankly are superb and edge of your seat! The historical environment and settings have been well researched to make the story lines so very believable!! I can hardly wait for what I hope will be many sequels! If you enjoy Roman historical fiction, you do not want to miss this series!"

Goodreads:

"... a very entertaining read; Haviaras has both a fluid writing style, and a good eye for historical detail, and explores in far more detail the faith of the average Roman than do most authors."

Sign-up for the Eagles and Dragons Publishing Newsletter and get a FREE BOOK today.

Subscribers get first access to new releases, special offers, and much more.

Go to:
www.eaglesanddragonspublishing.com

For my Father
Whose toil was great

Για τον πατέρα μου
του οποίου ο μόχθος ήταν μεγάλος

HEART OF FIRE

A Novel of the Ancient Olympics

ADAM ALEXANDER HAVIARAS

There can be no victory without sacrifice…

Chapter One

THE SACRED TRUCE

Η Ιερή Εκεχειρία

3 96 B.C.

THE SHIELD WALL BEGAN TO BREAK ALMOST RIGHT AWAY, AND the bragging between the two forces quickly turned to screaming as the blood flowed from the first wounds. On the edge of Ares' Dancing Floor, near Eleutherai, yet another battle had broken out.

It was the month of Thargelion, and men had already partly sated their winter's bloodlust. However, in recent years, when the memories of past alliances and betrayals still festered, when city-states still jingled purses before fighting men to gain the upper hand over their neighbours, peace was a rare thing, and bloody skirmishes the norm.

"Push forward!" yelled Stefanos, son of Talos, pentekonter on the right wing of the shield wall of Arkadian and Achaean troops. "Now!" he ordered, as he drove the three-meter shaft of his ash doru into the face of one of the men in front of him, pulling it back out of the gore for another strike. One of his opponent's spears slammed into the face of his hoplon shield, but it took the impact, the bronze and oak his constant protection over the years.

"Come on, peacock!" his opponent yelled, his voice a panting echo inside his bronze helmet as he thrust once more at the image of a lone peacock feather upon the hoplon. "We're in the land of Ares now, not of Hera!"

Stefanos ignored the personal insult to his goddess, and focussed on breaking the enemy wall.

"Forward! One!" he ordered, and the right wing pushed, their shields locked perfectly, their steps in concert. "Two!" They pushed again, the voices of the men before them cracking as they stumbled backward over the rocky terrain. "Three!"

The wall of spears and shields thrust forward one more time and the enemy's left buckled like a ship's hull, groaning as it breaks over the rocks.

"We've got them!" yelled Kratos, the man on Stefanos' left.

"Let's finish this!" added the Spartan, Pollux, on Stefanos' right. "I'm hungry!" he laughed as his red cloak rippled behind him.

With one more thrust, Stefanos drove the leaf-shaped blade of his spear up into the helmet of the man who had insulted him, and then gave the order, "Wheel to the left!"

The pentekostys turned in to hit the centre of their opponents' line, and then the real butchery started as infantry were caught between the shield walls of the centre and right as if between Scylla and Caribdis.

Stefanos, son of Talos began to laugh as the blood poured over his spear's shaft, and he stepped over the dropped hoplons of the fleeing men before him. The solid wall of the seventy two men under him gave him joy, even though some of them had fallen; he had only just met most of them, but the men he had known before still stood, the promachoi whom he commanded on that day.

"Running cowards!" Pollux yelled as he watched more of their opponents turn and run.

"They don't deserve to stand in a shield wall!" yelled Stefanos. "Finish them!" he yelled as his doru struck in and out of the bodies of men like an enraged viper with infinite venom.

Then, the sound of drums rang out over the field, the signal for an immediate halt.

"Why are we stopping?" Stefanos stood, his eyes on the remaining enemies several feet away as he turned to peer along the broken lines of bleeding, sweating, and heaving warriors.

"It's the Eleans!" someone called out from the next pentekostys, lowering his hoplon and spear, and pushing back his helmet.

Stefanos stepped out of the line and stared at the approaching line of white-clad priests and heralds who walked without fear between the two armies, their himations staining with blood and offal as they walked among the dead and dying.

"The Sacred Truce is declared!" said the lead herald, his voice high and clear above the carnage. "All hostilities are against the Gods' will, and must cease. Those competing in the Games must make their way to Olympia by the month of Skirophorion if they wish to win eternal glory. The Sacred Truce is declared!"

Stefanos stood his ground, barring the herald's way, his chest rising and falling calmly, his brown and green linothorax splattered with blood. He pushed his bronze corinthian helmet back on his head and stared at the herald and priests.

"You have a lot of nerve stepping in like this. We were almost finished," Stefanos hissed.

"No," the Elean herald said calmly. "You are finished. Now."

Stefanos leaned into the man with his blood-spattered hoplon, pushing him into the priest behind him.

"Stefanos! Let them pass! The battle is over!" yelled the lochagos from the centre of the line. "That's an order, soldier!"

Both sides stared in silence as Stefanos stood his ground, but after a few moments, the rage was leeching out of his veins.

"Come, Stefanos," came the voices of Kratos and Pollux beside him now, their hands on his shoulders pulling him gently out of the way. "It's over. Another victory."

Stefanos looked up at the sun, where its rays struck out from behind a cloud above the distant hills, and nodded as the herald and priests moved away from the battle, their duty done, to announce the Sacred Truce of the Olympic Games in other parts of war-torn Greece.

As the afternoon sun beat down on the gathering of men and carrion crows, both sides began to collect their dead and wounded from the field.

It had been an unplanned confrontation coming out of an accidental meeting of mercenaries, and a patrol of Theban and Attic allies. The cost had been great, but for the mercenaries on both sides, it had been another job, the last for a few months.

As the lochagoi made lists of the dead, noting their native polis, or deme if they knew it, the rest of the troops continued to pick up the bodies of the fallen and lay them in bloody rows beneath their shields.

Stefanos, son of Talos was quiet as he oversaw the men of his pentekostys. The living and the dead on that plain were faces he had seen before, fought with and against, over several years. There were many new faces too, young men, boys, for whom this had been their first engagement.

"Were we ever so young?" Kratos, Stefanos' best and long-

time friend said as he came up, wiping the sweat from his brow. "Seems hard to believe."

"I suppose we were," Stefanos said. "We were also better trained."

"We had more opportunity to fight then."

"There is always a fight to be had, even during the Sacred Truce," Stefanos said, slapping Kratos on the shoulder. He stretched out his arms and rolled his head from side to side. He felt good, young and limber, despite his forty years. All of the war over the past twenty one years, including the march on foot back from the heart of Persia, had taught Stefanos and Kratos that life was meant to be taken, and lived, that kings and politicians, tyrants and philosophers did not give a damn about soldiers. The latter were pawns in the great game, and if one was going to play the game, he might as well get paid well for it.

It had been some years since they had seen their native Argos. They had actually decided that summer that they would finally return to see their families, Stefanos to see his father, Talos, the bronze smith, and his sister Cleo, a priestess of Hera at the Heraion of Argos.

Kratos longed to see his mother, and the three sisters he had left behind, beautiful women who were as tall and lean as their older brother, and were more than a match for any man. It still chafed at Kratos, the way that Stefanos had moved from one to the other of his sisters in the course of one hot Argive summer all those years ago, but the fact that they were still the best of friends and none of the girls hated Stefanos showed how very close they were.

"You two still heading back to Argos?" Pollux said to them as he heaved the body of a fallen warrior by himself and tossed it onto the growing pile of dead, swishing away a swarm of flies with the hem of his red cloak.

Pollux had met the two older men on the march back from Persia. He threw his lot in with them, and they had been close ever since. Pollux was a Spartan through and through, and the mercenary life suited him, filled a void that was left when there were no more battles to fight. Only Sparta ever took precedence. He turned down any job that would pit him against his fellow Lacedaemonians.

Stefanos and Kratos had no such qualms about fighting against the men of their own city.

Pollux leaned his shield against the trunk of a nearby olive tree and removed his helmet, tying his curly black hair back with a leather thong. "I'll probably head back to Sparta," he said. "King Agesilaus is still in Persia, and Lysander has been sent back to Sparta to be kept out of the fight. Might be there's some opportunity there..." he mused.

"Don't get caught up in the politics, Pollux. Bad for business, you know," Kratos said.

"We're all caught up in politics," Kratos said. "It's just that Spartan politics is more fun!" he slammed his fist on the face of his hoplon which was decorated with two serpents facing each other, fangs bared.

"You three!" came the harsh voice of their Achaean lochagos. "How about you help us dig the burial mounds so we can all get out of here?"

Stefanos stood up and walked over to the man, whose bushy, greying beard sprouted out to tickle the top of his muscled cuirass.

"We're done here," Stefanos said. "We'll take our pay now."

The man reddened in the face. "What do you mean you're 'done here'? No one's done here until I say. I have rank."

"And we'll have the money you owe us for the last week," Kratos added.

"Fucking mercenaries. Don't you give a damn about anyone but yourselves? We need to honour our fallen brothers."

"They're not my brothers," Stefanos said. "And yes, we do care about more than ourselves." He put his fingers to his chin. "We care about food, wine... women... Maybe boys in his case," Stefanos nodded toward Pollux who shrugged. "Did I miss anything?" he asked Kratos.

"No, I think that about covers it."

"Well, you're not getting a stater until those bodies are properly honoured," the lochagos said. "Then you'll get your pay."

Stefanos' fist flung out so quickly that the man had no time to react and was on the ground before he knew what had happened. When he looked up through the daze of flashing light, he could see Stefanos holding the pouch of coins that he had been carrying at his waist.

"This should about cover it, I think," Stefanos said. "Next time, just pay right away and save yourself the headache."

The three of them walked back to the group of mercenaries they had been with and distributed the pay that was owed. Once that was done, they hoisted their shields and spears, and began the long march through Megara and back into the Peloponnese, leaving the cities to clean up their own mess.

Chapter Two

MEMORIES IN BRONZE

Αναμνήσεις σε Χαλκό

Megara was choked with a long file of warriors heading for the Peloponnese and the sanctuary of Olympia, or back to their native villages or polei for the period of the Sacred Truce. Most were in a jovial mood, and one would have thought that they had not spent the last few years plunging both spear and blade into the bodies of their fellow Greeks.

Stefanos, Kratos, and Pollux travelled without worry, the three hoplites walking over the rocky mountains with the islands of Salamis and Aegina set in a sparkling blue sea to the south. They passed by Kakia Scala where a great monster was said to have always lurked in wait for travellers, to apprehend and devour them before tossing their bones down the cliffs into the sea. Both Kratos and Pollux's grips on the shafts of their spears lessened as they passed safely through.

As their sandalled feet trod through beds of spring flowers of purple, red, and yellow, Stefanos shook his head at the light moods of all the travellers around them.

They would trade it all, the shield wall, the blood, the thrill of an enemy kill, for games. How can they so easily forget? he wondered.

The truth was that Stefanos, son of Talos had only known war since the age of nineteen when the Spartans attacked Argos at the battle of Hysiae, in the aftermath of their victory at Mantinea. Despite the horrors he had witnessed, including the death of many friends and neighbours, Stefanos had found he excelled in war, and the shield wall of the phalanx became his home.

But he did not remain in Argos. The elite force of the Argive Thousand had been, at the time, a close-knit group of men who seemed to spit at the efforts of anyone outside their circles, even if they had proved themselves worthy of the task.

Stefanos' family began to experience hard financial times after the death of his mother, Hermia, a priestess of Hera at the Heraion of Argos, and so he chose the mercenary's way of life. His father had been unable then, to carry out the bronze commissions that were coming his way, epinikion works among them, due to the sadness lodged deep in his creative heart.

Stefanos enjoyed the mercenary life, the independence of it, though it broke his father's heart that his only son had turned his back on the craft that he so revered and loved. Talos had never been the same since, and though he did begin to work again, his bronzes became more pained, and sinister, displaying the darker side of Eris and ponos, the strife and toil that were every man's lot in life.

Stefanos had competed in some of the crown games, and had been victorious in the javelin, hoplitodromos, and boxing at both Isthmia and Nemea, but he had never stayed for the victory feasts that came after the crowning. When the pine, and wild celery of Isthmia and Nemea had been placed upon his head, he had left the sanctuaries, his point made, offered his rewards to Hera at the temple where his mother had spent most of her life, and then got on with his own.

Sitting around a camp fire the night before they came out

of the mountains of Megara and into Isthmia, Stefanos, Kratos, and Pollux shared freshly-cooked meat and memories of recent battles.

The constellations in the cool night sky looked down on them as they leaned against a grouping of massive boulders that protected their backs. Each man's hoplon, doru, and xiphos were beside him, even though most of the travellers that night would not have dared to set upon three experienced hoplites of Argos and Sparta.

"How long since you've both been home?" Pollux asked as he tore into a hunk of steaming goat meat fresh off the spit.

"Six years," Stefanos said casually, as he ate.

"Long time."

"What about you, Pollux?" Kratos asked. "When was the last time you saw Sparta?"

"I see Sparta every time I stand in the phalanx shield wall," he said, smiling. "I've spent all my time with you amateurs, keeping you alive!" he laughed, his voice echoing off of the rocks about them, Stefanos and Kratos joining in. "In truth, I long to see the Eurotas valley again, to climb Taygetos and smell the fresh mountain air of my home, but I don't know how long I'll stay. Things are heating up with the Persian bastards again, so there might be a good bit of work to be done for Sparta. I assume you two would like to be a part of that should the opportunity arise?"

"You know us better than to ask a question like that," Stefanos said, tossing a bone into the coals of the fire and sending sparks into the night air.

"Actually, I was considering taking part in the Olympiad," Kratos said, causing the other two to look up at him.

"Really?" Pollux asked.

"Yes," Kratos straightened. "We're not getting any younger and, well, I think I could compete in the pentathlon. What better way to honour the Gods than to take all that I've learned on the field of Ares and win glory before the eyes of Zeus himself?"

Pollux nodded knowingly at Kratos, his pious Spartan side always seeing the right in honouring the Gods, but Stefanos shook his head.

"Why waste time at Olympia, Kratos? If King Agesilaus is waging war against the Persians in Ionia, then there will be work to be had, no? The Sacred Truce doesn't apply to Persians." Stefanos stopped eating and stared at his best friend. "Olympia is supposed to be hot and stinking during the Games. Why would you want to pack it in with all those crowds?"

"Why wouldn't I?" Kratos said. "If this is my last chance... I could die on the battlefield tomorrow, or the day or year after that. I don't want my legacy to be blood, and sacks of coin. I want to give some kind of glory to my family's name."

"You've never told me any of this," Stefanos said.

"I've been thinking about it the last few days. It makes sense." Kratos shrugged.

"Sense?" Stefanos said out loud.

"Makes sense to me," Pollux said. "What does it matter? If Herakles began the games to honour his father, that seems right enough."

"And, if I were to win, then any man in Argos would willingly betroth his daughter to me. I could finally have a family."

"You're both mad. A family?" Stefanos stood. "The fighting never stops, you know."

"True," agreed Pollux, "but the Gods are more important than butchery in the shield wall, and the Gods like the Games."

Stefanos turned from the camp fire, picked up his doru, and disappeared into the darkness beyond the light of the fire.

Kratos jumped up to go after him, but Pollux stayed him.

"Let him be. You know how he's always in his head. This is one of those times." They sat back down to finish eating.

Stefanos walked until he came to a rock outcrop jutting out over the clifftops to the sea below. The light of the moon and stars shone on the black depths and he stared at them, his spear across his shoulders, his arms up to hang from it.

He chided himself for being nervous to return to Argos, of seeing his sister Cleo, and his father. The last time he had been home, he had argued with Talos and they had parted with angry words. He loved his father dearly, admired his work, but he also resented Talos' lack of understanding or acceptance of his chosen life, a life that he had been forced into by circumstance and the Gods' design.

Seeing Cleo again worried him even more. The last time he had been in Argos, he had changed her life, and though he was sure it had been for the better, he feared that she did not agree with that sentiment.

Ocnus, son of Nemos, had always been a lying cheat, and cruel beyond measure. When Stefanos had returned to Argos after another campaign in Boeotia to find that Ocnus had made an offer to Talos for Cleo's hand in marriage, he had talked his father out of it, and at the same time, denied Cleo a family of her own.

The dowry offer had included, among other things, the bronze smithing business and family lands. Stefanos knew that Ocnus would treat Cleo like a slave, that he only cared for the profits in bronze and the selling of their lands.

Stefanos' father had told him at the time that he was going to accept Ocnus' offer because there was no chance that Stefanos himself would ever return to Argos to head the family, and because he was getting old.

But Stefanos had not wanted to see his father's artistic legacy, much as he did not want to be a part of it, turned over to a fiend like Ocnus who would transform it into a base smelting business, cranking out ingots instead of works of art. He did not see himself as a bronze smith, but he certainly could see the beauty in what his father created, even though he had never told him as much.

When Talos agreed to call off the betrothal, Ocnus went on a rant against their family in the Agora. It was then that

Stefanos approached him with witnesses, prodded him into attacking first, and then pounded his face into a pulp until he took back the things he had said.

The next day, Cleo, publicly humiliated, went into service at the temple of Hera.

Stefanos loved his father and sister, but the choices he had made, choices he had stood by, had caused them great pain. He had not been there for them, and the guilt, much as he hated it, was crushing him the closer he came to Argos.

Stefanos took a last look at the night sky, at Centaurus glinting down at him, and turned to go back to the fire and his friends.

As they came into Isthmia the following day, the welcome scents of pine and the salt-sea filled their nostrils.

Most of the travellers along the road carried on west to head over the mountains of Arkadia to Olympia, in Ellis, but Stefanos, Kratos, and Pollux turned south west toward the sanctuary at Nemea. Here, at the long altar before the temple of Zeus, they made offerings to the Protector of Travellers for helping them come this far, and asked that they might gain their destinations without worry.

With the sheep's blood still fresh on his hands, Pollux turned to Stefanos and Kratos. "I guess this is farewell for now, brothers."

The two men embraced their Spartan compatriot, not a little moved to see their warlike triad broken for a time.

"May the Gods guide us to you again soon," Kratos said.

"If they desire it," Pollux said plainly, "I'll see you. And I'll send word if there is room in the mercenary shield wall of Sparta."

"Yes, do, my friend," Stefanos said. "And forgive my glumness yesterday. Peace time makes me itchy."

"Sometimes I wonder if you're more Spartan than I am," Pollux laughed. He then turned to Kratos. "Good luck in the

Games. May the Gods grant you victory, and Nike's crown rest lightly on your brow."

With those parting words, Pollux hoisted his hoplon, satchel, and doru, and turned in the direction of Tegea, and then Sparta.

"I'm always sad to see that red cloak fade away," Stefanos said as he watched Pollux march down the narrow track away from the sanctuary.

"Me too," Kratos said, putting his hand on Stefanos' shoulder. "So, you ready to go home?"

"No. But let's go anyway."

Together, they took the Argos road directly to the south, their hoplons on their backs, and their spears pointing the way home.

"Six years..." Stefanos mused. "I wonder how your sisters are."

"Don't even think about it!"

THE NEXT DAY, WHEN THE PLAIN OF ARGOS OPENED UP BEFORE their eyes, both men stopped to look at it, quietly leaning on their spears in the fading light. The city was coloured by a pink sunset over the mountains to the West, and the smoke from the sanctuaries of Hera, Athena, Apollo and Aphrodite rose up over the city giving it a dream-like countenance.

High on the hill of Larisa, south west of the sanctuaries of the Aspis, the heads of sentries could be spotted along the fortifications where the Argive Thousand stood watch over the plains to the south and west, ever-ready to meet an attack by Argos' enemies.

"Looks the same as ever," Kratos said.

"Looks can be deceiving."

"They're your family, Stefanos. You've provided for them when they were in need, and whether Cleo likes it or not, you did her a favour. She's always looked up to you, my friend."

Stefanos nodded, unconvinced. "Maybe I can eat with your family tonight, and see mine tomorrow morning?"

"I don't think so," Kratos said, no humour in his voice this time as they continued on their way toward the city walls.

They entered Argos through the north gate, to the left of the great theatre, where the guards stopped them.

"What business do you have in Argos?" said the file leader.

"We're Argives," Stefanos said, eyeing the group of ten men.

"We've been fighting abroad. Just back from Eleutherai," Kratos added. "I'm Kratos, son of Lichas, and this is Stefanos, son of Talos. The Sacred Truce is on, so we've come home before heading to the Games."

Stefanos shot a look at Kratos, but said nothing. He could feel himself getting impatient.

"Mercenaries, eh?" the file leader said. "We don't need any trouble within the city walls. We've had enough outside of them."

"We won't be fighting in our family homes, if that's what you're worried about," Stefanos said. "Can we pass? We're citizens. You can't bar our entry."

"I can have your weapons though," the man said.

Stefanos stared at him and stepped forward to look him in the eye. "You've no need to do that, friend."

There was a lingering silence as Kratos and the other guards looked at the file leader and Stefanos.

"No need. You may enter. Welcome home," he said, his voice dripping with sarcasm.

Stefanos pushed past him and beneath the massive gate house, Kratos following.

"Your propensity for making friends never ceases to amaze me," Kratos said as they made their way to the agora through which they needed to pass to get to the neighbourhood where their families lived on the southern end of the city.

"They've no right to treat Argive citizens that way."

"No? Even though we've raised arms against Argos' allies?"

Despite the onset of evening, the city streets were full of citizens, and the agora filled with groups of men in heated discussion about everything from politics and war, to art, theatre, and the latest bronze sculptor to make a name for himself.

Stefanos and Kratos looked around at the familiar alcoves where they had run rampant as boys, the colonnades where they had played hide-and-seek, and the bouleuterion where they had first heard the news that Argos was officially at war with Sparta whose forces were making their way toward Hysiae.

The two armed mercenaries were met with not a few looks of anger and disgust as they made their way through the crowds. People cleared a way for them, some out of fear, others out of intense dislike, but Stefanos was not bothered. It made their progress that much easier.

When they reached the southern end of the agora, a group of men did stand in their way and Stefanos made directly for them.

"Here we go," he said to Kratos, who loosened the grip on his spear shaft. "Ocnus! Is that you?"

The group of five men stepped forward. Their leader, Ocnus son of Nemos, stood there in the uniform of the Argive Thousand, decked out in a matching blue and white thorax and cloak.

"What are you doing here?" Ocnus demanded.

"I live here," Stefanos said. "I see the Thousand's standards have dropped drastically."

Ocnus took a step forward, but Stefanos did not budge. Ocnus was a big man, but lacked the strength and confidence that Stefanos possessed, even though he feigned as much.

"I also see your own standards are the same," Stefanos

said, looking beyond Ocnus to the same four men that had always backed him up, Krikor, Biton, Ampyx, and Glaucus. "Boys," Stefanos nodded. "Still buggering this one?"

"Listen to me, you mercenary piece of shit!" Ocnus grabbed Stefanos' thorax and shook. "Things are different now, and you owe me."

"Owe you?"

"Yes."

"Maybe you're right," Stefanos said. "Here's payment with interest for laying your hands on me just now." Before Ocnus could react, Stefanos' head slammed into his face, crushing his nose and sending him back into his friends' arms as he howled. "I thought I'd reset it for you. I did a botch job last time."

Kratos laughed uneasily as people began to gather and stare at them. "Let him be, Stefanos. He's part of the elite guard now. He deserves our respect."

The two men laughed and continued on their way, but not before Ocnus stood up again, holding his bleeding nose to yell at them.

"Hope you enjoy your homecoming! The Gods have a sense of humour!"

Stefanos and Kratos continued on their way, but Ocnus' words thrust a sliver of dread into Stefanos' thoughts.

STEFANOS ARRIVED AT THE DOOR OF HIS FAMILY'S MODEST home where he stood beside the bronze Herm that warded off evil and guarded the home. He found he could not open the door immediately, and so he stood there, his hand fidgeting with the handles of his hoplon's grip and the shaft of his doru.

Some warrior... he chided himself. *I can face down elite infantry or Persian cavalry, but can't even knock on the door of my childhood home...*

Shaking his head, and laughing a little at himself, Stefanos raised his hand to knock on the door, but as he did so, it opened and out came a doctor in a rough-spun Ionic chiton. Stefanos stepped back, surprised, to allow the doctor through.

"Good evening," the doctor said, nodding and moving past Stefanos with his case to walk down the street.

As the door was closing, Stefanos put his foot in and pushed through.

"Doctor, did you forget some...thing..." a tired voice said, trailing off.

Cleo gasped and took a step back as her brother appeared before her, fully armed and armoured, as he had been the last time he had come into their home, six years before. Her hand shook as it covered her mouth, and tears began to pool at the corners of her brown eyes.

"Cleo. What's going on?" He looked at her, his heart tightening. She looked pale and tired, her once-shiny black hair gone to grey, even though she was three years younger than him. He leaned his spear and shield against the back of the door, and reached out to her.

Her arms wrapped quickly about his neck and she held him tightly, despite his thorax, as emotions swept through them both in the fading light of the small courtyard.

After a few moments, he held her gently at arm's length and looked into her eyes. "Cleo, what's happened? Why aren't you at the Heraion?"

Cleo nodded, wiped the tears at the corners of her eyes and spoke. "Father is dying, Stefanos. The Gods will take him soon."

"Dying?"

She nodded. "It is good Zeus and Hera have brought you home safely to you family." She began to walk beneath the small olive tree that stood in the middle of the dirt courtyard, and made for the open door that led into the stone house. "He'll want to see you..." she said as she disappeared inside.

Stefanos stood there for a few moments, trying to register all that was happening, afraid of what he might find beyond the door of his childhood home - a smell of death, and the angry words of a dying man? He was not sure he wanted to deal with that, but picked up his shield and spear and walked slowly after her, the branches of the olive tree brushing his hair lightly as he passed beneath it. He glanced at the bronze statue of the the goddess Hera which stood at the far end of the yard, beneath an arch of bougainvillea, and entered the house.

It was dark inside, but for a few oil lamps. The kitchen smelled strongly of herbs and the long table to one side was empty, except for a couple of wooden bowls with the remains of half-eaten barley broth, a plate with crumbs of bread, and a pitcher of water with a clay cup.

Stefanos leaned his doru and hoplon in a corner, put down his satchel and looked at Cleo. "Where is the slave that we hired last time I was here? She was supposed to help."

"I sold her when father became ill and could not work anymore," Cleo said, her voice harder now, drained of the shock and sadness of minutes before. Now she turned on her brother with hard, chiding eyes. "Six years, Stefanos... Six years!"

"It's as it has always been," he answered peevishly.

"Yes, but you could have stopped in Argos once in while. Even I know the fighting stops in the months of Gamelion, Anthesterion, and Elaphebolion."

"It doesn't stop for a mercenary. People don't stop having enemies in the winter months."

"Are you a common thug now, wagging your spear to collect overdue rents for others?"

"Mind your tongue, woman. I didn't come home to be chided."

"You didn't come to see our father dying either, did you? But you will."

Stefanos was silent. He did not want to fight with her. Not now. Not ever. But it seemed they would. "I guess you're still angry with me?"

Cleo looked up from the pot she was stirring above the fire and shook her head. "No. Of course not. Not for that."

"Are you sure? I just saw Ocnus in the street. He's still raging over it."

"The Gods know you did me a favour, exposing him to father. I have a good life, serving the goddess. I have food, shelter, and a means of helping others. It can be difficult, but it is right and destined."

"And that is your toil?" Stefanos said softly.

"Yes." Cleo nodded, resigned and determined at once, and walked over to her brother to lay the palm of her hand upon his rough, sun-darkened cheek. "You should go in and see him. But be quiet, and gentle. I don't want him over-excited."

Stefanos stared down the small corridor that led to their father's room. It was dark, but for the flickering of a single lamp which hung from the ceiling mid-way. Without another word, he walked toward the open, olive wood door and entered.

The room was full of the smoke from incense burning at a small shrine where statues of the Gods, Apollo, Asclepius, Igeia, and Hera peered from the smoke toward the narrow bed in the corner of the room.

Stefanos gasped as he laid his eyes upon his father, Talos, and had to lean against the wall to support himself.

The man who had once had hard, muscled limbs like Haephestos himself now lay there weak and white, his skin loose upon his bones, his once-kind, creative, and eager face now contorted and angry, even in sleep. His body shuddered with some sort of pain, but Stefanos wondered if it was not the regret and tortured dreams that the Gods felt compelled to send the aged as they walked towards the banks of the black river.

A wave of intense sadness swept through Stefanos, and he moved toward the bed to kneel beside Talos. He gripped the frail, calloused hand with his own, and leaned forward.

"Father?" he whispered. "Father, it's me. Stefanos. I'm here."

For a moment there was no reaction and if he had not seen the shuddering breath rising and falling in his father's chest, Stefanos would have thought him dead.

"All will be well, Father. I'm here. I can help."

The frail hand gripped Stefanos' suddenly, and Talos' rheumy eyes blinked open and closed a few times before they searched for the source of the voice and found it. They focussed on Stefanos beneath creased brows, and the hand pulled away.

"Leave me..." Talos croaked, before turning onto his side, his back to his son.

"Father, please. I'm home. I wish to make peace with you and see you well again. I didn't know..."

"You didn't care..." Talos accused. "Leave me. I need to rest."

Stefanos stood up, dizzy from the smell of dying that hung in the small room, and turned to make his way out. In the doorway, he turned back. "I'll be in the other room with Cleo if you need anything."

When he came back into the kitchen, he sat down to a bowl of steaming broth and a plate of bread and cheese which Cleo had set out for him. A small cup of wine had also been put out, which Stefanos took right away, tipping a little onto the floor before drinking.

"How long has he been like this?"

"Two months," Cleo said, sitting down opposite her brother. "He has good days and bad days. Today was a bad one. He's had more of those lately. But tomorrow, once he's registered that you've returned, I think we'll find he has a lot to say...and little time to say it in."

"What does the doctor say?"

"Just that it's the Gods' will, his time to go. The truth is that I think father has lost his will to go on. The best we can hope for is for you two to make peace so that he can go into the Afterlife with a measure of joy in his heart."

She sighed, and seemed to deflate before Stefanos' eyes. It was then that he realized the fullness of her despair, her loneliness, the burden he had left her with while he was away fighting on foreign fields.

"I'm sorry you've had to deal with this, but I can't apologize for following the path that the Gods have set before me."

Her stare was fierce, but only for a moment. Then resignation overtook her anger and frustration, the resentment she had stored away for the brother she had once loved and honoured above all others.

"But, I will make peace with him, whatever it takes," he said, a part of him knowing he would regret it. "How long do you have leave from the Heraion?"

"As long as it takes. The head priestess is very accommodating."

"Because of Mother?" he asked, and Cleo nodded.

Their mother, Hermia, had been one of the the most devout priestesses of the Heraion, a woman whom the goddess seemed to bless every day with skill and foresight, at least until the day she took her.

Stefanos and Cleo were silent, each staring at the table, alone with their own ghosts for a few moments. Then Stefanos stood and went to his satchel which he had deposited near the doorway.

"Well, this should help ease things and pay for a monument when the time comes," he said, removing a heavy leather purse from the satchel and dropping it on the table with a thud."

Cleo nodded but did not smile. "That will help." After a few moments, she rose from her chair. "I'll go and check on him."

Stefanos watched his sister go back down the dark hall to their father's room. "Gods help me in this."

After a few minutes, he finished the last of his broth,

bread, and cheese and leaned on the table, his eyes fixated on the fire. He felt warm all of a sudden and rose to unstrap the thorax which he had not taken off, so accustomed was he to wearing it at all times.

He laid it and his xiphos on the floor beside his satchel, hoplon, and doru. After unstrapping his greaves, Stefanos, now cooler in his chiton, went outside into the courtyard.

The stars were out, and as bright as he remembered from beneath the olive tree where he had sat so many years as a youth, contemplating his choices as every young man is bound to do in the life given him by the Gods. With his back to the trunk of the tree, Stefanos looked up at that night sky, the noise of Argos drowned out by thoughts of what he might say to his father the following day, if he yet lived, and what his father would say to him, if he chose to speak to him.

WHEN THE COCK CROWED IN THE YARD THE FOLLOWING morning, Stefanos was still abed, a single ray of sunlight angling its way into his plain room to light his face. The room felt stuffy after so many nights in the open air, lonely after countless nights in the arms of numerous women. He felt an urge for such a woman then, but suppressed it when he remembered where he was, and the situation in which he found himself. He sat on the edge of the small bed, rubbing his eyes and short beard. After relieving himself in the clay chamber pot, he strapped on his sandals and went out of the room.

Cleo greeted him in the kitchen, having laid out a bowl of beans, hard bread, and a cup of water.

"He's feeling better today," she said without preamble.

"Will he see me?" Stefanos asked.

"What do you think?" Cleo answered, watching as her brother began to eat and drink. "All I ask is that you don't upset him overmuch. Remember the man he was before mother passed, if you can."

Stefanos' mind ran over images of his father's workshop then, of beautiful bronzes in various stages of creation, the sweet gleam of the shaped metal, and the sparkle in Talos' eyes as he held his son in his arms and showed him around. The time when Talos had shown the finished statue of Hera to his wife and children stood out among the dusty memories.

That statue, he had told them as their mother smiled proudly, was going to stand in the Heraion of Argos for ages. It was Talos' crowning achievement, and even as a young boy, Stefanos remembered the pride that swelled in honour of his father then.

"I'll stay calm," Stefanos said to his sister, snapping out of his reverie, and finishing his final bites of food.

A FEW MINUTES LATER, HE WAS FILLING THE DOOR FRAME OF his father's room.

Talos was lying flat, staring at the ceiling, his face pondering some thought or design such as he used to when getting a new idea for a bronze. When he realized Stefanos was standing there, his eyes darted that way angrily and he fought to push himself onto his creaking elbows, to sit up and lean against the wall at his back.

Stefanos rushed forward to offer help, but his father waved his hands away.

"If I can hammer and shape the limbs of a bronze god, I can raise myself from my bed," Talos said, his voice and breathing laboured, though there was fire in its depths, once as hot and strong as the forge which he had pumped himself.

"Father, it's good to see you," Stefanos said, kneeling beside the old man. A lump caught in his throat as he reached out for the hand again, and felt the fragility of the once-strong bones. "I'm sorry I have not been home for so long."

"We all have to deal with our choices, but I am glad that you've returned now, before it's..." a few more breaths, "...before it's too late."

"Don't talk like that," Stefanos said.

"You can't escape your fate, son. When the Gods take me, I will smile at the beauty I have left behind, the beautiful bronzes that decorate sanctuaries, homes, agorae, and shrines from Corinth to Tiryns."

Talos smiled, and seemed to grow in strength a little before Stefanos' eyes, but the latter knew that meant he would be ready to argue.

"So, tell me of your battles then. Where has...where has your life led you?"

Stefanos stared at the aged eyes, the creased brow, and the tangled white beard stained with soot from the forges.

"I've just come from a battle near Eleutherai. A small skirmish. Kratos, and our Spartan friend, Pollux, have been going from job to job for some time during the Nicia's peace and -"

"You fight during the declared peace?" his father cut in.

"Yes, well sometimes. There is always fighting."

"And will you fight during the Sacred Truce that has just been declared?" Talos eyed his son angrily then, making it obvious that such an act would be a disgrace.

"Well...perhaps. King Agesilaus is in Ionia, fighting the Persians. The Sacred Truce does not apply to them. I'm sure Kratos and I will be able to find work there. My skills as a pentekonter in the phalanx are well-regarded."

"I see. You are friends with the Spartans still. I assume the memories of their atrocities at Mantinea and Hysiae have faded then."

"No. But neither have those of the Athenians I fought with on Melos, when they slaughtered the men and enslaved the women and children." Stefanos' face grew hard and angry then, he could feel it contorting at the memory and fought down the urge to yell, or hit something, minding his sister's wish to stay calm. "I set my shield and spear in the line of the side I choose, Father, those that pay well for my skills. The Gods honour prowess on the field of Ares."

"They also punish hubris, and you are dangerously close. I

am still saddened that you decided to take up arms with the Spartans under that animal Gilippus."

"We all do things we are not proud of."

"So there is some remorse?" Talos said, coughing loudly, and reaching for the cup of water on the table beside the bed.

Stefanos reached for it quickly and held it to his father's lips, letting him catch his breath afterward.

Talos looked back at his son. "Syracuse was many years ago, and you cannot have been fighting petty battles all this time. If you were not here, where were you?"

"I went to Persia, Father."

"Persia?" Talos was surprised at this, and sat up a bit straighter. "What were you doing there?"

"We took up arms with the satrap, Cyrus, a friend to the Greeks. We were to help him take the throne for himself."

"You fought for the Persians?" Talos turned away. "Son, you have shamed yourself..."

"Against Persians, Father!" Stefanos' said, his voice angry now. "I was fighting against the Great King. Would it be better to go back to fighting Greeks on Greek soil?"

"But you just told me that you have been doing so."

"I'm not going to argue with you about this for the thousandth time," Stefanos stood and leaned against the wall, distancing himself from his father in case he felt like striking the old man.

"You lost that battle in Persia, from what I heard."

"We were betrayed, yes. When Cyrus was killed at Cunaxa, all ten thousand of us had to march out of Persia with their cavalry and archers nipping at our heels the entire way. Only thanks to the skill and determination of a good friend were we able to make the journey home."

"Another Spartan?"

"No. An Athenian, who has befriended Spartans, as I have."

Talos' weakly clenched fist pounded the bedding at his side as if he was back in his forge. "You fought with Persians, eastern animals who burned the Acropolis and artistic treasures that stood there... And you befriend Spartans, a people who don't even believe in the merits of artistic endeavour, and have no art to speak of. They deal only in death, and the belittling of their fellow human beings."

"Glory on the battlefield is enduring, Father," Stefanos stepped closer now, feeling his long-held resentment creeping into his veins like an unstoppable poison. "It is what matters most in this world. We live in a world of war, and only the strong and skilled will be remembered!" His voice was a shout now, and he could hear Cleo's hesitant footsteps in the corridor. *Let her listen!* he thought.

Talos was shaking his old head now, his eyes not fiery or angry, but sad and despairing. "What you speak of, my son, is what matters least in this world. You've turned your back on the beauties of life, and the world around you. When the battles are finished, and the crows have gorged themselves on the dead, the remnants of war are but dust in time, carnage to fade away and be forgotten. And rightly so!"

Talos took a few more breaths, his lungs sounding like they were going to burst, but he carried on, desperate to speak his mind, as if he had thought it over all the years his son was away.

"Art and beauty in the world are what matter...they are the things that endure. The likeness of a god or goddess in bronze, a hero or victor crowned by Nike, will be remembered and admired, inspire others for ages to come. Can the same be said of a man who expertly thrusts his doru into the body of another man in the front line of a phalanx in a petty skirmish on the other side of the world?"

Stefanos did not answer. He was done with the conversation, and realized he had gone too far. His father had weakened before his eyes, the effort of their debate all too much for him.

"You should rest, Father." Stefanos said, helping to lay Talos back down, even as the old man's eyes stared up into his, pleading, willing him to understand the wisdom he had imparted to him. "I'll come back to see you later, yes?"

Talos nodded and closed his eyes, his rough breathing haunting Stefanos as he walked down the corridor.

"What are you thinking?" Cleo snapped as Stefanos came into the kitchen. "Are you trying to kill him?"

"I don't know what happened." Stefanos rubbed his dark hair in frustration as if harassed by flies. "He always manages to rile me. Even now, he's full of spite."

"No he's not, Stefanos," Cleo said, her eyes meeting his as she laid a hand on his hard, scarred arm. "He cares deeply for you. He's always wanted more for you."

"You think so?"

"I know it. He hates the world that forced you into war against fellow Greeks. To our father, the bronze of beloved Hera is not his greatest creation, Stefanos... You are."

Stefanos stared at her intensely, almost despising her for having said what she did, but he held back the vitriol that came to mind.

"I need to go out," he said, moving away from her to pull a small pouch of coins, and his grey chlamys from his satchel. "I'll see you later..." he said putting on the cloak and heading out into the grey day.

Stefanos moved through the streets of Argos in a daze, the oppressive clouds pressing down on him from above as thunder rolled in the distant mountains on the other side of the gulf to the south-west.

He walked quickly, making his way to Kratos' house several blocks away. His friend always had a good ear for listening, and understood Stefanos' divergence in belief from his father. If conversation was not needed, Kratos was always up for a good bout of drinking.

When Stefanos arrived at the door, he knocked loudly. There was a shuffling inside, and then hesitation behind the door.

When it creaked open, a slave stood there, head bowed low.

"Yes?" the young man asked.

"Where is Kratos? I must speak with him."

"Master Kratos is at the gymnasium. Training..."

"Training? For what?"

"For the Olympiad, of course," came another voice as the slave stepped aside.

The door opened to reveal one of Kratos' sisters standing there in a pale, rose-coloured peplos. Her blond hair fell about her shoulders, and her eyes stared unabashedly at Stefanos.

"Anticlea?" Stefanos said, smiling. "You're looking well."

"So are you, Stefanos. What do you want with my brother?"

"To talk. Has he definitely decided to go the Games then?"

"Yes. He has."

"When will he be back? I need to speak with him." Stefanos could not help looking over Kratos' younger sister, the curve of her breasts beneath the peplos, the soft shoulders and white skin.

Anticlea smiled. "He just left, so will not be back for some time," she said. "My mother and sisters are also gone, just now, to the agora. I'm afraid you won't be able to greet them for a long time either."

Her eyes stared at his again, and he felt his loins stir as he met her gaze.

"I'm thirsty. Might I trouble you for a cup of water, Anticlea?"

"It is no trouble. But the cistern is nearly empty. We do have some honeyed wine, though. Will that suffice?"

"I remember your honeyed wine. It was always the best," Stefanos said, walking over the threshold and following her into the living area as the slave closed the door behind them.

"Anthos, you may leave us. I will fetch the wine and serve our guest," Anticlea said to the slave.

Without a word, the slave slunk away to his own room, and when the door closed in the distance, Anticlea's arms wrapped quickly around Stefanos' neck and he pulled her in close to feel her body and lips pressed against him. She laughed as he hoisted her, and carried her down the corridor to the women's chambers where her sleeping area was.

For the next couple of hours, Stefanos lost himself in Anticlea's soft body and the pleasures of Aphrodite, managing to forget all the racing thoughts that had chased him to Kratos' doorway.

He smiled to himself as he walked through the wet streets of Argos. The rain had passed, the sun was coming out, and Anticlea had been as lively as ever. He knew Kratos would be furious, but that his anger would die away within hours.

As Stefanos rounded a corner, headed for the baker's shop on the road perpendicular to one of the local gymnasia, he bumped into Kratos.

"There you are!" Stefanos said. "I was just at your place looking for you."

"I wasn't there," Kratos said suspiciously. "I was at the gymnasium."

"I know. Anticlea told me," Stefanos said, unable to hide his smile. "She made sure to share some of her expertly made honeyed wine. True nectar!"

"She what!" Kratos roared, knowing the look that crossed his friend's features.

"Pandaros!" Stefanos suddenly yelled, seeing the man Kratos had been with coming around the corner.

"Stefanos!" the man named Pandaros said, walking up to the younger man and kissing him on both cheeks. "It is good to see you," he said.

Pandaros, a former victor at the Pythian and Nemean Games, had been a family friend of both Stefanos and Kratos' families, and had trained the boys in athletics from an early age. Even at the age of sixty, his body was still solid, well-muscled and well-proportioned. His hair had thinned to almost nothing.

"I was just helping Kratos with his training for the pentathlon at Olympia. Finally, he's going to compete in the Great Games," Pandaros said.

"Well, he could have no better trainer, my friend," Stefanos said. "You look well."

"The Gods have blessed me with the will to carry on training in my old age. I can't abide the life of laziness that makes so many men bulge in places they shouldn't."

"I hear honeyed-wine helps too," Stefanos said, glancing playfully at Kratos, the latter shooting him an angry look.

"I'll take your word for it!" laughed Pandaros. "Come, will you take food with me? I still receive free meals in Argos for my wins at the games, guests included!"

"How can we say no?" Stefanos said.

"After the workout you just put me through, Pandaros, I could eat a whole boar!" Kratos said. "Lead the way!"

"Pandaros! Take a seat!" yelled the tavern keeper when the three men entered the front room of The Iron Fist, and made their way to the inner courtyard where there were a few empty tables beneath a fig tree.

"Thank you, Iphitus!" Pandaros yelled. "I bring with me two former victors as well, though they've never been in Argos long enough to claim your hospitality!"

"You're all welcome. I'll bring food in a few minutes," Iphitus said, bringing over a krater of watered wine and three clay cups "Enjoy!"

"I should have claimed my victories sooner," Stefanos said.

"Yes," said Pandaros, "But from what Kratos has told me, you boys have seen so much action over the years, you would not have had the time."

"True," Stefanos agreed. "Steady work for men like us, from Syracuse to Babylon!"

Pandaros sipped his wine, opting not to say anything about that. "I'm just glad you're both back safely. I've heard stories of that march back from Persia...ten thousand men! The Gods must love you."

"Which is why I'm opting to enter the Olympiad this one last time," Kratos said. "I can feel it in my bones... Nike is waiting for me."

Stefanos looked at his friend and realized that he had never seen such sincerity and determination in his face.

"You're really going to do it?"

"Yes," Kratos said. "And you should too. You're one of the best boxers I know, and unbeatable in the hoplitodromos."

"I'm not interested," Stefanos said, sitting back and crossing his arms. He began to suspect that this meeting was not a coincidence.

"Your chances are good, Stefanos," Pandaros said evenly, leaning forward on the table, the veins in his thick, leathery arms pulsating.

"Can we talk about something else?" Stefanos said stubbornly. "We haven't seen you in years, Pandaros. What news?"

Pandaros sat back and went through the news about local athletes, his own training school, and his frustration with the local ephebes who seemed to be growing more fat and lazy. Once he had vented for a time, he turned to Stefanos once more.

"I'm sorry about your father, Stefanos. He has always been a good friend and supporter. I visited him last week after seeing your sister at the Heraion. I'm much saddened to see him in his current state."

"Thank you. I'm just glad I've come home now, though some things have not changed; we fight as much as we ever did."

"Such is the way between fathers and sons. But I know for a fact that he is proud of you."

"A noble effort, Pandaros, but my father made his thoughts about me perfectly clear this morning." He turned to Kratos. "That's why I came to your house."

"I see," Kratos crossed his arms. "Seeking comfort between my sister's thighs?"

Stefanos could see his friend's jaw set tightly and wondered for a moment if he would strike him, but Kratos held back.

"Well," laughed, Pandaros. "Such activities and urges are, I dare say, signs of a healthy individual. But really, Stefanos, your best friend's sisters?"

"They are the most beautiful women in Argos!" Stefanos said.

"Nice try," Kratos said, leaning back as platters of roasted meats, cheeses, and fresh bread were laid on the table by Iphitus.

"Enjoy!" the tavern keeper said, taking the krater to add more wine.

The three men ate in silence for a while, each busy enjoying the food set before them.

"I've seen some pretty amazing bouts on the skamma these last years," Pandaros said, going back to athletics. "One lad from Epidaurus defeated thirteen opponents in the boxing by exhausting them for hours, dodging faster than anyone I've seen, except yourself," he added to Stefanos. "He always won by single knockout."

"Why'd he lose on number fourteen?" Stefanos asked.

"Hubris set in, my guess is. Seems his opponent had learned his technique, and feigned ignorance of it. He play tired, having jumped around for a long time, and then, when the boy from Epidaurus let his guard down, he knocked the teeth out of his head with a single punch. Never seen anything like it."

"Gods. All his teeth?" Stefanos took note of the chewing he was able to do at that moment, and was grateful he was as fast as he was.

"I'll say it again, Stefanos," Pandaros added, throwing a

clean bone down on the table. "You were always one of my best students, and from what I can see, war has kept you strong."

"And I'll say it again, my friend. The answer is no."

Over the next few days, Talos' condition became worse, and Stefanos raged at his own incapacity to help his father.

In returning to Argos, wandering its streets, and hearing the familiar bustle of his childhood deme, Stefanos' memories, which he had buried deeply, had become chaotic in his mind, churned like the sand of a seabed when waves crash upon it, over and over.

He had decided to help Kratos train at the gymnasium for his upcoming competitions. There was still some time for the latter to get to Olympia for the Scrutiny, the time one month before the Games when the Hellanodikai decide who is eligible and worthy enough to compete.

Stefanos decided to help his friend for all they had been through over the years, and he could see how much it meant to Kratos. Besides, it passed the time, distracted him from darker thoughts, and helped him to stay fit for battle as he hoped to be heading for Persia soon.

However, he realized as the days passed and things got worse at home, he could not leave his father.

One day, after training with Kratos, and visiting the baths, Stefanos' steps led him to the Heraion outside of the eastern walls of the city. He did not enter the sacred precinct, but sat upon a boulder outside the sanctuary, his eyes taking in the gathering of buildings, the temple of Hera where smoke rose from the altar which sat before the aged columns.

He remembered his mother, Hermia, then, and how she had appeared in her white priestess' robes. He used to walk out to the very spot where he sat at that moment, surrounded by spring wild flowers, to watch for her, ready to walk home with her on the days when she returned home.

The wind whipped across the plain as Stefanos sat there, Zephyrus out of the mountains of the Peloponnese to the West. He sat there exposed, his head in his hands, staring at the Heraion, at the ground, at the sky above, tormenting himself with thoughts of happier, carefree times of which there had been too few in his life.

He had spent many more joyous moments in the shield wall during his life, revelling in the skill and strength that made him a terror on the battlefield to his opponents, and a strong ally to the men beside him.

"At least I have that..." he said to himself, suddenly missing the feel of his hoplon and doru in his hands.

For a moment the wind stilled, and the air grew cool around him, the light brighter, almost blinding.

Stefanos hopped down from the boulder into the grass, sending a snake slithering away. Then, he almost collapsed.

My son... I have missed you.

His mother stood before him, her once-white robes dirty and tattered, her skin as pale as chalk. Her face looked down at him pitifully, and she reached out to him.

"Mother?" Stefanos shuddered, backing away until his back was against the boulder. He closed his eyes.

Do not fear me, the shade said. *How I've missed you, my son...*

"Get a grip, Stefanos," he told himself, before opening his eyes to reassure himself it was just his own imagination.

When he looked up again, it was still there, watching him, mouthing words he did not want to hear.

"Why are you here?" he asked.

Talos' time is near, Stefanos. Your father will pass from the world soon. You must...you must...

"What must I do?"

Ease his passing...lighten his heart... The shade smiled sadly. *Make peace with him, Stefanos, for he has loved you since the day you were born, even more than the very fires of his own forge...*

Stefanos shut his eyes tightly, fighting the unfamiliar sting of tears in his eyes. He pressed the muscles of his back into the rough edges of the rock behind him, opened his eyes, and found himself alone again, the heat of the sun beating down once more, the wind wrapping itself about him. He stared at the distant Heraion as he stood up, brushing off his chiton, and turning to go back to the city.

He picked his way through the crowds of men, groups of boys playing, and packs of stray dogs and cats at their heels. After a time, his footsteps led him to his father's workshop, a place where he had spent many hours watching, and listening to his father speak at length about smelting, sculpting, and the beauty of bronze.

Stefanos opened the doorway to see the workshop dusty, cold, and unused. His nostrils filled with the familiar tang of molten bronze, his ears with the hammer and tap of tools to shape it. He could see his father's strong hands shaping the hard material into things of beauty and his heart was filled with a longing to see that man again, a man he had admired and looked up to like the heroes of the past.

The dark reality of that quiet workshop robbed him of the memories, and he was left staring at the unfinished lump of bronze on the dais at the centre of the room. He presumed it to be the last thing Talos had been working on, and moved toward it to pull the sheet off.

Dust fell all around him and he waved his hands to clear it away. When it settled, he stared at the unfinished bronze of what appeared to be a warrior, the feet bare, greaves leading up to solid thighs, a leather skirt and muscled torso. But there it ended, unfinished, unpolished and rough.

"Must be an Ares commission?" Stefanos said to himself, picking up the sheet and placing it back over the bronze. He walked over to the anvil where the heavy hammer lay, and slipped his fingers around it. It did not feel right in his hand. It had been too long. He was not his father.

Stefanos pounded the anvil once, the dead ring echoing in the workshop one time before he put it down and made his way to the door. Before leaving, he turned to look a last time at the dusty interior that had been lit by the fires of creativity and inspiration, then closed the door and went home.

"FATHER!" STEFANOS YELLED WHEN HE ENTERED THE courtyard, running past the olive tree and bursting into the kitchen where Cleo spun, surprised and putting her hands up.

"What is it?" she asked.

"Is he..." Stefanos panted. "Is he?" He could not say the word.

"He's as good as can be expected when the end draws near," she said, walking up to him and placing her hand upon his heart. "He's asked to see you as soon as you returned home."

Stefanos nodded, and took a few deep breaths before downing a cup of water.

"Where were you?" Cleo asked. "Not at the gymnasium the entire time?"

"No. I went to the Heraion...and then to father's workshop."

"I see."

Stefanos could tell that both those places haunted his sister as well, their measure and meaning morphing over time into something less than happy. He touched her hand, and turned to go to their father's bedside.

Stefanos found Talos sitting up, staring at his own hands, turning them over curiously, scrutinizing them.

"It's a strange thing to look at yourself and not recognize the person you have become," he said without looking up at Stefanos. "I've honoured the Gods all my life, enjoyed my daily toils. And yet..." he coughed roughly, spittle mingled with blood falling from his mouth. "And yet, the changes they have wrought upon me seem cruel reward."

"Father," Stefanos said softly, taking a square of linen from the table and dabbing at Talos' mouth. "Such changes are not wrought upon bronze, are they?"

"No!" Talos' face lit up, and he smiled. "They are not. Bronze, if cared for, is eternal, not this!" he said, pinching at the loose flesh of his arm. "Not this..."

Stefanos sat on the edge of the bed, hunched over, staring at the worn marble floor, rubbing his jaw slowly, listening to the shallow breathing behind him.

"I have always honoured Eris agathos," Talos said. "Good strife, is what makes a good man. It matters in all aspects of one's life."

"What are you getting at?" Stefanos sat up and looked at Talos.

"You are aner agathos...a good man. But you have honoured Kakochartos for too long."

"Kakochartos?" Stefanos repeated, his voice angry. *Why can't he just say something kind?* "My ponos, Father, has always been war. I have been on the front line of the battles of this world since I was nineteen. Twenty one years! How could I make statues when our people were slaughtered and enslaved at Hysiae!"

"Twenty one years of Kakochartos! Of exulting in bad things, of war, dissent, and destruction. You have lusted for bloodshed and battle, my son." Talos wept then, fear and regret layered over his face and the features of his body.

As the old man looked upon his son, it became apparent that he was not scared for himself, for the imminent approach of death and the long ride the Ferryman had in store for him. He was afraid for the son before him, and it tore him apart as surely as Cerberus' fangs.

"When you embrace Eris agathos, you are creative, productive, an example to all mortals for the betterment of this world. I have always striven to make this world a better place, to leave behind beauty, for I have..." he hunched over, coughing blood, his hands gripping Stefanos' arm tightly, desperately. "I have been blessed by the Gods, in my skill and toils, in my beloved Hermia, and my faithful Cleo...and in you, my son...in you..."

"Father," Stefanos' voice shook, and he felt the veins in his neck and head pulsating so much, he thought he would explode. "I've not known any other life. I don't know what else to do. The hoplon and doru are my tools, the thorax and greaves my clothing. I know I enjoy battle, and killing... It's what I am good at. It's who I am!"

Talos shook his head violently. "No. No!" He poked Stefanos in the chest. "Who you are is in here. A good man, with arete...kalos...aner agathos. You are all of those things. You have just wandered far from the path...but it is never too late."

"I told you. I don't know what else to do. What can I do for you, Father, to make you happy, to give you the peace of mind you want? Tell me what I can do?" His voice was almost a shout.

Talos did not flinch, however. Nor did he continue weeping. He gripped his son's arm tightly.

"Embrace Eris agathos, and the agon. You have always had philoneikia, the love of competing, and philonikia, that essential love of winning."

Stefanos stared at Talos, his racing heart slowing as his father's eyes sought his and locked onto them.

"Enter the Olympiad, Stefanos. Win. For you, for our family, for the Gods themselves. Win and redeem yourself. Shake off Kakochartos for something greater, nobler."

"The Olympiad? Father..." Stefanos shook his head slowly.

"Yes! And when you have won, and the olive crown has been placed upon your brow, I want you to commission the greatest epinikion bronze of yourself to stand in the Altis of the sanctuary for all time. When that happens, I will rest easy in Elysium."

"Father..." Stefanos looked at the old man before him, haunted by memory, by the shade of his own mother, by the faces of the countless men he had slain from Syracuse to Persia. They all stared at him now, expectant, mocking, pitying and vengeful.

Then he felt the hand gripping his arm tightly, desperately - the hand that had created beauty with a hammer in its fist. He wanted to help his father, to give him peace.

Talos' aged eyes stared expectantly at Stefanos, full of hope, but also of fear that his son would refuse his wish, the last he would ever make.

"I will go, Father...to Olympia. If the Gods grant me victory, and Nike crowns me, I'll erect a bronze as you wish."

"Thank you, my son. Yes...a bronze, beautiful, and god-like..." Talos released Stefanos' hand and lay back, relief washing over him, his wrinkled lips smiling beneath his beard. His eyes looked up at Stefanos again. "I have never stopped caring for you," he muttered, his eyes closing. "I tried finishing the bronze...of you...but my body was too weak. My son..."

Stefanos watched as his father drifted off to sleep, his mind going back to the unfinished statue in the workshop. It was up to him now, to finish his father's dream, make it his own.

THE NEXT MORNING, AS THE COCKS CROWED ACROSS THE CITY of Argos, from the hill of Larissa toward the gulf to the South, Helios' light filtered in through every window and door, bringing with it the golden light of summer. Birdsong filled the air, the streets, and gardens. The agora came slowly to life as the first of the vendors began to sing their own song to those passing by.

In their family home, Stefanos slept in the dawn light that touched his bed. It had taken him a long time to fall asleep, but even then he had been restless, his mind churning over the task that had been set for him, the challenge he had accepted. Then he remembered his father's face, the smile, the kind words that had finally come from his lips, and he had fallen asleep at last.

"Brother..." said a soft voice, after the second cock's crow. "Stefanos?" Cleo's soft voice said, her hand upon the bare muscle of his shoulder.

"What? What is it?" He opened his eyes to see her sad face staring down at him.

She had been crying, and now her eyes were red and telling.

"Father is gone..." she said, her eyes shut tight against another wave of grief.

"He can't be yet... He was smiling last night. Are you sure?" Stefanos, no stranger to death, found himself trying not to believe it. Even after the conversation, the coughing, the blood, he still hoped that Talos lived.

"The Gods have taken him. Come..." Cleo stood up, and held out her hand to lead her brother to the room.

She had lit incense upon a small bronze tripod with lion-clawed feet, and four oil lamps burned gently, one in each corner of the room.

The siblings stood there, looking down at their father, his face pale, and peaceful.

"I can't believe he's gone," Stefanos said, kneeling beside the body, feeling the stinging in his eyes. Though he was a grown man, in that moment he felt like an abandoned child, disbelieving, wishing he could undo the Gods' work.

But that would go against his father's final wishes. *No hubris...no Kakochartos...* In Stefanos' mind then, he began to hear the roar of a crowd, feel a crown of olive, and see the gleam of bronze in the sun's light.

"Thank you for making peace with him," Cleo said, kneeling on the other side of the bed, where she stroked Talos' hand. "I know it was not easy for you."

Stefanos did not speak, just nodded. He was suddenly sad for her as well, for when he left Argos, she would be alone, just her and Hera, and the likeness of the goddess that stood in the temple and that had been crafted by the man who lay peaceful and dead before them.

THEY WERE NOT ALONE IN BURYING THEIR FATHER.

The priestesses of the Heraion, as well as several well-known citizens of Argos, came forward to pay their respects in the days after Talos' passing. Many insisted on contributing to his memorial stele in the necropolis, as well as the coffin for the inhumation. However, Stefanos would have none of it. As Talos' son, he saw to it that a smooth larnax of olive wood was produced to hold his father's remains, and that a tall, marble stele with a forge fire and hammer in relief upon it were made ready. All of the artisans involved did their utmost for their former colleague whose name was now etched upon the simple monument.

Three days later, Stefanos and Cleo stood, dressed in black himations, at the head of a large group of Argives in the necropolis of Argos to lay their father to rest beside their mother.

Sacrifices had been made to appease the dead and honour the Gods who would carry Talos to the Afterlife. A brilliant golden drachm had been placed in Talos' mouth to pay the Ferryman who would row him across the black river Styx.

Cleo wept in the darkness of the epeblema that covered her head and face, but Stefanos' tears had dried up days before, his sadness replaced with determination and the thoughts of ponos ahead of him.

When the rites were finished, the meat of the sacrifices distributed to the gathered mourners, and the fat and bones left to the sacrificial flames for the Gods, Cleo turned to Stefanos.

Her eyes stared at him from behind her veil, and her hands gripped his tightly as she looked up.

"May the Gods guide you, Stefanos," she paused, fighting back more tears. Then she looked up again. "Win. Win for us. Win for him!" She looked to their father's dirt-covered coffin, then she hugged her brother tightly, as she had so many times before when he left for battle.

Stefanos held her small body close, uncaring of the stares of those all about them. They were all they had left.

When Cleo left to accept the condolences of other mourners, Stefanos turned and went over to where Kratos stood with Pandaros, beside the grave.

"I'm coming with you," he said.

They nodded.

Chapter Three

THE PRINCESS

Η Πριγκίπισσα

"We can't miss the Scrutiny," Pandaros said as they walked along the road west from Argos a few days later. "The Hellanodikai are pretty ruthless in their eligibility requirements. The Scrutiny takes time, so that's why they want all competitors there a month before the games."

Stefanos and Kratos gave each other knowing looks as they walked behind their trainer. Pandaros had not lost any of his intensity and seriousness over the years; once it was agreed that he would accompany them as their trainer, they felt like they were in the gymnasium of their youth again, under his hard tutelage. It did not matter one bit that they were both veteran hoplites with their bronze shields on their backs, and their dorata in their hands. They were once more Pandaros' students.

"The Olympiad is much bigger than the Nemean and Isthmian Games, and the sanctuary is larger and busier than any of the others. Your opponents will be in your faces all of the time, and they will try to taunt and intimidate you to no end, as you train, as you eat, as you bathe. This is the ultimate agon, lads, and the best promachoi from all over the Greek world will be there to compete for the olive crown before almighty Zeus!"

As they reached the edge of the plain, Stefanos stopped to look one last time at Argos, the smoke rising from the agglomeration of clay rooftops, sanctuaries, and temples. Whenever he left Argos, he wondered if he would ever see it again.

"She'll be fine, Stefanos," Kratos said. "Cleo has always been stronger than anyone gives her credit for."

"I know."

Kratos smiled reluctantly. "My sisters wanted me to wish you luck." He cleared his throat. "They said they hoped you will visit with all of them next time."

Stefanos smiled and laughed, despite himself.

"Are you two women coming?" Pandaros yelled from atop a large boulder as he pointed at the mountains of Arkadia. "We need to reach Artemisio in three days."

Another knowing look, and the two friends hoisted their hoplons and satchels, and followed after their old trainer.

THE DAYS WERE GETTING HOTTER AS THE MONTH OF Skirophorion was coming to an end, and the Peloponnesian landscape grew drier, browner, the array of wild flowers shrivelling under the growing intensity of the heat.

The mountain paths that Stefanos, Kratos, and Pandaros took smelled strongly of olive, hot pine, and wild thyme. Grasshoppers flung themselves across the men's path as they plodded up goat tracks, and game ways. The route to Artemisio had been more like military training than a country stroll.

Pandaros told the two men to move ahead at a pace until sundown, at which time they were to prepare a camp for his arrival, with their only food to be something killed with a thrown rock, spear, or javelin. They had no wine, only the water from mountain springs, still cold and clear from the winter's runoff.

Artemisio had been their first destination, not Mantinea, which would have been the more direct route.

"Too many spirits from that battlefield linger there," Pandaros said. "I don't want anything affecting your performance. Besides, the climb over the mountains will be good training."

Stefanos and Kratos, did not argue with Pandaros' reasoning. They had their own terms with the dead, but strolling through the plain of Mantinea where so many had met their end in slaughter seemed to be tempting things, especially as they were Argives who had befriended Spartans, the latter having slaughtered their opponents in that battle.

From Artemisio, the real climb into the mountains of Arkadia began, and barren rock gave way to denser pine forest, and scrubland. Once they passed through Orchomenos, where the people looked upon the two hoplites with great suspicion, Pandaros began putting them through their paces.

Both men were made to run in their full armour up the mountainside, at times for a long distance, others as a sprint; more than once did Stefanos or Kratos slam bodily into a rock face, or cling desperately to a tree root or fallen log on the other side of a long jump across a gap between two cliff faces.

Pandaros had them lifting variously-sized rocks and boulders too, as they marched along the paths overlooking the plains below. Their ruthless trainer had returned with a vengeance, pointing out random boulders and telling them to dead-lift them, even if they were to be pried from the land's embrace.

In the evenings, while the meat they had caught cooked over a fire in the camp they had built, Pandaros had them spar with each other. Kratos was not the boxer that Stefanos was, but his fighting skill, combined with his wrestling training proved useful enough a test for Stefanos. To make things more challenging, Pandaros would swing a long, thick branch at Stefanos' head as he was sparring with Kratos.

"What are you doing, old man?" Stefanos yelled the first time the branch caught him by surprise on the side of the head.

"Training you!" Pandaros raged back. "You're slower than you used to be. What happened to your battlefield training? When you get in close, and only your xiphos can be used, I'm sure you aren't facing just one opponent, are you? A hit could come from anywhere, and some opponents will be fast enough to hit from one side, step behind you and hit again before you have time to spit out your teeth! So..."

Kratos swung and caught Stefanos on the arm, the latter ducking under another swung branch, and parrying the follow-up punch from Kratos who reeled backward when Stefanos landed one on his jaw.

"That's it!" Pandaros yelled. "Good, good." He nodded and helped Kratos up from the ground where he sat rubbing his face. Then he turned to Stefanos. "It's no use standing there to take all the hits your opponent has to offer, waiting for the moment when you can land one. Your vision and your aim will just get worse. Stick to your style, Stefanos, weave, dart, move out of the way, but don't waste energy dancing around unless you have the energy to spare. It will be a lot hotter on the skamma of Olympia than it is here in the fresh mountain air."

Pandaros walked over to the fire where a small boar Kratos had brought down with his spear was roasting over the fire, the fat crackling and spilling into the flames. "Food's ready."

The two younger men came and sat down slowly on the ground opposite Pandaros, who began to cut pieces of the hot meat from the roasting beast. The smell of game filled their nostrils and they found they were both starving, no longer distracted by the intensity of their training.

"I'm proud of both of you... I never thought to be able to

train you again. However..." he smiled, "it's not just about eumorphia - anyone can be in good shape. This is about philoneikia, and philonikia; you must love to compete, and to win. You must embrace Eris agathos, and make your toils a part of who you are, in those places that only the Gods can see. Then the goddess Nike will come down out of the heavens to crown you and raise you above all mortals, just as Herakles was, or Pelops who drove his chariot across these very mountains and valleys that we cross."

"Don't tell me you're going to run behind us now, Pandaros, poking us in the back with a spear, just like Oinomaus did," Kratos said, chewing.

"Would it make you work harder?" the old man raised an eyebrow in the fading light.

"Yes," Kratos acknowledged warily, looking at Stefanos.

"If it will increase your toil, and drive you to run faster, to move quicker, we should do it."

"Very well," Kratos said, dreading the next day already.

"Every man's ponos is increased when he has something to lose," Stefanos said, his face serious. "If we've seen anything in the battles we've fought, it's that the winners are often those who fight with the greatest will, and who stand to lose everything."

"Very true," Pandaros agreed. "Though the Gods have a way of negating that hypothesis."

"I'll be back," Stefanos said, rising from the ground and walking away from the fire.

"If you see an Arkadian bear, use him for boxing practice," Pandaros called after him.

Stefanos walked close to the edge of the cliff where a cold spring gushed out of the rock, and plunged his fists into the icy water for as long as he could stand it. His body was feeling Pandaros' training, from the swelling in his fists, to the steady throbbing in every muscle, to the blisters on his heels, but he knew it was worth it, knew that he had met even greater hardship, especially on the march back from Persia with his friend, Xenophon.

As Stefanos stared at the clear night sky, with Libra and Centaurus lighting the dark above the mountains and valleys, he began to wonder if he would be able to keep his promise to his father, and honour his memory with the Olympic victory Talos desired.

Stefanos looked out at the land, pulled the hem of his chlamys up over his head, raised his arms to the sky, and whispered.

"Father Zeus... Mother Hera... Guide me in this endeavour. Help me to honour my father's memory and my family's name. I know that I've not always been the man I should, or could have been. I am mortal and, in my life, have honoured your son Ares more than most." He closed his eyes tightly, the faces of his own mother and father floating before him. "Please help me to reach for something more in this life, to be aner agathos... I honour you... Guide me to Olympia, Father Zeus, Protector of Travellers...and to victory..."

After a few more minutes, Stefanos turned and walked back to the camp where Kratos was already sleeping beside the fire, and Pandaros was poking at the hot coals with a stick before putting another log on. The old man smiled sadly as Stefanos walked up.

"I know that your father, Gods keep him, put a lot of pressure on you with his dying wish."

"Yes," Stefanos answered. "He did."

"But he knew you were capable of victory, Stefanos. He knew it! And I know it. The Gods have set this before you for a reason, my boy. Victory is within your grasp."

"I'm glad you think so," Stefanos said.

"I know so," Pandaros said intensely. "And you have to know it too."

. . .

It took Stefanos some time to fall asleep, which was unusual as he had become accustomed to sleeping anywhere at any time on the march over the years, stealing sleep whenever he could. That night, the hoot of owls on the hunt sounded in the mountain forests, and the blood-curdling screech of foxes ripped the air.

Eventually, exhaustion and Morpheus overtook him and he nodded off, still wearing his thorax, huddled beneath his chlamys.

Some time later, he was awoken by a sound of galloping, and cries somewhere on the mountain track above their camp.

Stefanos sat up and looked at Kratos and Pandaros who both slept soundly beside the dying embers of their fire. He grabbed his doru and plunged up into the moonlit darkness of the forest until he reached the side of the mountain track.

The sound was getting louder and louder, and Stefanos wondered if he had happened upon some lost group of centaurs in this remote region, perhaps chasing the local maenads. He gripped his doru easily, ready to thrust at any time.

The air grew suddenly cold, his breath appearing before his eyes, even as the thunder of hooves got closer and became louder.

Down the path, a charioteer was whipping the reins of a team of four white stallions, his long hair billowing behind him as he turned every now and then to look behind him from the cab of his chariot.

"Hold, friend!" Stefanos yelled, but the charioteer paid him no heed, and sped right past him. Stefanos jumped out of the way just in time.

He returned to the track to stare at the back of the madman, then turned when a rumble of more hooves came, followed by maniacal laughter. Stefanos turned to see a bearded man driving a chariot pulled by winged horses through the forest. He sneered as he saw Stefanos and pulled back a great spear, ready to throw, and launched it with all his might down the path before him.

Stefanos raised his own spear, the end planted in the ground, just as he had always done to repel cavalry on the battlefield, but he missed and tumbled out of the way, the wheels tearing by his head only by inches.

Then there was a scream to cow even the bravest of men, choked by blood, and followed by a gloating laughter.

"Kratos!" he yelled, but his voice was hoarse, his throat cold and tight. He stood in the middle of the road, shaking, looking after the last driver until it was quiet again.

It took him some moments before he became aware that he was still standing on the roadside. He felt a nudge on his forearm, and looked down to see what looked like a satyr skitter away behind a tree, the dark eyes and heavy brow peering at him from behind a mountain oak.

Leave now! the satyr warned. *They are coming!*

"What?" Stefanos began to approach the satyr, squinting his eyes, but stopped when the sound of hooves cracked the night air again from behind him. There was a sound of whipping, a man's voice with a woman urging him on.

They came on a chariot pulled by brilliant white steeds, racing as though a hydra's jaws were snapping at their heels. They came into view some distance away, but Stefanos could see them clearly, the man strong and muscular, wearing a skull cap over his short hair, bare chested, and the woman behind him in a flowing peplos, her arms holding onto him as she stared into the darkness behind them, her surprise as the chariot behind them came into view, pulled by winged black horses whose eyes burned with fire the nearer they got.

Stefanos recognized the second charioteer, the beard, the wicked laughter, and prepared to plant his doru in the ground when the first chariot passed.

"Not this time!" he yelled, his limbs shaking as he gripped the ash spear shaft.

The first chariot did not slow down when they saw him,

but sped past, the wheels seemingly on fire, lighting the darkness. The woman in the back, her long hair whipping about her face, looked at Stefanos then, her face intense, a sheen of sweat showing on her brow in he moonlight. There was fear there, but more determination than anything else.

Stefanos turned, his doru planted strongly in the earth, to face the oncoming charioteer.

The man sneered at him as his stallions raged toward him, their hooves cracking the rock beneath.

Stefanos wished he had taken his helmet with him, but it was too late. He braced for the impact, sighting the chest of the stallion on the right side and held fast.

Suddenly, one of the chariot's wheels collapsed on its axel. The man raged for a moment, his spear falling from his grasp.

Stefanos changed the angle of his spear and drove it deep, surprised at the ease with which he did so.

In that moment, the chariot splintered and flipped through the air, directly over Stefanos' head. He dove out of the way as the chariot came crashing down to explode on the spot where he had been crouched, and he fell down the steep incline beside the road, careening against logs, and boulders, and the trunks of squat oak, and mountain ash.

As he tumbled, he thought he could see the raging driver flying ahead of his team to land on the path just before the horses who then trampled him while he screamed and raged, his body bloody and pulped.

Stefanos lay among dead leaves on the forest ground, straining to see up the mountainside to the road above for a few moments before his vision blurred, and he fell unconscious, cold on the ground.

"STEFANOS! WAKE UP!" THE VOICES SAID, SOUNDING AS IF they were underwater. "Another day of training, Stefanos!"

He felt rough hands shaking him, and then his xiphos was in his hand, the tip of the blade pointed at Kratos' throat.

"Easy now... easy. Stefanos, it's me."

Kratos' face and long dark hair came into view, his eyes wide and wary with the tip of the leaf blade pointed at his throat.

"Put it down, Stefanos. You've had a dream."

Stefanos looked around him and saw the burned out fire, their camp, Pandaros staring at him over Kratos' shoulder.

"Easy, lad. The exhaustion has taken over your senses," Pandaros said. "You're on the mountainside with me and Kratos. We're on the road to Olympia, remember?"

"Yes," Stefanos said, lowering the blade quickly and releasing the rim of Kratos' thorax. "How did I get here?"

"What do you mean?" Kratos said, standing up again and stepping back. "You've been sleeping for hours. We thought we'd let you go a little longer."

Sunlight angled into the clearing where they were and Stefanos squinted, rubbing his eyes. How is this possible? "Didn't you hear the screams? The sound of the horses on the road? I called for you, but you two slept through the entire thing?"

"The night was as quiet and peaceful as we could ask for," Pandaros said, concern showing on his face.

Stefanos got up, looking himself over for signs of blood, scrapes, or broken bones, but he could find none. "The Gods sent me a dream then, I suppose."

"Keep it to yourself," Pandaros said quickly. "If it was as bad as you seem to think, you should think it over in your own mind."

Stefanos nodded, but did not reply as he set to eating a bit of leftover meat from the spit before gathering his things and preparing for the next part of their training march. As Pandaros picked up his own spear, a flash of his dream of the night before sent a chill down Stefanos' spine.

. . .

The descent out of the mountains into the valley took them longer than they had expected. The paths had been washed out by winter rains, and were strewn with downed trees and boulders which Pandaros immediately set the two armoured men to clearing as they went.

By the end of a second day of labouring before Pandaros' spear point, they finally reached the valley floor near to Heraia, on the banks of the Alpheios river. Pandaros raged that they were going to miss the Scrutiny, and Kratos ran, jumped, and threw discoi and javelins on the flat lands along the river.

Stefanos trained too, sprinting in his full armour, and sparring with Kratos, but always with the thoughts of his experience on the mountainside, wondering why the Gods had shown him such things. He had come to the realization that perhaps he had seen the chariot race between Pelops and Oinomaus; Pandaros had said that the legendary race had taken place along the route they were following.

But it was the face of Hippodameia that haunted Stefanos. From where she stood in Pelops' chariot, staring backward, her hair whipping about her, the intense eyes, the will to take control of her own life... Stefanos felt as if she were staring directly at him, and he could not shake the vision of that lively woman.

It was not something he would dare mention to Kratos or Pandaros. Kratos and he had shared many of their hopes and dreams with each other over the years, but some things were meant to stay in one's heart. Besides, they might think him crazy.

When they arrived at Heraia, where a small settlement clustered around a sanctuary of Hera, the men made their offerings to the goddess. They had come a long way over the mountains on their journey, trained on the edges of dangerous precipices, and come down into the lush river valley of the Alpheios.

Stefanos spent a long time over his offering to the goddess, the blood of the hare he offered soaking the field flowers and herbs on the altar before him. He felt Hera's eyes upon him, more than he had in many a year, not since he had last knelt in the Heraion of Argos where his mother served.

Mother Goddess...guide me on my path. Help me to honour my family in the Games on the banks of sacred Alpheios. Also...help me to understand what I saw on the mountainside. My mind is unfocussed, and it frightens me, despite all that I have seen... Mother Hera, I carry your symbol upon my hoplon with pride. I honour you, oh Goddess....

When Stefanos left the sanctuary, the sun was low in the West, casting orange light over the green fields and hills of Ellis and Triphylia. Olympia was out there, closer than ever, and Stefanos could feel a rumble in the veins of the earth as they neared their destination.

He glanced at an olive tree beside the road and saw Kratos and Pandaros sitting, waiting.

They stood when they spotted him and walked over.

"The roads are more empty than they should be. I fear we are late. Everyone is probably already there."

"If we hurry, we should just make it," Kratos said. "Doesn't it take the Hellanodikai a long time to see all the potential competitors?"

"If the Gods are kind, yes," Pandaros said. "We can walk for another hour perhaps, but then we'll need to make camp."

"Let's get going," Stefanos added. "Pandaros, you've got some blood on your neck," Stefanos pointed out.

"That bird I offered had more blood in it than I thought possible," the old man said, wiping at his neck.

They camped on the slopes of a tall hill overlooking the snaking river where it was flanked by flat, green fields on either side, dotted with oak, cypress, and plane trees. Each man fell asleep quickly beside the small fire they had built.

THE ALPHEIOS VALLEY WAS FILLED WITH A RED LIGHT AS DAWN crept over the world. Morning doves began to coo in the tree tops, and the fields steamed as the rising sun burned away the dew that night had left behind.

The morning peace was broken by the sound of charging hooves, and voices, of short commands, and grunts of effort and delight.

Stefanos opened his eyes where he slept against a fallen tree trunk, and looked around. His chlamys was damp, and he hung it on a nearby branch to air out. Laughter reached his ears and he cocked his head to listen - it was coming from down in the valley.

"Women?" he said to himself, looking at the stirring forms of his companions, and smiling to himself, before grabbing his doru, and stepping out of the ring of their camp to walk to the edge of the trees where there was a view of the field below. The Alpheios sparkled in the early morning sunlight, along an expanse of green grass dotted with olive trees at the edges.

"Jumping!" a stern voice commanded, and there was laughter again, playful and melodic.

Stefanos looked in the direction of the voices as his eyes alighted on a group of four young women exercising beside the riverbank.

They were naked, their skin tanned to a soft olive colour, their bodies firm, vibrant, and athletic. Three of them were dark-haired, except the youngest whose blond hair was tied in a thick tail with a thong. The four of them jumped up and down continuously, their heels slapping their bare bottoms rhythmically, and in concert. They spun, and jumped, and raised their arms with beautiful ease, a sheen of sweat forming on their bodies.

Stefanos stared at the group, suspecting that he had come upon a group of river nymphs. He debated whether he should approach, wondered what pleasures might be had of such creatures if they were willing.

Then there was a thunder of hooves from out of the olive grove and the commanding voice bellowed once more, strong, and confident, a voice used to being obeyed.

Stefanos tore his eyes from the nymphs to see a tall, lean, strong woman riding a huge black stallion toward the group of girls. His smile faded as he took in the sight of her raven-black hair which fell wildly down to the small of her toned back, stray strands falling forward over her pert breasts as she reined in hard before the younger girls, dismounting with a leap to land and roll with the skill of Artemis herself.

All Stefanos could do was stare at the heavenly creature before him as she eclipsed the girls with her presence, beauty, and power. He felt his loins stirring as he leaned forward for a better look. *A goddess?*

"Pirro!" the woman called as she held the reins of her horse.

A lanky young man with flaming red hair and a limp came hobbling quickly from beneath the broad leaves of an aged oak tree to stand at the woman's side, his head bowed.

"Take Xanthus to the river for a drink, and brush him down. He did well this morning," she said as she stroked the stallion's forehead gently, whispering something inaudible to it.

"Yes, my lady," the young man said, taking the reins and leading the stallion away.

The woman immediately joined the younger girls in their exercises, her tall body jumping higher, and her legs moving faster than any of the others as her feet slapped against her buttocks with intensity and speed.

Stefanos watched as if in a dream that he could not shake, even after waking. *Who is she?* he wondered. It was as if some god or goddess was whispering into his ear from behind, urging him on to action, the hair on the back of his neck prickling and writhing despite the growing heat of the morning.

Far to the left, out of sight from his perch, Stefanos heard a flock of birds disturbed, their group flying suddenly into the air from a copse of plane trees. His senses perked up and he tore his gaze from the woman who also seemed to have noticed the noise, for she stopped her jumping and stood before the young girls, a xiphos suddenly glinting in her hand.

Stefanos stared from her to the trees, and then he heard it, the clatter and grunt of running men. He stepped forward, scanning the descent before him quickly, a boulder, a log, a flat space where he could gain speed. He gripped his doru and jumped.

The men came at the five women quickly, spears and daggers pointed at them, lascivious grins on their faces as they ran.

"Five of you take the leader," one man yelled as they ran. "The rest of you take the horses. Kill the others!" The group roared and rushed upon them.

Stefanos' legs pounded toward them, his presence as yet unnoticed by the women who were moving back toward the oak tree where the red-haired boy held the big black stallion and three other black horses. Stefanos came at the group from the side, just before they collided with the girls. He saw the woman's eyes glance at him, but pressed his charge and slammed into the leader so that the leader crashed into three of his fellows, taking them out momentarily.

Stefanos' doru swung in a deadly arc, slicing across the throat of one of the men, like a scythe across winter wheat. Then, he pulled it back and thrust into the chest of another, sending him screaming backward. The sound of clanging weapons told him that the girls were engaging some of the other men rather than cowering behind the tree or horses.

"Kill him!" the leader yelled, pointing at Stefanos.

A dagger slammed into Stefanos' side but his thorax turned the blade.

The man fell, grasping at a thrown dagger that protruded from his neck, and the voice of its wielder yelled. "Protect the horses!"

The surprise of Stefanos' initial attack had worn off now, and the seven remaining brigands were regrouping before him.

He stood there, eyeing each of them, his armoured bulk a wall between the two parties, blood dipping from the tip of his spear.

"Leave, stranger! This isn't your business. We'll kill you next!"

"I'm not that easy to kill," Stefanos said calmly.

"He's right, stranger. This isn't your fight."

The words came from the huntress, and Stefanos turned to look at her, sweat upon her face and chest, and a sort of joy on her face. He lost his concentration with that look and the brigands charged.

Stefanos felt his doru gripped by two men so that he could not use it, and chaos ensued as the group clashed again.

"Stefanos!!!" Kratos yelled as he and Pandaros came running down the hillside and across the grass. Kratos launched a javelin and it took one of the men in the side of the head, blood exploding from the other side.

Pandaros hacked his way to the centre of the brigands, his xiphos slashing, taking out two of the men, before a third set upon him.

Stefanos felt his spear shaft wrenched from his hands and turned to his fists, feeling the connection with the face of the other man before him, one, two, three, before turning to another who fell before he could land a punch.

The huntress stared wildly at him, angry that he had almost taken her kill. "I told you to leave!" she ordered.

He stared at her again, a confused look upon his face, comic almost as she laughed and slashed at another brigand without taking her eyes from him.

Two men were left facing the group and when they saw Stefanos and Kratos regroup, they turned to flee back into the trees.

"They won't be back," Kratos remarked, but even as the words left his lips, the huntress and one of the girls had stepped forward with a javelin each and launched them at the retreating men.

The shafts arced over the dewey field to ram into the men's backs, sending them face down into the dirt where they lay motionless.

"A good throw, Euryleonis," the huntress said as she turned casually back to her girls. "You see what happens when one retreats? That!" she said, pointing at the distant bodies.

The girls nodded, and began securing the area, and putting their chitons back on.

"What just happened?" Kratos said to Stefanos as he stared at the women who seemed unconcerned with them.

"You robbed us of a good lesson," she said to Stefanos without looking at him.

"We saved your lives!" Stefanos replied.

"But not your own," she answered.

Dread grabbed hold of Stefanos as he turned to the mass of bodies.

"Where's Pandaros?" Kratos said, as they both rushed to the pile of carnage where the main fight had taken place.

"I'm...here..." a hoarse voice croaked. Pandaros lay beneath the body of one of the men he had killed.

"Pandaros..." Stefanos said, tossing the body to the side and kneeling in the blood around them.

"Where are you hurt?" Kratos asked.

Pandaros shook his head. "I won't be...going...to Olympia," he said, shaking his head slowly and removing his hand from his stomach where a deep, wide gash spouted blood from his abdomen.

Stefanos realized they were kneeling in Pandaros' blood, and looked sadly at the old man's pale face.

"You old fool..." he said sadly. "Why?"

"Why...not?" Pandaros gritted his teeth and his eyes began to stare at the sky. "You are my best...students..." he said.

"The Gods are calling to him now," a woman's voice said beside Stefanos then. "It is his time."

Stefanos looked up at the huntress then, his eyes angry and incredulous at the interruption. Before he could speak,

Pandaros' old hand gripped the edge of his thorax and pulled him closer.

"Win glory for us..." he said as his last breath escaped his body and his eyes strayed to the bright blue of the sky above.

Stefanos put his hand on the old man's chest and closed his eyes.

"You see," the woman said as she turned to walk back to her girls.

"Who do you think you are?" Kratos yelled at her as Stefanos rose and began to walk toward her, his fists clenched.

"You watch a good man die so casually? When he died trying to save you?"

The woman turned from stroking the muzzle of one of her horses, her eyes stern, fearless, and critical as she took in Stefanos' person.

"You fought well-enough, but your friend was old, and had no place in our fight, as you did not."

"He's dead because of you!" Kratos said, stepping up to stand beside Stefanos.

"No," she said. "He's dead because of himself. It was the Gods' will."

"Maybe it's the Gods' will that we take you and your horses as payment?" Kratos said, stepping forward.

"Get back!" a new voice said from behind the women.

Stefanos put his arm in front of Kratos as he spotted the red cloaks approaching, a line of spear points and bronze helmets arrayed before them. The troops marched directly to stand before the women, the leaf-shaped blades pointed at Stefanos and Kratos' throats.

The half enomotia of Spartan warriors stood still and calm before the two Argives, their eyes cold beneath the burnished bronze of their helmets.

A massive man with a crimson-crested helmet stepped forward, their enomotarch. He looked from the women and horses, to Stefanos and Kratos, and removed his helmet. His long dark hair fell about his shoulders and his beard gave his scarred face and grey eyes a look of cold brutality.

Stefanos stared back at the Spartan warrior, trying to see if his doru was within easy reach.

It was not.

The man stared at Stefanos, his warriors still unmoving behind him.

"Kill them," he said before turning casually as if going back to his breakfast.

"No," the woman commanded, and the warriors stopped immediately, even as their dorata were poised to pierce Stefanos and Kratos.

The enomotarch turned to her. "They cannot be permitted to live."

"And I said *No*, Typhon." The woman stepped forward, her black hair tied back so that her face and neck were revealed fully. She met the cold eyes of the warrior directly, with unyielding will.

Stefanos looked at her, the sway she held over these men of Sparta, and wondered again who she was, a woman who could speak to men in such a way, and not be punished for it.

The enomotarch pursed his lips and nodded once. "As you command." Without another word, the enomotarch put his helmet back on his head and turned away, his men following.

The horses were led away by the girls and the red-haired boy with the limp, flanked by the Spartans, leaving only the woman standing there, barefoot on the bloody grass.

"I am sorry for your friend," she said to Stefanos, ignoring Kratos.

"Sorry?" Kratos said, anger in his voice again.

"He died well," she said, her blazing blue eyes meeting Stefanos' directly for the first time, and lingering there for a moment.

Before Stefanos could say anything, express his anger at her curt dismissal of all that had happened, she turned and walked away to join her people. Only the young girl

Euryleonis waited for her beneath the broad branches of the oak tree. Together, the woman and the girl walked away, leaving the two Argives staring after them.

Before they disappeared, the woman cast a quick backward glance to see the two men picking up the body of their fallen friend.

Chapter Four

OLYMPIA

Ολυμπία

Stefanos and Kratos did not train that day, but spent the time building a pyre on the green field for Pandaros.

After washing the body of their friend, and placing a gold coin in his mouth, they said the prayers they knew in honour of their friend and trainer, to Zeus, Herakles, and Hermes who would take his soul to the Underworld. They watched for some time as the fire burned, choked by anger and smoke, and when the flames had fully consumed the body, they left that field behind to follow the line of the Alpheios on the final leg of their journey.

Neither man said much. They would be late, and they had no trainer. Already, they were ineligible. But they marched on anyway, doing as Pandaros would have had them do, training, testing themselves as they went, envisioning the victories that seemed even more out of their grasp, and to Stefanos, even less important in the face of what had happened.

Had we not set out for Olympia, Pandaros would be alive.

. . .

It was midday, two days later, when they approached the confluence of the Kladeos and Alpheios rivers, and the rooftops, sacred groves, and smoke from Olympia came into view, with the tree-clad Hill of Kronos looking down on the sanctuary. They approached from the east, following the line of the Alpheios river, the very first thing they could see being the high banks of the hippodrome on their right side.

The sound of harsh voices and neighing of horses could be heard in the air as they walked slowly beside the river, the two of them now blending in with other men coming to seek entry in the Games.

Stefanos stopped at a tree beside the river to stare up at the banks of the hippodrome. What he saw that night in the mountains of Arkadia came rushing back to him, the rumble of hooves and the scream of chariot wheels as those ghostly apparitions plunged insanely down those mountain tracks.

"You coming?" Kratos said, shaking his friend.

"Oh...ah, yes. Yes."

"I've never seen you look so white. You're not nervous are you?" Kratos laughed.

Stefanos shook his head, the weight of the bronze helmet tilted back on his head feeling heavier than ever. "Of course not."

"Then let's go," Kratos said moving into a crowd of people that got thicker as they reached the end of the hippodrome and the beginning of the small sanctuary of Hestia where sweet smelling smoke rose from the altar before a small temple.

They followed the people until they came to the southern stoa which was the entrance to the sanctuary. Here the crowds were thick, and the contemplative quiet of their journey shattered by the raised voices of athletes and their trainers or chaperones trying to gain late entry to see the Hellanodikai in the bouleuterion where they administered the Games and swore in competitors.

"The Scrutiny is finished!" they heard someone announce

above the heads of the crowd, only to hear the man booed, his voice drowned out by desperate cries of anger and frustration.

"You must account for Poseidon's wrath at sea!" pleaded one voice.

"The Arkadians slowed our progress on purpose!" yelled someone from Corinth, his hands waving.

"Looks like we're late," Stefanos said.

"We have to try," Kratos replied. "Pandaros didn't die so that we turn back now."

"No. He didn't." Stefanos pushed through the crowd that stood before the white marble columns and high walls of the stoa until they reached the main entrance. With their hoplons and spears, the two warriors garnered many wicked looks as they used their bulk to shove aside votive vendors and others who had come to the sanctuary to ply their wares. A group of kinaidoi lined the walls to one side, trying to attract the attention of the many paiderastia who might seek their companionship, and alongside them a philosopher talked about the purity of the Sacred Games, and the need for men to honour the Gods honestly and fairly.

"Out of the way!" Stefanos said, pushing aside a young boy who approached him, naked, baring his buttocks in the midst of the crowd.

"The little buggers are more aggressive here than at Nemea," Kratos observed as he kicked another boy aside to get through.

They finally broke through the press of flesh in the stoa to join the line of men seeking an audience with the Hellanodikai. The latter were the judges of the games, those men of Ellis who supervised the Scrutiny, and who had the power to admit or turn away any would-be competitor they wished. As such, the courtyard of the bouleuterion was more sedate and respectful than the stoa, men not wanting to anger the judges who sat at tables wearing their official purple cloaks over their white himations.

Stefanos and Kratos lined up and waited for their turn. As

they waited, they observed the men about them - a few other hoplites who, like them, had come almost directly from the battlefield, some bulky villagers, apalaistroi, who did their best to display their arete, their manly excellence, by standing calm and tall with arms crossed as they waited patiently for their turn to approach.

The gymnasiarchos of Olympia, the official who saw to the upkeep and fair use of the facilities of the sanctuary, moved along behind the tables of the Hellanodikai, providing occasional input as needed.

"Next!" called one of the Hellanodikai, not looking up as Stefanos and Kratos approached and put their hoplons down to rest against their greaved legs.

"Stefanos, son of Talos, and Kratos, son of Lichas, both of Argos," Stefanos said.

The judge looked up, his bald head burnt by the sun, the colour intensified by the purple of his cloak.

"You are late," he said.

"We were waylaid on the road from Argos."

The judge shook his head. "I've heard it all today. He put down the bonze stylus with which he had been making notes on a roll of papyrus. "You look like you've just come from the battlefield. Do you swear before almighty Zeus that you have been training for the past ten months for these games?"

"War is training, so yes," Stefanos said, staring down at the man, feeling frustration at his disdain toward them working its way quickly into his blood.

"So you say. Where is your trainer?"

"He was killed two days ago when we were attacked outside Heraia. We had to give him the proper rites before we could leave."

"That is why we're late to the Scrutiny," Kratos added, standing beside Stefanos.

"Perhaps it was the Gods' will that you not reach Olympia in time to compete," the judge said bluntly, leaning back in his chair.

"The Gods' will?" Stefanos said, gritting his teeth. "Our trainer is dead."

"And you must have one to compete."

"What was your trainer's name?" came the voice of the gymnasiarchos who now stood beside the judge. He was a grizzled, strong looking man, a man who had seen war and competition for long years by the look of him.

"Pandaros of Argos," Stefanos said.

"I'm sorry to hear it," the gymnasiarchos said, lowering his head. "He was known to me. A good trainer and competitor. He was a man of arete and andreia." He leaned over and spoke close to the judge's ear. "If you would like my opinion, these men look more than fit for competition, and their former trainer was a man of excellence. The Gods will be pleased by their entry in the Games."

"I don't want your opinion. You have no say in these decisions!" he hissed at the gymnasiarchos.

"They tell the truth," said a deep, rumbling voice behind Stefanos and Kratos.

All four men turned to see the Spartan enomotarch they had met two days before on the road when Pandaros was killed. He came from the neighbouring table where he had just put his name on the list of competitors, his red cloak hanging about him, his helmet tucked beneath his left arm. His dark eyes stared at the judge who looked up at him with less disdain and more fear than he had the others.

"Allow them to compete," the Spartan said. "I saw their trainer killed. They speak true."

"They are still late for the Scrutiny," the judge said stubbornly, his eyes less certain.

"As am I, yet I have entered, as have my comrades."

"I think, our Spartan friend has helped to aid your decision," the gymnasiarchos said, smiling.

The judge did not speak for a few moments, perhaps unable to as the Spartan stared down at him.

Stefanos tried to meet the Spartan's eyes, but the man

would not acknowledge him, rather continued to stare at the judge, waiting for the man to capitulate.

"Very well," the judge said. "They can compete."

The Spartan nodded, turned, and left the bouleuterion.

"What events will you be competing in?" the judge said, inviting Stefanos and Kratos to enter their names.

"That was strange," Kratos said as they left the bouleuterion a few minutes later. "Why did the Spartan help us?"

"Don't know." Stefanos stopped and nodded to where the Spartan was walking back toward the hippodrome with the red-haired youth he recognized from the attack. "Let's ask him!"

Stefanos began to walk quickly, pushing his way through the crowd after the Spartan. "Enomotarch!" he yelled, several men about him turning to look at him. "Spartan!"

There was sudden silence around them as men stopped moving about and stared. Ahead of them, the enomotarch stopped and turned slowly to look at the two Argives. He eyed them for a moment.

"We would speak with you," Stefanos said, walking forward.

The Spartan stared at them for a second more, turned, and began to walk away without another word, the red-haired youth shuffling along quickly beside him.

"Guess he doesn't want to talk," Kratos said, his hand on Stefanos' arm. "Come. Let's find the Argive camp. The judge said it was just the other side of the Alpheios."

Stefanos tore his gaze from the back of the red cloak and they went back in the direction of the stoa.

As they did so, a voice called out to them.

"Stefanos! Kratos!"

They turned to see a slightly younger, strong, smiling man coming toward them along the back wall of the bouleuterion.

His sandy hair hung down to his jaw to blend with the thick beard that looked like he had just come out of the sea. He wore only a chiton, and seemed quite comfortable as he moved through the sanctuary, as though he had been there for some time already, and did not worry about enemies within the crowd around them.

"Zeus Saviour..." the man said.

"...and Victory!" Stefanos and Kratos replied, striding toward him and laying their dorata and hoplons against the wall of the bouleuterion to embrace the man warmly.

"Xenophon, son of Gryllus!" Stefanos said out loud, his voice full of affection. "It's good to see you, my friend!"

"And you both!" Xenophon said, one hand on each of the two men's shoulders.

"Last we heard, you were in Ionia with the Spartans," Kratos said.

"I was! But Agesilaus wanted to return for the Olympiad, and asked me to accompany him. So, I did."

"Rubbing shoulders with the Spartan king now, eh?" Stefanos said.

"He's become a good friend," Xenophon said in earnest.

"Is he a good king though?" Kratos asked.

"I believe so. He's good for Sparta, and even though he's only been Eurypontid King for two years, he's showing much more promise than his half-brother Agis ever did."

Stefanos and Kratos shifted uneasily at the mention of King Agis of Sparta who had soundly defeated Argos at Mantinea years before.

"Well, we can only hope Agesilaus crushes the Persians," Kratos said.

"Not before we can get in on the action!" Stefanos added quickly, and turned to Xenophon. "How's the fighting in Ionia?"

"Heavy fighting. Good fighting," Xenophon nodded, his beard swaying as he did so. "Agesilaus is a good tactician. He's giving Tissaphernes a lot to worry about."

Stefanos slammed the butt of his spear into the ground. "Gods I wish I could wade through Persian blood after all we've been through. Rather than playing at war for no pay."

"I know," Xenophon said. " We all do. And maybe we will. But, I have to say, I'm surprised to see you both here. Are you competing?"

"Yes," Kratos answered. "We were late arriving, but were able to convince one of the Hellanodikai to allow us in. Our trainer was killed on the road here."

"They believed you?" Xenophon said. "I've heard they are especially rigid in the Scrutiny this year."

"The judge was about to turn us away, even though the gymnasiarchos of Olympia spoke in our favour," Kratos said.

"Then a Spartan enomotarch walked up to the judge, spoke true on behalf of our story, turned, and left. We were just trying to get his attention when you walked up."

"If he didn't stop, he had other business," Xenophon said, waving a hand. "As long as you are entered in the lists."

Stefanos thought of the woman he had seen in the field at that moment. In truth, he had been unable to forget her, the forceful demeanour, her athletic body, the anger she had stirred in him when she had dismissed Pandaros' death in aiding her.

Kratos elbowed Stefanos. "You awake?"

"Oh...yes," he shoved him back. "Forgive me," he said to Xenophon. "It's been a long road."

"I can see that," the Athenian said, smiling. "Well, you are both here, and that's what matters. Are you staying in the Argive camp?"

"Yes," Stefanos said. "We're told it's on the other side of the Alpheios. You? Are you with the Athenians?"

"Ha! No," Xenophon replied. "My fellow citizens shun me for befriending the Spartans. I'm in their camp on the other side of the Kladeos; they like to keep to themselves."

"Well, if you see Pollux, tell him we're here," Stefanos said.

"I will. He's on guard at the king's tent."

"So he did come?" Kratos said. "It'll be like old times!"

"Between your training, that is," Xenophon said. "From what I've seen of the other competitors, it's going to be hard-going this Olympiad."

"We can handle it," Stefanos said. "Let's meet later to catch up. I want to know how to get in on the Persian campaign. I'm sick of things here," he added intensely.

Kratos looked at his friend, and Xenophon noticed, but said nothing.

"I'll send word when you should come to the Spartan camp. I'll introduce you to Agesilaus." Xenophon waved to someone in the distance who had been trying to get his attention. "I've got to go now. See you soon?"

"Yes," they answered, watching him cut through the crowd to a man waiting in the distance.

"Good to see him," Kratos said. "He looks older than us though."

"You would too if you had to lead ten thousand men out of Persia and back to Greece on foot." Stefanos picked up his hoplon and doru. "Let's find the Argive camp," he said.

"Think there will be anyone we know there?"

"Unfortunately, yes," Stefanos replied.

THE ARGIVE CAMP WAS LOCATED JUST SOUTH OF THE Alpheios, beside a copse of beech and oak trees. Men were everywhere, talking with their trainers, exercising, readying themselves for the upcoming games. They stood around makeshift skammae, watching men spar at boxing, wrestling, and pankration. Pairs of ephebes and their trainers or chaperones stood by to watch the older, more skilled men in order to learn techniques that might gain them their first Olympic victory.

The skammae were dotted around the camp which was mostly a large conglomeration of tents, and shelters. Altars had been set up where men could sacrifice to the Gods in the hopes that they would grant them a victory. There was also the usual array of vendors on the outskirts to cater to the needs of the men of Argos for the duration of the games - sellers of votive offerings, sacrificial animals, food, oil for their bodies, hand braces for the pugilistic sports, and harness for the equine competitions. Prices were as high as the expectation in each man whom the Hellanodikai had admitted to the competition.

"Looks like all of Argos is here," Kratos said as they walked past a row of men working on a series of korikoi hanging from three trees, their fists pounding into the bags filled with sand and seed with lighting quick speed.

"Uh huh," Stefanos grunted, staring past the training men to see the large grouping of blue and white tents where members of the Argive Thousand were encamped, no doubt with members of the Argive council; everyone would want to be at Olympia, and not just for sport. The Games were always an opportunity for alliances to be made against common enemies, for ideas to be spread among the greatest warriors of the Greek world, and plots to be hatched. War may stop during the Sacred Truce, but the fighting was always worse after the Olympiad.

Stefanos knew that with all of the bitterness of the last several years, tensions would be running high on and off the sand.

"We need to find a tent or shelter," Kratos said, wiping sweat from his brow.

"Doesn't look like there are any left," Stefanos said as he scanned the tents. The Argive council always provided a certain number of tents for the men representing the city in the Games, but this Olympiad looked to be the highest in attendance for many years. "We'll have to check with the vendors over there." Stefanos pointed to the long row of sellers who had set up shop.

They walked over to one who had supplies for tents and shelters, and waited in the line that had formed before his stall. The man looked to be from Cyrene, and he had an array of poles, staves, ropes, and fabrics of many colours and designs set out.

Stefanos and Kratos could see men shaking their heads and arguing with the man, but his confident demeanour did not waver, even before the muscular men threatening to rip him apart for his thievery. The men walked away with a tent nonetheless, and soon enough Stefanos and Kratos approached the bearded man who was handing coin over to his helpers to stow somewhere safe.

"What do you need?" the man said without preamble.

"A tent," Stefanos said. "How much?"

"A tent big enough to hold two warriors such as yourselves, as well as your equipment, will cost you fifty drachmae."

The two men could not speak for a moment, for that sum would wipe out almost all of their funds.

"Ten," Kratos said, leaning on the board of the seller's counter.

The man smiled and crossed his arms. "You can appreciate that I will not be able to consider such a sum. Look around you..." he pointed. "Men are here from all over the world for the great games of Zeus. They will not turn away from glory because of the price of a tent where they can rest out of the blazing sun between competitions, or rest in peace at night so that their bodies are ready for the trials they face in the days to come."

"You're a thief," Stefanos said plainly.

"Perhaps," the man said easily, "but you are in more need than I am. Will you sleep exposed to the gaze of your competitors? Your enemies?" He smiled again, his eyes roaming past the two men. "From the looks I see your fellow citizens giving you, I should think you need to be behind heavier fortifications than even my canvas can provide."

Stefanos and Kratos turned around, the bronze helmets upon their heads glinting in the sunlight, to see men darting looks at them. Some averted their eyes, but others continued to stare, especially one group in particular.

Stefanos turned away from the vendor and made for the group without pause, Kratos following, shaking his head and gripping his doru.

Ocnus, son of Nemos, stood at the head of his small group of friends, Krikor, Biton, Ampyx and Glaucus, all of whom were still sweaty and dirty from their exertions, except for Ocnus himself who was still in his blue and white uniform.

"Don't you five ever get out of each other's holes long enough to make some new friends?" Stefanos said, his eyes looking directly at Ocnus.

"Trouble finding shelter, Stefanos?" Ocnus said, laughing, his friends following suit. "I could put in a word with the council members here to provide you with a tent, but I don't think you'll last long in the Games. They should spare themselves the expense."

"Which member of the council did you allow to bugger you so that you can wear that nice, clean uniform?"

"I earned my place in the Thousand."

"Sure you did, but I'm sure your superior's spear thrust is far better than your own. I'm surprised you can still walk and stand under all the weight of that fancy armour!"

"How was your visit home then?" Ocnus said, spying the twinge in Stefanos' jaw. "I hear your father finally crossed the river. A shame his business is no more. And your sister...so alone...so pious," Ocnus laughed. "What will she do without aged Talos? Who will look after your family estates when you set off to fight for the Spartans again, or the Persians?"

Ampyx, a big blond Argive spat at Stefanos' feet then, challenging him to approach, sneering at him along with the four others.

"Careful, boy," Stefanos said. "You don't want to miss your competition because of a stupid decision now." He could feel Kratos closer to him, ready to restrain him. The mastigophoroi, the whip-bearing police of Olympia, were extremely rigid in their enforcement of the peace at the sanctuary.

"Why don't you kinaidoi move along and leave the men to their own business?" Kratos said, standing in front of Stefanos.

Ocnus laughed again. "We'll see each other again," he said, "But I would be surprised if you slept well at all. You never know what can happen outside the boundaries of the sanctuary."

Stefanos watched Ocnus turn and leave, followed by his friends, the one named Ampyx staring back over his taught shoulder to stare at Stefanos and Kratos.

"Should have known they'd be here," Kratos said.

"Let's find some shelter," Stefanos said, returning to the vendor, fire in his eyes.

The vendor ended up selling Stefanos and Kratos a thick square of plain canvas, two poles and a length of hemp rope for a sum that would allow the two men to have funds for the entirety of the Games. The negotiations had been slow and stubborn at first, the vendor refusing to budge on his extortionate price, that is until Stefanos' fist reached out, viper-quick, to grab the man's chiton and whisper that he would report him for having brought Persians to the sacred games.

"I see your boys back there," Stefanos said through gritted teeth as the vendor squirmed. "How long will you be able to remain here to bleed the competitors in the Gods' games when you have brought three xenoi here?"

The vendor relented and gave them the items they desired for ten drachmae.

They found a spot where they created a lean-to beneath the thick limbs of an oak tree, somewhat apart from the mass of the Argive camp.

"You think Ocnus and his boys will try anything?" Kratos said, holding his spear and staring at the sea of tents.

"I don't think so. They're cowards, that uniform doesn't hide the fact."

Kratos looked doubtful, but did not say anything as they set up their camp and unstrapped their thoraxes for the first time in many days.

AT DUSK, STEFANOS MADE HIS WAY TO THE SANCTUARY AND the temple of Zeus to make an offering for their safe journey to Olympia.

Kratos had already made his thank-offering at the altars within the Argive camp, and now stood watch over their camp.

The evening was humid, and a mist formed along the banks of the Alpheios as Stefanos crossed the river, holding the small goat he had purchased from one of the vendors within the Argive camp. He carried the beast tightly beneath his left arm, leaving his right free to grab for the dagger which hung at his belt.

It felt strange to wear only a chiton, to leave his thorax and greaves behind in the camp. He did not like the feeling, and his eyes scanned the mist before him where dots of orange torch and campfire glowed, the raucous voices of men and boys everywhere around him. The sun was dipping red in the distance beyond the river Kladeos, and Stefanos wondered briefly when he would catch up with Xenophon again, his friend encamped with the Spartans to the west of the sanctuary. He smiled at the thought. It had been a long time.

Stefanos walked through the stoa and around the back of the bouleuterion until he reached the sanctuary of Hestia and the entrance into the Altis where he paused before setting foot in the Olympic sanctuary. In the dim light, the statue of the goddess Nike soared atop her triangular pedestal, ready to crown the victors with an olive bough. All about her, dotting the Altis, were the bronze statues of past Olympian victors, their shadowed faces and bodies seeming to move and observe the mortals about them in the glow of the firelight.

Stefanos thought of his father's wish, the reason he had

come to Olympia, and the weight of it felt as though it would push him into the ground. The bronzes standing silent all around the Altis seemed to mock him, their eyes doubting his skill, especially the Diagorids of Rhodes, that family of boxers and pankrationists that had been winning at Olympia for close to one hundred years. Stefanos wondered if he would meet any of them on the sand, and flexed his hands as he thought of it; Diagoras, Akousilaos, Dorieus, and the young Eukles had all been crowned and their statues now towered over the mortals walking through the sacred precinct.

The poet's voice in the dim light brought Stefanos out of his thoughts, and he recognized one of Pindar's odes.

"Of garlands from these games hath Diagoras twice won him crowns, and four times he had good luck at famous Isthmos and twice following at Nemea, and twice at rocky Athens. And at Argos the bronze shield knoweth him, and the deeds of Arcadia and of Thebes and the yearly games Boeotian, and Pellene and Aigina where six times he won; and the pillar of stone at Megara hath the same tale to tell." The poet paused, letting his words settle on his listeners before continuing.

"But do though, O Father Zeus, who holdest sway on the mountain-ridges of Atabyrios glorify the accustomed Olympian winner's hymn, and the man who hath done valiantly with his fists: give him honour at the hands of citizens and of strangers; for he walketh in the straight way that abhorreth insolence, having learnt well the lessons his true soul hath taught him, which hath come to him from his nobles sires..."

Stefanos pushed past the group of men listening to the poet, and made his way beneath the statue of the goddess Nike to stand before the entrance to the temple of Olympian Zeus. He paused there, the goat struggling with futility beneath his muscular arm as the scent of blood and smoke reached its nostrils.

Massive bronze tripods blazed with fire either side of the

ramp leading up to the temple, casting an ethereal light upon the east pediment where Zeus stood with both Oinomaos and Pelops on either side of him, along with Sterope, Hippodameia, and the horses and chariots of that legendary race ages ago.

Stefanos looked upon the scene with curiosity, suppressing the wave of prickling that ran up his spine and at the base of his neck, memories of what he had seen in the mountains coming back to haunt him. Not one to be cowed, he pressed on up the ramp indicating his offering to the two theokoloi who stood beside one of the massive Doric columns either side of the bronze doors.

"I wish to make an offering to Zeus in thanks for my safe journey here," Stefanos said to the first priest.

"Come with me," the man said, moving in front of Stefanos, and pushing through the bronze doors, his white robe dragging along the marble floor, the hem stained with blood about the bottom.

They entered the temple and immediately the sounds of the crowds outside became muted, the world became still. Stefanos could hear only his breath and the beating of his heart as he walked across the floor and approached the titanic ivory and gold statue of Zeus at the far end. He felt like dropping to his knees then, and nearly did, his legs stopping and his knees feeling weak for a moment as he took in the glistening skin and muscle of Zeus seated on his golden throne, his crowned head reaching all the way to the temple's ceiling.

The god seemed to breathe before Stefanos, more lifelike than any bronze or marble statue he had seen, so much so that he felt the artist must have used some form of strange magic to breathe some of the god's essence into the statue itself. Zeus's left hand held a giant spear topped by his eagle, and his right, outstretched hand, held Nike herself, winged, beautiful, ready to descend to crown the victors at Zeus' behest.

"Approach," the priest said, standing beside the marble altar behind which was a pool of olive oil that, along with the fiery tripods to either side, cast a shimmering light upon the bearded face of Zeus.

Stefanos approached, his eyes looking up, and handed the goat to the priest who took it from him and held it upon the altar.

"Speak your words to almighty Zeus," the priest said, his eyes looking up as well, his grip upon the sacrificial beast solid and unwavering.

Stefanos looked from the priest to the statue and raised his arms, feeling small beneath the gaze of the king of the Gods.

"Father Zeus, Protector of Travellers... Accept this beast in thanks for our safe arrival at Olympia and the games begun by your son Herakles. I honour you, mighty Zeus... Help me to fulfill my father's wishes in the contest, whatever the cost... Grant me victory..."

The temple was silent, still. The flames flickered violently either side of the enthroned god. The priest looked at Stefanos to make sure he was finished, and then his blade slashed the goat's neck deeply so that the beast convulsed for but a moment before going limp, its lifeblood running freely over the marble altar to run in hot streams along the channels and onto the floor.

Stefanos was still then, his eyes open, then closed, off and on until the priest had finished his probing of the guts and organs.

Then the man stopped, his hands still, his head down, silent.

"What is it?" Stefanos asked.

The priest did not answer, but raised his hands dripping with blood to Zeus, his voice whispering so lowly that Stefanos could not understand what he was saying. Then, the man turned and walked directly to Stefanos, his eyes staring into his.

Stefanos felt strength welling inside him then, something he had never felt before. It was as though Zeus himself was reaching out to him then, touching his forehead with his mighty, blood-soaked hand.

"Go unto your agon, Argive, and seek your victory."

Stefanos felt the trickle of blood down his cheek then and began to back away from the priest.

The man's eyes stared at him, still and intense, as though he were in a daze, standing still in a pool of blood.

Thank you, Father Zeus... Stefanos thought as he turned and went back into the dusk light.

Once outside, Stefanos stood still at the bottom of the ramp beneath the lofty statue of Nike. The Altis was quieter, but for a few groups of men admiring the epinikion statues of past victors that adorned the grounds. He felt his limbs hard and strong then, the blood pulsing through his veins as though of fire, and he began to believe that winning was possible as his gaze travelled to the high altar of Zeus, just to the north of the temple, near the temple of Hera, and beside the Pelopion.

Fire and smoke rose high into the sky from the altar which was reached by a winding path around it. The smoke settled over the sanctuary and weaved its way over roofs of the naiskoi and oikoi of the Terrace of the Treasuries, up the slope of the Hill of Kronos and beyond.

Stefanos began to make his way to the temple of Hera when he saw a head of shocking red hair bobbing as the owner limped along the south wall of the temple toward the baths and the river Kladeos. He followed, through the darkness and smoke. As he got closer to the youth, his feet quick and quiet in the trodden grass, he recognized him as the boy who had been with the Spartan woman the morning Pandaros was killed.

He could see the untrusting eyes of fellow competitors watching him as he walked among them, curious as stags watching an aged lion walking among them. Stefanos ignored them, and pressed on until he reached the banks of the Kladeos where the red-haired boy crossed the river and pressed on toward the distant glow of another camp, a stade away.

Stefanos slowed his pace and went more cautiously then. He was getting far from the sanctuary and the darkness about him was thick among the trees. He knew there would be Spartan sentries everywhere, especially with King Agesilaus present.

The boy paused before reaching the Spartan camp and turned south west.

Stefanos considered leaving off his pursuit, but something pushed him on. He knew he should return to his own camp and Kratos, who would be worried about his long absence with their enemies so near, but he did not want to stop. When the boy disappeared beyond the tree line and into an open field, Stefanos stopped and watched, his eyes scanning the torchlit precinct guarded by an iron ring of Spartan hoplites.

The neighing of horses could be heard within, and the familiar commanding voice of a woman.

Stefanos knew it would be madness to approach any more and so decided to climb up the limbs of the strong oak tree beside him to get a better view. He reached for the first limb and pulled himself up, careful not to make so much noise as to alert the guards. When he reached a safe perch, his eyes immediately locked onto the four-horse chariot speeding back and forth in a deadly ellipse and driven by the woman he realized he had been hoping to see.

She wore only a short chiton and her black hair whipped in the breeze behind her as she sped back and forth, watched by her entourage of girls and the big guard that had spoken for Stefanos and Kratos at the bouleuterion.

"You see?" the woman yelled. "Give them their heads in the turns and their instincts will carry them through at the correct speed!" she said as she pulled her team to a halt before the spectators, the horses panting and snorting as she got down.

Stefanos watched her long lean legs and felt himself stirring again. There was something about the woman that he did not quite understand, though he knew he was drawn to it. The sight of her also angered him, for she had been dismissive of Pandaros' death, even when it was in helping her and the girls with her.

The woman walked around to the front of her team, stroking the head of each horse and speaking softly.

"The Gods have blessed you," she said, her black hair blending with the black mane and coat of the stallions and mares of her team whom she had reared and trained from foals. "Xanthus," she spoke to the first stallion on the outside. "The Gods have given you the speed of an immortal stallion. You are fast and fearless," she whispered, moving to the two middle horses, stroking each of their foreheads with her hands. "Zoe, Phaedra... you will keep the pace steady, the lines straight, giving order to the team together. My girls..." she smiled, turning to the last stallion, the one who would be on the inside of the hippodrome.

"Acheron, you will be steady, and strong, and anchor the team in the turns so that you reach your final destination. Without you, my friend, we are lost. Hold true..." She put her forehead against the stallion's and closed her eyes, uncaring of the eyes of the mortal men and women all about her. She only ever felt at home with her horses.

"Princess Kyniska," said the red-haired youth as he passed the bodyguard, and approached the woman.

"Yes, Pirro," she answered, opening her eyes and turning to face the boy. "Is everything in place?"

"Yes, my lady. Both teams are enlisted with myself as the driver."

"Good," she said, her blue eyes blazing in the firelight. She stepped closer to the boy who bowed as she approached. "Did you also visit the temple of Hera?"

"Yes, lady."

"And? Is the portrait of me visible within the temple? From my victory in the Heraia?"

He nodded. "Yes, though not at the front. It is closer to the cella."

"That is well," she answered, nodding. "Then the Gods will see that it was I who ran to victory in those games." She smiled. "My offerings on the altars of Zeus and Hera were accepted then?"

"Yes, lady. The Gods seemed pleased," Pirro answered, taking a brush from the younger girl, Euryleonis, and beginning to brush down Xanthus.

"Good," Kyniska said, turning quickly to another one of the girls. "Thais, have my whites harnessed and ready for training. I want Adonis, Zeta, Hippolitus, and Pasiphae to get some more in tonight.

"Is it not too dark, my lady?" asked the girl.

"No," the woman said flatly. "Do you think that Pelops and Hippodameia stopped when Oinomaus was closing on their backs with his spear poised?"

"No," the girl replied, shrinking a little under her mistress' intensity.

"No." Kyniska smiled once more, her hand on Thais' blushing cheek. "If they thunder past the Taraxippos before the first turn in the hippodrome, do you think they will shy away from the evil that haunts that spot and terrifies other teams who train only in the day?"

"No, my lady," the girl said now, meeting the older woman's gaze and smiling back at her, reflecting the pride in the teams they all cared for. "They will not."

"Training in the dark helps them to rely less on their sight, though horses are visual animals. The darkness is a good substitute for fear, of which mine have none. Now, go and get them."

Thais ran off, passing some of the guards, to the stabling area.

"Pirro," Kyniska said, turning to the young man. "Take them around three more times before you stable them for the night. They've given much today," she said with pride.

Kyniska took a hemp bag from the girl named Helle, who was waiting for her, and plunged her hand in to take out an apple for each of the horses.

Never once did she move abruptly around her animals. Her voice to them was alway soft and soothing.

"Yes, lady..." the boy said as he handed the brush to one of the other girls. He made his way to the front of the team and spoke to each of them, his lanky frame limping before them as he reached up, the horses nudging him playfully as he passed.

Pirro mounted the cab and took the reins in his hands, wrapping the leather about his wrists three times and gripping them tightly. He set his good leg forward for support, then trotted the team back out onto the track.

As they had been talking, torches had been lit around the perimeter, casting an orange glow over the grassy field beyond the Kladeos.

Pirro stood poised for the moment Kyniska gave him the signal to start, his eyes reaching between the dark necks of Zoe and Phaedra. He was small in the cab, but it was more his home than any other place, and every time he stood there, he did it for the woman who had never given up on him, who had saved his life.

Pirro stood where he did at that moment, always, because Kyniska had saved him in Sparta. Ever since that day when the horses had threatened to stampede through the city, trampling dozens of Spartan women and children, Kyniska had kept the boy close. He had stopped the horses with a word, saving many lives.

Kyniska had known immediately that the boy had a talent for speaking with her equine brothers and sisters. Never had she seen such skill in contact with horses, except for herself. When she had offered to have him stay with her and train as a driver for the Olympiad, he had accepted immediately.

Pirro eased the blacks into a gentle walk, then a trot. They moved like water and Kyniska, despite having seen them run countless times at her behest, never tired of seeing their flowing manes and tails, or hearing the sweet sound of their hooves pounding the hollow ground.

Before the horses knew it, Pirro had them running, diving into the turns and firing out of them faster than a Spartan spear thrust.

Kyniska watched them closely, how they moved together, worked together. She searched for any flaw that might hinder them in their pursuit of glory, the smallest infraction, but none could be seen. They were healthy and strong.

It's time, my children. It's time.

Up in his tree, Stefanos continued to stare at the Spartan woman.

A part of him wanted to drop down and confront her about her behaviour when they had saved her and her girls. *Pandaros is dead!* he thought, anger filling him once again.

He saw the Spartan enomotarch standing nearby, still in the shadows near a torch. The man's eyes never left the woman, and Stefanos wondered if they were lovers. After all, he had heard that Spartan women were able to chose whomever they wished to share their bed.

Stefanos' eyebrows peaked at the thought, but he was still angry and before he knew it he was dropping out of the tree onto the damp grass, just as the chariot team was rounding the turn nearest to him.

The horses cried out in surprise and shied away from the man that had dropped out of the tree.

"My lady, no!" the enomotarch was yelling.

Stefanos turned from the horses to the woman rushing straight at him and before he could speak, her foot had landed in his gut full force, sending him flying backward into the trunk of the oak tree.

"Step away," she said , her voice on the edge of more violence, so much so that Stefanos forgot his gut and rose again to stare at her.

"I...I wanted to thank..." Stefanos' voice trailed off as he looked upon her, unsure of what to say, his anger forgotten.

"You're not welcome here!" the enomotarch said as he approached, his spear pointed at Stefanos.

To the side, the boy, Pirro, was trying to steady the horses, their neighing echoing over the moonlit field.

"Careful with that," Stefanos said to the Spartan facing him as more guards came up to stand behind their enomotarch. "You could get hurt."

Kyniska turned from the horses to look at the two men facing each other. *What does he want?*

"You challenging me, Argive?" the Spartan said, smiling beneath his helmet.

"I've laid bigger lads than you in the dirt," Stefanos replied, crossing his arms, even as the spear point hovered a foot from his neck. Then the tip came closer.

"Typhon!" Kyniska said sharply, coming to her guard's side. "We may not be in the sanctuary, but this is a sacred time and I don't want to anger the Gods."

Typhon continued to stare at Stefanos, his black locks hanging around his shoulders, the oil on them glistening in the torchlight. "What do you want here?"

"Pirro, hold them still," she pat the horses and walked over to Stefanos again.

Stefanos could feel the burn in his gut where she had kicked him. "Why did you attack me?"

"Why did you drop out of the tree?" she replied quickly. "Trying to steal glimpses like a thief?"

"I was out for an evening stroll. On my way back from the temple, I saw your driver there," he nodded toward Pirro, " and thought I would follow him to say thank you." Stefanos eyed the group all about him, noticed they were itching for a fight.

"So?"

"Thank you," he said, gazing back at the woman before him, her dark eyes darting at him from beneath her knitted brows and dark wisps of chestnut brown hair. He forced his eyes to look up.

"You've said it. Now you may go," Kyniska said.

"No."

"She told you to leave," Typhon stepped closer, handing his doru to the man behind him and getting in Stefanos' face.

"Ease up, friend. I'm not finished. I expected you to offer me a friendly word for saving your life the other day, even at the cost of one of my oldest and dearest friends."

Kyniska laughed, her voice beautiful and mocking all at once. "I have thanked you three times already."

"I didn't notice," Stefanos said.

"I'm not surprised," she said, smiling back at her girls who were all waiting near the horses, the team of whites now brought up to join the others. "I thanked you when my men did not kill you along the river the other day. I thanked you by having Typhon here speak for you during the Scrutiny as to why you were late."

"And the third time?" Stefanos asked, sure he had her now, surprised that he was enjoying this banter, despite the danger he had put himself in.

"By not allowing my men to cut you to pieces here and now for interrupting my team's training."

"Your team?" Stefanos looked at the horses and the two light chariots that rocked back and forth a few feet away. "Are you a rich lady then? You must be to have a half enomotia of men at your command."

"I am rich. And your life is getting shorter, Argive." Kyniska turned away from Stefanos and went to the white team that had been brought up, speaking to each of the horses.

"Well," Stefanos said to Typhon who still stood directly in front of him. "I guess we're finished. My thanks, friend," he said, slapping Typhon on the shoulder.

There was murder in Typhon's eyes, but Stefanos ignored it and turned to walk away, back toward the river Kladeos.

In the dim firelight, he could see the outlines of the Spartan guard watching him, waiting to see if he would leave or not.

He did, but not before catching a final glimpse of the woman in the chariot cab, driving her team of whites gradually faster around the dark track, her voice loud and confident in the dark.

THE SANCTUARY WAS MORE EMPTY WHEN HE WALKED THROUGH, back the way he had come, but for a few groups still lingering outside the baths from which the sound of splashing and conversation emanated.

As he walked, pairs of mastigophoroi patrolled the grounds, their long whips visible in the shadow, ready to strike at anyone who dared to disturb the peace of the sanctuary.

When he arrived back at camp, Kratos jumped up, his xiphos in his hand.

"Where in Hades have you been? I thought something happened to you!" Kratos said, his eyes wide, his face angry in the orange light before their lean-to.

"I've been playing with the Spartans," Stefanos said.

"Playing? Hmm," Kratos pursed his lips and flung back his long hair. "You're going to get yourself killed even before you compete," he said, his finger pointing at Stefanos.

"I wanted to thank the enomotarch who spoke for us."

"It was obvious he didn't want to speak with us, don't you think?"

"It's all for show. They're really gentle creatures, the Spartans."

"And my sisters didn't bed with you," Kratos laughed.

Stefanos smiled. "Don't tease me," he laughed. "Of course they did!"

Kratos' fist flew out playfully and caught Stefanos in the stomach, causing him to grunt in pain. "What's wrong with you. You hurt? Who did you fight with this time?"

"Some woman," Stefanos said, smiling through the pain. "Come on. Let's get some sleep. We need to hit the skamma tomorrow." Stefanos laid himself down on his mat and looked up at the sky, his lids feeling heavy, but his mind racing.

Don't forget what you're here for, he thought. *Father, I won't let you down.*

Back on the dark field, the chariot still made the rounds of the track, the sound of the wheels cutting through the earth and grass soft and lulling combined with the pounding of horses' hooves.

Pirro, and the girl Euryleonis watched from the fence as Kyniska drove the animals around the track in darkness but for a few torches. The beasts' white bodies flashed in the light occasionally before disappearing again, their mistress' voice encouraging them with every hoof beat.

"She's distracted," Pirro said to Euryleonis.

The girl did not smile. She could see it too. "Yes. The incident with the Argive. She should have let Typhon kill him."

"I will," Typhon said, his dark form coming out of the shadows. "That Argive has pushed me too far."

"Surely he meant no harm," Pirro said. "In truth, had he not been there the other morning, who knows what might have happened before you and the guards arrived?"

"Careful, boy," Typhon said, towering over the young man.

"I am," Pirro said, his face reddening in the darkness. "I know my job, Typhon. Do you know yours?"

"I might just end your life, cripple," Typhon's voice was so full of menace that Euryleonis backed away.

"You could, I know," Pirro answered. "But you won't until I drive my lady's chariot to the heavens and back." Pirro stood, small and insignificant before the warrior, but with the courage of a thousand lions behind him as he turned away from the Spartan and made his way to the track where Kyniska was waiting for him.

"Zeta is a little hesitant so close to the inside," she said. "Tomorrow, let's try moving her to the right, switching with Pasiphae."

"I agree," Pirro said, "She seems to have been taken lately with Adonis more than Hippolytus." He smiled.

"You noticed?"

"Yes."

"Of course you did." Kyniska ruffled his red hair and stepped back. "Take them around a few times to cool off before stabling them. They've earned their apples."

"Yes, lady." Pirro took the reins and clucked lightly, setting the whites off at a slow walk.

Kyniska stared after them with pride. They were her younger team, more inexperienced, but if it came to it, if something happened to her blacks, they would be able to hold their own in the Games.

Before returning to Euryleonis, who was waiting to attend upon her for the night, Kyniska stared at the tree which the Argive had fallen out of.

"Fool," she muttered, as she walked away.

Chapter Five

THE GREEKS

Οι Έλληνες

The serenity with which the Gods blanketed the sanctuary of Olympia in the morning belied the noise and intensity of the day ahead. It was thus every day.

When Stefanos and Kratos woke beneath their shelter, it was to the sound of birdsong, the sight of soft sun rays angling their way through the mist that drifted up the banks of the river Alpheios.

Once men woke and broke their fasts, the days were filled with the harsh voices of their trainers, and the grunts of exertion from the athletes. In the stadium to the east, the quick steps of the runners could be heard, along with encouragement from the sloping banks where a few scattered spectators and followers sat in comment. At the same time, a short distance away in the hippodrome, the thunder of hooves shook the earth as charioteers and their teams took their practice runs on the course, assessing their readiness for the great Games.

Around the Altis, the theokoloi, those priests of the Gods

who dwelt in the theokoleion to the west of the Altis, made sacrifices upon the altars of the Gods, including Olympian Zeus, inviting them to witness the upcoming games so that they might choose the best from among the Greeks. The smell of burning herbs, meat, fat, and bone was constant around the sanctuary, as much as the jockeying of the vendors who sought to sell the athletes and their followers every manner of product from the latest discoi and javelins, to the most blessed oils with which the men could anoint themselves.

The sanctuary of Olympia exploded into being every day.

"I don't think we should leave all our belongings here," Kratos said to Stefanos as they finished their breakfast of cheese, bread, and fresh figs. "The kinaidoi will rob us blind while we're gone, and our armour and weapons will be lost to us."

Stefanos looked at the pile of his thorax, greaves, helmet, hoplon, doru, and xiphos. He shook his head. "You're right, but carrying these things around all day with us...it's going to be difficult. We'll have to put them down at some point to train. And since Pandaros was killed, let's face it, our training has suffered."

Kratos nodded. "We need to make him proud."

"Yes. The apodyterium of the baths or gymnasium isn't safe either."

"There's always the camp of the Argive Thousand," Kratos laughed.

"I don't think so!"

"What about one of the treasuries?"

"I don't think there is one belonging to a city that would be friendly to two mercenaries. No. Looks like we'll need to carry them with us and keep a watch."

"Long days ahead," Kratos muttered as he doused the fire and hoisted his things.

. . .

THE TWO MEN LEFT THE ARGIVE CAMP, HOPING THAT AT LEAST their shelter, which they had bargained hard for, would not be stolen while they were in the sanctuary for the day. The Sacred Truce did not seem to apply to thievery.

They crossed the river over the foot bridge along with many others who made their way to the training grounds of Olympia.

"There's the gymnasiarchos!" Kratos said, pointing with his spear toward the west end of the stoa. "Let's ask him where the palaestra is."

Stefanos sped up to catch the man who had just finished chiding an athlete and his trainer for refusing to wrestle with some of the peasants present in the training area.

"The Gods will laugh at you!" he yelled to their backs. "Stop complaining and compete!"

"Ahem," Stefanos said, as he walked up.

"What is it, Argive?"

"Just wondering where the palaestra is, so that my friend and I can train."

"Walk straight back, along the western side of the Altis until you see the training area on your left. I've installed rows of korikoi and enlarged the skamma, so there should be plenty of room."

"Is there a space for javelin?" Kratos asked.

"Along the river, other side of the palaestra," the gymnasiarchos said. "Watch yourselves out there, men," he said, his voice lower. "The wars have made men angry and hateful. Many have forgotten Eris Agathos. Let me know if there's trouble."

"We will," Stefanos said, smiling as he and Kratos walked away. "He's naive if he thinks he can stop fights breaking out."

"Hopefully men will remember the real purpose for being here."

"What's that?" Stefanos said, his father's voice in his ears.

Kratos stopped. "Why, for the glory of our city, our families, and the glory of the Gods themselves."

Stefanos was taken aback at the intensity and sincerity in his friend's face and voice. He reached out and pat Kratos on the shoulder.

"Then let us honour the Gods and our families."

"What of Argos?"

Stefanos did not answer.

They continued to walk, and the crowds got thicker as they passed the processional gate to the Altis and the House of the Phaidryntai, those servants of Olympia who cared for the colossal chryselephantine statue of Zeus in the great temple. The phaidryntai stood beside the building that had served as the workshop of the artist, Pheidias, who had sculpted the marvel within the temple.

The crowds were almost unbearable now, made more so by the equipment that Stefanos and Kratos carried with them. Athletes walked about naked or in their loincloths, just prior to practice bouts, and observers and others stood watching them, assessing the skill and bodies of the competitors from other cities.

Beside the circular Heroon, where the altar to the unknown hero was located, a large crowd was gathered around a massive man wearing a lion skin.

Stefanos stopped in his tracks, shaking his head for a moment, trying to imagine how he could possibly be seeing Herakles.

The man stood there, recounting feats to do with a lion, and something about killing three Persian Immortals with his bare hands. The crowd about him was rapt by his booming voice, the sound of which seemed accompanied by the flicker of his muscles. The only thing missing was the hero's club.

"Who in Hades is that?" Kratos said out loud.

"Don't you know?" said a young man carrying a discus who happened to hear the question. He looked at Kratos and Stefanos as if they were from some other world. "That's Polydamas of Thessaly, of course. He won the pankration twelve years ago! He killed the lion he wears, with his bare hands on the slopes of Olympus itself, and he defeated three of the Persian king's best all at the same time." The young man shook his head. "Who is that?" he muttered as he ran over to join the crowd.

"Oh," Kratos said. "*That* Polydamas!"

Stefanos laughed. "I think we've been in the field much longer than all these young pups."

"Gods help me," Kratos said. "If it had been the real Herakles, then I'd have been impressed."

They walked by the crowd of people who seemed to be reaching out to Polydamas as if he were the son of Zeus himself, each stretching out his fingers to touch the hero.

They arrived at the palaestra in time to find places for their things along the wall surrounding the skamma where men were boxing and wrestling, lifting weights and stretching. On the east side of the palaestra hung several korikoi, the bags filled with either sand or seed, where competitors in the boxing and pankration were warming up.

Stefanos and Kratos watched them for a minute before removing their tunics and sandals. They noticed some of the Hellanodikai on hand, sitting to the side wrapped in their purple cloaks, observing the competitors who would bleed before them in days to come.

"Come, let's get ready. I'm sure our things are safe with them here," Stefanos said, eyeing his hoplon with the peacock feather upon it.

They entered the elaiothesion, the room where amphora of olive oil had been set aside for the athletes to use. The smell inside the room was pungent and heavy, and they both caught their balance as their bare feet trod across the oily, marble floor.

Stefanos dipped a ladle in and brought it up to see the golden liquid draining back into the jar. "Good stuff," he said, taking some in his hand and beginning to rub it the length of his limbs, his scarred muscles glistening in the light coming in through the door.

"Are we really here?" Kratos said. "I've been wanting this for so long, Stefanos. I'm having trouble believing it."

"Then snap out of it!" Stefanos said. "Pandaros would flay you if he knew your head wasn't in this."

"I know. Be in the moment, every hour of every day, he would say." Kratos' hands stopped. "I still can't believe he's gone."

"He's not gone to Elysium yet," Stefanos said, smiling. "I'm sure he's got Charon waiting until the Games are over, just so that he can see if we win or not."

"If?"

"When."

They both laughed and then went out onto the sand.

ARETE WAS SOMETHING THAT EVERY MAN AND BOY AT OLYMPIA observed with curiosity and care. They assessed, they learned from, and they observed the level of each competitor's manly excellence, their physique, the way they carried themselves, how they cared for their bodies as well as their minds.

One was as likely to be engaged in a swift discussion of technique, as much as observed by one's foes for the method of fighting, grappling or throwing.

Stefanos and Kratos kept to themselves as best they could, warming up with some running around the sands, before lifting the stone and lead weights that were available. They sparred with each other, testing each other's quickness in boxing and wrestling, just as Pandaros had had them do on the road.

Before long, the sweat was pouring off of each man and they took a break in the shade of the peristyle, drinking water from clay cups. When their thirst was quenched, they went to the konisterion to dust their hands and legs with powder so as to have a bit more grip against the sweat that ran all over them.

After that, Stefanos went to his satchel to pull out his

himantes, the hardened hide strips that boxers wrapped about their fists and forearms before stepping onto the sand.

"I'll see you later," Kratos said as he picked up a javelin. "I'll be by the river, practicing."

"Good luck," Stefanos said as he held one end of linen between his teeth. "I'll be at the korikoi." He pressed the strips of hide tightly to his fists, flexing and bending his hands to get the right feel and flex. He felt power in his hands with the himantes on, and turned to one of the vacant bags which still swung from the last user's abuse.

He gave it a jab with one hand, then another, getting the feel of his inanimate opponent. He began to dance slowly, his feet fast and light, belying his bulk. Then he launched into a flurry of hits, mock parries and skiamachein, the method of shadow skirmishing that Pandaros had taught him to use over the years when he did not have a sparring partner.

Stefanos, son of Talos, thought of his father with every punch, jab, and grunt. After all, he was the reason he was there.

Suddenly he felt eyes on him, and turned to see a man standing naked, several feet away. His long dark, oiled hair was tied back, and his arms were crossed over his chest, his himantes red with blood from a recent bout.

"Argive," he said.

Stefanos stared at him for a moment and then recognized him as the Spartan enomotarch that had been guarding the Spartan woman. *What's her name? Kyniska?* he tried to remember.

"Spartan!" Stefanos answered loudly, causing many of the men on the skamma to turn and look.

Typhon did not move. "Why don't you practice with me instead of those korikoi?"

Stefanos walked up to him, his eyes assessing his opponent. He'd boxed Spartans before and knew they were well-trained. He'd also beaten them before too.

"You sure you're up for it?" Stefanos replied.

"Mercenary!" came another shout from across the palaestra.

Typhon looked curiously over Stefanos' shoulder. "Seems I'll have to stand in line to pommel you, Argive. That one seems desperate."

Stefanos turned to see Ampyx, one of Ocnus' cronies coming toward him, shoving aside those who were in his way and gathering angry retorts in his wake.

Stefanos glanced at the Hellanodikai and noticed them observing the scene with disdain. All eyes were on them at that moment.

"What do you want, Ampyx? Where's your master? Off the leash are you?"

Ampyx flexed and rolled his shoulders quickly, his long blond hair waving from side to side as he did so. "Ocnus' duties require him elsewhere."

"What a shame," Stefanos said, smiling. "And you? What battlefields have you been on these last years?"

"Shut up, Stefanos. It's time you got a lesson." Ampyx put up his fists, ready.

"You don't waste any time," Stefanos said, walking slowly toward him. "Remember to mind your posture, and don't give away your move with your leading foot."

Ampyx rushed in with a furious swing and upper-cut combination which Stefanos dodged as easily as if he were taking a stroll through the forest.

"Not bad," Stefanos said, feinting so as to lure Ampyx in again.

Ampyx attacked with another combination, this time with four hits.

Stefanos barely dodged the third and fourth, but did not allow a fifth. A double-feint threw Ampyx off his guard and then Stefanos' hide-covered fist slammed square into the man's face. Blood exploded in all directions, and Ampyx flew backward several feet, to land on his back in the sand.

"You're too angry, Ampyx," Stefanos said, standing over

the howling man. "You weren't ready. All that fanciness is going to get you hurt. Next time I won't be so gentle on you."

Stefanos chuckled to himself as some other men dragged Ampyx away, arms flailing. He turned to speak to Typhon, but spotted Pirro speaking with him.

"Your beating will have to wait," Typhon growled at Stefanos, before leaving with Pirro.

"But I'm all warmed up!" Stefanos called after him to no avail.

"I'll spar with you!" bellowed someone who had just come onto the skamma.

Stefanos turned to see a massive young man. He wondered at the youth's size, for he had never seen such a beast.

"Where are you from, friend?" Stefanos asked, sizing him up.

"Pelopidas of Thebes," he said, stretching his limbs and twisting his trunk-like torso.

Great. Thebans, Stefanos cursed his luck.

"You ready, Spartan lover?" called one of the men who was with the giant youth.

"Shouldn't you be fighting kids your own age?" Stefanos asked as they circled each other.

Pelopidas laughed. "This is my first Olympics," he said. "I don't know all the rules." He swung, and the massive arm reached over Stefanos' ducking head, a swing to take down a horse.

"Time for your lesson then!" Stefanos said, wishing he'd been boxing Typhon instead.

"What were you thinking, Stefanos?" Kratos said as he looked at Stefanos' bruised ribs. "You're lucky that gorgon didn't break anything."

"If I'd been slower, he would have," Stefanos winced.

"Just be careful. This is meant to be practice for the main

event. You don't want every boxer in Olympia to discover your tactics. Remember what Pollux says? *Never let the same enemy see you fight more than once.*"

"Good advice," Stefanos said, standing up and gathering his things. "I'll remember that next time. For now, I need a soak in the baths."

The two of them walked out of the palaestra to the bath house located between the river Kladeos and the Heroon.

The baths were crowded inside, but not as much as the swimming pool beside it. With the midday sun pounding down on Olympia, it seemed that every athlete and his trainer had packed into the relatively small structures to wash away the morning's dirt and discuss what they had learned, what needed to be improved upon, who were the ones to beat, and who fought dirty.

"There's an obol for you if no one touches our things," Stefanos said to one of the young boys in the apodyterium where they undressed and left their things.

As they stepped into the bathing area, they scanned the perimeter of the water where groups of men stood about talking, oiling themselves, and scrubbing their skin with fine sand or with a strigil, beside large basins filled with water.

The pools of warm and cold water were packed to capacity, and the two men were hard-put to find a space to drop into.

"See anyone we know?" Kratos asked, splashing himself with water from a newly refreshed basin.

"Not yet," Stefanos answered, walking across the mosaic floor that was covered with dirt, oil, and hair from all the bathers. The smell of olive oil and sweat was overwhelming, but it was nothing compared to the smells one encountered in the shield wall during a battle. As promachoi, Stefanos and Kratos would have seen it all - new recruits pissing and shitting themselves at the sight of oncoming cavalry, the punctured guts of the first enemies to go down beneath the blades of their dorata, the tangy stench of vomit when it all became too much for some.

"Stefanos! Kratos!" came a familiar voice from the far side of the pool beside them.

The two men turned to see Xenophon, his long hair and beard soaked, giving him a poseidonic quality.

They walked around the edge of the pool and slid into the water to stand beside him.

"I've never seen it so crowded," Xenophon said. "Everybody's here!"

"You seen anyone from the Persian march?" Stefanos asked.

"If I did, I might not recognize them. We've all changed so much.

"I heard what happened," Xenophon said, pushing away a drift of oil that floated by on the surface of the water.

"Heard what?" Stefanos asked.

"About the palaestra, and how you knocked down one of your own Argives with a single blow."

"That just happened!"

"News travels fast here. Already, you're the man to beat."

Kratos laughed. "I told you!"

"Fantastic." Stefanos hung his head. He had wanted to be less obvious until the day of the Games. *Too late...*

"Never mind. Oh, gods..."

"What?" Kratos said to Xenophon.

"Eteocles."

Stefanos turned round at the name and felt his blood boil.

"He's coming over," Xenophon said as a tall man with a pointy nose and broad swimmer's shoulders came wading over to see them.

"And here they are, the Spartan lovers!" Eteocles said, looking down his long nose at the three men.

"Eteocles," Xenophon greeted him. "What brings you to the Games?"

"What brings me?" he laughed. "Why, everyone is here!

And word is the Spartans will be humiliated. Why should I miss that?"

"I thought you'd be slaughtering more women and children on some remote island," Stefanos burst out. Even though it had been almost twenty years since he had sailed with the Athenians to the island of Melos, he could still hear the cries of the women and children as they watched their husbands and fathers slaughtered and were themselves thrown into the awaiting slave ships.

"Ah yes, the Argive who disliked my methods. I see you are none the wiser. Turned from your city to bed with the Spartans, eh?"

"Better the Spartans than a coward who slaughters helpless islanders." Stefanos could feel Xenophon's fist gripping him under water.

"Helpless?" laughed Eteocles. "Who's ignorant now? Never mind. I'm sure you and I have more in common, what with your activities in Sicily."

Stefanos' eyes went wide.

"Oh yes. I know the things you've done, Stefanos son of Talos. Many do, and the Gods punish such things."

"Then I guess I'll see you in Tartarus," Stefanos said, moving closer to stare up at the taller man.

"Really, Xenophon, you should pick more civilized company...oh, wait...you've also turned against your city, haven't you? What would Socrates say?"

"Don't you mention his name," Xenophon answered, his voice angry for the first time.

"That's right, I forgot. You were not there for him at the time of his death. You must feel so guilty, especially after selling yourself for hire to the Persians when he advised you against it."

Xenophon got control of the anger that was simmering inside of him, though it took great effort. "If Socrates were alive, he would say that I have pursued virtue beyond the walls of my city, a place where justice is wounded, and corrupt men make it a slave to their benefit and not that of the people."

"You're losing your touch," Eteocles mocked. "Too much time with your laconic friends." Eteocles turned to look back and waved to three of his friends. "I must be going now. I look forward to seeing the Spartans fall in the Games." He looked at Stefanos and Kratos. "As well as some Argives..." With that, he turned haughtily and waded back across the pool, his naked form disappearing out the door and into the apodyterium.

"I hate that man," Stefanos said.

Xenophon sighed. "Me too." I'm sad to say he is the worst of Athenians, and there are more and more like him. Perhaps it's best that Socrates is gone... I can't believe it's only been three years since the trial."

"What of your friend, young Plato?" Kratos said. "I remember you speaking very highly of him. "Has he not been able to sway the youth of Athens to better thoughts?"

Stefanos leaned back against the wall of the pool, his mind wandering as it often did when the discussion would turn to philosophy.

"So soon after the trial?" Xenophon said. "I think it wise if Plato keep quiet for a time. After all, that's the charge they brought up against Socrates... corrupting Athenian youth."

Xenophon was quiet for a few moments, his long hair giving him an air of sadness that the other two men had rarely seen in him, even in their darkest days on the march back from Persia.

"Come," Stefanos said, patting the two other men on the shoulders. "Let's get out of here and go find a shady spot and a pitcher of wine over which we can reminisce about shield walls and spears, the sting of Persian arrows, and the speed of horses!"

Xenophon smiled. "Excellent idea!"

. . .

THEY SAT IN AN AREA TO THE SOUTH OF THE BATHS AND swimming pool, a spot along the river where wine, pastry and meat vendors had set up shops to cater to the crowds. The three men obtained the last table along the riverbank and sat down.

Xenophon gazed at the pile of their weapons, armour and satchels. "Why are you carrying all that about with you?" he asked.

"Let's just say the Argive encampment is not at all welcoming or friendly to mercenaries," Kratos said as he bit into a pastry filled with cheese.

"Or Spartan-lovers?"

"I don't know that we are that either," Stefanos said, "but they certainly think of us as such."

"You need to rest and train in peace for the great Games, don't you?"

"We do what we can," Stefanos shrugged.

Xenophon was silent for a minute, rubbing his beard. "It's not right, but I know what it is to be ostracized by your own city. If I were in Athens, I would have a hard time of it, though I do miss it." He went back to rubbing his beard but said nothing more for a bit.

"You know who else is here?" Xenophon said.

"Who?"

"Thrasybulos."

"That must make you uncomfortable," Stefanos said, aware of the great Athenian general and how he had opposed the thirty tyrants installed in Athens by Sparta only eight years before.

"Discomfort is something I've come to accept more easily, thanks to the example of our Spartan friends," Xenophon laughed.

Stefanos looked at his friend and knew that the laughter could not hide the fact that he did not like the idea of being in the same space as Thrasybulos, a general and Athenian democratic hero who had commanded alongside Alcibiades, and who had taken Piraeas from the tyrants with only a thousand men.

"How did Agesilaus take this news?" Kratos asked.

"He shrugged it off. This is the time of the Sacred Truce, and our Spartan brothers believe everyone should honour the Gods and hold to the peace."

"Tell that to the Argives," Stefanos muttered.

Xenophon leaned over and slapped Stefanos on the shoulder. "Don't worry about it! It may be that things are not as bad as you think. Once everyone gets into the mindset, and are overcome with thoughts of victory, they will focus their energies on their training and winning, rather than their hatred of you."

They finished their wine and food in silence, their eyes watching the crush of men and boys as they passed in front of them, some heading for the stadium, others the hippodrome, while most made their way to the palaestra for afternoon training, or into the grounds of the Altis to admire the statues of past Olympians beside the altars of the Gods.

Xenophon stood up, followed by Stefanos and Kratos.

"I must be going, but I'll see you soon," Xenophon said. There are some horses I wish to see."

"Horses?" Stefanos asked.

"Yes. To be honest, my friend, my favourite event of the games is the tethrippon. I love the skill with which those drivers take their four-horse teams around the hippodrome. Amazing!"

"You always liked horses," Kratos said, remembering Xenophon talking about it all the way back from Persia: the skill it took to raise and train a horse, the mastery of skill to ride a horse so that it moved naturally.

"Yes, well. That doesn't mean I won't come to your bouts. Now, I really must go."

Xenophon turned and left, making his way across the sanctuary toward the stoa and the hippodrome beyond.

"You going to train more?" Kratos asked Stefanos when they hoisted their things again.

"I think I'm good for today," Stefanos said, feeling his ribs on fire from his encounter with the Theban youth, Pelopidas. "You go ahead."

"I should. I need to dedicate more time to each of my events."

"All right. I'm going to rest. I'll see you back at camp then?"

"Yes," Kratos said. "Just try to stay out of trouble."

"Me?"

"Yes, you!" Kratos said shoving Stefanos as they went their separate ways.

Stefanos walked slowly through the crowd, eventually making his way to the Altis, where a forest of magnificent bronzes rose up like trees around him, each dedicated to an Olympic victor crowned by Nike herself. It was peaceful there, the sound of birds on the rooftop of the temple of Zeus floating over everything.

The afternoon light set the Altis aflame. Stefanos yearned for such peace inside his heart, but images of his father, as well as his sister, tormented him as he walked.

He hated Ocnus, for what he had done to Cleo, for what he was. Stefanos also realized with distaste that some of that hatred was owed to himself. Cleo was alone. Ocnus was right about that, and part of the blame, Stefanos knew only too well, was his own.

He came to the back of the temple of Zeus where the sacred olive tree sprouted out of the earth, its roots ancient and deep. From the boughs of that tree, countless champions had been crowned. He stared up into the silver leaves, set against the backdrop of the blue sky.

There is nothing wrong with being alone and enjoying one's life, he told himself, wondering at the same time if Cleo truly enjoyed her service to Hera, as their mother did, or if she would have been better off with a cruel husband, birthing his children and taking his abuse. *Likely not,* he thought.

Stefanos sighed and walked on around the back of the temple, passed the shivering tree until he faced the Pelopion near the great altar of Zeus. He stopped, the hairs on the back of his neck standing on end as he faced the ancient, barrow of Pelops, whose remains were said to lay in the earth beneath, surrounded as it was by a pentagonal wall.

Stefanos forced himself to go closer and walk up the steps of the small entrance where a few people stood idly, watching him curiously, this hoplite carrying his weapons and armour with him.

"Show the hero respect," said an Elean man, as Stefanos passed between the columns supporting the tile roof of the propylon.

Stefanos looked sternly at the man, but nodded, remembering how seriously the Eleans took their ancient overlordship of this land. Once within the small compound, the sounds of a man's voice echoed throughout, softened by the rise of the grass-covered barrow in the centre. It was surrounded by an ancient stone wall, and topped by a grouping of cypress trees that seemed to stretch to the sky, to the stars themselves.

Stefanos moved to one side, found a space along the wall near a couple of Arkadians, and put down his load. He watched the priest as he raised a triangular, bronze dagger and sliced it across the neck of a black ram that was held in place on the altar by his two attendants.

"Mighty Pelops, we offer this black ram to you, hero of our ancestors and forebear of the house of Atreus. With this, your own dagger, we give you the blood of this ram that you may bless these games held in honour of your race across the land."

"That's Pelops' blade?" Stefanos whispered excitedly to the man beside him.

"Shhh!" the Arkadian said, his muscular arms crossed in

front of him, a scowl on his bearded face. "Yes," he added. "It is the hero's blade."

Stefanos looked back to the altar which was now running red with blood that dripped along the channels to the edges and down into the grass at the base of the altar, around the priest's feet.

The sound of screaming horses erupted in Stefanos' mind, and the sound of grinding chariot wheels whipped around the small enclosure. He looked around frantically for the chariot, but no one else seemed to notice anything.

From around the back of the barrow there appeared a woman in a long white peplos, with long hair as wild as a horse's mane, running down her back and over her shoulders. No one looked at her either, but she looked at Stefanos, tears running down her face as she ran one hand along the wall surrounding the burial mound.

Stefanos thought he recognized her, but could not remember for a moment. Then, it dawned on him. *Lady*, his mouth whispered, but made no sound.

She turned toward him. She was tall, and slender, her cheeks red, her eyes wet.

The neighing of horses grew louder and louder then, and Stefanos watched as she walked directly toward him. He was unable to move, unable to speak, even as she reached out to touch his face. In her eyes, he could see mountains, and trees passing by, flying spear shafts, and a man's shoulders as they strained for dear life against the reins of a chariot. A man's yelling, and pain, so much pain mingled with victory...

Stefanos shut his eyes tightly.

"Are you unwell?" the voice cut through the fog, muffled and faint. "Argive?"

Stefanos opened his eyes to see the priest standing before him, wiping his bloody hands on a white towel that one of the attendants had handed to him.

The enclosure was empty now, the onlookers having gone

back out into the Altis. Stefanos was the only one remaining but for the priest and his helpers.

"Do you need some water?" the priest asked him. "The day is hot, and can be doubly-so within the walls of the Pelopion."

"No," Stefanos said, shaking his head and gathering his things quickly. He felt his tunic soaking with sweat, his face running wet and clammy. "No, I must go. Now."

"Go then," the priest said, eyeing him.

Stefanos went out of the propylon and turned right. He made his way across the ground, passing beneath the boughs of some trees, shoving a couple of people out of the way as he caught his breath.

"Argive boor!" an Athenian said, before rejoining his group.

Stefanos ignored the man and arrived breathless at the side of the temple of Hera where he sat on the steps beneath the temple's high doric columns.

He looked back the way he had come and saw the group the Athenian had been with, a whole mass of neat white chitons and himations surrounding a tall, thick man dressed in a bronze cuirass and still wearing a helmet. Obviously, the man had just arrived.

Stefanos heard the name Thrasybulos said out loud, and then a deep voice in reply to the crowd. Even with the Altis, men did not shrink from seeking powerful sponsors and useful connections.

He began to catch his breath and lowered his head for a few minutes, the stone of the temple behind him a comfort at that moment.

"You look unwell, Argive," a soft voice said.

Stefanos turned to see a delicate pair of sandaled feet on the step beside him, the long flowing folds of a cream-coloured peplos gathered about the ankles.

He dared not look up for a moment, wondering if it was

the apparition from the Pelopion again, but then he felt a hand on his shoulder, and he turned.

"Do not worry. I am the priestess of Demeter Chamyne. It is my duty to be within the sanctuary."

"Should you be touching me, priestess?" Stefanos asked the younger girl whose face lightened at his awkward tone.

"I was tending the altar of the goddess when I felt an urge to come outside. The first thing I saw when I came out was you, stumbling toward this spot from the Pelopion. What happened?" The priestess sat down beside him, her leg against the hoplon where it leaned against the bottom step of the temple.

"It was nothing. An ill feeling came on because of an injury to my ribs this morning."

"The Gods reveal much to us through pain, do they not?" she smiled.

"Eris and ponos?" Stefanos laughed.

"Yes. For the Gods have willed them upon us from the beginning, so that we may become stronger, wiser, and more knowing of ourselves."

"I doubt the man whose face I fractured this morning learned much about himself."

"Such things happen at Olympia. Always. Truly, I think the test of the Games starts well before the first day of competition, don't you?"

Stefanos' face contorted, not because of what she had said, but because of an acute ringing in this ears. He shuddered as the priestess' hand grabbed his wrist, stronger than a vice.

"Hey..." he began to protest but her eyes were still and locked upon him in a way that forbid speech or movement. They were wide, and blue, and gazing beyond him, beyond the space in which they found themselves.

"You are drifting upon the waves... Set your heart to the task at hand... You do not... you will not... fight for yourself alone..."

Stefanos stared at the priestess, unable to pull his eyes

away from her. "Stop," he said, but her eyes made no sign of recognition. He tried to nudge her leg with his, but his foot grazed the hoplon with the peacock feather upon it, and it fell to the ground, away from her leg.

The priestess' eyes shot wide and her face reddened suddenly. "Forgive me," she muttered, embarrassed.

"Why did you say those things?" he asked.

"I said nothing."

Stefanos was going to say more, but decided against it. He looked up at the temple of Hera again, and felt its draw.

His attention was taken away by the group of theokoloi on the other side of the Altis who were staring at them.

"I must go!' the priestess said hurriedly. She began to walk away when she stopped and turned. "There is something about you, Argive. You are being watched." She paused a moment and looked again at him. "Make these days the greatest of your life."

Stefanos gathered his things again and ploughed through the crowds of newly-arrived Thebans, Athenians, and others until he was on the other side of the stoa and crossing the river back to his and Kratos' camp.

The Argive camp was bustling when he arrived, full of new spectators eager to secure a spot and meet with those from their allied cities, in order to conduct business and establish new relationships.

Once at the shelter beneath the tree, Stefanos set his things down and started a fire. The flames caught quickly, everything was so dry, and soon he was sitting against the bole of the tree staring into the crackling heat, his mind caught in a web of wonder and doubt as to all that had happened that day.

Stefanos reached over to grasp the shaft of his doru and laid it across his lap, more at ease with the weapon in his hand.

Great Mother... Oh Hera... I know my prayers do not reach you as often as they should. I feel more alone than ever now. I thought I liked it that way, being on my own, but... for the sake of my own mother and

father, help me to understand what I'm supposed to do here. Gods know I've embraced Eris...but have I been kakochartos? Or is there some remnant of Eris Agathos in me? I don't know anymore. The priestess was right. I am drifting...ever since Hysiae, when I first took up the hoplon and doru in the name of my city. I have been lost...

Stefanos' lids were heavy as he stared at the dancing flames before him. There he saw a man and woman in a chariot drawn by four horses, tearing across the land, spear shafts raining down on them, threatening to pierce them both but for the speed of their team.

He shook his head, trying to reclaim his consciousness, but the woman stepped off of the chariot and pointed at him from the flames.

Leave me alone... he thought.

She continued to point at him, and then, from behind her back, she held aloft an olive crown, fresh, and shivering, newly made. She held it out to him, willing him to take it.

Take it...son of Talos... he heard her say at the back of his mind.

Take it...

"Good morning."

Stefanos looked up from where he lay beneath his chlamys, his doru still grasped tightly in his fists.

Kratos stood on the other side of the fire pit, trying to light it again in the damp morning air. "What happened to you?"

Stefanos turned away from his friend and stared at the ground for a moment, trying to recollect the night. He realized his eyes were wet and he quickly wiped them before turning and sitting up.

"I overslept, I guess."

"You must have been more hurt than we thought," Kratos said, handing him a skin of water. "I didn't think you took a hit to the head."

"I didn't," Stefanos said. "I was just tired." He stood up, and went around the back of the tree to relieve himself. When he came back, he looked at his friend. "Where did you get to?"

"I ended up training with some of the other pentathletes. A few of them are from Argos. Do you remember Telamon?"

"The son of that banker?"

"Yes. He's here. He almost won at the last Olympiad. Said he would tell me what to expect. Then he wanted to see what whores were still available to the north of the sanctuary, and well...we found some nice ones. I looked around for you - I know you never miss a chance like that - but I couldn't find you in the Altis or anywhere else."

"Don't bother. I wasn't feeling great anyway." Stefanos stretched his arms up to the sky and bent sideways back and forth to try and test his ribs.

He felt fine.

"You all right? You look like you've seen a ghost," Kratos said.

"Pa!"

"You up for training today?"

"Yes, I think I am," Stefanos said, feeling better, enjoying the waves of strength that flowed through him. "I'm ready."

After they ate a good breakfast of cheese, bread, and dried meat, Stefanos hoisted his things and followed Kratos back into the sanctuary to the palaestra.

As they reached the entrance, Stefanos stopped his friend.

"You go ahead. I'll join you shortly. I want to make an offering in the Heraion."

"Sure," Kratos said, waving to Telamon who was already inside with some of the other Argive athletes.

"I'll catch up with you," Stefanos said as he strode across to the Altis and along the side of the temple of Hera. He went up the steps and passed between the thick columns of the goddess' dwelling.

It was dark inside, and incense curled about the columns

supporting the cedar roof within. It smelled sweetly as he walked toward the altar beneath the statue of the goddess.

No priestesses were present, nor any competitors. His footsteps echoed on the floor as he walked forward, his eyes taking in the painted images of female champions of the Heraia which hung on several of the columns leading to the altar.

Hippodameia came to his mind, she who had helped Pelops to victory in defiance of her father, and who had established the Heraia in honour of the goddess. He had heard that there was a wooden couch within the temple that contained the heroine's bones, and sure enough, there it lay, ancient and cared for, to the right of the altar.

Stefanos felt his spine tingle as he stopped before the altar and placed his armour, satchel, and weapons on the floor. He took the hoplon that hung from his back, that which had shielded him and the men beside him through countless battles, its surface dented and slashed with a thousand death blows that had never seen home.

"Goddess Hera. Thank you for watching over me. I know you are guiding me, somehow...and I will seek to understand. I will also claim victory for my family if it is offered to me. Great goddess, I offer you this hoplon, emblazoned with the peacock feather that is your emblem, which I have ever carried into battle. Grant me victory in the agon to come in these ancient games."

Stefanos stopped, unsure of what else to say. He held the hoplon up above his head, offering it to the goddess as she looked down at him from painted marble eyes, and laid it upon her altar.

He was silent for a few more moments, his thoughts of his mother and father, of his sister yet living.

After a time, he began to back away from the altar, his satchel, weapons, helmet and armour on his person once more. He backed away, watching the large round shield he had offered as the torch-light played upon its surface. Then, he turned, and left the temple, feeling strong and full of purpose.

When the temple was empty and the flickering of the flames in their braziers could be heard again, the shadows stirred and a solitary form emerged from behind the ancient couch to stand before the altar.

Kyniska, dressed in men's travel clothes, slid back her hood and looked up at the goddess. Her dark hair fell in wild wisps about her face, and her dark eyes went from the goddess to the shield upon her altar.

For a moment she turned to look at the temple's entrance again to see if the Argive was still there, but he had disappeared into the light of day.

"Goddess...beloved Hera...grant us both victory..." she whispered, her voice hoarse.

Chapter Six

THE SPARTANS

Οι Σπαρτιάτες

For the next two weeks, the regimen was strict for every man at Olympia, but for none more so than Stefanos and Kratos.

Every day they would wake as Helios' fiery chariot broke over the eastern horizon, its golden rays slicing through the mist that blanketed the Peloponnese from Argos to Elis. They would eat a light meal, and then they would gather their things and head for the Altis to observe the morning rituals.

The Gods were watching Olympia now, and every man there knew it, could feel their eyes upon him as he sought to win the sacred olive crown.

Kratos was now storing his equipment in the tent of his friend Telamon, but when he invited Stefanos to do the same, so that he would not have to carry it around, the latter declined.

"I don't know Telamon much, but some of his friends know Ocnus' friends, and that's reason enough for me to keep my distance."

"Suit yourself, but the crowds are thicker than they were when we first arrived, haven't you noticed? It seems like the whole world is here!" Kratos said as he gazed at the bustling sanctuary.

"It does. But I'll carry my things," Stefanos insisted.

"You know," Kratos said, "I know you don't like Ocnus. I don't either, but he actually hasn't been that bad."

"Drink too much again last night?" Stefanos said, eyeing his friend cautiously.

"No. Well, yes. Maybe... Anyhow, I think your things would be safe."

"Thanks anyway," Stefanos said, turning to go toward the temple of Hera. "I'll see you later?"

"Yes. I'm training with Telamon again, but I'll see you on the palaestra?"

"I'll be there."

"Are you thinking of him?" Kratos asked before turning to go.

"Who?"

"Pandaros. His voice is in my mind, goading me on like I was sixteen again."

"Of course." Stefanos smiled. "Except in my mind, we're on the mountain, running over logs and boulders with his voice echoing behind us in the wood. *Come ladies! You can do better!*"

Kratos laughed. "Old bastard..." He shook his head.

Stefanos watched Kratos go, then turned to make his way up the steps of the Heraion.

It was the same every day, except after a while, Kratos began to sleep longer, his nights with wine, women, and boys in the Argive camp catching up with him.

Stefanos tried to warn him of it, that he was not as young as he used to be, but Kratos waved him off.

"I'll vomit, then I'll be good as new," he muttered from under his chlamys.

It came to the point where Stefanos did not even bother

waking his friend, and just set off for the sanctuary himself. He knew they each had to pursue their own path to victory or defeat. He also knew that for him, the latter was not an option.

As the Games drew closer, more and more boxers from the various camps made an appearance on the palaestra to either check out the competition, or intimidate their potential opponents.

The young Theban, Pelopidas, was a regular fixture, his fists always bloody from his latest bout. Whenever he spied Stefanos, he nodded gravely, with a shocking display of respect. Neither of them wanted to fight the other again, mainly for fear of getting injured so close to the start of the Games. Stefanos felt the memory of throbbing in his ribs whenever he saw the Theban, and Pelopidas' hand automatically went to his now-crooked nose which Stefanos had fixed him with.

Stefanos felt life flowing through him when he was on the palaestra, his wrapped fists pounding the extra-heavy korikoi that the gymnasiarchos had set up for the heavier fighters among them.

One day, when Stefanos finished his training, he sat down to watch some of the practice bouts between other competitors. He sweat profusely, leaning his muscled back against the wall of the peristyle that was lined with benches.

"You know something, Argive?" the gymnasiarchos said, sitting down beside him, his legs spread, his thick hands on his knees.

"What's that?" Stefanos answered, water running down his chest between his muscles to his groin.

"You could win. You know that, don't you?"

Stefanos turned to look at the older man carefully. "What makes you say that?"

"Look at the men around here," he said in a low voice, indicating the various men and boys standing about the skamma, flexing, stretching, lifting, and sparring. "Swollen ears and broken faces, all of them. And to hear them talk, you'd think they'd been born dumb." He lowered his voice even more. "If they'd been born in Sparta, they'd have been killed at birth."

"You Spartan?"

"Yes. What of it?" the gymnasiarchos demanded.

"Nothing, friend. I've no problem with the Spartans."

"I think you're the only Argive to say such a thing." He waved his hand. "Anyway I look at you and I don't see a broken face. Your ears aren't swollen, and your nose has only been broken, what? Once?"

"Twice."

"That's normal. Some of these lads couldn't get out of the way of a bee."

"They seem pretty good to me," Stefanos said, watching a bout at the far corner where an Arkadian was pounding the ribs of one of the Macedonian athletes.

"You're fast. You get out of the way. But you also hit hard, and when it counts. I've been watching you, and I can tell my old friend Pandaros trained you."

"You knew him well then?" Stefanos asked.

"Yes. We met on the skamma many times. He was a man of true andreia and arete. Always focussed. We never got distracted by the kinaidoi parading themselves before us like these paiderasts and erastai."

Stefanos did not say anything, though his mind thought briefly of Kratos and his activities of late.

"There's a reason competitors need to report to the Hellanodikai a month before the Games."

"Isn't it to ensure that everyone is here in time so that the Games take place at the right time?"

"No. These weeks before the sacred Games are the true test for many. It's hard to stay focussed in this chaos - so many vendors, and whores - so much to pull your attention away from the true agon."

"What is the true agon then?"

The gymnasiarchos paused, his wrinkled, sun-worn face staring at Stefanos. "The true agon is the one you face with yourself everyday you draw breath upon the Gods' earth." He stood up and slapped Stefanos' scarred chest. "You could win."

Stefanos watched the gymnasiarchos leave, his words ringing in his ears as he watched the sunlight angle its way onto the sand.

STEFANOS TRAINED ALONE FOR THE NEXT SEVERAL DAYS, declining when anyone asked him to spar with them. The other boxers mocked him, some of their scarred faces raging at the insult so much so that their swollen, crushed ears became as red as tomatoes.

From then on, his training was mental. Stefanos felt strong, but he knew that he needed to believe, to strengthen his resolve and faith in the gifts the Gods had given him.

It was as if the gymnasiarchos had channeled Pandaros from across the Styx, and with those words of encouragement, the seedling that he had planted weeks before now sprouted, and he began to nurture it. The altars of Zeus, Hera, Demeter, and Estia burned with his offerings. His prayers left his parted lips to the spirits of Herakles, and those of Pelops and Hippodameia.

Every night, as he lay back on his mat, his hands grasping the shaft of his doru, Stefanos looked up at the stars until his lids grew heavy and his mind wandered away from prayers to thoughts of battles-past, of blood and agony, those things that he had known since the days of his youth. No true glory could be found there, he knew.

His father had been right. Kakochartos had dominated him for too long.

He did not see much of Kratos either, for the other did not want to spar anymore, fearful that he would injure himself so close to the start of the Games.

One morning, as Kratos came to gather his things, Xenophon walked up to their camp.

"Stefanos! Kratos!" Xenophon called as he walked across the flat area of dry grass and dirt toward the two men.

"Xenophon!" Stefanos called back. "I thought you'd left! We haven't seen you anywhere."

"I've been holed up with Agesilaus. Talk of going back to Asia and how we can use cavalry to better effect against the Persians."

"You've missed the training, and the events at night in the sanctuary. Some great plays have been put on!" Kratos said, smiling as he picked up his things.

"I know. But, Agesilaus is very persuasive, and a good friend," Xenophon added. "But, I'm glad I found you both. I told Agesilaus that you were not at home in the Argive camp, and asked if it would be possible for you to stay in the Spartan camp as my guests."

"I'm guessing he said no," Kratos laughed.

"Actually, he said *yes*. I told him how much you had fought with Sparta in recent years, and how we marched back from Persia together. He said any friend of mine was welcome to be a guest."

"That's…" Stefanos looked at Kratos, "…very generous. You know, I think I'll take you up on that," Stefanos said, feeling an odd wave of relief wash over him. If anything had been wrong, it was that he was not sleeping well enough, his unconscious mind always distrusting of the Argives about him, especially Ocnus and his friends.

"Wonderful," Xenophon added, his long hair hanging down to frame his bearded face as he looked to Kratos. "And you, my friend?"

"Thank Agesilaus for the offer, but," he looked at Stefanos, "I'm going to stay here with the people of my city. "Telamon has offered me a space in his tent since one of their group has had to withdraw from the Games due to an injury."

"You sure?" Stefanos asked. "We'll be safe in the Spartan camp with Xenophon. We'll actually be able to sleep!"

"I'm fine here, my friend," Kratos told Stefanos. "You go ahead."

Stefanos wondered at the change in his closest friend, and had no doubt that certain other Argives continued to paint a grim picture of Stefanos. That Kratos was buying such lies was a brutal surprise, if that was the case.

"Listen," Kratos said, looking up from the ground. "I'm training with Telamon and the others now, heavily, every day. I need to focus on that. I can't sit around the campfire reminiscing about our childhood."

"Reminiscing?" Stefanos said, trying not to sound enraged. Is that what you call remembering those that have gone before us?"

"Yes. It makes me feel weak, and I can't have that now."

"Well, it makes me strong," Stefanos said. "It gives me purpose."

"I know," Kratos said, putting his hand on Stefanos' shoulder. "I'll see you," he assured. "I just need to focus on training, as do you."

"Of course," Stefanos said. "Well, good luck," he said in a clipped tone as he swept past Xenophon.

"Stefanos, come on!" Kratos called after him, before looking at Xenophon. "There is a lot on his mind."

"I gathered," Xenophon said. "If you change your mind, you know where to find us?"

"Yes."

"Good luck, Kratos," Xenophon said, smiling at Kratos one last time and then turning to go toward the river and follow after Stefanos.

"What was that about?" Xenophon asked Stefanos.

"I don't know. He's become close friends with a group of Argives. They drink and whore all night."

"I seem to recall you liking both of those things more than most," Xenophon said, his eyebrows raised.

Stefanos looked askance at him. "Yes. But things have...changed...lately. I've got other things on my mind."

"Then that is to your credit, my friend," Xenophon said, taking the satchel from Stefanos' shoulder and carrying it as they made their way across the Kladeos to the Spartan camp. "I know the Games are a week away now, and that your mind is swimming with thoughts of blood and victory, but I think I know just the thing for you."

"Oh yes? What's that?" Stefanos said.

"A symposium...tomorrow night."

"I haven't been to one of those in a long time. Besides, my mind is not in it. I decline, my friend."

"But, you can't," Xenophon said, smiling.

"Why? I don't want to hang about talking about the state of the world and how everyone knows how to make it better."

"You need to come."

"Again, why?"

"Because King Agesilaus is your host, and he invited you."

XENOPHON'S TENT WAS LOCATED IN A CLUSTER OF CLIENT-KING and guest tents to the north of the main Spartan camp on the other side of the river Kladeos. The walls were leather, and it was about double the size of a regular campaign tent, the sort they had used on the way to Persia.

It lay unguarded. There was one thing Stefanos noticed right away - there were not the loiterers that were common to the Argive camp, and no doubt the Athenian and other camps. The Spartan camp was quiet, but for the sounds of men training for the Games, and the crash of xiphos upon hoplon as they trained for war.

The Spartans never stopped training for war.

An uneasy peace lay over the Spartan camp, but Stefanos was grateful for even that. They were a harsh people, he knew that much, but he also liked to know how he stood with people. With the Spartans, Stefanos had never been in doubt about his place and how they felt about him. Only by his skill with doru, hoplon, and xiphos had he gained respect among the red cloaks of the Spartan shield wall, even though he was only a mercenary.

"What do you think?" Xenophon said, shuffling some papyrus sheets on his writing table which stood directly opposite the tent entrance.

Stefanos walked in and looked about, ducking to avoid a hanging oil lamp in the shape of a satyr's face and mouth.

It was exactly what he might have expected, though a bit more plush. Behind the large writing table were three shelves which were full of scrolls, tablets, and bronze styluses. A large chair sat behind the desk where Xenophon bent over his papyri, and there were two more in front of the table. To the right of the table, a wooden dummy stood with Xenophons' deep red thorax with blue trim, a gorgon roaring upon the chest.

Stefanos remembered the armour, greaves, and blue-crested helmet well, having fought beside them all the way from Persia, his own shield often locked beside that of Xenophon's with its gorgon head to match that upon the thorax.

Stefanos looked at the lamps hanging from the ceiling, and the two couches in front of the entrance to the right-hand chamber.

The tent had sixteen poles as thick as a pugilist's arms holding it up. To either side were separate sleeping chambers, and Stefanos assumed one of these to be his.

"Fancier than what we were used to on the march," Stefanos said, picking up a green and red cushion that lay on one of two couches to the right, beside the entrance to a second chamber where a bed was.

"True," Xenophon laughed. "But I daresay, we'll be back to sleeping rough in a short few weeks. Persia beckons to Agesilaus again. He wants to see Tissaphernes pay, and he wants to be the man to make him do so."

"He's going to ask me to join the expedition, isn't he?" Stefanos said, still standing there holding his doru and satchel.

"Yes."

"I need to focus on the Games. Then I'll think of war and pay again."

"Our Spartan friends never stop thinking of war. The Olympiad to them is sanctioned battle for the Gods' entertainment. War without the death."

"But with much blood."

"You should know. I've been hearing stories about the old Argive mercenary who trains alone since he nearly killed a couple of men on the skamma. I guessed it was you they were talking about."

"Old?" Stefanos shrugged. "I'm ready for this, my friend. I can feel it. It's just..."

"What?" Xenophon stepped forward, his face actually concerned. "You can tell me, Stefanos. For so long on the march, we stared at each other's tired, emotion-ripped faces across the camp fire while the Persians hunted us. I know you by now. You seem different."

"It's not that easy to explain," Stefanos tried to force a smile, but it would not come. The thoughts surfaced every now and then when he stopped training, to torment and frighten him, a man who thought he had stopped being frightened.

"The Gods...they've been showing me things."

"What things?" Xenophon turned to pour some water from a pitcher on his table into two, orange, earthenware cups. He handed one to Stefanos. "What are the Gods saying to you?"

"I'm not sure. Do they ever speak plainly?" Stefanos dropped the large satchel with his armour in it and leaned his doru against one of the tent poles. "Before Pandaros died on the road, I had a dream of a chariot race across the Peloponnese. I saw Pelops and Hippodameia being chased by Oinomaus."

"Their spirits no doubt still race across the land," Xenophon said, his eyes staring at Stefanos. "Pelops won the race. Perhaps the Gods are saying to you that you will win in the Olympiad?"

"I don't know. My father...it was...his dying wish that I do so, that I erect a fine epinikion bronze in the Altis afterward."

"I'm sorry for your father, my friend. I know you had unfinished business with him." Xenophon put his hand on Stefanos' shoulder. "But it's easy for the dying to make demands of the living. By all means, strive for victory, but do not let the dead torture you from across the black water. You'll never rest."

"You turning into a realist?" Stefanos asked.

"No. Just a man who has seen and dealt too much death."

"And you do not regret the demands the dying have made of you?" Stefanos asked. "What of Socrates' advice that you not go to Persia? Don't you wish you had listened?"

"No," Xenophon said without hesitation. "I don't. The path that led us east taught me a great deal. It made me the man I am today, a man that not only my father, Gryllus, can be proud of, but also a man that I can be proud of."

"Sometimes, lately especially, I wish I had stayed with my father and sister in Argos," Stefanos said, looking up at the tent ceiling rising and falling slowly in the hot breeze outside, as if a titan were plucking the rooftop. "But I went to war instead."

"And have become the man you are as a result. Your own Odyssey, my friend. We must all have one. It's the Gods' will."

"And now?"

"Now that I hear you say these things?" Xenophon bent to pick up Stefanos' satchel for him. "I think you had better win these Games, for your father's soul, and your own."

Xenophon walked across to the left side of the tent where there was a second chamber with a bed behind a curtain of blue canvas. He placed the satchel down on the ground beside the bed.

"My home is yours, Stefanos. Rest, and train, and rest some more. I can promise you that there are no daggers in the dark here." He smiled, if not a little sadly.

"I'm grateful for the space. I won't get in your way, I promise."

"Ha. Don't worry. Most nights, I'm not even here. Agesilaus keeps me up all night talking of warfare and battle plans. We discuss the running of Sparta - the subject fascinates me - and the story of his succession."

"Anything about Lysander?" Stefanos asked, referring to the former Spartan general who had brought Athens and her allies to their knees, and who, in turn, Agesilaus had tamed, even though the man had put the lame king on the throne.

"There is always talk about Lysander," Xenophon said. "But, tomorrow night, don't bring him up unless the king does. It can be a...touchy...subject."

"I'll remember that," Stefanos said.

XENOPHON DID NOT COME BACK TO HIS TENT THAT NIGHT, AND Stefanos found himself enjoying the solitude of that fine dwelling.

Food was waiting for him on a small table beside the couches in the middle of the tent when he awoke, and after splashing his face with water in the bronze basin on the ground beside his bed, Stefanos sat down to eat the bread and cheese drizzled with honey. There was also a bowl of bean soup which he ate with relish, knowing that soon his exertions on the palaestra would make him ravenous.

The training would be shorter today, he knew, for he would have to visit the baths, and then make his way back to the Spartan camp for his audience with the king.

Stefanos was in no mood for a symposium with the Spartans. In fact, he had not thought they went in for such things.

As he walked into the palaestra that day, exceptionally lighter than before, he removed his tunic, sandals, and loincloth, and got oiled up before beginning his opening warm-up, running around the perimeter of the sand.

The day was hot, and the cicadas in the pines and poplars dotting the sanctuary were deafening. It did not take long for the sweat to begin pouring off of him as he ran, and lifted, and stretched his limbs. When he finished, Stefanos began to strap on his himantes, his knuckles well-used to the strips of hard hide now.

Father Zeus...give me strength and skill, he thought as he stepped up to one of the korikoi.

STEFANOS DID NOT THINK ON THE EVENING DURING HIS training that day. Instead, he went over the scenarios he imagined himself living through on his way to victory. The men he would have to defeat, or bring to near-death. He imagined he boxed taller men, heavier men, faster men, every conceivable variable, trying to determine an outcome, to see it and make it happen in his mind.

Some men thought he was mad as they watched him, dodging and feinting, striking the bags as if his life depended on it. Others observed with keen interest, the more experienced among them seeing something in the Argive's form and stance that they knew was something to reckon with.

Stefanos ignored them all, and punched, blocked, and pounded until the sun began to dip into the west in earnest. He was one of the last to leave the palaestra.

"Good night, Argive," the gymnasiarchos said after him.

Stefanos lifted an arm in farewell as he went out and turned right to go to the baths.

He soaked for a long time in the water, letting it refresh and rejuvenate his body.

An enormous splash startled Stefanos.

"You should spar, Argive," said a great booming voice. "What are you playing at? How can you know how you will stand up to your competitors by only taking part in skia-machein? The shadows don't hit back."

Stefanos turned to see the titanic, scarred bulk of Polydamas of Thessaly sitting a few feet to his right in the pool.

"My methods are my business," Stefanos said, closing his eyes and returning to his thoughts.

"Your methods are going to get you killed!" Polydamas said, running a beefy hand over his balding head and beard.

Stefanos opened his eyes and looked at the former Olympic champion. His head was large and round with the swollen ears so normal in boxers and pankrationists. He imagined the champion standing there, taking hit after hit until he decided he had humiliated his opponent so much that he would take him down in one punch. His chest stood out from his body, a mass of muscle that could have been a bull's. His eyes were laughing.

"Do you know who I am, Argive?"

"You're Thessalian from the look of it," Stefanos teased.

Polydamas looked down at his naked body and began to laugh.

"I like you, Argive. You don't pander like all the rest."

"That's reassuring," Stefanos said.

"However, if you want to rub against me, I won't complain," the big man laughed.

"I don't think so," Stefanos said, his brows creased as he realized his relaxing soak was over. "I'm sure there are many kinaidoi outside who would be happy to oblige, but if you make that offer again, you'll regret it."

"Don't get uptight!" the man said. "Just being friendly. I'm an Olympic victor," he boasted. "Many men and women have yearned for the honour."

"I'm happy for you. Now, I must be going. I have an important appointment."

"As do I, but they will wait upon my leisure."

Stefanos got out of the pool and walked away, sensing the big man's eyes upon him as he left. As he made his way to the apodyterium, he realized he did not have that much to wear to an audience with the king of Sparta.

"MY LADY, IT IS NEARLY TIME FOR YOU TO GO," SAID EUNICE to Kyniska as she brushed down her blacks whom Pirro had just finished taking around the track. "The king has commanded your presence." The girl's blond hair was stuck to her brow, sweat glistening on it after a day of exercise with the others.

"Commanded?" Kyniska rounded on her protege. "Do I look like a woman of Athens, or Corinth?"

"No, my lady." Eunice hung her head.

Kyniska came up to her and stood before her. "Am I soft of flesh? Is my skin pale and unused to the light of the sun?"

"No!" Eunice looked up, shocked. "You are not any of those things."

Kyniska softened her look and put her hand under the girl's chin. "We are Spartan women. Remember that." She turned to Helle, Thais, and Euryleonis who were standing to the side. "You would all do well to remember that. We cannot be strong only some of the time. We are not commanded."

"Even by the king?" Helle asked.

"In that, I speak for myself. And the answer then is, yes. Even by the king." Kyniska turned to watch Pirro bringing the whites up to speed around the track. "Slow Hippolytus a bit more going into the corner!" she yelled, before turning back to the girls.

"My lady?" said Thais.

"What is it?"

"Who is that man in the trees on the other side of the track?"

Kyniska whipped around in time to see a man in a plain chiton and long dark hair throwing something onto the track in front of the charging whites.

"Pirro! Stop them!" she yelled. "Typhon, in the trees!"

The enomotarch and three others were charging across the track toward the trees when the horses began to scream, the inside stallion bounding and thrashing, pulling them along faster.

Typhon and the guards dove out of the way just in time, the horses' hooves narrowly missing the three men, and Typhon rolling and continuing on into the trees, his doru hungry for the intruder. He disappeared.

Eunice screamed as the chariot came careening toward them, Pirro struggling to rein in the horses who were losing control as Hippolytus went wild.

"My lady, no!" Helle cried out as Kyniska ran toward the chariot and leapt up into the cab to grab the reins from Pirro.

The chariot went into the far turn again, balancing on one wheel as the inside stallion surged forward.

"No!" Kyniska spotted several shining objects in the dirt ahead of them and pushed Pirro out the back of the cab before gripping the reins and pulling against the soft sides of her teams mouths.

The horses screamed and then, on the outside, Adonis crumpled and the chariot exploded up.

Kyniska released the reins just in time, but she could not stop herself soaring over the heads of her team. The world turned over and she tried to keep her eyes on the ground as she flipped, even as the limbs of her bloodied and broken team tangled behind her.

"Kyniska!" Euryleonis yelled as she ran across the field, the others behind her. "My lady, no!"

Kyniska lay some distance away. Her head was spinning but she forced herself to her knees, taking a mental note that nothing felt broken. A searing pain across her arm and face told her that something had dug into her. She looked down to see a caltrop sticking out of the muscle of her arm. She pulled it out and stared in fury at the bronze star. Then she looked to her team, ignoring the girls fussing around her, pulling at her, and ran toward the flailing horses whom Pirro was trying to calm with every ounce of his skill.

It was dangerous to get close to such large animals, but Kyniska did not heed such advice, her fury clouding her mind as she approached.

"Shhhh..." her voice shook. "Steady now," she said taking in the wreckage.

Amazingly, Zeta and Pasiphae had been unharmed, but on either side, the stallions were badly hurt. Hippolytus tried to right himself but kept falling down, unable to stand upon his injured hoof.

As Kyniska looked to Adonis, her breath caught in her chest and she struggled for control.

The stallion's two front legs had snapped and he lay broken upon the dirt, his eyes wide and glossy.

She went directly to him and leaned over his head, whispering into his ear.

"Shhh, my friend. Shhh. I'm here," she said, closing her eyes and feeling the rushing of the beast's heart in his muscular chest. "I'll find out who did this to you. I will. And I'll feed them to the hounds of Hades so that they never have rest."

"My lady!" Typhon's voice called over as he came up with two of the other warriors. "We've got him!"

Kyniska stood up, and spoke to Thanato who was standing with the girls. "Get more of the men!" she ordered.

"Yes, lady." He ran off.

"Are you hurt?" Typhon asked, his voice uncharacteristically concerned.

"No," she answered. "Who is this?" she said suddenly, staring at the limp body between the two troops following Typhon.

"A slave. He almost got away, but I took him down."

"He's dead, Typhon!" Kyniska yelled. "How can we find out who sent him now?" she raged. "Didn't you think?"

"My lady, he was getting away. I had to take him before he

escaped into the sanctuary." Typhon stood motionless before her. "Would you anger the Gods so close to the Games?"

Kyniska turned away from her enomotarch and stared at the shuddering bodies of her horses.

Pirro had unhitched Zeta and Pasiphae and was leading them away.

"Helle, and Thais," she said. "Take the mares to the stables, feed, them and give them water to calm them. I'll be there shortly. Euryleonis, take the blacks far from here. I don't want them frightened any more."

"Yes, my lady.'

"Pirro, do you think Hippolytus can limp away from here?" Kyniska asked.

"He might, my lady," the young man said, wiping a streak of blood from his own forehead.

"Do it," she said.

Pirro went over and unhitched the harness from the stallion, Eunice running to help him. Together, they soothed the stallion and turned him away from the one still lying on the ground.

After stumbling a couple of times, Hippolytus managed to limp away.

Kyniska said nothing as she watched them go. When they disappeared, she turned back to Typhon and the others.

"Does he have any slave markings?" she asked, pointing at the man hanging between the two Spartans, a large red patch of blood from where Typhon's spear had spitted him through the back of his tunic.

Kyniska walked over, and ripped the tunic away, looking at the dirty, naked and cowardly form.

"Nothing," Typhon said.

"Quiet!" Kyniska roared. "We could have questioned him."

"I did what needed to be done," he answered stubbornly.

"You disappoint me, Typhon." Kyniska turned to look her bodyguard in the eyes. "Give me your xiphos," she said, her eyes looking at the cherry wood handle of the sword at his waist.

He looked down and then back at her. "Let me do it for you," he said.

"No. I will." She reached for the sword handle without waiting for him, and slid it away from his side. "Leave me. Take that filth away."

The two men carrying the body dragged it away, but Typhon remained.

"You too. I wish to be alone."

"Kyniska..." he began to say.

"Are you deaf? I said leave me!"

Typhon hoisted his bloody doru and whipped round to follow the others, his red cloak swaying angrily as he went.

Kyniska felt the blood running down her left arm where the caltrop had stuck into her, but paid it no heed. "I will bleed with you," she said as she knelt beside Adonis' shuddering body. "They will swim in rivers of blood, my friend."

Kyniska stroked the stallion's white, blood-stained coat. He was sweaty, his eyes beginning to roll imploringly.

"Shhhh," she soothed as she raised her arms to the sky, the one bleeding, the other holding the leaf-shaped blade. "Oh mighty Poseidon, tamer of horses and lord of the deep. Oh Earthshaker... Take this stallion into your herd to run with you for all time in the wine-dark deep. Bless him..."

Kyniska reached up with her bloody hand to grasp the handle of the sword, with the blade down. Droplets fell upon her face, but she did not care as she looked down and placed the tip of the blade against the soft part of Adonis' skull, just before the ear.

"Farewell, my friend..."

She leaned with all her weight on the blade and felt the metal slice through, grating bone until it punctured the brain clean through.

The body shuddered powerfully for a few moments, but

she held on until it ceased. Her breath was heavy and rapid and she felt her throat tighten.

You can't! she commanded herself. *No weakness!*

Kyniska stood, placed her foot upon the dead beast's neck, and pulled the xiphos clear of the head.

Her hands shook as she looked down at the horse she had trained from a foal, who had listened to her every command, who had been the one to carry her whites to victory in other contests. But she did not cry. No tears, even as she knelt down and kissed the broad white brow one last time.

"Go with the Gods..." she whispered staring up at the emerging stars in the sky above.

Kyniska turned away, and walked in the direction of the torches not far off, where Typhon and an entire file of her guard stood waiting.

"Here," she handed Typhon his blade back, and flinched away when he reached for her. She stopped and stared at the men around her. "I want all of you guarding the other horses all night and all day until the Games are finished."

"What of our own competitions, my lady?" Typhon asked. "We need to train as well."

"If you do, you are no longer in my guard," she said before walking in the direction of the stables to check on the others.

"The king is waiting!" Typhon called after her.

"Let him!"

"I DON'T HAVE MUCH IN THE WAY OF CLOTHING," STEFANOS said to Xenophon as the latter emerged from his chamber in the tent wearing a white chiton hemmed with red wave patterns, and a pair of sandals.

Xenophon waited for Stefanos to finish rummaging through his things and smiled to himself as he poured two cups of wine.

"You've been wearing armour for far too long."

"I prefer it," Stefanos answered, his voice frustrated.

"We're not going to fight."

"I prefer fighting," Stefanos said as he came out from his chamber. "How's this for an audience with the king of Sparta?"

Stefanos emerged wearing plain grey tunic with blue lines dyed around the edges. It was a bit worn in places, but it was clean and unstained. He too wore sandals, the same he wore into battle.

"It's all I have," Stefanos said.

"Trust me, it's perfect," Xenophon said, a big smile on his face.

The two friends made their way in the gathering dark, passing Spartan citizens and hetairoi who roamed the rows of the camp to try and lure some business. Pots of food cooked over camp fires wherever they looked as the athletes born in the shadow of Taygetos gathered after their exertions.

Men stared at the Athenian and Argive as they passed, those who recognized Xenophon greeting him curtly, others directing outwardly aggressive looks.

"Our friends are ever apprehensive of outsiders," Xenophon said. "Even after we've been through so much."

"Too much for comfort, I would say," Stefanos said, eyeing the massive tent directly ahead of them.

"Too true, my friend. But we can mend things. We must."

"Yes, but with whom?" Stefanos said. "The Spartans, or our own people?"

Xenophon did not answer.

Agesilaus had arrived not long ago, having come directly from Persia for the sacred games. His tent dwarfed all others in size, but it was of like simplicity, a titanic leather beast, dark-skinned and worn, supported by about twenty thick trunks of wood.

A ring of red-cloaked guards stood about the tent, and as they approached, Stefanos recognized Pollux to the left of the main entrance. Pollux, like the other guards, carried a bronze-headed doru that gleamed in the firelight, as well as the hoplon of the royal guard, a red shield with the image of a tripod upon it.

"Ah! Pollux, son of Milo," Xenophon said. "On guard duty tonight?"

Pollux relaxed when he saw who the two men approaching were. "It's fine," he said to the guard on the other side of the entrance. "They are friends of Sparta, and guests of the king."

Stefanos could see Pollux's raised eyebrow through the eye holes of his helmet.

"It seems like it," Stefanos said. "You going to join us in there?" he asked hopefully.

"Not that I know of. There's been an incident and we're on the alert."

"What's happened?" Xenophon asked.

"Not for me to say. I'm sure the king will tell you all about it. You can go in. The king will join you shortly."

"Thank you, Pollux," Xenophon said. "After the Games, we must all sit and drink together." He went in.

"Where's Kratos?" Pollux asked.

"With the Argives. I'm staying here with Xenophon."

"Strange."

Stefanos shrugged and took a breath before entering, puffing out his chest and holding his head high.

"Enjoy!" Pollux teased behind him.

THE INSIDE OF THE TENT WAS SPRAWLING. A MISTY WORLD OF golden light, wood, bronze, and leather. Braziers burned in symmetrical positions throughout the massive, square tent of the king of Sparta. In the shadows, Stefanos spotted more of the king's guard, their forms blending in with the sixteen tree trunks that held up the hide walls and ceiling.

It was hot inside, and this coupled with the heady scent of myrrh fluting from a tripod at the back made Stefanos' head spin for a few moments.

People stood in scattered groups, cups of wine in their hands as they spoke in whispers and darted suspicious looks at every newcomer.

"The king is not yet here," Xenophon whispered to Stefanos. "I will go and see him. Stay here."

Stefanos stood in the middle of the tent, his eyes taking in the faces of the people and the layout of the space. He had never seen such a big tent, and would have expected such a thing to be a thing of extreme regality. However, its occupant was a Spartan and such things were beneath them.

There were rows of wooden couches and a few chairs toward the center at the back of the tent, all facing a large wooden chair made of smoothed olive wood. Behind this was a large black krater of wine with reliefs of the labours of Herakles around its rim. Two slaves stood to either side of the krater, ladling out wine into plain kylixes that were brought out by slaves and handed to guests. Stefanos accepted a wide kylix from a passing slave in a brown tunic and walked slowly around the tent after tipping a drop of wine onto the floor in honour of the Gods.

Beside the krater was a wooden frame where the king's armour hung between two dorata, their deadly points glinting. The thorax was plain, absent ornamentation but for the outline of muscles in the bronze. There was no back plate, and the front was riddled with cuts and scratches from numerous battles as promachoi. The helmet on top had a tall, bristling red crest above the shadowed eye slits.

Hoisted beside the armour was the king's hoplon, polished and scratched, but larger than normal, and heavier than the average. On its face was a massive swirl of white, red and black that seemed to move as Stefanos stared at it.

More people were filing into the tent then, and Stefanos turned to see the massive form of Polydamas of Thessaly striding toward him.

"There you are, Argive!" the Olympic champion bellowed as he walked through the crowd, men heaping compliments upon him as he smiled and nodded, and exchanged some good-natured words with some of them. Polydamas wore a lion skin in emulation of Herakles, leather breeches, and sandals, but little else. His pectorals jutted out from beneath the lion paws that dangled before him, and laughter lines creased deeply about his eyes as he smiled.

A few men stared at Stefanos as he turned to look for Xenophon but could not find him anywhere in the mass of men and slaves slinking in and out among the guests.

"Looks like the Gods have decreed we should be friends!" Polydamas said as he arrived beside Stefanos and slapped him on the shoulder. "It would seem we are both guests of the king of Sparta."

"So it does," Stefanos answered. He scanned the room again and spotted Xenophon speaking to one of the slaves standing at the back of the tent where an exit let into a separate set of rooms. "Excuse me," Stefanos said quickly, breaking away from Polydamas and making for Xenophon.

"There you are!" Stefanos said. "I can't believe I let you talk me into this."

"There was no talking, my friend. Agesilaus wanted to see you."

"Where is the king?"

"Delayed. Some of the Spartans were attacked earlier and he is raging for justice. He's gone to the bouleuterion now to speak with the Hellanodikai."

"Even the king of Sparta can't force the Hellanodikai to do something," Stefanos said, remembering what Pandaros had said about their age-old rights to administer and judge at the sanctuary.

"Agesilaus can be very persuasive," Xenophon said seriously. "An attack on Sparta during the Sacred Truce, and just outside the sanctuary, is a supreme sacrilege in Agesilaus' eyes. You know how they handle insult."

"I remember, yes." Stefanos looked over to a row of three tables where slaves were laying out platters of steaming lamb and beef, hot breads, cheeses, and bowls of Laconian olives. Stefanos' mouth began to water. "Are we permitted to eat?" he asked Xenophon.

"Yes...but..."

"But what?"

"You'll see. Agesilaus is a good host, but a harsh judge of his guests. Refrain for now."

The two men moved away from the tables groaning with food, and walked along the side of the tent, glimpsing some familiar faces of Argives and Corinthians, Thebans and Athenians.

"Anyone important?" Stefanos asked.

"Yes." Xenophon spotted two men who had just entered. "I can't believe he's come," he said, standing on his toes to see over the other guests' heads.

"Who?"

Xenophon was already moving into the crowd to greet the two Athenians who had just arrived. Stefanos followed, eyeing Polydamas in the centre where he was surrounded by his admirers.

"Plato!" Xenophon said as he came up to one of the two men. "It is good to see you!" Xenophon kissed the newcomer on both cheeks and stood back to look at him.

Plato, Stefanos knew from his conversations with Xenophon, was a philosopher and student of Socrates, a man and teacher whom Xenophon and many others had admired very much. Plato was not tall or short. He wore a clean, off-white himation that revealed the lean muscle of his one exposed shoulder. His hair and beard were short and sandy and of similar length, the one running into the other to give his entire head a sense of uniformity.

"Xenophon," Plato said, smiling, despite the dark circles beneath his eyes. "It has been some years, has it not?"

"Not since before the trial," Xenophon answered. "I still grieve for beloved Socrates."

Plato looked up into Xenophon's eyes and nodded, his

own eyes watery, but their dams reinforced. "It has been three years, and yet I feel his loss as though it were yesterday," Plato said.

"Too true," Xenophon added. "The Gods did indeed allow the inexplicable then. I still regret that I was not able to be there for the trial."

"As do I," Plato said.

"Socrates would not want his star pupils to be moping about as if bewailing the loss of a child now, would he?"

Stefanos jumped at the sound of the high, gravelly voice that emanated suddenly from Plato's companion, a slightly older man wearing a grey himation with mud stains about the bottom hem.

"Ah, where are my manners?" Plato said, his voice picking up from the note of despair that had inhabited it only moments before. "Isocrates of Athens, another student of Socrates."

"Of course, Isocrates," Xenophon said, reaching out to take the man's hand. "I remember reading a pamphlet of yours that I greatly admired, about the need for Athens and Sparta to unite against their common enemy."

"Thank you, son of Gryllus. I remember Socrates speaking highly of you, and trying to talk you out of going to Asia to fight for that same enemy." Isocrates' over-large brow wrinkled in accusation as he stared at Xenophon, his patchy beard and receding hairline adding to the effect of his unhappiness.

For Stefanos, he could not get past the man's voice and looked away for a moment to bite his lip.

"Different times, Isocrates," Xenophon said mildly, used to defending his actions and opinions to his fellow Athenians for some time. "A path set before me by the Gods, and one that taught me a great many things, and introduced me to new heights of strength in my fellow man." Xenophon turned to Stefanos and pulled him into the circle.

"May I introduce my good friend, Stefanos, son of Talos of Argos."

"Talos, the bronze smith?" Plato asked.

"Yes," Stefanos said, his head rising a little higher.

"I believe your father created the magnificent bronze of the goddess in the Heraion of Argos, no?"

"Yes, he did," Stefanos answered, feeling a tightness forming in the middle of his chest.

"Is your father still creating? I would love to visit the artist himself the next time I am in Argos."

"My father died just recently," Stefanos said.

"I am sorry," Plato responded. There was a kindness in his eyes that Stefanos appreciated, though he would never have shared the observation.

"Thank you."

"Do you follow in your father's footsteps?" Isocrates asked, Stefanos turning to face him. "Your build is not that of a bronze smith. Usually their arms are disproportionate to the rest of their bodies."

"I'm a soldier," Stefanos replied. "Have been since I was nineteen."

"Argos has not seen as much of war as Athens these many years," Isocrates said. "What else have you been doing?"

Stefanos took a breath. "I never said I fought for Argos alone."

The circle of men was silent for a moment before Xenophon jumped in.

"Stefanos marched back from Asia with me. We learned the lessons the Gods set before us together, through fire and sand."

Isocrates continued to stare at Stefanos. "And before your glorious march from Cunaxa? Where were you?"

"Melos," Stefanos said, mentioning the slaughter of the Melians by the Athenians.

"Really?" Isocrates seemed surprised.

"And Sicily," he added.

Silence again.

"With Demosthenes? How did you escape?"

"I fought with Gilippus."

"The Spartans?"

"I think we should leave aside our martial histories for the time being," said Plato, laying a hand on Isocrates' shoulder and stepping forward. "I'm sure as the evening wears on, discussions of war will become inevitable."

"I'll leave you to handle this little philosopher," Stefanos whispered to Xenophon, before nodding to Plato and backing into the crowd.

"It's the shifting of mercenaries back and forth that disallows the victory of democracy," Isocrates muttered.

"Oh, come now," Plato said. "Much more is to blame than that. Come, I see the priestess of Demetra Chamayne has entered. Let us greet her. Xenophon," Plato nodded and took Isocrates away to meet with the one woman who was permitted to attend the sacred games of the Olympiad.

"I forgot your impatience with philosophers," Xenophon said as he came up beside Stefanos toward the back of the tent.

"How could you forget that?" Stefanos said, his thick arms crossed over his chest. "He's going to say one word too many."

"And Plato?"

"I don't mind him. But is he ill?"

"No. But the death of Socrates hit him hard. He left Greece for Egypt and Cyrene afterward, a time to travel, to gather his thoughts and seek guidance."

"Rather like marching to war with the Persians?" Stefanos said.

"Quite," Xenophon answered, smiling.

"Make way for the Eurypontid King of Sparta, Agesilaus II!" a guard called from the back of the tent and stepped aside to make way for the king of Sparta.

Stefanos felt his heartbeat quicken as he and Xenophon

stepped back from the entrance and bowed their heads slightly.

Agesilaus limped briskly into the room, and were it not for the guard's announcement of the king's arrival, one would not have thought he was a king at all, nor even a noble.

Agesilaus, apart from having a lame leg, which was unheard of in Spartan warriors, was short and at a glance, unimpressive. That is, until his eyes fixed upon you, and he spoke.

The king of Sparta was not dressed in expensive linens, nor did he adorn his person with any jewels or gold, not even a simple bracelet.

Agesilaus II, half-brother to the late King Agis, and son of the former King Archidamus II, wore a simple crimson chiton, cinched at the waist with a brown leather belt that matched his leather wrist guards and sandals. He stopped and looked about the tent, his gaze feline and alert as he took in every person there.

Stefanos observed the king as discreetly as possible from his unnervingly close vantage, and thought that the king seemed to have memorized the list of every person who had been invited.

Agesilaus' face was a little long, with high, bony cheeks in which his light palor seemed at war with the sun he had seen campaigning in Asia. His thick brows came close to meeting in the centre of his face above a long nose, but none of them could distract one from the king's pale, blue eyes which turned on Xenophon and Stefanos after raking the gathering.

The king smiled broadly. "My friend," he came to Xenophon who nodded his head slightly in as much obeisance as his Athenian morals would allow him. "This must be the man I have heard you speak so much about." Agesilaus turned to Stefanos. "Stefanos, son of Talos?"

"Yes...yes..." Stefanos jibbed, unsure how to address the king. "Thank you for your hospitality this evening...sire."

"Think nothing of it. It is the time of the Gods' Sacred

Truce, and Sparta honours it. Even here," the king indicated the three of them, "we have a Spartan, an Athenian, and an Argive in close company, and without weapons drawn."

There was some laughter about the room, but Agesilaus did not smile. He looked at the room. "Continue your conversations!" he said loudly. "The king is coming!" He turned back to Xenophon and Stefanos.

"We were told that there was an incident in the camp," Stefanos said conversationally.

Agesilaus fixed on him. "Yes. And I'll see justice done on the perpetrators." He eyed the room again. "Imagine, Spartans attacked on the edges of our own camp!" The king's fist began to clench and unclench, despite the calm demeanour of his face.

Xenophon reached out and put his hand on the king's shoulder. "I'm sure the Gods will throw the guilty parties at your feet, my friend."

Agesilaus looked up and smiled, his teeth white and hungry. "Yes. They will." He waved his hand and a slave came with three cups of watered wine. Each of them took one, and then the king raised his cup, tipping some onto the ground. "To the Gods..."

"To the Gods," Stefanos and Xenophon followed suit, spilling some of the red liquid at their feet before drinking with the king.

"I must greet my guests," Agesilaus said, "but we will sit together later. I would hear of your battles, Argive. Xenophon tells me that you fought with Sparta in Sicily, under Gilippus."

"I did," Stefanos answered, though the memories of slaughtered Athenians in the bogs and fields of Sicily were little better that those of slaughtered Melians at the hands of the Athenians.

Agesilaus nodded and moved away to greet a group of Corinthians who were standing nearby.

"We can eat now," Xenophon noted.

"How do you know? Did he notice that we had not touched anything yet?"

"Oh, he noticed."

OVER THE NEXT HOUR, AS AGESILAUS MADE HIS WAY AROUND the tent, which was by this point, filled with a smell of sweat and smoke, to greet various men from his allied cities, as well as men from those cities with whom Sparta had spent decades at war.

There was a tension in the air that made Stefanos uncomfortable, for it resembled the tension before a battle. He felt sure the incident that the king had mentioned contributed to it, and perhaps the king spoke at length with his guests in an attempt to decipher if the guilty parties were present.

Standing over the table laden with food, Xenophon and Stefanos looked at the simple fare on display. Their eyes rested on the steaming black cauldron of blood broth which most men avoided touching.

"We should have some," Xenophon said.

"I've had my fill of that on campaign," Stefanos answered, gazing into the thick black liquid where bits of offal bobbed slowly on the surface.

"Here," Xenophon handed Stefanos a bowl and took one himself.

Stefanos took the wooden ladle and dipped it in, drawing out a steaming portion for each of them.

At the end of the table, in conversation with two Thebans, Plato glanced at them and smiled.

Stefanos nodded back and brought the bowl to his lips.

The hot liquid tasted of iron and raw meat, nothing else. He gulped at it, trying not to chew as he did so and allow the foul mixture that was the main staple of the Spartan diet to run quickly down his gullet. After what seemed like an eternity, the bowl was empty.

"Glad to see you enjoying our Spartan fare," Agesilaus

said, coming up between Xenophon and Stefanos, and filling his own bowl which he downed slowly and noisily, wiping a drop of the liquid from the corner of his mouth afterward. "Not many here have dared to try it."

"Their loss is our gain," Xenophon said ironically, smiling at the king.

"Ha! It's probably the safest thing here, as my cooks are unused to making any of that other food." Agesilaus laughed, turning back to look at Plato who had also filled his own bowl and was drinking slowly. "You surprise me, philosopher!" Agesilaus said.

Plato finished and handed the bowl to a slave. "Good. I am pleased not to be predicable."

"Ha!" Agesilaus actually seemed to like Plato, or at least be more interested in him, but his attention was pulled away by a loud, brash voice at the entrance to the tent. "Thrasybulos has actually come."

"Remember the peace, my friend," Xenophon whispered, knowing Agesilaus' hatred of the Athenian general who had helped break the thirty tyrants' hold on Athens.

Without a word, Agesilaus moved into the centre of the tent to meet Thrasybulos face-to-face.

"This bears watching," Plato said, still smiling as he moved closer to where Isocrates was, already moving in to get the ear of both Sparta and Athens at once.

"King Agesilaus," Thrasybulos said as he stopped in front of the king of Sparta.

"Thrasybulos, son of Lycus," Agesilaus replied, looking calmly up at the face of the Athenian general. "In the name of Zeus Xenios, I welcome you to my tent."

Thrasybulos looked around the large, plain tent and the faces of the crowd staring in his direction. "Thank you. I must say, your invitation took me by surprise." He chuckled, his strong bearded face placid. "By the looks of my fellow guests here, it would seem you have surprised them as well."

Agesilaus laughed. "I honour the Gods' Sacred Truce, as should we all."

"Agreed," Thrasybulos said, extending his arm and grasping Agesilaus'.

Stefanos watched the two men stare at each other and felt as though he could cut the tension with a dagger.

"Wait a moment, philosopher," Agesilaus said to Isocrates who had begun to move in to speak. "Let the general have some food and wine first."

Thrasybulos eyed Isocrates a moment, for he knew him well, and moved into the crowd to be swarmed by Thebans, Athenians, Argives, and others.

As soon as the meeting was over, a troupe of three flute girls came into the tent, two playing the aulos and one the lyra. Stefanos set aside his food and had his kylix refilled with watered wine.

Aeson of Thessaly, who arrived just after Thrasybulos, was deep in conversation with the latter. He was younger, but intense in his demeanour and the way he went about conversing with those around him, a distinct contrast to the Athenian general who was, by now, well-used to the presentation of his person.

"How many more people are supposed to come to this?" Stefanos asked Xenophon.

"There is just one more person of note, but I've been asked not to speak of it."

"Why? Who?"

"You'll see," Xenophon said, his mysterious smile making Stefanos slightly uncomfortable. "Some of us will be sitting soon," he added. "Enjoy the entertainment for now. I want to speak with Plato about his travels."

"I'm fine," Stefanos said, impatient to be gone, to rest before training the next day. He knew he had neglected his running, and hoped that he was sufficiently prepared for the hoplitodromos. War was training enough for that, as had been his march across the Peloponnese with Kratos and Pandaros.

At that moment, one of the young girls appeared before him, as if out of the earth. Her aulos fluted from her mouth, its notes playful and rhythmic as she danced before him, her corn-gold hair whirling in wisps about her face, as thin and fine as the tiny white strophion she wore.

Stefanos looked at her as she spun about him as if weaving her notes like rope about his person. She was young, and lean, and the lines of her body ignited his insides. He smiled at her, noticed her lips puckered against the mouthpiece of the two flutes as she played one last note for him alone before dancing away to entertain some of the other guests.

For some time Stefanos went round the room, avoiding the blustery oaf, Polydamas, and watching Agesilaus manoever his way among men who, only days before, would gladly have plunged a blade into his back and down the length of his spine.

The king's lameness gave men a sense of superiority, Stefanos could tell, a false sense of strength over the Spartan. But Stefanos knew better than to make such judgements.

From what Xenophon had told him, and from what he had heard, Agesilaus was a fine warrior, and a cunning intellect who never shirked from a fight, verbal or martial.

Stefanos wondered if Agesilaus had quite forgotten about him, if he might escape the king of Sparta's questions, but that hope was soon shattered when one of the slaves came up to him.

"Stefanos, son of Talos of Argos," the helot said, head bowed as he leaned in to speak to Stefanos.

"Yes?"

"King Agesilaus requests that you sit with him and some of the other guests."

"Me? Where?" Stefanos felt suddenly conscious of numerous eyes upon him.

"This way," the slave said, walking slowly away from the tent entrance where Stefanos had been skulking, to the couches set out in a long oval at the centre of the tent. "This one is yours," the slave indicated a couch with a thin cushion beside which was a small rectangular table with three legs.

Stefanos looked about the circle. He was sitting at the far end, directly opposite Agesilaus who was himself sitting down with Xenophon on his right. The couch on his left was vacant for the moment, but beside the latter sat the Priestess of Demetra Chamayne, and then Thrasybulos, Aeson of Thessaly, and Polydamas of Thessaly.

"Argive!" Polydamas bellowed, tapping Stefanos' couch. "We can talk now."

Stefanos looked away from the Thessalian to his left where Isocrates sat scowling, ignoring him and speaking with the Priest of Zeus to his left, between himself and Plato, who sat to Xenophon's right.

The circle complete, but for the empty couch beside the king, Stefanos realized it was indeed an odd assortment of guests, least fitting of all, he felt, was himself. He represented Argos, it seemed, though that confounded him as, being a mercenary, he had shown little loyalty in the past to his polis.

Thebes seemed to have been ignored, as was Corinth, while Athens and Thessaly were well-represented.

"To Father Zeus!" Agesilaus said, raising his kylix to the group and spilling some wine onto the floor.

The guests followed suit and then everyone drank. Around the fringes of the tent, those guests who had not been invited to sit with the king, were mingling and whispering, some leaving as the evening wore on into its next phase. As the girls playing the aulos and lyra moved to a corner to play a slow, steady tune, the king, with his armour and shield glinting bronze in the firelight behind him, looked at his guests.

At first, no one spoke but for the general murmur of those watching from the thinning crowd at the fringes. More incense was placed in the braziers, and more wine added to the krater behind the king.

Stefanos watched as the king took imperceptible sips, if

any, of the stronger ratio of water and wine, while some of the others, especially Polydamas beside him, gulped thirstily.

Aeson of Thessaly looked to his countryman to his left, gave a slight shake of his head, but said nothing. His eyes stayed on Agesilaus and Thrasybulos.

"This is a unique experience you give us, King Agesilaus," Plato said, smiling and lifting his cup to his lips. "Athens, Sparta, Thessaly, and Argos have often been at bloody odds. Now we share wine and the potential of learning from each other. Shall we trade ideas rather than spear thrusts?"

"Too much talk, can lead to misunderstanding, don't you think?" the priest of Zeus said beside Plato, crumpling Isocrates' face with his words.

"With respect, if we all talked more, perhaps we could get past our collective differences and direct our warlike energies against a common foe. Persia for instance?" Isocrates said.

Agesilaus turned toward Isocrates. "I have already done so. All year Spartan troops have been trading ideas with the Persians on the battlefield. A shame Athens was not there to be a part of it?" Agesilaus turned to Thrasybulos who was waiting for the assault.

"Why did Sparta turn to war against the Persians, when not long ago your city sought help from them against Athens?" The general stared at the Spartan king who sat up, in his plain clothes, pretending, Thrasybulos believed, to be an exemplar of Spartan virtue.

"Why then, the Lacedaemonians are Medising!" Isocrates blurted, his face a shade of red yielding to purple.

"Philosopher," Agesilaus said. "I say not! Rather, the Medes are Laconising!"

There was laughter from the Spartans about the tent, but none spoke, the sound of Thrasybulos' laughter drowning them out.

"Well said!" the Athenian general replied, raising his kylix to Agesilaus.

"And what has the fighting been like in Ionia?" Aeson asked, as Polydamas crunched on a chicken bone.

"The Persians stick to the sea when they can, refusing to fight us on land. But we draw them in. Our campaign against the satrap, Tissaphernes, in Sardis, was a success. They now take Sparta seriously again."

"As they did after Thermopylae and Plataea," Xenophon added with a nod to the king.

"Let us not forget Salamis either," Thrasybulos said.

"Those battles were a generation ago!" protested Isocrates. "I speak of the moment. Today! But you are correct to mention those glories of Greece's past, for those are the partnerships we must return to."

"Is it partnership, or true democracy for that matter, when some democrats in Athens swear to kill all who oppose her?" Xenophon added. "How can we expect Sparta, or others," he nodded to Aeson, " to join forces with Athens if there is such talk? The powers that be in Athens now are not what they used to be. Glories cannot be built on hatred, for those foundations will shake the world until all that is left is rubble. Look what those in Athens did to our friend, Socrates!" Xenophon's words struck many in the room, for there were men in that tent who had known and admired Socrates, a man who fought and thought, a man who had supported the thirty tyrants set in place by Sparta, but who had been betrayed by the very city he had sought to educate over his lifetime.

Agesilaus spoke. "I have learned much of Socrates from my friend here, and though he sounded like he was as good at making enemies as he was at thinking and questioning, it seems to me that it was a mistake of Athens' to force his death."

"A death he went to willingly," Plato added, his face back in a state of exhaustion and sadness. "Perhaps our answer lies in the Olympiad itself?"

"What do you mean?" Aeson of Thessaly said.

All this time, Stefanos looked about the circle of guests,

watching them, wondering who would speak next. Polydamas continued to eat, as did the priest of Zeus, though he could do quite as he pleased in his high station. The Priestess of Demetra was quiet, and ate slowly and methodically, mostly grapes from a platter.

"What I mean is," Plato continued, "that we should go back to the ideals these games exemplify. We need only look to Eris."

"Yes!" Isocrates exclaimed. "Eris Agathos and Kakochartos. Our world has been shattered by the latter, this constant exultancy in war and dissent, and the lust for battle and bloodshed. It holds us back!"

"Careful now," Agesilaus sat forward a little. "Do you point your finger at Sparta? For war and battle is the toil of the Spartan man. It is what makes our armies undefeatable."

"Careful, Agesilaus," Thrasybulos warned. "I know you are pious, and the Gods won't reward Hubris."

"Not Hubris. Fact," Agesilaus said plainly.

Stefanos suddenly found himself clearing his throat. "Is not Athens' and Thebes' hatred of Sparta and their wish to kill all who oppose the democrats Kakochartos as well?"

The gathering turned to Stefanos who felt like he had just thrown a spear across the room with the looks he was getting from everyone.

"And what would a mercenary know of this?"" Thrasybulos said.

"I've seen Kakochartos on both sides of the conflict in many battles. All of our cities have exulted in the evils of war, as...as have I, I admit."

"And what battles have you seen, Argive?" Aeson challenged. "As far as I know, Argos has let others do most of the fighting for it."

"I've fought for Argos, true." Stefanos sat up, and put his hands on his knees as everyone stared at him. In his mind, he could see his life of blood as if in a maelstrom of memory, as if it were akin to what the Gods would glimpse when they judged him... The tramp of thousands of feet, the clash of dorata upon hoploi, the cries and grunts of men as phalanxes collided...the screams of the wounded...the wailing of women...the cries of babes ripped from their mothers' arms...

"I have lived without loyalty," he began, the words like a mouthful of sand, "but this has given me a unique perspective. I have -"

Stefanos stopped speaking where he sat, the powerful, the holy, and the brilliant turned toward him. He looked beyond the king to where a woman and two young girls entered.

Kyniska had entered the tent, her tall form slipping past the king, with Eunice and Euryleonis following at her heels, their heads high.

Stefanos continued to watch, as did many of the others in that tent, as Kyniska came around and seated herself between the king of Sparta and the Priestess of Demeter.

Agesilaus turned toward her, his face clearly annoyed. "You're late," he said through gritted teeth.

"Forgive me, brother. I was washing the blood from myself and binding my wound after the attack." Kyniska said, her eyes looking up finally from the floor to stare at the faces about her.

The tent was dead silent.

"Attack?" Plato said, Xenophon sitting up beside him, concern spreading on his face.

"Yes!" Agesilaus said out loud. "It seems someone attacked my sister and her driver while they were training on the track."

"Training?" Polydamas spoke for the first time. "A woman?"

"My chariot team," Kyniska said directly to the big Thessalian who continued to look confused, even as he continued chewing.

"Are you quite hurt?" Xenophon said looking across at Kyniska, at her bandaged arm.

"It is nothing. A caltrop in my arm and a few scratches,"

Kyniska waved her hand, but her face was intense. "But I lost two of my team tonight. Two stallions whom I have trained for years. One of them, I had to kill myself."

Men looked about the room at each other, as if trying to ascertain the guilt of the others.

"Who would violate the Sacred Truce in this way?" said the priest of Zeus. "Sacrilege!"

"I agree," Agesilaus said, his gaze hard on the assembly.

"Sister?" Stefanos blurted out, unable to tame his whirling thoughts. *The king's sister?*

"Of course," Agesilaus said. "I'm sure many of you are wondering why a woman, other than Olympia's revered priestess, has just joined our symposium. My sister, Princess Kyniska, daughter of Archidamus II, Eurypontid King of Sparta, is a competitor in the four-horse chariot race in this Olympiad. She has raised and trained her teams herself, and breeds the finest horses in all of Greece."

"Forgive me, but I do believe our Thessalian horses will outrun yours, Princess," Aeson said, eyeing Kyniska intently from his couch.

"The Gods will show you the fault in your claim, Lord Aeson, on the day of the race." Kyniska said, her eyes glancing quickly at Stefanos before going back to her brother.

"But you said your team was lamed?" Plato asked.

"My second team. My first team is safe and sound, and surrounded by my bodyguard. If anyone tries to harm them, they will get a foot of Spartan bronze in their guts." Kyniska put out her hand and a kylix of water was handed to her. "But I was late, and you were in the middle of a conversation. Please continue, Argive," she said, looking directly at Stefanos.

Stefanos felt his neck grow hot as he looked back at her, his train of thought shattered at the sight of her, the long red peplos, and the bloody bandage around her left arm, covered only slightly by the long strands of her dark hair.

Kyniska's dark eyes challenged Stefanos to continue, as if

she enjoyed watching him squirm in such company. A company she had just handled as deftly as her brother.

"The Argive seems to have lost his thoughts," Aeson laughed. "No battles to speak of then?"

Stefanos was on his feet, but Polydamas was up then too, standing between him and Aeson, his overlord.

"Sit back down, both of you," Agesilaus commanded.

Stefanos looked at the king and nodded. "Forgive me, my lord," he said through gritted teeth." Stefanos turned and sat back down. "To answer this young pup's question, yes, I have seen battles."

Aeson sat up, his eyes full of loathing.

Stefanos noticed the smirk on Agesilaus' face and continued.

"I was eighteen when I went to war after the battle of Mantinea when Argos was crushed by Sparta." He looked at Agesilaus and Kyniska, the two girls behind her staring defiantly at Stefanos over their mistress' head. Such brazen defiance would never have been seen in the behaviour of other women. "I was nineteen in my first battle, when Sparta attacked the village of Hysiae - we fought Sparta off then. My first time in the phalanx, I knew I'd found what I was meant for, that the Gods had given me purpose."

"To kill?" the priestess of Demeter said, her face sad and pale.

"It was my destined struggle," Stefanos defended.

"Kakochartos!" Isocrates spat, but Stefanos ignored him.

"After Hysiae, I joined with Athens as a mercenary on the Melian campaign."

"A sad affair," Plato acknowledged, his head hanging. "I remember hearing of it. All the men slaughtered, and the women and children sold into slavery."

"I thought I would find greater camaraderie among the Athenians than I did among the Argives," Stefanos said, "but I was wrong. I found only greed, and slaughter." He turned to Isocrates. "You speak of Kakochartos? The battle of Melos was one of the worst examples of the war. After that," he looked up at Agesilaus, "I joined Gilippus' forces and sailed to Sicily."

"You joined the Spartans?" Aeson said. Several men from the crowd behind Stefanos murmured angrily at the memory of the campaign in which Athens' armies were slaughtered across the sea.

"Yes. Whether you like it or not, our Spartan brothers know the value of a warrior. They also know how to fight."

There were loud protests at this and the noise in the tent rose to a new level.

Xenophon looked to Stefanos as if asking why he was goading the assembly thus, but the latter shrugged and continued.

"I won't deny it. The slaughter of my fellow Greeks across those rocky landscapes and bogs of Sicily disturbed me. But I was paid well by Gilippus to do what I did best. When that job was done, I marched east with Xenophon and others, Spartans, Argives, Thessalians, Athenians, Corinthians, and other mercenaries, to join Cyrus' armies and set him on the throne of Persia."

"Shame!" someone yelled at the back of the tent.

"Shame, you say?" Stefanos stood. "In our mercenary ranks, we stopped fighting each other at last. In Persia, we fought against Persians." He looked down at Isocrates. "You yourself said that we should fight the Persians, not each other."

"Not for Persian benefit!" Isocrates spat.

"Nonetheless, we fought, and bled, and returned together!" Stefanos turned on the spot, eyeing everyone who seemed to challenge him.

From her couch, Kyniska watched the Argive plead his life, though for what reason she knew not. He was tall and strong, and though older than most in the tent, his form spoke the truth of the life he had led. Every scar seemed to glow red in testament upon his arms and legs, the muscles of his shoulders and neck, the areas where his thorax had left him vulnerable.

"You hide behind the Ten Thousand!" someone yelled.

Xenophon was up in a moment. "Who said that?" he yelled, demanding the person come forward. None did. "I'll have you know that Stefanos, son of Talos, a mercenary yes, as I was, is the best pentekonter in all of Greece's armies, not for any loyalty to his city, but for his loyalty to the men at his side, and his will to get them to Hades and back alive and victorious!"

"So says the Athenian traitor!" another burst out, and at this, Agesilaus was on his feet.

"Enough!" Agesilaus said from the centre of the tent, his presence enough to stifle the insults. "Nobody shall disregard the laws of hospitality in my tent. I'll not have the Gods insulted here!"

At that, several men at the back of the tent left, the crowd thinning considerably.

"It seems, Argive," Polydamas said, sitting up and setting his bone-strewn plate on the table before his couch, "that you are adept at making enemies." He looked at Stefanos and Xenophon, then to the king. "It is thus with all who are great and touched by the Gods. Is that not so, King Agesilaus?" the Olympic champion said.

"I have found it so, yes." Agesilaus nodded, turned to look at his sister, and then sat back down.

"Then let us return to our conversation," Plato added. "Our Argive mercenary has shown us that the opposing faces of Eris are present in every man, for he admitted to revelling in bloodshed, though his regret is plain enough to see. Am I correct?" He looked at Stefanos.

"I don't know. Were I finished fighting, I believe I would miss it," Stefanos said honestly.

"It is not that you fight, for that is noble," Isocrates said, calmer now. "It is where those fighting energies are directed that determines which face of Eris you honour."

"Indeed," Plato continued. "On our journey here, Isocrates and I have been discussing the ponos of men...and women," he nodded politely to Kyniska whose face was still and attentive. "Man's toil is, one could say, ruled by just and unjust action or pursuits, Eris Agathos or Kakochartos."

Stefanos and Xenophon were sitting again, each drinking from their newly replenished kylixes.

Stefanos looked around the tent and noticed that very few men were left, other than those who had been sitting, and a few Spartans, Thrasybulos' friends, and some Thessalians. Behind Kyniska, Eunice stared intently at her mistress. Euryleonis, however, looked at each speaker in turn, her interest or disagreement plain upon her young face.

"We are at the great Games," Plato said. "Let us look at pursuits other than war." He looked to Agesilaus for approval and the king nodded. "Socrates used to say that to injure a friend or anyone else is unjust, and that justice is doing good to your friends and harm to your enemies."

"That depends," Xenophon said.

"On what?" Plato asked.

"On the nature of the person to whom the harm is being done," Xenophon answered. "Let us use the Melian campaign Stefanos referred to."

Kyniska watched Stefanos at that moment, the tensity of his jaw as the battle of Melos was mentioned again, and for a moment she thought him weak. Then she remembered what she had heard of the Athenians' actions, the injustices done to women and children who had been Sparta's allies.

Would I have thought differently if they were Athenian allies? she wondered to herself as Stefanos sipped his wine.

For a moment, their eyes met, and he quickly looked away.

Xenophon continued. "It was badly done. The Melians could have been taught a lesson without enslaving the women and children. Much better to be just toward them, as that would have imparted harmony and friendship."

"Which is the nature of justice," Plato said. "Injustice is

ignorance. It is divisive, and creates hatred and fighting and prevents a city, people, an army, or others, from acting together."

"As the Greeks should act. Together!" Isocrates said in his grating voice.

"But, without the threat of injustice, by your definition," Aeson said, "there would be chaos."

Stefanos began to feel his head spin with such talk. He hated philosophical discussion, and this was one in which he unwittingly found himself at the centre.

"We are, I fear, heading back into the realm of war, gentlemen," the priest of Zeus said where he lay back in his white robes. "I thought we were steering our way back to a discussion of the great Games, of the skills that are given us by the Gods themselves."

"Very well. Forgive me," Plato said to the priest. "Let us say that injustice prevents a man from pursuing his fated ponos, that it leads to Kakochartos."

"Whereas," Xenophon jumped in. "Justice encourages men to nurture Eris Agathos, to pursue the nature that the Gods intended for them, and so make the world about them a better place."

"You idealize, my friend," Agesilaus said to Xenophon, a knowing smile on his lips.

"Precisely!" Plato said, "Why should we not strive for perfection, for the ideal situation? Every pursuit, be it government, kingly rule, hoplite warfare, sculpting, boxing, or horse racing, has an ideal, something to strive for. If all men were permitted to fight for such things, how would we find the world about us?"

"As Sparta is," Agesilaus said. "You cloud the issue. I had this same discussion with my father, Archidamus, when I was young. What you say is impossible, for one man's justice is another man's injustice, one's man's pursuit and ideal another man's hatred."

"Do you not enter the conversation, Princess?" the

priestess of Demeter asked Kyniska quietly, leaning over to speak to her.

Kyniska looked at the priestess, her pale skin, soft body, and prematurely lined face. "She who knows how to speak, knows also when," Kyniska said, staring into the priestess' eyes. "They are not ready for a woman's word at this point."

The priestess smiled and nodded. "I understand you. Though I think the Argive has an interest in what you would say."

Kyniska looked at Stefanos and caught his eye again. Beyond the Argive, she spotted Typhon watching her closely and looked away, annoyed at his attentiveness. Ever since the attack, he had been unbearable.

Thrasybulos spoke to Agesilaus. "You speak of Sparta being the ideal, Agesilaus. Explain what you mean. How is Sparta any better than Athens? I would know your mind." Thrasybulos put a piece of cheese in his mouth and looked to the Spartan king for an answer.

"You talk back and forth about Eris Agathos, Kakochartos, a man's ponos, and more until the issue is so clouded you cannot see the true importance of a man's existence. In Athens, men," he said the word with not a little disdain, "have various professions. They may be potters, or sculptors, poets or philosophers, teachers or doctors. And these same men may, when needed, take up arms for their cities."

"Yes," Thrasybulos said. "Every male citizen contributes in various ways to his polis, to his society."

"True. But these same men lack focus. They cannot achieve perfection in any one area because they are spread too thinly. They cannot hope to attain the heights of glory that the Gods have destined for them. And so, they mock the Gods."

"And how does this differ in Sparta?" Plato asked.

"In Sparta, every male citizen is trained to fight, to hold his shield in the phalanx wall, to protect the man at his side, and thrust his spear for Sparta. And that is all he need do. There is focus, and so with his toil dedicated to a single goal that is both honourable and pure, he can achieve the perfection that is pleasing to the Gods."

"And what is that goal, King Agesilaus?" Thrasybulos asked.

"To fight and die for Sparta. To achieve a beautiful death."

"Is that all there is in the world?" Isocrates asked. "Death? Would you leave nothing behind?"

"If I have done anything noble, that is a sufficient memorial. My actions for Sparta. If I have not achieved anything, then nothing can preserve my memory."

Kyniska looked at her brother, but he did not acknowledge her. She had to admit to herself that the conversation was not a smooth one. It was filled with jabs and insults, all cloaked in philosophical dialogue that just barely stayed together.

"And what happens when there is no more fighting?" Isocrates asked, and everyone stared at him as if he had just challenged the king of Sparta to single combat.

"There will always be fighting," Agesilaus answered.

The slaves came around with some more wine and placed platters of fruit and nuts on each of the diners' tables. In the background, the flute girl began a soft tune once more, an attempt to still the aggression in the air, though Agesilaus seemed quite content with things.

Plato then sat up on the edge of his couch. "Our venerable Priest of Zeus had the right of it. We should speak of the Games and the toil men go through to get here. If we cannot steer the conversation away from war, then perhaps we should all agree with King Agesilaus in that true perfection can only be attained in combat. In Sparta, warriors seek perfection in battle. Yes? What of other pursuits?"

"Every athlete seeks perfection in his chosen event," Xenophon said, "and the ideal state of that pursuit is victory at the Olympiad."

"Every artist, and by that I mean artist, athlete, or warrior, has an inherent interest in being the best at what he does," Thrasybulos said.

"Yes. Let us take horsemanship," Plato said, nodding to Kyniska who had been silent the entire time.

She looked at the young philosopher keenly from across the circle and he smiled.

"I have heard of your great skill in raising and training horses, Princess. I assume you would not be here unless you wanted to show that your horses are the very best in the Greek world, yes?"

All eyes turned toward Kyniska and she felt her neck grow hot. She took a casual sip of watered wine.

"I believe in the skill the Gods have given me, and in the spirit of my horses. They seek perfection as much as I do."

"I see that in Sparta, the women have other pursuits than the men," Aeson said. "So much for Spartan perfection, Agesilaus."

The group stared at Aeson who now seemed to have crossed an invisible line.

Agesilaus stared at the man and then back to Kyniska, but Plato spoke first.

"Aeson, I'm afraid you are oversimplifying things. In Sparta, the women train for war in other ways. They are the garrison when all of the Spartan men are away. Is that not true?" Plato asked Kyniska and Agesilaus.

"Quite," Agesilaus said. "Though they know their place as well," he added with a look at his sister.

"Back to horsemanship," Plato continued casually. "Princess, when you are training your teams, when you are striving for the perfection you seek, that the Gods have set before you as a possibility, is the focus of your art not the perfection of the art of horsemanship, and all that considers the interests of the art of horsemanship?"

From his couch, Stefanos watched Kyniska and felt like he was watching a cornered lioness surrounded by jackals. He remembered how he had been furious with her, so much so that he had wished he had not come to her aid that first time outside of Olympia. But now, he found himself wishing she would tear them apart, though he knew not why. He tried to meet her gaze, but she would not look his way. She stared directly at Plato.

Agesilaus answered before she could. "Of course she does, just as a warrior perfects all that is of interest to his skill, such as a spear thrust, or the push of his hoplon, so too does the horseman consider how he sits on a saddle, the harnessing of a team to a yoke, how best to use the beasts to win the battle or the race."

Plato continued to stare at Kyniska, a slight smile upon his face.

"No," she said, not looking at her brother. The art of horsemanship is not how best to consider using the animals. The true art of horsemanship is to ensure that one considers the interests of the horse. I get to know each horse that I train from birth. I nurture them, discover their strengths and nurture those. Some may be faster, others more reliable and sturdy. The art of horsemanship is of course, important, but the true art is understanding those I am relying on and who rely upon me."

"I agree! Definitely!" Xenophon clapped his hands loudly and smiled at Kyniska. "You have touched upon the true secret of horsemanship, Princess. Would that all men dealt so with their neighbours." He looked at Thrasybulos who stared back at him.

Kyniska smiled briefly at Xenophon then turned her gaze to Stefanos, briefly before whipping around to look at her brother.

"If only life were that simple, If only ruling were that simple," Agesilaus said, crossing his arms.

"But the Princess proves that it can be by the fact that she is here to compete in the Olympiad, does she not?" Stefanos put in.

Everybody turned to look at him.

Agesilaus laughed. "I must make something clear to you

all. Chariot racing is not a true contest for a man. The horses do all of the work."

Kyniska stared wide-eyed and furious at her brother, just barely managing to contain her rage, her hand gripping the edge of her couch.

"Warfare and kingship are a definite art. But horse and chariot racing is not. The reason I have allowed my sister to compete in the Games is more to humiliate and discredit those rich buffoons who seek superiority over others by having their horses win for them. These men of Athens and elsewhere," he did not hide his dislike here, "refuse to step onto the skamma to trade blows with men like Stefanos, son of Talos, for instance, men who are of lower social standing because they believe it is beneath them."

Stefanos felt himself growing angry and noticed Xenophon's eyes pleading with him to keep his composure.

Kyniska looked from her brother to Stefanos and back. She had wondered when her brother would show his true nature, but the lies he told of her achievements rallied her hatred of him. *Our father, may the Gods bless him, would never have insulted his family thus, or guests for that matter...*

"And so," Agesilaus continued, "these men pay for expensive horses to bring them victory in the Games, and then claim that the goddess Nike crowns them for their achievement. Not the drivers' achievement, but their own. My sister will win because she knows something of horses and has enough gold left her by our father to buy the best breeds and equipment." He paused and looked directly at Kyniska. "But she is no Olympic champion. To say so dishonours the Gods' games."

Nobody said anything else.

Kyniska stared at her brother who smiled back at her and sipped his watered wine.

Agesilaus waved to one of the servants who ushered in a man with a clean-shaven face and wearing an Ionic chiton.

Stefanos wanted to rise from his couch and slam his fist

into the king of Sparta's face. *How can he dishonour his sister like that? I would never have done such a thing!* he told himself, thinking of Cleo and feeling a pang of anger for Kyniska.

Kyniska stood, ready to retaliate. She saw Aeson and Polydamas giggling as she stared around the tent, and Typhon who stood with his arms crossed, unwilling to meet her gaze. She was about to leave the tent when Stefanos sat up and spoke.

"King Agesilaus," he said. "What of the origins of the Games? Is it not true that Pelops, whose remains lie within the sacred sanctuary, raced his chariot across the Peloponnese with the woman, Hippodameia? A race against her father Oinomaus? Surely the Gods intended for such an event to be a part of the Games. Was it not one of the original events?"

"Ha! Our Argive mercenary believes in bedtime stories!" Thrasybulos laughed.

Stefanos turned on him. "Yes I do," he said. "Would you mock the Gods and heroes who have gone before us, Athenian?"

"A hero who won by deceit!" Thrasybulos countered.

"As I have seen many battles won by deceit." Stefanos crossed his arms and looked down on the big Athenian general. He looked up to see Kyniska leaving with Eunice and Euryleonis from the back of the tent, her back just disappearing into the dark.

"Let us not trade insults," Plato said, a little uneasy now. "The truth of our various arts piques my interest immensely. For I heard Socrates speak about it on many occasions without a sufficiently satisfying conclusion."

"If you must," Agesilaus said. "But I warn you, I'm not in the mood for further lessons."

Agesilaus stared directly at Stefanos then, and the latter felt the full meaning of those cold eyes.

"Very well," Plato said. "Would you say that the art is superior to the artist?"

"It depends on the artist you are speaking about, for all

men are different," Agesilaus said. "Until an artist perfects his art, he is the lesser, but once he reaches perfection, he is the personification of that art's ideal. Just as Achilles was the perfect warrior."

"And yet, Achilles was flawed," Thrasybulos said, "and his anger almost lost the Greeks the war."

"Only because he had to deal with lesser men," Agesilaus said.

"And does not a perfect warrior, or ruler for that matter," Plato said, pulling thoughtfully on his beard, "have to deal with and consider the interests of his brothers-in-arms, or his subjects? Even though he may be far more skilled than them?"

"It depends on his brothers-in-arms, or his subjects. The interests of some, slaves, women, allies who want your help, those who are weaker, are in your thrall and so need to consider the interests of the stronger. But, when it comes to one's fellow citizens, one's equals at home or in the shield wall, then yes, their interests must be considered for the good of all."

Stefanos began to tire quickly of the company then, for there was much being said that was not actually said, and he had never had patience for such talk. It was one of the things that had kept his fellow Argives out of the true battles that needed to be fought.

He stood as discreetly as he could, and made for the tent entrance.

"Argive!" Agesilaus called.

Stefanos turned.

"Where are you going?"

"I must consider the needs of nature," Stefanos said lightly, bowing his head.

Agesilaus laughed and waved him away, before returning to his conversation with Plato, the others waiting for the time to insert themselves.

"I think," Plato said, "that we have come back to our previous discussion of justice and injustice."

"Did we not say before," Xenophon put in, "that justice is doing good to your friends and harm to your enemies?"

"Yes," Agesilaus said. "But I still believe that justice is the interest of the stronger. And so, it is just in the Gods' eyes that those who are weaker or lesser consider not their own interests so much as those of their superiors, for their interests are naturally those of the stronger."

"Really?" Plato said. "Would you say then that because Polydamas, our champion pankrationist here," he nodded to the big Thessalian who was beginning to nurse another plate of food which he had demanded of one of the slaves, "that because he is physically stronger than all of us, and finds the eating of beef makes him strong, that if we ate beef also we too would be as strong? If our interests were identical to his, would we find ourselves in his exact situation?"

"No. Men are different. As are governments, be they democracies, tyrannies, oligarchies, or aristocracies." Agesilaus adjusted his seating position and straightened his plain clothing.

"Yet," Plato said. "Each form of government makes laws that some might consider to be unjust."

"By whom? Those who are weaker."

"Are we to judge?" Plato raised his eyebrows.

Everyone stared at Agesilaus.

"No," the king said. "But the Gods certainly do in the end, don't they?"

"And the Gods are superior to us all, wouldn't you agree?" Plato asked.

"Absolutely!"

"And would you say the Gods are just?"

"Yes, of course."

"And is it possible that, as they are superior to us, that the Gods might also consider any man, be he ruler, noble, peasant, or slave, in the wrong if their actions were unpleasing to them?"

"Yes," Agesilaus said, hesitantly this time. "What are you implying?"

"I imply nothing," Plato said. "As we have been talking, I have had a thought forming in my mind that if, as we agree, the Gods are just, it follows that those who are unjust, those who create division, hatred, ignorance, and who thrive on Kakochartos, are naturally the enemies of the Gods."

STEFANOS FELT THE WELCOME RELIEF OF THE COOL NIGHT AIR fill his lungs and caress his sweaty skin after the stuffiness of the tent. Though the wine had been watered, it had clouded his thinking and judgement, and he did not enjoy the feeling when in such company.

He did not want to return to the symposium, though he wondered if it could even have been called that. *What was she doing there?* he wondered, for he had never been to a symposium where a woman, let alone two, plus the two young girls, had been present. How happy would the king of Sparta be if he did not return? He wondered if they would even notice he was gone.

"You're not going back, Argive?"

Stefanos felt a prickle on the back of his neck and turned to see Kyniska approaching him in the moonlight, Eunice and Euryleonis a short distance away with Typhon and a few guards.

"Are you?" Stefanos asked as she came up beside him.

"I've had enough of their talk," she said, a definite edge to her voice. Her anger still simmering beneath the surface of her beauty.

For she was beautiful. Closer now, Stefanos could admire the smooth line of her jaw and neck, the curve of her lean shoulders and the lustrous hair running down between her shoulder blades.

Kyniska's brows knitted as she stared at the sky, almost as if she was not aware of his presence beside her.

"I don't blame you," he said. "I can't take any more either. I'm surprised your brother is willing to go through such talk. It doesn't seem very...Spartan."

"My brother is full of surprises," Kyniska said. "As are you."

She was looking directly at him now, her eyes locked onto his as surely as if she were a goddess come down to torment him.

"Why did you speak up? What sort of man are you, Argive?"

"Stefanos. Call me Stefanos. Argos is just another city to me these days."

"Why did you speak?"

"I only spoke as I felt compelled."

"Why?" she persisted, her eyes boring deep into his, interest and anger there, yes, and curiosity.

"I've seen things. I've..." Stefanos tore his gaze from hers and shook his head. He looked up at the sky, at the myriad stars that pocked the heavens above them.

"Tell me."

"On the journey here I saw... They are not just stories. The great race. Pelops and Hippodameia. I saw them in the mountains, their shades. They are still racing."

Kyniska took a step backward, her eyes intent upon the man before her.

"Also, something in the Pelopion. I saw her... I could hear her screams."

"You imagine things in the sanctuary. All men do-"

"No," he said quickly, looking back to her. "I didn't. And in the mountains..." Stefanos turned to face her. In the distance, Typhon began to stride toward them. "The morning after I saw Pelops and Hippodameia racing over the mountains... That's the morning I first saw you."

This time, Kyniska shook her head, her jaw working, her brow creased even more.

"I can't make sense of it," he said. "I've seen many things

in my life, great feats of bravery and cowardice, experienced moments in which I felt the Gods had utterly abandoned me, or handed us victory out of certain defeat. But that night in the mountains...here in the sanctuary...they have shown me things that I can't explain."

"Why are you telling me this?" she said angrily. "Why did you speak up in there?"

Stefanos shrugged and attempted to smile. "Maybe I felt that that was the just thing to do."

"You are not my defender. I'm a Spartan woman, I don't need you to defend me." Kyniska took a step closer now.

"I know," Stefanos said. "I wanted to."

Kyniska stared at him again, the strong shoulders and taut arms, his chest where it bulged beneath the plain tunic he wore.

For a moment, the world around them muted itself. She could feel her lips wet. *Take him if you want. You're a Spartan!* she yelled at herself inside, but something held her back. She felt as though she finally saw Stefanos, son of Talos, and she wanted to reach up and touch his rough face to ensure he was not some apparition sent by the Gods to distract her from the perfection she sought, her victory at the Games.

Stefanos saw her eyes change and he felt an uncontrollable urge to take hold of her, to kiss her and sweep her up in his arms.

"Princess!" the harsh voice came from behind Kyniska, and their reverie was shattered.

"What is it, Typhon?" Kyniska answered, her jaw clenched tightly, her eyes dark and stormy once more.

"The king commands you to come to his quarters. He wishes to speak with you about the incident earlier today."

"He can wait," she said.

"He commands it. Now." Typhon said, earning a hateful look from the princess.

"Go," Stefanos said. "We will see each other again."

Kyniska looked at him a few moments longer and then turned to go.

Typhon remained facing Stefanos for a moment. "You are to go back to your tent, Argive. The king is finished with your company tonight."

"Thank King Agesilaus for his hospitality," Stefanos said. "I need to sleep for training tomorrow anyway."

"I wonder if we'll meet each other on the sand, Argive?" Typhon said, squaring up to Stefanos.

"If that happens," Stefanos answered, "then the Gods will have abandoned you."

Typhon's fists balled and he was about to lunge at Stefanos.

"Typhon!" Kyniska's commanding voice shattered the dark and the enomotarch stopped in his tracks.

"I'll see you on the skamma, Argive," he said, before turning to go.

Stefanos watched Kyniska depart with the two young girls, surrounded by her guards. When they were gone, he made his way back to Xenophon's tent where he lay down and stared at the wavering roof as the night breeze played with it. Soon, his eyes closed and he fell into blissful sleep.

Chapter Seven

THE OATH-TAKING

Η Ορκωμοσία

The day of the Oath-Taking arrived and the tempest of arrogance and bluster that had blown about the sanctuary of Olympia was now muted and awed.

All felt that the Gods were now in attendance, and so every man trained with quiet intensity, anticipating the contests to come, the hoped-for elation at a bout won, a throw to match all others, or a stride faster and farther than everyone else.

Hope warred with doubt in each mortal man's heart as he oiled his naked body in the elaiothesion, and then dusted himself in the konisterion, the rituals before competition and practice.

Most of the noise came from trainers who offered last minute advice to their athletes, adjustment in technique, or hints as to how to best their competitors.

Early in the morning, Stefanos left Xenophon to his writing and made his way to the palaestra where he oiled and dusted himself before jogging around the perimeter of the peristyle. Once he was warm, he ran faster and faster until the sweat ran fluid down his body and he could feel it on his ankles.

A few men arrived after Stefanos, only to find him already warmed-up, stretching and lifting stone weights.

Stefanos felt good, even better than he had in a long while, and he could not quite explain it. He had been revitalized.

As he stood on the edge of the sand, drinking water from a clay jug, he looked up beyond the tiled rooftop to the trees above. Their tops swayed in the hot breeze and he thought back to that night not long ago, the night of the symposium in Agesilaus' tent.

His mind wandered, and he thought of Kyniska then, imagined her training her team of horses for the great race. He thought he could almost hear her voice high and lovely in command as she instructed her charioteer, even above the thunder of horses' hooves...

Stefanos had not seen Agesilaus since the symposium, but when he spoke with Xenophon the following day, his friend had warned him that the king of Sparta had been somewhat displeased, saying that he should not have invited his sister to join them.

"He was more than a little upset with you, Stefanos," Xenophon said.

"Me? Why?"

"Because of what you said about Pelops and Hippodameia and chariot racing."

"But it's true, isn't it?" Stefanos protested.

"Yes, but Agesilaus was trying to make a point to the Athenians and Thessalians, not make a decision about chariot racing or his sister."

"But he was wrong, and...she didn't deserve what he was saying."

"She's a woman, Stefanos, and Agesilaus is the king of Sparta. Just let it be." Xenophon paused and looked Stefanos in the eyes. "Agesilaus is also my friend. He has welcomed you in his camp. You should not cross him."

"I suppose not!" Stefanos said, throwing up his arms and remembering how much he disliked tyrants of any sort. Gods knew he had fought for enough of them.

"Just focus on the Games," Xenophon said, truthfully. "The Oath-Taking is almost here."

"I know..." Stefanos had said. "I know..."

AFTER TRAINING THAT MORNING, STEFANOS BATHED AND WENT back to the tent to dress for the oath-taking.

Xenophon was not there, and Stefanos figured he was with Agesilaus, for the king of Sparta had taken Xenophon into his confidence since Lysander had been dismissed back to Sparta.

It was, Stefanos thought, a dangerous business to become closely acquainted with the powerful men of the world. Lysander was a prime example, a great Spartan admiral with many victories to his name, relegated to menial status.

Look at all those Greek generals who led us to Persia and had supported Cyrus...dead in the sand at Cunaxa...

He did not want to end up dead in the dirt for any man, no matter how powerful, nor however many favours he might heap upon him. Stefanos knew at least, that even if he had lived in the shadow of Kakochartos for most of his life, at least he had done so at his own bidding. The choices had been his.

He sat on one of the stools in the middle of the tent with a cup of wine and looked about. He had never had such a clean dwelling on campaign. But then, Xenophon was from a wealthy family. He wondered how Kratos was doing with his training, or if he was drinking away his days and nights with the Argives.

Stefanos knew he resented Kratos for the friends he had chosen. He also knew that he should not do so. They were all at the Gods' whims, and he was used to his solitude, at peace with it. That is, until he met Kyniska.

His thoughts went back to the Spartan princess. *A princess!* He wondered what the Gods were playing at, putting her in his path. Since they had met that first time, when he had come upon her and her girls exercising naked in the morning mist, she had come in and out of his thoughts like a mysterious daemon, a memory of both pain and pleasure.

"Pandaros," Stefanos said, his eyes roving over to his thorax, greaves, helmet, doru and xiphos none of which he had picked up in days. "Even if Kratos lets you down, I won't."

In the distance he heard a sound of horns and drums calling the Olympians to the Bouleuterion where the Oath-taking was to occur.

Stefanos laced up his sandals and, wearing his plain chiton, tucked his leather pouch in his belt, and strode out of the tent into the blazing sunlight.

All about him, red cloaks and tunics could be seen streaming toward the river Kladeos.

"Stefanos!"

Stefanos turned to see Pollux jogging up to his side. "You off duty?" Stefanos asked.

"Of course. Anyone who is competing must take the oath, even the king's guards." Pollux smiled and looked Stefanos up and down. "You look different."

"Really? Tired maybe. A lot on my mind."

"I'll bet," Pollux smiled as they walked over the wooden foot bridge to the other side to join a crowd of Athenian athletes making their way to the area before the Bouleuterion and the altar of Zeus Orkios, God of Oaths.

"What do you mean?"

"Come on, Stefanos. I've known you too long not to see what's occupying your thoughts."

"The Games, yes. But I don't think I'm alone in that."

"Not the Games. I can see you are fit and full of confidence, so long as you don't have to fight me," he laughed and ribbed Stefanos playfully. "No," he said, his voice more serious.

"You're not speaking plainly enough for a Spartan again, Pollux."

"How's this then? Forget about her," he said, his voice low.

"Who?" Stefanos asked, though inside he knew what his friend meant.

"I'm not stupid, my Argive friend. I know how much you like women, and I saw you speaking with the princess the other night outside. You forget?"

"No. I don't. But you're imagining things. She is beautiful, yes, but nothing could ever come of that."

"I'm glad you see reason," Pollux sighed. "I'm sure the king has his own plans for his sister, and besides, I don't think Typhon would take kindly to it."

"Typhon? Her bodyguard?"

"Why do you look surprised?" Pollux turned around to see if the enomotarch was nearby. "She's a princess, and a Spartan woman. I've told you how things work."

"Then why should it matter?" Stefanos asked, pushing aside two men ahead who had stopped to argue in the middle of the throng.

"Because she's a Spartan. That's why." Pollux slapped Stefanos on the shoulder. "Besides, if you win the Games, imagine all the women you will have! Now that's something worth fighting for, no?"

"Not very pious of you, is it?"

"Ha. The Gods always come first," Pollux retorted. "And if they want to see a man bedded with many women, or men, then they will make it so. Come on. They're starting!"

Stefanos and Pollux pushed through the crowd until they could see the white robes of the theokoloi. They were gathered with their attendant wood cutters, animal rustlers, meat cutters, staff bearers and more, in a group around the large marble altar that stood beneath the towering statue of Zeus Orkios.

Stefanos looked up to see Zeus, his muscular body taut, beard long and full, staring down on the gathered athletes and trainers.

The king of the Gods held two massive lightning bolts, one in each hand, ready to strike down any who cheated or blasphemed the Sacred Games in any fashion.

It was hot, and the muttering of the crowd grew even louder than the whirring of the cicadas in the pine, oak, and plane trees that dotted the sanctuary.

When the drums and horns that had called all men to assemble before Zeus halted, a hush fell over the crowd as the most senior theokolos stepped forward, his arms raised, a staff in one hand, and a clutch of oak and olive leaves in the other.

A younger priest then stepped forward bearing a large bronze horn upon his shoulder. He took a deep breath and blew loud and hard so that the sound could be felt in the chests and hearts of every man there. Three long, lingering notes to call everyone's attention, and notify Zeus that they were ready to offer their oaths to him.

The head theokolos turned from the crowd of men to face the altar behind him and look up at the statue of Zeus.

"Zeus Orkios, father of your people and of these sacred games... We honour you..."

All of the theokoloi raised their arms to the statue of Zeus, as did their helpers.

The assembled athletes, coaches, and chaperones did likewise, and so every man and youth had his arms raised to the father of the Gods.

"Bless these competitors, Father Zeus!" the priest said. "Bless these Olympic Games!" He nodded to a man standing by who promptly disappeared around the side of the Bouleuterion. "May Nike, our supreme goddess of victory, crown the noble victors and smite those who bring dishonour to the Games!"

Stefanos felt a chill run down his spine at the words. He was sure every man did. There seemed to be a humming in the very air around him, the sound touched only by the heartbeat and breath of the men all about him.

A few feet away, Stefanos spotted Pirro, the red-haired charioteer. As he looked at him, Pirro turned to see Stefanos.

The boy's face was grave. Yet he seemed confident, even as a cripple, towered over by the men around him. He nodded a greeting to Stefanos and then turned his gaze back to the altar.

A sudden shriek pierced the air about them. Many men looked up, one muttering something about harpies, but after a few moments it became evident that it was the sacrifice.

From along the north wall of the Bouleuterion came six of the theokoloi's animal wranglers.

"It's the boar," Pollux whispered to Stefanos as they both stood on tiptoe to see over the heads of those in front of them. "The theokoloi's servants catch one on the slopes of Mount Erymanthus every Olympiad for this sacrifice alone."

"It's massive!" Stefanos said. "I've never seen a boar that big in all my life."

"Nor have I," Pollux said, his voice drowned out by the almost human screams of the tusked animal.

They watched as the six big men pulled the boar forward, bound by chains, his tusks, and body tied tightly so that he would not gore anyone.

Stefanos wondered if the beast was a descendant of the one Herakles had slain in the stories, and once he saw the beast hoisted onto the huge altar, pulled upward by the chains, he had no doubt that it was.

One of the tusks lashed out and narrowly missed the face of one of the wranglers. Extra ropes were hurriedly thrown over the beast to allow the priest to approach with a straight, long-bladed dagger. The bronze glinted in the sunlight and the boar screeched even more loudly, deafening the assembly as if it knew what fate the Gods had in store for it.

The wranglers, all of whom were large and well-muscled, strained at the chains and ropes, their bodies taut as Herakles' bow, their limbs shaking with the effort of holding the beast steady.

The head theokolos raised his arms to the statue of Zeus, the bronze blade pointing downward at the animal.

"Father Zeus! Accept this offering. Know that we honour you, Lord of all the Greeks, King of the Gods!"

The old man thrust the blade downward into the top of the boar's head and the animal writhed for a moment before going limp and groaning.

The priest withdrew the blade quickly, and even more quickly, the wranglers moved in to grab hold of the tusks with thick leather gloves and pull the head back.

With practiced precision, the priest put the blade to the boar's neck and sliced it deeply across the thick muscle of the neck. He drew the blade away quickly and the blood began to flow thick and red over the pure white marble of the altar of Zeus Orkios.

Stefanos stared at the massive body that appeared to die so easily with six men holding it down. A sacrifice to honour the king of the Gods, and seal their oaths in blood.

Two of the other theokoloi moved in with gleaming bronze to begin cutting the animal into sections, their robes soaking crimson.

The head priest then plunged his hands into the body and withdrew them to hold them up to the men who intended to compete in the Olympic Games. His red palms, thick and dripping with gore, faced them all.

"Father Zeus will have your oaths, competitors and coaches...mortal Olympians..."

Stefanos felt his father near in that moment, was back in the room in Argos, swearing to his father that he would go to the Games, that he would win for his family's honour.

The priest seemed to stare each man in the face,

unrushed, his eyes wide and brilliant, blood running down his forearms to disappear into the sleeves of his robes.

"Do you all swear that you have been training in your chosen events for the past ten months?" he demanded.

"We swear!" everyone answered.

"Do you swear, before almighty Zeus, that you will compete honourably and to the best of your abilities?"

"We swear!"

"Do you swear not to shame the Sacred Games?" the priest's voice was loud and rebounded onto them all from the neighbouring walls of the stoa to their right and the Bouleuterion before them.

"We swear!"

"Father Zeus!" the priest turned again to face the statue. "The men of Greece swear to uphold the sanctity of your Olympic Games! May you and Nike decide who is best among them, and crown them with eternal glory!"

Everyone was silent for a minute as the priest stood still, his arms up to Zeus, his mouth moving silently in whispered prayer.

Then, the horn-blower sounded another long, sombre note and the theokoloi set about preparing the fire that would roast the animal for all men there, while the wranglers began to cut the sacrificial corpse, setting aside the thigh bones wrapped in fat for the Gods, and the rest of the animal for men.

Soon the men began to breathe normally, and mingle amongst themselves. The smell of roasting meat wafted among them and water was passed around.

Stefanos spotted Kratos on the other side of the crowd and waved.

Kratos waved back, but then Stefanos spotted Ocnus beside him, as well as Krikor, Biton, Ampyx and Glaucus. They all stared his way, hatred in their eyes and demeanour. Kratos appeared surrounded by the blue cloaks of the Argive Thousand.

"What's he doing with that lot?" Pollux asked, handing Stefanos a jug of water. "Thought he hated them?"

"So did I," Stefanos answered.

"Well, this is the Sacred Truce now," Pollux warned, "and no matter how much you want to pound them to bleeding chunks, and I know they deserve it, you have to respect the Gods, my friend. Stay away from them. They'll only try and dishonour you. After the Games, I'll help you crush them."

Stefanos looked at Pollux and knew he spoke true, about the sanctity of the Games, but also about crushing them. He had seen Pollux destroy men with his bare hands when all weapons were broken or lost. In Persia, they had both been up to their elbows in enemy blood at their most desperate times.

"Kratos can choose what friends he wishes," Stefanos said, turning from his fellow Argives to face the Spartan. "I've got other things on my mind."

"The Games begin tomorrow," Pollux said. "May the Gods bless our limbs and our spirits."

They drank and Stefanos turned as Pirro passed by, his eyes catching Stefanos'.

"Is your mistress well? Pirro, is it?"

The young Spartan stopped suddenly and looked up at the Argive. "Yes. She is strong," he said calmly, unworried.

"What's that on your face?" Pollux said.

Pirro reached up and touched his face, smearing the glob of blood that had landed on him. He looked at his hand and for a moment, his eyes were fearful.

"Here," Stefanos offered him his water jug and the young man poured some on his hand to wash it away and wipe his face.

"What's this?" said a big Arkadian behind them. "A cripple competing in the Sacred Games?" The man looked disgusted and spat at Pirro.

The young man spat back without hesitation and the Arkadian lunged at him, but not before Stefanos stepped forward quickly and shouldered the man sideways so that he missed Pirro and ended up on the ground.

"Careful there!" Stefanos said to the man as he scrambled to his feet. "Mind you don't hurt yourself, or someone else. The Gods are watching you." Stefanos pointed, without taking his eyes off the man, to the statue of Zeus Orkios towering above the bloody altar.

"I know you, Argive!" the Arkadian hissed, his shoulder muscles up and rounded like an angry animal. "I've seen you training on the skamma. You haven't got a chance."

"That's up to the Gods."

"We'll see," the man said, eyeing Pirro who stood beside Pollux. He laughed. "What have the games come to, when a cripple drives the chariot of a woman?" he spat, and there was real hatred in his voice. "You'll crash in the first turn," he said over his shoulder before going back to his group.

Stefanos looked about and noticed several groups watching him and Pirro - Spartans, and Thebans surrounding the titanic youth, Pelopidas, Corinthians, and Athenians, some of whom Stefanos recognized from the Melian campaign, though they had been younger then.

He also saw Ocnus and Kratos looking at him, the latter looking ill-at-ease where he stood, like a man who has obviously lost sight of his loyalties.

There is no loyalty among mercenaries, Stefanos told himself, turning to see Pollux walking away. He turned back toward the altar to see Pirro looking worriedly at the blood that was still on his hand, trying to wipe it away.

The young man looked up, his red hair wild, his freckled face panicked. "It was blood from the sacrifice. It splattered across my face."

"Don't worry yourself," Stefanos said, patting him on the shoulder. "A little blood won't keep you from winning, will it?"

He smiled, albeit reluctantly. "No."

"Stefanos," Kratos' voice cut between them. "I...I wanted to wish you -"

Stefanos looked up. "What? What did you want to say, Kratos...friend..."

Kratos shook his head and his long hair waved about. "Stop it. They're really not that bad. There is, I've found, a camaraderie to be found among the people of one's polis."

"You sound like one of their bum boys already, you know that, don't you?"

"Enough." Kratos' voice filled with bitter severity, as a man who has been called out on a lie he has been clinging to.

"All those years fighting together, training. And now you're befriending the man who would gladly put a knife in my back."

"We don't speak of you or your family."

"Good. I don't want you to say anything about my sister to him. Can I ask that of you at least?" Stefanos stood beside Pirro, his arms crossed.

"Of course. Cleo is my friend too."

"Friend? Yes. She is kind, and deserved far more than that sadistic mule could ever have given her. You remember that will you, when you're cheering him on in the Games?"

"I only wanted to say that I wish Tyche is with you the whole of the Games and that you make your father's wish come true."

Stefanos stood staring a Kratos for a moment before nodding. "Get back to your friends," he said, his voice low and sharp. "They're waiting for you."

Kratos nodded, his head hung slightly before turning. "The Gods have a plan, Stefanos. And we are playing it out."

Stefanos watched Kratos walk away and join Ocnus and the others.

"Fortune favours the bold," Pirro said, more to himself than anyone else.

Stefanos looked down at the crippled charioteer and nodded. "Yes. It does."

"I must go. My mistress is waiting for me," Pirro said. "Thank you."

"Don't thank me," Stefanos answered. "He was all bluster. Men like that are easily cowed when reminded that the Gods are watching them."

Pirro began to walk away and Stefanos suddenly felt like he had no business there, among the athletes of the various cities. "I'll walk with you," he called after Pirro, taking two pieces of meat from the platter of one of the theokoloi's meat servers and handing one to Pirro. They strode across the grass, through the south processional gates, and past the House of the Phaidryntai.

When they crossed the river, Pirro turned to Stefanos.

"I really must go. Thank you again."

"Have you seen Xenophon today?" Stefanos asked. "He was not in his tent this morning."

"I believe he was with the king, this morning. But, as I was leaving for the Oath-taking, he arrived at the track to speak with my mistress. For an Athenian, he is quite knowledgeable about horses, almost as much as she is."

Stefanos laughed. "Yes. In fact, I think he is part centaur at times. He's always taking notes about horses. I'm sure he wants some ideas from Kyniska." *It feels good to say her name...* The thought surprised Stefanos and he noticed Pirro frowning up at him.

"Do you mind if I come with you, in case he's still there? I also wouldn't mind seeing you race. I have to admit, that I'm impressed you can control four horses."

"It's not about controlling them!" Pirro was suddenly lively, the sunlight flashing in his eyes. "It's about understanding them and learning how to talk to them."

"All right then."

"Shouldn't you be training anyway, Argive?"

"Call me Stefanos." He nodded. "I've been training in war for a long time. The Games begin tomorrow. It's in the Gods' hands now."

Pirro nodded. "Come."

· · ·

"In all of my travels, I've never seen such magnificent horses," Xenophon said, walking around the big black, Acheron, as he waited to be hitched to the chariot yoke. "Did the incident the other evening upset them all very much?"

Kyniska stood with her back to Xenophon, harnessing Phaedra second last. Euryleonis and Thais stood in front of the horses stroking their muzzles and whispering to them.

Xenophon waited patiently for her to answer, and she appreciated his calm around the animals. She wished, however, that he had not come the day before the start of the games to press her with his questions, but her brother had given his permission. Indeed, he had encouraged it.

Normally, Kyniska would have welcomed a conversation with a man who was obviously nearly as well-versed as she in the breeding, raising, and training of horses, but she wanted to be alone with her team. Even the proximity of her attendant girls annoyed her, though it was no fault of their own; they were as perfect as ever and, as usual, the only ones to come close to understanding her, especially Euryleonis.

"They are not themselves," she answered finally. "I tried to get the blacks away as quickly as possible, but they could sense the horror of what had happened. They smelled the blood on the grass. That's why I've moved to this track farther down the river, away from the noise and stink of the sanctuary."

She could still picture it, the sword she had grasped in her hands, the deep breath, and the force it had taken to plunge the blade into Adonis so that it was over quickly. She kept her back to Xenophon.

She had not been ready to receive guests; she still wore the sweaty, plain brown chiton that allowed her the most ease of movement. She was training too, and had been working with the horses while Pirro had been at the Oath-Taking.

I hope the Gods have found favour in the Games, she thought, looking up at the sky. The sun beat down on her and she closed her eyes for a moment, trying to think of flying manes and cries of victory, rather than screams, and blood, and death.

"Has your brother found out who did it yet?" Xenophon asked.

She turned to look at him. "Don't *you* know? I would think you are closer to my brother than I am, Xenophon. Doesn't he tell you everything?"

Xenophon smiled, maybe a little knowingly, but not in an unkind manner. "Perhaps. I suppose. Though why, I can't imagine."

"I can," she said. "I'm just here to show the Greeks that chariot racing is not a real contest." Her voice dripped with sarcasm.

Xenophon said nothing. He knew she was right, or at least that that was what Agesilaus believed and wanted. He looked again at Acheron and brought him over once Kyniska had finished harnessing Phaedra.

"The King of Persia would pay you handsomely for these mounts," Xenophon said.

"And I would spit in his face," she answered.

"I don't doubt it," he laughed, a little uncomfortable. "At any rate, I was hoping to ask you how you pick your horses. I'm compiling a work on horsemanship and I would like your input."

She turned finally. "What? A woman's input?" she played aghast.

"A *Spartan* woman's input," he corrected.

She nodded. "First off, you want a horse who can adapt to different terrains, so, the knees and ankles must be flexible, but thick. You want ease of movement, but not weakness. Some horses can run like the wind, but their legs are so thin that they can snap like a twig if they were to get caught somewhere."

"I agree."

"You don't want a horse that is skittish. It'll throw you in battle, or baulk at the sight of a snake on the path."

"Yet you don't want a horse that is oblivious to all around it either."

"Exactly," she smiled, at ease in the conversation now. "Strong, quick, and alert. That is what you strive for."

"Difficult to find all of those in one beast, though, isn't it?"

"Yes. That's why I breed and train my own." She reached up to stroke Acheron's powerful neck. "What is it, boy?" she said as the stallion tossed its head and pounded the ground with his hoof. "Eager to get running?" Kyniska turned to look down the river in the direction of the sanctuary.

"Where is Pirro?" she said as she searched for the red hair amongst the Spartans returning to the main camp from the ceremony within the sanctuary.

"He's probably at the feast with all the other competitors." Xenophon said.

"No," she said firmly. "He would come back to train."

"Does your charioteer have any life outside of racing and caring for your horses, Kyniska?"

"No. He cares only for them," she said firmly. "As I do." Kyniska nodded to Euryleonis and Thais.

Immediately, the girls tossed her the thick leather reins and she caught them deftly in her tanned, slender hands.

"Can you control the team with your wound?" Xenophon asked, his glance moving to the bandage on her left arm.

"Of course!" Kyniska said, turning in the cab and pointing the horses down the track.

The light chariot pivoted, the spoked wheels rocking easily on the dry, cracked ground.

"Do they require a hard lash?" Xenophon said, marvelling at the ease with which she stood in the cab, like an Amazon queen.

"I thought you knew about horses?" she said, her brow creased for a moment before her face relaxed.

Xanthus, Zoe, Phaedra, and Acheron stilled, and their ears perked up as if listening for something on the wind as their manes and tails twitched, their muscles ready to fire at any moment.

Kyniska clicked a sound with her mouth, not even a word, and the four horses went into a walk, that turned into a canter, the chariot wheels whirling more quickly to either side of the princess.

"No whip is needed when you know your horses, son of Gryllus," Euryleonis said as she and Thais stood beside him watching their mistress lead the team around the new track.

In the distant trees, along the edge of the river, the red cloaks of some of the men of her personal guard could be seen standing sentry.

"Good to see her guards are here now," Xenophon said, making idle conversation as his eyes took in the sight of the Spartan woman speeding around the track.

"The king insisted," Thais added. "If any xenoi show up in the Spartan camp uninvited, then they will be taken."

"Then it's good I have been invited, isn't it?" Xenophon laughed.

"Yes. Else you would be beaten," Euryleonis added.

"The Argive is safe too," Thais assured.

Xenophon looked at the young girls who watched their mistress with awe and appreciation. He could not blame them, for even he, a man who had seen all in war and peace across Greece and into the heart of Persia, even he could not take his eyes from her as she clicked and whistled, sending her team into a charge that was worthy of the greatest chariot races he had seen in his day, and still the reins were not as taut as one might expect. There was no whipping. She knew her team.

"The Games have begun!" Stefanos said suddenly, coming from behind with Pirro and Typhon. The latter looked thoroughly perturbed at his being there.

"Stefanos!" Xenophon answered. "I wondered when you would come back."

"I thought I would see you at the Oath-Taking," Stefanos said.

"Me too. However, watching Princess Kyniska handle her team of horses is much more interesting. The Gods have truly touched her with skill and intuition. Pirro, Typhon..." Xenophon greeted the other two.

Pirro smiled distractedly and limped quickly by Xenophon to stand at the side of the track and watch the team.

Kyniska spotted him as she came around the last bend, but offered him only a quick glance. Instead her gaze lingered on Stefanos as she sped by, her head turning briefly to pick him out among the others.

At that moment, Stefanos stepped forward, unaware of what Xenophon was saying to him. *It's just like...on the mountain. The woman...* he thought, a fiery feeling in his gut as he remembered dark eyes, as intense and willful as a storm.

"She taught me everything I know," Pirro said to Stefanos beside him. "I'm going to win for her."

At that moment the blacks thundered up to them, their hooves pounding the earth into submission as they slowed at their mistress' command.

"Pirro!" Kyniska called.

Immediately Pirro stepped out and, as the chariot came by, he grabbed the rail and hopped up, defying his disability.

As he did so, Kyniska leapt down with a whistle to her team that seemed to indicate she was handing them off to Pirro.

Sweaty and smiling, stray strands of her hair stuck to the sides of her face, Kyniska strode barefoot directly over to Stefanos.

Thais smiled, but Euryleonis watched the Argive suspiciously.

"I can see now that you fully understand your horses," Stefanos said, unable to take his eyes off of her.

"You can see, can you?" she laughed. "Then you will see my team run to victory in the Games."

"I don't doubt it," Stefanos said, moving closer, just as a thick hand grasped his shoulder.

"Typhon!" Kyniska said. "Get back! The Argive is my guest."

Her voice was so commanding, so certain of every word chosen, Stefanos was forced to pay attention to everything she uttered. He wanted to.

"Are you the reason that Pirro was late for training?" she demanded.

"No. The Oath-Taking is a long ceremony," Stefanos said.

"The Argive nearly came to blows with an Arkadian during the ceremony. He almost got Pirro expelled from the Games," Typhon muttered.

"Are you sure about that, Enomotarch?" Stefanos said. "Where were you when the Arkadian attacked Pirro?"

"Attacked?" Kyniska's face lit with fury. "You're supposed to watch over him, Typhon."

"I'm supposed to watch over you, my lady. Not your charioteer. Besides, I was there to swear the oath as well." Typhon puffed up his chest and crossed his scarred arms.

"Pirro and I are one when it comes to the Games, Typhon. If anything happens to him, you will pay the price."

"Princess, I -"

"Leave me!" she dismissed him and turned to watch Pirro speeding around the track now, testing out turns, seeing how the team was working together.

Typhon stared at her back, unmoving, He hated how she seemed to lean in to the Argive.

"Are you still there, Typhon? I told you to leave," Kyniska said without turning.

As they watched, Stefanos looked down at Kyniska. "Does your team get a chance to run the hippodrome before the race?"

"Yes," she said without looking at him. "Once. But that is not relevant. A well-trained team will be able to handle any terrain, any track, as long as the driver knows them well, and can anticipate for them. Besides, would your chances of fighting be better if you were to train in the stadium rather than on the skamma of the palaestra?"

"No. I suppose not. I must be able to fight and run anywhere."

"The same with horses." Kyniska stepped forward, not to yell commands to Pirro now, but as if to check the fine details of the movements of her team, the horses she had raised and trained so that they would arrive at the Olympiad in their prime.

After a few more laps of cantering and then walking, and many plumes of dust rising into the sky around them, Pirro brought the team to a standstill before Kyniska.

"Good," she said to the horses, shooting a smile to Pirro. "You're all ready." Kyniska walked up to each horse and stroked their soft muzzles and cheeks. "Nike will crown you with eternal glory. I feel it."

Stefanos and Xenophon, who had been standing in the background, moved forward to look at the horses up close.

The beasts were taller than the two men. Xenophon busied himself with admiring their form and skeletal structure, the powerful limbs and hocks, while Stefanos watched Kyniska with them, mesmerized as one might be when seeing a loving mother care for her child.

"You amaze me," he whispered.

She glanced at him, but her gaze did not linger.

Stefanos followed her along the row of horses, watched her bare arms as they reached up and stroked them, and they leaned into her. He stood beside Phaedra. "May I?" he asked.

"Slowly," Kyniska said, obviously wary. "Do you know horses at all?"

"I admit, no. But I've always admired them and their spirit."

"The spirit is different from horse to horse," she said abruptly. "Just as it is with men and women."

Stefanos looked at her across Phaedra's neck. *I don't doubt it.*

He reached up and ran his hand down the length of the mare's shiny black coat. It shone in the dying light of the day. There was a musty smell of sweat upon his hand as he touched the animal whose bulging eye watched him.

There was a loud neighing behind him and Stefanos felt himself pushed hard. He bounced off of Phaedra and jumped out of the way just as Acheron's massive head darted in to nudge him again.

"Is he trying to bite me?" Stefanos laughed, rubbing his shoulder.

Kyniska chuckled, though she seemed acutely interested in this behaviour. "I don't believe it."

"What?"

"He's playing with you," Kyniska came around to stand with Stefanos before the big Acheron. "What is it boy? You like this Argive?" Kyniska asked, her face breaking into a smile so lovely that Stefanos never thought to see one like it again.

Acheron nudged both of them, and they each reached up to stroke his forehead at the same time, Stefanos' hand covering Kyniska's.

Their eyes locked, and to his surprise, the princess did not pull her hand away. Her fingers moved beneath his, entwining awkwardly against Acheron's pitch black coat.

"My lady, I've never seen Acheron so taken with a stranger before," Thais said excitedly from behind them. "That's amazing!"

Kyniska slowly withdrew her hand. "Help me stable them," she said to Stefanos.

"I would like that," he answered, smiling. "Just tell me what to do."

"Walk for now. This way." She pointed toward a group of tents surrounded by guards. "The horses' tents are near mine," she said, walking in front of him, her dark hair trailing down her back. "Pirro," she called over her shoulder. "Bring them. Thais and Euryleonis, go and get Helle and Eunice and have them prepare food and wine in my tent."

"For you, my lady?" Thais asked, smiling.

"For two."

As they walked toward the large ring of tents and the red cloaks surrounding them, Typhon came walking towards them.

"I can help you, my lady," he said, his dark locks falling over his shoulders like a lion's wet mane. The enomotarch, Stefanos noticed, was back in his armour and red cloak, his doru clutched tightly in his right hand, his helmet resting atop his head.

"No need. Stefanos, son of Talos will help me," she said.

"Him? You can't, my lady. The King -"

"He is a guest in our camp, and he saved my life. Or have you forgotten? I trust this man, and that should be enough for you, Typhon. Now, arrange for the night watch and let us be."

Typhon froze on the spot, his face growing an angry red, his fist white around the shaft of the spear. His eyes bored into Stefanos as he walked by, and the latter could not help eyeing the Spartan back.

The stables, or rather massive tents that had been cordoned off, smelled of sweet, dry hay. They were aglow with light from several hanging bronze oil lamps in the shape of horse heads. In the orange light, Stefanos could see that each horse had its own stall.

The heads of two whites jutted out to watch the others approach, and Stefanos noticed one more white stallion lying on the ground.

Kyniska went straight to this one and laid her hand on its cheek.

"Is this the other that was injured in the attack?" Stefanos asked, kneeling in the straw beside her.

"Yes. This is Hippolytus. There, there... I'm here..." she whispered softly to the animal.

"They're like your children," Stefanos ventured.

"Yes. They are." Kyniska kissed the white stallion and

stood slowly. "Though I fear that he is done for. The leg is not healing as it should."

"It has only been a few days, though," Stefanos said. "Surely it would take longer than that?"

"Yes. But as soon as the Games are finished, we must travel and he cannot be transported yet."

"It's in the hands of the Gods," Pirro said, walking up to them. "They are ready, my lady."

"Good," Kyniska touched Pirro's face gently with her hand and he appeared to lean into the caress like one of the horses. "What is this on your face?" she said, rubbing her thumb on his cheek.

"Oh, ah, during the sacrifice I was..." Pirro began to look afraid. "I was standing close when the priest slit the boar's neck. He drew the blade too quickly and splashed blood on people. It was only a drop."

Kyniska stared at the young boy, her lips parting as if to say something, but deciding against it, their red lines shutting tightly.

"He's right. It was only a little," Stefanos said, his hand on Pirro's shoulder. "The priest was sloppy if you ask me."

Kyniska turned to Stefanos. "Can you unharness Acheron for me? He seems comfortable with you and should let you do so.

"Of course," Stefanos said, going over to Acheron and stroking him before unbuckling the straps that attached the chariot arms to the yoke about the stallion's neck.

Stefanos watched out of the corner of his eye as Kyniska took Pirro aside. She seemed angry, worried, and Pirro pleading, defensive. They both looked at Stefanos and then Kyniska put her hands upon both of Pirro's shoulders and hugged him close.

"I know you can do this. They're fools, all of them. They don't know your gifts. You will drive, and you will win," she whispered to him. "And when Nike crowns us, then we will make them pay."

Pirro nodded and took a deep breath as he stood before her.

"Make sure they have all the food and water they need," she said. "The Argive and I will brush them down."

Kyniska turned and strode over to Stefanos who was just undoing the last buckle.

"Pirro said you kept some Arkadians from attacking him."

"He was ready enough to fight, I can tell you," Stefanos answered. "But it would not have been fair, or right in Zeus' presence."

She put her hand upon Stefanos' chest and felt his heart beating beneath his muscle. "Thank you. He doesn't have many allies in this world, especially in Sparta."

Stefanos knew that in Sparta, Pirro should have been thrown from the cliffs as a child, or left exposed on the mountainside. He was not fit for the Agoge, the Spartan school of war.

But the Gods, it seemed, knew what they were about.

"The only ally he needs, it seems, is you..." Stefanos' voice trailed off and suddenly they were very close. For the first time, he saw Kyniska's strong exterior crack.

She smiled, nodded, and busied herself with the other horses' harness. "Come, Argive, there are other arts in the world than standing firm in the shield wall."

"Odd thing for a Spartan to say," Stefanos laughed.

"Spartan women know things Spartan men do not," she said, a playful look in her features, like the leaves of a slender tree rustled for the first time on a long, hot summer's day.

"Here." She tossed the yoke from Zoe's neck to Stefanos, the latter catching it sloppily as she busied herself with the next one. "Hang it beside her stable."

Stefanos walked across the straw-strewn floor and hung it on a wooden peg that protruded from one of the main posts. When he turned, Kyniska was already hanging a second one.

Her movements, he noticed, were quick and graceful. Not

feline, like other women, for he had always believed that implied something hidden.

No. Kyniska did not hide behind any mask. Her movements, her words, told only truth. In the way she took care of her team, it was obvious to Stefanos that she loved doing even these seemingly menial tasks. She was efficient, no time or effort wasted, but she was enjoying it. Or was it his presence she was enjoying? He was not so sure, for she seemed attracted to him one moment, and then unimpressed the next.

"Help me brush them," she said as she tossed Stefanos a round brush which he caught deftly this time, moving to Acheron's side. "Long strokes, with the coat, not against," she instructed.

Stefanos set to it, and stole glimpses of her over the horses' backs. "Wouldn't it be more appropriate for your slaves to do this work? You are a princess, after all."

"No. These are my family, my children. Only my maids and Pirro care for them besides me. They know them, and how to treat them. And my horses know that I trust them."

"What do other Spartan women do then? Those who don't have horses?"

"They raise young men before they go to the Agoge, and they train their girls." Kyniska did not look at him.

"Do you have...I mean, do you have children, Kyniska? Are you married? I would think your father or brother would have wanted to marry you to some great warrior?"

"I am not married. Nor do I have children. Only my horses."

"Why?" Stefanos stopped brushing and leaned against Acheron's great rib cage.

Kyniska looked up. "All men who came forth weren't good enough."

"Really?" Stefanos looked surprised. "I thought all Spartan men were great?" he said sarcastically.

"Martial prowess is important, but it is not all. Were I to

marry, I would want to marry my equal, as well as someone who understands my world, my reason for living."

Stefanos scoffed and Kyniska's eyes filled with anger.

"No, no! I'm not laughing," Stefanos protested. "I'm only thinking how in Athens or Argos, or anywhere for that matter, you would never hear a woman speak like that. I know Spartan women are supposed to be different...I've known a few..." he cleared his throat and moved on quickly. "I mean...what I'm trying to say is that it seems to me that you're different even from Spartan women. I don't doubt that you cannot find your equal. Why would you want to tie yourself to a mule when you can race like the winds on these?" He gestured to the four blacks between them.

Stefanos felt awkward then, like he did in his first boxing match, all flailing limbs and inaccurate punches. He was relieved when Kyniska's face relaxed and the makings of a smile pulled gently at her slightly dimpled cheeks.

Together they finished brushing down the horses and led them to their stalls. Fresh hay and water were given to each, as well as some special oats that Kyniska had prepared earlier.

Normally, Stefanos would have found this work boring, the smell of the stable stale and pungent, but he found himself enjoying every moment of it. Every action of Kyniska's, of his own, seemed heightened. He felt more aware of everything, just as in a battle when all senses are accounted for.

If she had been any other woman, he would have grabbed her then and there, pressing his mouth to hers. But he could not do so with Kyniska. She commanded his attention, his respect, for the woman she was, for the ponos he could see she had been suffering through all of her life.

He went over to each of the horses and pat them. "Thank you for not kicking me," he smiled at Acheron and the stallion nudged him playfully as he rubbed his neck.

Kyniska in turn watched Stefanos with the team. She surprised herself in trusting this stranger with her family. She watched Stefanos in the orange light of the lamps, the way his muscles fired with every movement, the way his shoulders relaxed and tensed as he reached up to place his arm about Acheron's neck, the way he laughed like a little boy who has his first close experience with a great horse.

Kyniska was used to taking what she wanted, to taking men when she had need, but as she watched the Argive before her, a man she had told herself she hated the first time they met, she realized she did not want him to leave just yet. She wanted to get to know him more, to find out more about him.

She knew many men, but this one puzzled her to no end.

"Come. I've had the girls set food aside for us in my tent."

"Not more blood broth, I hope." Stefanos smiled.

"No. Although if that is what you would like, I can arrange it," she laughed.

"Surprise me," he answered, and she led the way out of the stables. "Pirro will be with you shortly," she said, turning to look at all of the horses. "Good night."

Outside, Kyniska found Pirro talking with Helle.

"You can go in now, Pirro."

"Yes, my lady," the young man smiled. "Typhon asked me to inform you that the guard is set and that they will be surrounding the tents all night."

"Good," she answered.

"He also said he will accompany the Argive back to Xenophon's tent for you."

Kyniska turned to Stefanos. "Do you wish to leave now?" she asked him.

Stefanos held her gaze and shook his head slowly. "No. Not if you don't wish it."

"Tell Typhon to wait outside the stable door when he returns."

"Yes, my lady," Pirro said as Kyniska and Stefanos went under the awning before the tent and disappeared inside.

Helle looked at Pirro and smiled knowingly, even as she wrapped her arms about his neck and the two of them went into the stables together for the night.

THE OATH-TAKING

. . .

THE INSIDE OF KYNISKA'S TENT WAS MUCH SMALLER THAN that of Agesilaus', but it was certainly more ornate, though not opulent.

They had left the gathering of tents, and walked into a world of firelight, scented smoke, wood, and fluttering linen.

Stefanos was blinded for a moment by the light and smoke from the bronze brazier that burned directly ahead of the main entrance to the tent which was supported by four massive poles at the corners and one in the centre. The cream coloured linen was decorated with blue meander patterns at the top and bottom with red acanthus designs bisecting them at chest-height.

As Stefanos went deeper into Kyniska's world, he passed a statue of Poseidon on one side of the central post, and another of Artemis. The two statues were smaller than he had seen elsewhere, and they were not of marble but of aged bronze which he stopped to admire.

At the very back of the tent, Kyniska spoke with Euryleonis, Thais, and Eunice in whispers. She looked over the food they had set out on the table between two couches at the back and nodded to them.

All three girls bowed to her and padded by Stefanos on their way to the entrance. Thais and Eunice smiled at him, but Euryleonis scowled appraisingly at him before turning, grabbing hold of both the leather entrance flaps, and closing them with a snap.

As Kyniska poured wine into two silver cups decorated with charging horses and charioteers, Stefanos glanced around the tent. To the left was a long curtain wall behind which there was a soft orange glow, and to the right was another curtain wall that was dark. At the back of the tent was another bronze, this one of a magnificent stallion that seemed to be flying over a grassy plain, free of harness, rider, or any other burden.

Suddenly Kyniska was at his side, a silver cup held up to him.

"The bronzes were all my father's. He left them to me."

"Did King Archidamus have a love of horses too?" Stefanos asked, moving closer to the one of the stallion to admire the workmanship.

"Yes, though he only ever really spoke about it to me. He gave me my first horse. I was in love with them from then on."

"A wonderful gift," Stefanos said raising his cup. "To Poseidon and Artemis," he said, pouring a little to the ground before sipping.

"To the Gods," Kyniska said, following suit. She sipped, and Stefanos watched as her lips touched the silver rim. "Eat," she said suddenly, seeming to enjoy the increasing hold she had on him. "No blood broth," she smiled.

She indicated a couch to the right of the table that stood before the statue of the horse, and she reclined on that to the left.

"Eunice is a good cook, so I think you will enjoy this, if you have digested your sacrificial boar."

"I didn't have much," Stefanos said as he took a few grapes from a clay platter. "You didn't need to put all this out."

"I didn't. Eunice did."

Stefanos looked at the table of cheese, figs and grapes, bread, honeyed chicken, and nuts.

"Simple fare," she said smiling, "but not very Spartan."

"No. But greatly appreciated," he said, not wanting to take too much, though his stomach growled at the sight of it. He also eyed the large pitcher of wine beside the one for water and told himself he should be careful.

"Would your brother be upset to know you dine on such food with an Argive?" Stefanos asked, smiling, though he was in dead earnest. He needed to know if he could relax or not. Being in the tent of his friend Xenophon within the Spartan camp was one thing, being alone in the tent of a Spartan princess, the king's sister no less, was quite another.

"Yes," she answered. "But I am free to invite whom I choose."

"I don't think I've ever eaten such a meal alone with a woman before," Stefanos said.

"You have no woman then?" she asked casually, brushing aside a strand of her hair that had fallen before her face.

"No. Well...no. Just my sister."

"What is her name?"

"Cleo."

"Is she married?"

Stefanos was silent a moment, then shook his head. "No. She was to be, but I put an end to that."

"Why?"

"The man was unworthy and would have been cruel to her."

"Aren't many men cruel to their women?"

"Not to my sister if I can help it."

"And you did. Was she angry with you?"

"At first," he said taking a sip and then reaching for a piece of meat from the platter. He put it in his mouth and his eyes widened at the explosion of flavour on his tongue. "This is good!" he said.

Kyniska smiled. "You can tell Eunice. Is your sister still angry with you?"

"No. She saw the right of it. She's priestess at the Heraion of Argos now, as my mother was."

"They are both there?" Kyniska nodded gravely, her respect for the Gods evident in her manner as they spoke about it.

"No. My mother died many years ago. My father died just before I came here."

"I'm sorry," she said. "It is not easy to lose a kind father."

"How do you know he was kind?" Stefanos asked.

"I can see it in you." She looked at him as if observing a thing of beauty, intense in her appraisal, as if assessing a new champion for one of her teams. "Your father was a bronze smith?"

"How did you know that?"

"You're Argive, and you had an eye for my statues here." She smiled. "So tell me, Stefanos, son of Talos... Why are you competing in the Olympiad?"

"What do you mean, why?"

"You're older than most of the competitors, about my age, and you are a mercenary who seems to have enjoyed the life he has chosen to some extent. Why are you here?"

Stefanos sighed and put down his wine cup. He stood and walked to the bronze horse.

"I ask too many questions," Kyniska said. "My father always said I was too curious for a woman, even a Spartan woman."

Stefanos turned and looked down at her. "I'm here because I swore to my father on his death bed, just before the Gods took him, that I would fulfill his wish of me having an Olympic victory and of...of mounting an epinikion bronze in the Altis dedicated to our family." Stefanos smiled and shook his head. "He loved bronze..."

Kyniska said nothing, and all that could be heard was the flickering of the flames in the bronze tripod, and the rustle of the tent walls in the breeze coming from the distant sea to cool the valley beneath the Hill of Cronos.

"What of your own father?" Stefanos broke the silence. "What would he think of his daughter competing in the Olympiad? Your brother doesn't seem to think much of it."

"Agesilaus thinks only of war and strengthening Sparta's position in Greece."

"He's right to. There are many cities that want to wrestle that power away from Sparta."

Kyniska took some cheese and held it as she answered. "You're right. He's surrounded by enemies in this place."

"As are you," Stefanos nodded to the bandage around her arm where the caltrop had punctured her tanned skin.

"Everyone has enemies," Kyniska said. "But you cannot turn from the path the Gods have laid before you to avoid them. They're part of the journey."

"As are friends, I hope."

"Do you have many friends? I imagine a mercenary has a hard time keeping friends."

"You're right. The man I travelled here with - Kratos."

"What of him?"

"He's now training with the man whom I prevented from marrying my sister."

"Here?" Kyniska's face was wary.

"Yes."

"And Xenophon? Isn't he your friend?"

"Yes. We've been through much together. But then, so had Kratos and I."

"That's why I love my horses. You can count on them until the death. Love and respect them, and they will give you their undying friendship and love."

"If only mortal men were like that," Stefanos mused.

They were silent for a few minutes then, but not uncomfortably so. They sipped their wine, ate, and gazed at the flames of the lamps flanking the equine statue.

Stefanos stole glimpses of Kyniska, and remembered flashes of her in his mind - when he had spied her exercising on the field along the river, when she had been insulted by her brother before the symposium guests, her face in the moonlight that same night, her smile as she interacted with her team. He also saw the face of the woman he thought was Hippodameia. He looked across the table at Kyniska again.

She seemed lost in thought, a troubling one.

"What?"

She looked up from her wine cup and stared across the table at him, a hint of awe in her face, across her brow.

"Have you seen her again?"

"Who?"

"Hippodameia. You told me the other night that you believed you saw her."

"You think I'm mad," he said, a little too defensively.

"No!" she said quickly. "Not at all. I've just... I've never seen her and I...I don't know. Have you again?"

"Not since the Pelopion. But I can say this: it was not a soothing experience. I don't know what I saw, but that was the second time and there was..." He wondered how he could find the words to describe the experience. He was no playwright or tragedian. "I had an overwhelming sense of sadness when she appeared. Her arms were outstretched, and she wept."

"This was in the grounds of the Pelopion?" Kyniska asked.

"Yes."

"Perhaps she wept for her dead husband?" The stories speak of great love between them. A love that drove her to betray her father for Pelops."

"Her father was cruel."

"That too."

Stefanos sighed. "I've never had such an experience before. Gods and heroes have never shown themselves to me, not in battle, not at home as a child."

"Perhaps they did and you never noticed before?" She smiled. "The Gods show themselves to us in many ways, everyday. I see them in the running of a horse, or hear about it in the unimaginable turn of a battle. Even in..."

"In what?"

"In your coming to my aid that first day along the river when those bandits appeared. Typhon never leaves my side. That was the first time."

"What are you saying?" Stefanos was sitting up.

"I'm saying that...that you should," she looked distraught for a second then sighed and lay back against the arm of the couch. "You need to pay attention to these things. The Gods send us messages in many ways. You are here, at the Olympiad for a reason. You must discover what, besides glory for your family, that reason is."

He had hoped for something more. He did not know what, but something more flattering, not a lecture on omens and the ways of the Gods. *Spartan piety!* Stefanos was suddenly angry and he did not quite know why.

"Why are you here then, at the Games? Haven't you won in other games, like the Heraia?"

Her long neck straightened and she became alert to his tone. "Yes. I've won every competition I've entered, including the Heraia. But this is the Olympiad. All the Greek world is here, and I would show them what a Spartan woman can do."

"And what about Kyniska?" Stefanos asked. "You're more than just a Spartan."

"As you are more than just a mercenary from Argos, playing at champion?"

He did not answer.

She continued. "I would show the world what Kyniska can do, what her horses can do, and what a crippled charioteer with a heart bigger than every warrior here can do!"

Kyniska was standing without knowing it, her fists clenched at her side, her hair wild about her face, and her eyes ablaze with passion. Stefanos stood to walk over to her, but as soon as she registered his approach, she turned away quickly and walked over to the statue of Artemis, the Huntress's eyes looking upon the mortal, almost with an accusing glare, or was it a question or challenge?

Stefanos approached her slowly. He knew she did not want him to see her face, her armour broken. She was strong and stubborn, and he was the same.

"It seems that the Gods have set both of our hearts on fire, Kyniska. Our ponos is similar. Maybe it is Eris Agathos after all?"

He thought of all the accusations that had been levelled at him, like the shafts of enemy spears at his heart. All the times he had been revelling in horror, and when people had told him so, he had raged for the truths they flung at him, withdrawing to another battlefield for another city or empire. He had never stopped to challenge his accusers.

He now realized that the Olympiad was where he was to prove his mortal worth, or else fall through the halls of Hades to the darkest depths of Tartarus for all the pain he had caused in his selfish life.

Kyniska saw the dawning of truth and realization in Stefanos' eyes, and when he looked at her, she slapped him across his jaw.

"You can't do this to me. I cannot be weak, Argive. Not now!" Her voice was like a distant sound of thunder, buried deep within iron-grey clouds.

"Neither can I," he said moving closer, only to be stopped by her outstretched arm pressed forbiddingly into the muscles of his chest. He did not move more, but looked to her arm which was bleeding through the bandages.

Stefanos reached out and took her left hand, her right still holding him back but beginning to bend as she turned her head away to look at the image of Artemis once more.

The hunter, Acteon, had once come upon that fell goddess when she was vulnerable, and she had killed him for it.

Should I do the same? Kyniska asked herself, though she already knew the answer.

Stefanos raised her left arm and, more gently than she could have imagined, he kissed her wound, drops of her blood warm upon his lips.

"The Gods curse you, Argive," she said softly as her right arm bent and went up around his neck to pull him in.

Suddenly their lips were together, their tongues sliding in and out of each other's mouths, at first slowly, and then with greater intensity and longing.

Kyniska felt his strong arms wrap themselves around her and hold her as close as possible, her entire being set alight with his touch.

As he lifted her off the ground and felt her strong, willowy arms wrap around him, Stefanos thought that he had never experienced such a heady feeling to wipe away all other cares and worries.

They kissed for a long time, neither wishing to break the spell. Nothing mattered - the late hour, the start of the Games, the tramp of horses' hooves, the ring of red cloaks and bronze-tipped spears that surrounded them. None of it.

Kyniska broke away from Stefanos for a moment, her arms grasping his torso, her eyes determined and inviting.

"Come..." she led him to the back of the tent and then through the flap to the left which led to her sleeping quarters. She did not release his hand.

They walked past a flickering oil lamp on a bronze tripod in the shape of a rearing horse, and a wooden rack where a xiphos and short javelin lay at the ready.

Kyniska stopped before a large, square bed covered in two single linen sheets from Aegyptus.

Stefanos stood facing her, and once again she extended her arm to push him back a little, this time her face less severe, and even more inviting.

Kyniska stepped up onto the bed and stood before him, a goddess from the heights of Olympus.

Stefanos could feel his heart pounding like a war drum in his rib cage as she reached up for the clasp of her peplos and let the garment drop around her ankles and onto the floor. At seeing her naked body, Stefanos' breath caught in his throat. She was a goddess in mortal disguise for all he knew, her tall body shaped to perfection by years of toil and passion.

As he looked up from her legs, to her waist, to her perfect breasts, and up to her face, it was all he could do not to run at her immediately. Instead, as she watched him expectantly, playfully, he lifted his chiton up over his head and let his braca fall to the ground.

"You should be careful," she warned. "You'll make the Gods jealous."

"Too late. You've already done so yourself," he said as he moved closer to touch her as she stood on the edge of the bed.

The sound of the flames in the oil lamps seemed loud in his ears as he kissed her lips and neck, and travelled down the Elysium lengths of her body, his hands gentle, betraying their pugilistic nature.

Kyniska moaned, and pulled his head close to her, gripping his head as he explored below her navel and waist. After a few minutes, she lay back on the bed and pulled him into her, their limbs clamping tightly, desperately, about each other as if to prevent a destined separation.

They melded into one body, moving in divine concert, the mortal man within the mortal woman, but both feeling as gods in those stolen moments when there was no world beyond the bounds of their lovemaking.

Some time later, when the moon was high in the night sky, and nymphs and satyrs danced along the banks of the distant Kladeos and Alpheios rivers, Kyniska and Stefanos lay sweaty and asleep, their limbs wrapped about each other in calm and bliss.

Chapter Eight

THE OLYMPIAD

Η Ολυμπιάδα

It was the sound of mourning doves that first broke the peaceful screen of Kyniska's dream as she lay upon her bed, comfortable, and unwilling to open her eyes.

She could feel the heat of morning light across her neck and chest, before the neighing of one of her horses sounded loud from the stables beyond.

Kyniska kept her eyes closed and found that she was smiling to herself. She felt alive, more so than she had imagined possible, but also swept up in a sense of joy at the dream some god had sent her. She sighed a little and turned to the tent wall, her hand going down to touch herself, the sensation one that sent new spasms of pleasure through her body.

The horses neighed again, and she opened her eyes to stare at the canvas of the tent, lit up by Helios' chariot in the East.

She paused for a moment as her mind began its exodus from the fog of her dreams, and as her smile threatened to fade, she felt a strong arm slide around her waist to cup the muscles of her tummy.

She turned quickly to see Stefanos leaning on one elbow, his brown eyes like honey in the sunlight, his smile a welcome she had never before experienced.

Her smile returned, broad and in earnest, as she turned onto her back and he leaned down to kiss her, no words, no laughter, just the feeling of intense closeness that they had shared the night before, and which still burned within both of them.

"Good morning," Stefanos said, his hand going from her waist to her shoulder, caressing her long hair, a finger running along her jaw to her lips.

"Is it morning?" she pushed him over and moved on top of him.

"Where are we?" Stefanos asked, his voice sounding as if the question were absolutely sincere.

"You..." she said, beginning to slide on top of him until he was inside her and the muscles of his shoulders and neck tensed, "...are in my tent. You are mine to do with as I please," she said, her smile morphing into an expression of the pleasure she felt rushing through her.

"Oh..." he smiled and sat up to kiss her lips, her neck and breasts before she pushed him back down and their bodies began to remember the night before, to re-enact what had not been a dream but reality.

After several minutes, they fell back again, breathing hard and glistening in the morning light.

There were many voices out in the camp by then, the neighing of horses louder and more urgent as they were fed and prepared for the day by Pirro and the girls.

"My lady?" came a whisper from within the main area of the tent.

Kyniska looked at Stefanos and sighed. "Seems we must awake."

Stefanos nodded and watched as Kyniska walked naked to the curtain that led to the other room.

"What is it?" she said.

"Forgive me my lady," Thais said, sneaking a glimpse of Stefanos as he stood from the bed, but quickly looking away. "The hour is very late, and Pirro is taking the team to the hippodrome for their test runs shortly. He said you should see them before...reassure them."

Kyniska seemed to shake her head rapidly, as if coming out of a pythian trance.

"What day is it?" Kyniska asked.

"What day?" Thais' eyes bulged unbelievingly. "My lady, it is the first day of the Games!"

Kyniska was still for a moment, her body visibly tensing before Stefanos' eyes. She turned to look at him, her eyes wild and awake.

"You must go now," she said.

He was already putting on his chiton and sandals. "I'm going to miss the Kleros," he said, rushing, despite his intense urge to remain behind. "I could stay with you," he said.

"No! The Gods are watching. If you miss the Sorting, you'll be disqualified from the Games!" Kyniska was now putting on her peplos. She could hear Thais setting out water and food in the other tent. She turned and Stefanos held her fast.

"I don't want to go," he said.

"How can you say that? Would you fall out of the Games? Lose your honour for a night of pleasure?"

"Stop. I'm going. But don't send me off like that. I..." Stefanos struggled as to what to say. The moment was too rushed, Kyniska too distracted by the neighing of horses in the compound of tents.

She took a deep breath and looked up at him, her lips pressed suddenly to his. "Go. I will see you later."

He nodded and smiled. "I would the Gods speed the time

for us," he said before pushing aside the flap to the other room and leaving her.

Kyniska stood there, alone again, as she was often used to, but this time it was not pleasant or welcome. It was as if a part of her had just been ripped from her flesh. "Don't be stupid!" she chided herself.

Meanwhile, Stefanos took a piece of bread from the table Thais had just set up and began to walk out of the tent, nodding to the young, wide-eyed girl who stood there gawping at the man who had, unusually, spent the entire night with her mistress.

He pushed the tent flaps aside and stepped out onto the sunlit dirt.

"Argive bastard!"

Stefanos felt something collide with the side of his head, making him drop his bread and sending him staggering into the dirt, his vision dazed for a fraction of a second.

Quickly, he shook his head and rolled away to gain his feet, his fists up.

Typhon stood there breathing rapidly, his own fists up and ready, his black hair dangling about his neck and shoulders. Behind him, several of Kyniska's guards stood with their dorata ready.

"You'll regret that," Stefanos said, coming closer, his eyes scanning the postures of the men behind the enomotarch. "Not very brave of a Spartan to hit a man from behind when he doesn't expect it," Stefanos said to Typhon who looked even more enraged at the accusation.

"Then I'll kill you face to face," Typhon spat. "Filthy Argive, defiling our princess!"

"That is not your business," Stefanos growled, stepping in to engage the Spartan.

"Stop!" Kyniska yelled, throwing herself between the two men. "You disobey the Sacred Truce!" she raged at both of them.

"I was just asking your enomotarch how he feels about

actually fighting someone face to face," Stefanos said, lowering his fists.

Kyniska looked at him, and noticed the red on the side of his head, then turned to Typhon.

"Are you brawlers or Olympians?" she demanded.

"This Argive disrespects Sparta," Typhon growled.

"On the contrary, he has fought for Sparta and respects its warrior ways more than you do, it seems."

"Excuse me?" Typhon said, his anger with Kyniska unshrouded.

"You know my meaning," she said. Kyniska turned to Stefanos and nodded. "Go. I will see you later."

Stefanos nodded, his eyes going from her to Typhon and back to her. Then he looked to Pirro who was now standing nearby. "Good luck in the trial run, Pirro."

The red-haired youth nodded his thanks and they watched Stefanos pick his way through the crowd of gathered Spartans to Xenophon's tent as horns blared in the distant sanctuary of Olympia.

Kyniska turned to Typhon. "You are a disappointment."

"And you," he whispered through clenched teeth, "are whoring yourself to that Argive!"

Kyniska's hand swept across his face without warning, her eyes ablaze. "You think because I used you in my bed a couple times before, that you are my lord and master?" She laughed, making him more angry. "You forget yourself. I can have whichever man I want."

"Whore," he said again, his fists balled up.

"You said that already, and I could have you stoned for it. Agesilaus wouldn't care. But I won't."

She saw Typhon's eyes relax, the arrogance returning.

"But you are no longer my enomotarch. In fact, I no longer want you in my guard. Twice you've failed in your duty - once along the river when it was the Argive who saved me, and then the other day when my team was attacked right here."

Kyniska stepped around Typhon and went to the men behind him.

"Ajax," she said to a tall, tree-like file leader. "You are enomotarch of my guard now. Earn it. And assign a new file leader to take your place."

"Yes, my princess," the tall Spartan said, leering a little at Typhon who stood there facing his former tent mates.

"Typhon is to move all his belongings and business to the main Spartan camp. I don't want him anywhere near me."

"Yes, my princess," Ajax said again, moving toward Typhon who was already on his way to his tent to gather his things, curses upon Kyniska and Stefanos dripping from his mouth as he stormed off.

Kyniska dismissed her men and went over to Pirro and her team to look them over and reassure them. Once she was beside them, caressing their strong necks and feeding them apples from the bag Euryleonis held out for her, she felt better.

"The day did not start like this," she whispered to Acheron, her forehead on his neck.

It took Stefanos some time to find out where the Kleros was taking place in the sanctuary. He first ran from his tent, across the river, past the pool, and along the wall of the House of the Phaidryntai until he reached the Bouleuterion, but no one was there.

There were few people around and the sounds that he could hear, of heckling and argument, were far distant.

"The Kleros takes place in the stadium," said one of the men Stefanos recognized as a wood cutter from the day before. "You'd better hurry!" the man said animatedly.

"Thanks!" Stefanos shot off, turning left at the sanctuary of Hestia and then running through the Altis until he reached the krypte leading into the stadium.

The roar of the crowd thundered at the foot of the Hill of

Kronos as he plunged into a sea of white chitons and muscled torsos to find the tables for his events.

"Where is boxing?" he yelled.

"Over there!" one of the Hellanodikai pointed toward one of the largest gatherings.

"And the hoplitodromos?" Stefanos asked again.

The man waved him over. "This is the table. Start here, Argive. The line over there is much longer."

Stefanos stopped and turned to run over to the table where about sixty men were lined up.

They eyed the newcomer as he approached, breathing heavily, some smirking, others nodding a curt greeting.

Stefanos nodded back and stood waiting for his turn to step forward. He eyed the men about him.

These were no shepherd boys, he knew, but battle-hardened veterans like himself who felt most at home in a thorax and helmet, carrying a doru and hoplon.

They were silent for the most part, quiet and determined - Spartans, Argives, Athenians, Syracusans, and Ionians. A group of Thebans stepped up to join the line then, and Stefanos noticed the Spartans there stiffen and turn their backs to face the table.

The hate was tangible.

Isocrates' dreams of everyone joining together against the Persians will never happen, he told himself, standing in the middle of all those men, for whom he had fought on both sides. He was grateful he did not know any of them.

Stefanos craned his neck to see if he could spot Pollux or Kratos in the crowd of athletes, but it was impossible to say. There were so many competitors grouped all together.

The sun was beating down by then, the comfort of dewy morning gone. Stefanos looked around at the men he might have to race or fight, and felt a sense of power that encouraged him. Yet he remembered Pandaros' warnings about such a thing.

Never assume you are better. Assume you will have to give your all in a fight or race, and let the Gods decide. Many men hide their skill well until you are on the skamma. Don't be blind to their skills, especially at Olympia. Those who compete in the Sacred Games are the best in the world.

Stefanos remembered his trainer's words and forced himself to look at the men around him. Some slouched or looked tired, but when they moved, even a little, their muscles snapped into action quickly.

The eyes... Stefanos thought. *It's in the eyes...*

He could see some of the men already visualizing victory, as if by thinking over it again and again, they were creating it, moulding it out of nothing but their struggles to get there.

Yet, it was not the feel of dirt beneath his running feet that Stefanos felt, nor the satisfying connection of his wrapped fist shattering another man's face that he thought of.

His mind pulled him back to Kyniska, to her voice, her lips, her hair, the passionate look in her eyes. Like a Siren luring him onto the rocks, thoughts of her pulled him away from the competition, and possibly from victory.

"Argive?" a voice said. "Argive, you awake?" the Hellanodikai said, hoisting his purple himation over his shoulder. "What is your name?"

"Oh, ah...Stefanos, son of Talos... of Argos," he said, stepping up to the table.

"Finally," the judge said. "Take a token from the jug," the judge indicated a deep clay jug that sat on top of the table.

Stefanos reached in and felt around the bottom for a sherd of pottery, pulled it out, and looked at it.

"Beta," he said, showing the Hellanodikai who marked it down on a list.

"Listen all of you!" the judge said when he had marked the last man's name. "The hoplitodromos is on the third day of the games. You will run in heats of twenty. Don't be late! Arrive with your trainers, in your own armour, greaves and helmets, but not your hoplons! You will use the shields that are kept in the temple of Hera. Understood?"

The judged looked about and when a few men muttered or nodded their understanding, he waved them off. "Go on! Those of you who have other events to sign-up for better get moving!"

Stefanos turned away from the group of hoplite race competitors and made for the large crowd gathered to sign up for boxing. The men here were harder looking, more motley. Whereas in the hoplitodromos, one had to have a certain amount of wealth in order to possess the armour for racing, all a boxer needed were his fists, and the hide himantes for wrapping them.

He recognized several men from the palaestra. They eyed him suspiciously but turned to look back toward the front as he approached to line up.

"Thought you wouldn't make it!" a gruff voice said beside Stefanos. The gymnasiarchos slapped him on the shoulder. "Just don't be late for competition. The Hellanodikai make no exceptions for disregard of the rules."

"I was signing-up for the hoplitodromos. Got the 'Beta' heat."

"Out of what?"

"Sixty men."

"Three heats. That's good. You'll have the advantage of the first heat going tentatively, but have time to rest before you go again."

"If I go again," Stefanos said.

"You'll upset Pandaros' shade with talk like that. Not exactly the talk of hero Olympian."

Stefanos nodded, moving along the line, the gymnasiarchos following him, eyeing the competition. "I've never asked your name, Gymnasiarchos."

"No. You didn't." The man smiled.

"What is it?"

"Call me Axion," he said.

"Still think my chances are good?" Stefanos whispered as he looked up and down the lines.

"Yes. As long as you stay focussed, Argive. Notice you're the only one here without a cabbage head? These shepherds and smiths can pound away and take a blow, but you have the advantage of battle. Many of these," his voice was really low now, "have never been in true battle. For at the end of the day, these are games, make no mistake."

"I won't underestimate them either," Stefanos said, remembering Pandaros' words.

"Nor should you," Axion agreed. "You have money from war, but many of these peasants having nothing but a few sheep or goats which they protect with their fists on the hillsides and mountains of the Peloponnese. A victory here is their only way out of the shit. They'll fight hard, and fight until they can't get up."

"Then I'll have to fight until they can't get up."

The man in front of Stefanos heard this last and turned to scowl at him, avoiding the gymnasiarchos' eyes. "The Gods will punish you for your hubris, Argive."

"Hubris?" Stefanos said. "Turn forward little man. No one is above the Gods, not even me."

The man shook his head and moved forward to dip his arm into the clay pot.

"I must go," Axion said. "I'll expect to see you at the palaestra."

Stefanos nodded and moved forward. So many men had gone before him, most in fact, but there were still many behind. The boxing competition would be long, and fierce. He spotted the long lists of names of men he might meet on the skamma on the fourth day of the Games.

He reached into the jar and pulled out another shard of pottery.

"What does it say?" said the Hellanodikai sitting before him.

"Psi," Stefanos said, showing him the token.

"Why, me too!" said a voice from the table beside where the other line of boxers waited.

Standing there was Ampyx, Ocnus' friend, a fellow Argive.

"Looks like you'll be out sooner than you wished, Stefanos," the big blond laughed, his thick muscles swollen and sunburnt. "You'll regret ever coming here," he spat.

Stefanos smiled and looked back at the table where the judge watched the two men. "Old friend from the palaestra back home." He leaned down. "Still upset I slept with his sister," he said, winking.

"You're dead!" Ampyx said, pointing. "Dead."

"And you're an oaf," Stefanos said casually.

Ampyx lunged, but the Hellanodikai shouted loudly. "Any man who brawls within the sanctuary before the competition will have his name struck from the lists of competitors and pay a fine!"

Ampyx stopped himself, just short of ramming into Stefanos who was ready to react should he have to.

Ampyx glared at Stefanos one more time before leaving to join Ocnus and his group of friends where they waited for him in the middle of the stadium. They all looked back at Stefanos and laughed among themselves.

"No fighting," the judge said warily to him from where he sat. "The Gods will punish it."

"I'm not here to brawl," Stefanos said to him, gripping the two sherds of pottery in his hands. "I'm here to win."

Stefanos left the table and walked down the line of other event tables, ignoring Ocnus and the others as he passed them. At the end, back toward the crypte to the Altis, the last table was filled with men signing-up for the pentathlon.

"Kratos!" Stefanos called, feeling a sudden urge to speak to his friend.

"Stefanos," Kratos greeted him, though Stefanos did not fail to notice the glance he cast past him at Ocnus and the others. "You all signed-up?" he asked, shaking the other's forearm.

"Yes. Just. You?"

"Yes. Pentathlon starts tomorrow morning."

"What's the first event then?" Small talk seemed the most comfortable thing at that moment, which was odd because they had always been frank with each other. But, something had changed. Stefanos could see it.

Kratos rolled his shoulders as he looked at the ground, unable to meet Stefanos' eyes. "The foot race is first, followed by the jumping, discus, javelin, and wrestling last. Will you be watching?"

"Yes. I've trained all I can."

"I suppose you've been busy," Kratos said, smiling.

"What's that supposed to mean?" Stefanos said, coming a step closer.

"Well... I heard that you and the Spartan princess we rescued are, well, keeping each other company." Kratos leaned in and elbowed Stefanos. "Mingling with royalty, eh? Is she good? I mean, you know what they say about Spartan woman."

"Watch your mouth, my friend. We've been through a lot together, but some things are beyond my limits."

"What?" Kratos looked genuinely shocked. "Since when do you have limits? You always talk about your women, even my own sisters!"

"And how did you know anyway?" Stefanos asked, glancing back at Ocnus and the gang who were moving out of the stadium. "My business is my own."

"Come on! You don't really expect to keep such a thing secret. I heard how you defended her at the symposium, in front of the king of Sparta no less! You should watch yourself, my friend."

"I can take care of myself, thanks, without your advice." Stefanos could feel the resentment flooding into his mood, his words. The thought of Ocnus' smug look was enough to drive him to murder.

"I saw that enomotarch too, Typhon. He was raging. Almost started a fight right here just before you arrived. I saw a few Spartans pull him away."

"So, what's that to me?"

"Really? Surely even you could see how he watched the princess. He's been fucking her, obviously."

Stefanos's fists shot forward and bowled Kratos back several feet, drawing looks from some of the other pentathletes.

"What's wrong with you?" Kratos shouted, silencing everyone about them.

"Why don't you go join your new friends?"

"Oh, that's it? Not that I talked about the woman, but that you're upset I've been training with them? The men from our own city?"

"You're an idiot," Stefanos mumbled.

Kratos brushed the dirt from himself and walked away from the stadium, disappearing into the krypte.

Most of the competitors had left the stadium by that point, and the Hellanodikai were filing out, a row of purple cloaks, their heads together, discussing the competitors they had seen, the matches they foresaw, and their guesses as to whom the Gods would crown.

As they went past, Stefanos nodded to them, wanting to be alone on the field.

The sun was almost at its zenith as he stood there, feeling the heat on his bare skin, the sweat gathering along the edge of his hairline. A hot breeze blew across the stadium from the north side of the Hill of Kronos and kicked dust up all around Stefanos where he stood.

He closed his eyes and gripped the two sherds of pottery in his hands, the one red, the other black. He felt the wind on his face and inhaled the dry air of the stadium.

This is the place, he thought. *Eris Agathos,* he told himself. *Good strife... Good.*

He opened his eyes and began to run around the edges of the stadium, just before the grassy embankments where, tomorrow, thousands of men would be cheering on the men of their cities, their chosen champions beneath the Gods' gaze.

As Stefanos ran, he wondered if anyone would cheer for him, other than the gymnasiarchos, Axion.

He ran faster and faster, pushing away thoughts of spectators and hated men. And there were many whom he hated that would be among the spectators. Even as the thought came to him, he knew there was one person he wished could watch him in the Games, and she was not permitted in the sanctuary.

Kyniska flooded his mind then and he found himself running faster, his heart pounding, strong, vibrant, intense and full of life, his legs taking him faster and faster down one side of the stadium and up the other.

Other athletes began to flow out of the krypte to take a last opportunity to train on the field before the Games began. Stefanos slowed when they came into view, some of them pointing at him. He ignored them and continued running, his legs and arms pumping faster until they were an absolute blur, and then he slowed, his breath quick, sweat pouring from his brow.

He made his way out of the stadium and ended up at the hippodrome to the south. The sound of charging horses reached his ears as he crested the top of one of the embankments in time to see ten chariot teams taking their practice runs on the sand.

He searched the groups for Pirro and the blacks and spotted them in the middle of the pack, like pitch shadows among chestnuts, dapples, and whites. They seemed to be lagging, and Stefanos stood there, willing them to pull ahead, worried about what it would mean if Kyniska's team did not win - humiliation, defeat, anger, waste.

"Come on, Pirro!" he yelled, but the chariot remained where it was, in the middle, average, the horses shying in the Taraxippos where the shade of Oinomaus was said to haunt the hippodrome, ready to strike fear into the bravest of teams and cause chaos.

Stefanos watched the heat come to the finish line and saw Pirro drive the horses slowly off the track. *Oh, no...* He was suddenly very worried for Kyniska, for her dreams that, from what he saw just now, were set to be trampled in the dirt.

How were his own odds shaping up? He wondered at this as he made his way back to the Altis. Now that the bluster and cockiness of his fellow competitors had begun to abate in the face of Olympia's solemnity, he could see how truly determined each man was, how years of practiced skill, struggle, and a deep-rooted love of winning had brought them all to this place to compete beneath the Gods' gaze.

He strode past the statues of the Zanes, bronzes of Zeus that were created from the fines imposed on those who cheated in the Sacred Games, who broke the laws of Olympia. Every image of Zeus seemed to threaten or accuse passers by, warn them that to flaunt the laws meant severe punishment.

Stefanos walked along, directly for the temple of Hera. He stopped before the steps and looked up at the acroterion of the temple, the great, painted fan of peacock feathers set atop the pediment.

He went up the steps and into the temple. A few men stood silently in the aisle, whispering prayers to the goddess, but Stefanos went directly to the main altar where a priestess stood her head bowed, smoke whirling about her long robes.

Stefanos recognized her as the priestess of Demeter Chamayne from the symposium. He waited a moment before approaching, hoping she would leave so that he could make his prayer in peace, but she remained where she was.

He stepped up and put down a few drachmae which he had fingered out of the pouch that was tucked in the belt of his chiton.

"Goddess Hera, accept my offering and my prayers..." Stefanos said, his mother and sister coming to mind even as he said the words. It was as if every time he prayed, they were there, praying with him.

The priestess beside him looked in his direction, but did not speak.

His voice was low as he spoke. "Goddess, the day of my trial approaches. Help me to be strong, my goddess. Guide me. Help me to make my father's wish come true." He stopped for a moment, feeling as if his words were not quite sincere, and he apologized inwardly for it. "Goddess Hera, please watch over her..." Kyniska was in his mind, strong, a force of nature, but also vulnerable and worrying. "Let her be victorious in the Games. Ask Poseidon to goad her horses on."

A hand suddenly grabbed hold of his and he felt suddenly very hot, as if his skin were burning.

The priestess was gripping Stefanos' arm tightly from where she stood and her head turned slowly to face him.

Hippodameia.

She was as he had seen her on the mountainside, sweaty and scared, her hair wild, as if she were caught up in the act of keening.

"What...who?" he tried to speak but the words died in his throat as her eyes held his like a spot of fire in the dark of night.

Her hand shook and tears ran down her cheeks.

"Why do you weep?" he asked trying to pull his arm away, but unable to do so.

She shook her head, then the eyes changed.

"You?" she said, her eyes looking away suddenly and her grasp releasing.

Stefanos looked at her and saw the priestess of Demeter again, her face older, confused, and embarrassed.

"Forgive me, I think I felt faint," she said, swaying a little on her feet. "I've been here for hours."

"Are you unwell?" he asked, not knowing what else to say, wondering whether the look on his own face would alarm her.

"I am...fine..." Now she looked at Stefanos closely and her

eyes widened. "You must hear the Gods, Argive. Heed their counsel."

"I do," he said.

"No. Do heed their counsel, your heart...for both your sakes..."

"What? Why are you saying this to me?" he demanded.

The priestess shook her head and turned to leave, her footsteps echoing loudly in the temple as she ran past the two men whispering at the far end near the entrance.

Stefanos watched her disappear outside into the blinding sunlight and then turned back to look up at the statue of Hera and his hoplon resting against the base of the statue with her symbol upon it.

"Goddess..." he said. "What is happening?"

"How did the training run go? Were they all right in the turns with the other teams around them?" Kyniska asked Pirro excitedly as he rode up, even before he had a chance to dismount from the cab and greet her.

"They are hesitant in the Taraxippos, as were most of the teams. The other horses don't bother them, but the whips the other drivers were using gave them a fright. They were like cracks of lightning.

Kyniska pat each of the horses and spoke softly as she did so. "The Gods are with us, friends. Don't be afraid. We've worked long and hard for this... all your lives...."

"My lady," Pirro said. "Acheron seemed most disturbed and was pulling us toward the inside, away from the Taraxippos. When twenty teams race at once, chaos will reign and we'll get into an accident."

"Did you speak to him during the race, try to allay his fear?"

"It was so loud, I don't know if he heard me."

"Of course he heard you."

"Well, we could -" Pirro stopped abruptly and bowed low,

as did Eunice, Euryleonis, Thais, and Helle who were standing nearby, behind Kyniska.

Kyniska turned to see her brother coming toward them. "Agesilaus," she said, her voice cold and calm.

The king of Sparta approached his sister slowly, smiling but a little, with Xenophon, and some of his royal guard in tow.

The Spartans stationed around Kyniska's camp all bowed and then stood back to attention as their king came into the space between the tents.

Agesilaus approached Xanthus and raised a hand to pet the animal, but the stallion pulled away from him.

Kyniska took a quick step forward but stopped herself. "They don't like you, brother," she said, taking Xanthus' bridle and soothing him as she watched her brother back away.

"Useless beasts," the king said. "I hope they prove better on the track during the Games than they did today. I've laid quite a challenge before the rich men of Greece by allowing you to race."

I would have raced anyway, you arrogant shit! is what she wanted to yell, but she held her tongue, unused to doing so as she was, for she saw the look in her brother's eyes. He could withdraw her from the competition if he wished it, or dismiss her guard leaving her open to the enemies who had not yet been caught.

"Have your men discovered who attacked me and my team?" Kyniska asked. "Sparta has been offended."

"Sparta is always offended in the face of lesser people," he replied.

"You still haven't answered my question," Kyniska countered. "Have you discovered who did it?"

"No. I have better things to do besides starting a war within the sanctuary of Olympia. I'll not offend the Gods in such a way." Agesilaus turned to Xenophon and smiled, his back to Kyniska. "Afterward, however, there will be war enough for Thrasybulos and those upstart Thebans."

"You know Father would not want that."

His steely eyes turned on her and she could see the anger and resentment in their depths. "Father is dead. And I inherited the mess he left us."

"The strength of Sparta's army, which he left you, I think you mean." Kyniska hated when her brother spoke ill of their departed father, knew that her brother looked down on Archidamus' initial reluctance to enter into the war with Athens.

"Which I will use to crush the other cities," he said casually.

"But first, Persia!" Xenophon said, coming to stand beside the two royal Spartans. "We are still going there, are we not?"

Agesilaus smiled. "Oh yes, and I'll be happy to have you in my ranks and by my side," he said, slapping Xenophon on the back.

"What about Persia?"

Kyniska's face turned quickly in the direction of the voice to see Stefanos walking toward them. She wished he had not come at this time, for she immediately saw the look in Agesilaus' eyes change, exhibiting an extra degree of anger and annoyance.

"Speaking of upstarts," Agesilaus said to Xenophon as Stefanos approached. "Argive! Will you come to Persia with me?"

Stefanos slowed his pace as he approached, his eyes going from the king, to Kyniska, to Xenophon, and then back to the king.

"I don't know, King Agesilaus. When are you leaving?"

"Immediately after the Games." Agesilaus stared at Stefanos, defying him to say 'no' to him.

"I'll have to think about it," Stefanos said. "Who knows what the Gods have in store for me?" He could not help it. He had glanced at Kyniska even as he said it and the king and everyone else noticed.

But Agesilaus said nothing for a moment. Then, "You are right. Who knows the Gods' will other than the Gods themselves?"

"Exactly."

"Stefanos, shouldn't you be training?" Xenophon interrupted. "Your first competition is on day three isn't it?"

"Yes, my friend. But I'm as prepared as I can hope for."

"Let us hope you don't find yourself face-down in the dirt, Argive. Otherwise you'll find yourself fighting for the Thebans next," Agesilaus said.

"They don't pay nearly enough," Stefanos laughed.

Agesilaus nodded slowly and then walked toward Stefanos, leading him by the elbow. "Walk with me."

Stefanos walked slowly beside the king of Sparta, wondering how he would deal with the inevitable outburst that was due to come from his host.

"When I was a boy, I used to visit a helot's daughter, a slave, and bed her before I went to my mess hall in the evenings. She was young, willing, and not put off by my infirmity. We fucked like wild animals and we enjoyed it."

"Sounds like evenings well-spent, my lord."

"Yes. Until my father found out that I had been bedding a slave."

"What happened?"

"I came to my father's house to find the girl tied to a stake, her back bare to me, and my father holding a lash which he handed me. He said I had not been discreet enough, and that the slave girl had developed an attachment to me that was not fitting for a prince of Sparta. She was not Spartan."

Stefanos could feel his anger rising and he fought to keep it down. Just barely as the king stopped walking and looked him in the eyes.

"My father made me whip the girl until she was dead, her body limp upon the poll to which she had been tied."

"A terrible way to die," Stefanos said, staring the king in the face.

"Yes. Even my father's eyes were wet. He had hoped for more from Sparta."

"He wept for the girl? A helot?"

"Of course not. He wept for me. You see, my eyes were dry. I found that I didn't care. I knew I could find another girl, and that I would be more discreet."

Stefanos wanted to punch the little Spartan king in the face. He hated his arrogance, hated his whole person then.

"My father was kind, and my sister praises him for it. But as for me? I fully admit that I am not. Kindness is weakness, Argive. And betrayal is punishable by death in Sparta."

Stefanos refused to look away from Agesilaus then, but he could not help noticing Typhon standing in the background, having arrived with the king's men, along with Pollux.

"My sister can fuck whom she chooses, Argive. I don't care. But if the animals she takes between her legs get ideas above their stations, then not even the Gods themselves could save them."

Agesilaus actually smiled then, and pat Stefanos' shoulders with both hands.

"Good luck in the Games, Argive. We'll be watching you."

With that, the king of Sparta strolled away from Stefanos, followed by Xenophon and the rest of his guard.

Stefanos stood there for a few minutes looking after them, part of him wishing he had a spear in his hand at that moment, but knowing the futility of the thought.

It was Kyniska's grip on his hand that brought him to, that soothed his raging mind. She stood there, holding his arm tightly as Pirro and the girls went about unharnessing the horses, each of them watching her with this mysterious Argive who had touched a part of her mind in a way that no other man had ever done.

"Your brother is a wicked man," Stefanos said later that night as he and Kyniska lay naked in her tent, she on top of him, their bodies melded together in the lamp-light.

Kyniska looked distracted as she traced the lines of the

scars on Stefanos' shoulders with her finger, her eyes partially concealed by the strands of her long hair.

"Did he really do those things to that slave?"

"Yes."

"And your father handed him the whip?"

Anger swept across her lovely face and she rolled off of Stefanos. "My father was trying to raise a king who would take responsibility for his actions." She sighed, a heavy weight upon her shoulders. "But you are right, of course. My brother is a dangerous man. I fear that one day his arrogance and stubbornness will be the downfall of Sparta."

"Sparta?" Stefanos laughed. "It will live forever. The men are strong."

"Men are only as strong as their leader," Kyniska retorted.

Stefanos wondered what had got into her. The strong, iron-willed woman he had first met seemed worried now, to be caving beneath some titanic weight.

"Well," he said. "If Sparta were led by you, it would fare better."

Kyniska turned toward him, leaned over, and kissed him on the lips. "You flatter like an Athenian sometimes."

"I'm serious. I've fought for many leaders, and I've led men myself, and I see more of the qualities needed for leadership in you than I have in most others, including Agesilaus, Aeson, or Thrasybulos. You are stronger than Queen Gorgo."

"She was a great woman," Kyniska said, remembering her father's stories of the Spartan queen. "But Gorgo had a Leonidas at her side, a Spartan king by which all others are measured, but none can equal."

"You don't need a king to be strong."

She looked at him intently, but did not voice the thoughts that crept over the distant borders of her mind. "Is your sister a strong woman?"

Stefanos sat up and took her hand. "Yes. But not like you are. Cleo is devoted to her duty. She does not take what she wants, but she accepts her fate with grace."

"It is a sacred thing she does, as priestess of Hera," Kyniska said. "But it must be a lonely life. Is she lonely?"

"Yes. Lonely and sad," Stefanos shut his eyes for a moment, fighting back the sadness and guilt welling up inside him. "If I can win at the Games...I..."

"What?" Her hand touched his face, gentle and lithe.

"I fight not just for my father's wish. Nor my mother's memory. I hope that, maybe I can help Cleo somehow."

"You will!" Kyniska held his face in both hands. "Nike will come down from Olympus to crown you victor, I can feel it, Stefanos."

"As I hope she will crown you."

Kyniska was quiet.

"Are you worried?" he asked.

"The Gods will do as they see fit. I've trained them for years for this moment in time. I've tried to protect them by placing a guard on them all day and night. My prayers to the Gods are sincere. I can only keep training them until the final day."

For a few moments the two of them lay back in silence again. The camp and the sanctuary beyond were unnaturally quiet. The night before the Games were to begin, it seemed every competitor was holding vigil with himself and his gods.

Stefanos thought of Kratos, of all the years they had been friends, had trained together. It hurt that Kratos had abandoned him for Ocnus and his friends, but then, he had always sought approval in Argos, the accolades of his polis, even though he had never outwardly admitted it. Stefanos realized that he should be there to cheer Kratos, even if the latter had turned away from him. He was happy at that moment, with Kyniska lying beside him, his heart full of something he had never felt before.

"Will you go to the Games tomorrow?" she asked, as if reading his thoughts.

"Yes. Then I'll train. Then, if you'll have me, I will come to watch you."

Her eyebrows raised playfully, and the slight grooves of her dimples flexed. "Careful, Argive, lest I tire you out for your race."

She kissed him then, and his strong arms wrapped around her waist, pulling her close as the flames of the oil lamps sputtered and began to fade, throwing them into impassioned darkness.

THE FIRST DAY OF THE OLYMPIAD DAWNED WITH GOLDEN LIGHT suffusing the sanctuary, as if the Gods' very presence lit the mortal world with an empowering light.

There was a palpable excitement in the air, quiet and simmering, as if the world were anticipating the emergence of heroes, ready to bear witness to deeds that would be celebrated in song and poem for ages.

Stefanos whistled as he walked from Kyniska's camp to Xenophon's in order to prepare. He had already eaten some of the fruit, cheese and oats which Helle had prepared for her mistress and him, and all that remained was to put on a clean chiton, gather his training satchel, and head into the sanctuary for the beginning of the pentathlon.

As Stefanos stepped through the threshold of Xenophon's tent, he saw his friend sitting at his table rifling through some papers, making notes on a flattened sheet of papyrus.

"Don't you ever stop writing?" Stefanos said, his smile broad, his mood light.

Xenophon did not look up right away, but kept writing for a minute before answering. He put down his stylus and stared at Stefanos who was washing his face in the basin that sat atop the tripod near the bed he had not slept in.

"What in Hades do you think you're doing?"

"Washing my face."

"Not that. I mean, what are you doing with Kyniska?"

"That's not your business, my friend."

"Ah, but it is when the king of Sparta, my own friend,

chided me for having you as a guest in his camp." Xenophon was now standing in the middle of the tent facing Stefanos, his arms crossed, his long hair dishevelled, his face contorted in frustration.

"She and I have grown close."

"You mean you're fucking her," Xenophon said, his usual propriety forgotten.

Stefanos dried his face and turned to face him. "Careful."

"You're the one who should be careful. I tried to warn you."

"She can take care of herself."

"I'm not talking about Kyniska, though she is far above your station, and she's a Spartan."

"I thought you liked Spartans."

"I do. But they don't like others."

"Agesilaus likes you."

"And he hates you now. You shouldn't have spoken against him at the symposium. He was your host."

"And he was wrong."

"Kyniska is his sister and subject."

"Kyniska is a strong woman, a Spartan woman, who makes her own decisions." Stefanos stepped up so that he was in Xenophon's face. "Look. I don't want to fight with you. You're one of the only friends I have left in this world. But you can't tell me that Agesilaus is a good man, or that it's fair the way he's manipulating Kyniska."

"Listen to yourself!" Xenophon said. "She's a woman, Stefanos! Since when does a woman decide her life's course?"

"She's not like other women. The Gods have blessed her in ways I cannot describe or understand."

"Oh, now you speak of gods?"

"Yes." Stefanos took him by the shoulders and held him fast. "Since I left Argos to come to Olympia...since I've begun to dedicate myself to Eris Agathos, I've felt the Gods closer than ever before. It's as if they're trying to tell me something. I feel like I have a purpose."

"You do!" Xenophon said, shrugging off Stefanos' hands. "But your purpose is not to end up with a Spartan doru through your guts because you slept with the king's sister! Do you realize that every man in the Spartan camp hates you right now? And you walk about whistling and smiling, rubbing their faces in it. They all desire her, and yet they are all afraid to approach her because her brother is Agesilaus."

"I'm not afraid of Agesilaus, or anyone else. You should know that."

"And what if she bears the brunt for your daring? What then? Do you think she is safe just because the king is her brother?"

Stefanos felt a prickle of dread for Kyniska then. He remembered how coolly dismissive of Kyniska Agesilaus had been at the symposium. He began to hate the king of Sparta. He looked at Xenophon for a moment and saw something in his eyes, in the way he held himself and the way in which he pleaded with Stefanos to abandon his attachment to the Spartan princess.

"You want her for yourself, don't you?" Stefanos stood back, looking at Xenophon. "Has Agesilaus promised her to you?"

"What? No!" Xenophon said too quickly. "I won't say I'm not fascinated by her, but the king has made no promises."

"But you want her." Stefanos shook his head. "Of course you do. But not for the strong-willed person she is. She's just a woman!" he mimicked. "You want her for her knowledge of horses, but more so for the ties that would bind you to the royal house of Sparta and Agesilaus."

"Don't be ridiculous!" Xenophon waved him off, and returned to his table.

"Now I see. Why not? Athens has turned you away, and you need a new home. It makes sense."

"This is how you thank me for my hospitality?"

"Look," Stefanos tried, despite his anger and jealousy. "I didn't mean for this to happen. The Gods have arranged it.

They arranged that I rescue her on the road here, that we meet."

"Maybe the Gods are playing with you?"

"Maybe, but I won't gainsay them."

"Stefanos. What of your father's wish? The reason you're here? This is your only chance to win glory in the Olympiad. You're not getting younger."

"No, I'm not. But I'm ready. I know my path. Do you know yours?"

"No man can know for sure, Stefanos."

"You once told me of Plato's idea that for each of us, there is another half in the world waiting to be found. What if Kyniska is..."

"What? Your long-lost half? I think you misunderstand Plato's theory."

"No. I don't think I do. I finished lying to myself not long ago. My family and Kyniska helped me to see things right. Can you say the same thing, Xenophon? Can you claim to be completely honest with yourself?"

Stefanos pulled his chiton over his head, bent over and picked up the satchel with his thorax inside, the belts holding his xiphos and dagger, his helmet and doru.

"What are you doing?" Xenophon asked.

"I've outstayed my welcome," Stefanos said. "I wish you well, brother. I'm sorry it had to be this way."

Xenophon watched Stefanos walk out of the tent into the sunlight toward the sanctuary. Shaking his head, he sat back down at the table and slammed it with his fist.

THE CELEBRATORY MOOD OF THE GAMES WAS SOURED FOR Stefanos as he walked with all of his belongings toward the palaestra where he found Axion, the gymnasiarchos, just about to make his way to the Altis for the sacrifice to Olympian Zeus.

"What are you doing here?" Axion asked. "You're not leaving Olympia?"

"No. I've just disagreed with my host," Stefanos said. "Do you have a safe place where I can keep these for the day?"

Axion hesitated a moment, watching the last of the men making their way to the Altis. "Sure. But let's be quick. We don't want to miss the sacrifice."

Axion went back the way he had come, his footsteps slapping on the marble beneath the peristyle of the palaestra until he came to a wooden door with a lock on it. He pulled a key from his belt and opened it. "Put them in here," he said, stepping aside to let Stefanos in.

The room was filled with amphorae and pots containing oil and chalk, rods for judges, and extra korikoi filled with sand. There were medical instruments too, and bandages for binding wounds that men received on the skamma.

Stefanos leaned his doru in the corner and placed his satchel, helmet and weapons on the ground in front of it. "Thanks," he said to Axion as the older man locked the door again.

"You shouldn't be carrying weapons around the sanctuary anyway. If they think you've some ill-intent, they banish you from Olympia." They began to walk back toward the Altis. "Do you have somewhere to put them later?"

"Yes," Stefanos said, thinking of only one place where he was welcome.

The Altis was packed almost to capacity, the great temple of Zeus surrounded by athletes, coaches, and supporters of the various cities, all vying to get as close as they could to the men who had already won renown, or to catch a glimpse of the Hellanodikai in their purple cloaks on the steps of the temple, alongside the theokoloi in their white robes as they called for the Games to commence.

The priests processed down the steps of the temple directly to the altar of Zeus which rose up out of the ground, built upon ages of sacrificial bones and detritus to tower over the Pelopion and the statues of Olympic heroes dotting the Altis. A black ram was brought to the top of the sacrificial mound.

The theokoloi held it fast while the head priest slit its throat and the blood poured over the altar.

Snatches of epinikion odes by Pindar were sung as the priests cut up the animal and wrapped the thigh bones in fat to be laid upon the altar and set alight for the Gods' pleasure. The smoke rose high into the air and it seemed as if the breeze responded by blowing it toward the stadium where the first events of the day were to take place in the shadow of the Hill of Kronos.

A cheer rose up to the heavens and all men there, young and old, noble and commoner, raised their voices to the Gods.

Best is Water of all, and Gold as a flaming fire in the night shineth eminent amid lordly wealth; but if of prizes in the Games thou are fain, O my soul, to tell, then, as for no bright star more quickening than the sun must thou search in the void firmament by day, so neither shall we find any games greater than the Olympic whereof to utter our voice: for hence cometh the glorious hymn and entereth into the minds of the skilled in song, so that they celebrate the son of Kronos...

STEFANOS WALKED WITH THE REST OF THE CROWD, ALONE again, having lost Axion in the mix. He glanced toward the temple of Hera and saw the priestesses standing on the steps of the temple watching the men move to the stadium.

The priestess of Demeter Chamayne broke away from the small group of women and joined the procession of the Hellanodikai into the stadium. As the priestess of Demeter, she was the only woman permitted to observe the Games, with her own marble seat reserved for her amidst the roar of men and competitors.

Stefanos stopped when he saw her and let the crowd move around him, like a rock in the midst of a tumbling stream. When he was alone in the Altis, but for the theokoloi who continued with their offerings and other duties at the altars, he walked back, past the temple of Hera, beneath the gaze of the priestesses there, and back to the square enclosure of the Prytaneion, just behind the temple.

He stopped for a moment before the entrance, and then stepped over the threshold to stand before the sacred flame of Olympia.

The sound of the outside world disappeared behind him and he could only hear the flickering of the flame. It held his gaze for a few minutes. He thought he saw something move inside the fire, galloping horses, chariot wheels, and a weeping woman.

Stefanos stumbled back and tripped on the threshold to land on his backside upon the marble slabs. The fire rose up then, higher than it had been, but still, not violent.

Then he felt hands reach under his arms and pull him up.

Stefanos turned, dazedly, to see Pirro standing behind him, a look of concern upon his freckled face.

"All will be well," the young man said. "The Gods are on our side."

Stefanos nodded but looked back to the fire which was low again. "Do you really think so?"

"I know it," Pirro said, his eyes bright and lively. "As surely as that flame burns for all time, I know we can do this!"

"Thank you," Stefanos said, feeling odd at his weakness before the younger man.

"We'll do it for her," Pirro said, his voice hoarse and full of pressure and pride.

"For her," Stefanos repeated.

THE SPECTATORS AROUND THE BANKS OF THE STADIUM ROARED encouragement at some and cajoled others. The pentathlon was a popular event, and some of the greatest athletes in all the Greek world had come forward to show the variety of their strength and skill.

Heats of men were gathered at the nearer end of the stadium, their bodies now naked as they waited for their group to take part in the first competition, the two-stade sprint.

Pirro had left Stefanos to go back to Kyniska and train with the team.

Stefanos came out of the krypte into the stadium, and moved to the left where he found a vacant spot among the men of Corinth, just beneath the Hill of Kronos. He was almost parallel with the grooved stone starting line where the mechanism had been set up, a rope running across the stadium to prevent anyone from charging off before the others.

Men sang songs in the stands or chanted the names of their favourite athletes and comrades, waving to them if they were waiting, encouraging those who stepped up to the line for the first heat.

There would be no definite winner as yet in the pentathlon, as that could only be decided when all five events had been completed. If a man did not do well today, he had four other events in which he could always make up the points.

However, as the music of tambourines and double-flutes rang out over the stadium, and as the crown pulsed with excitement, it became evident that a good showing in the first event would be an advantage to the competitors.

One of the Hellanodikai stepped up to the end of the starting mechanism, put his hand on the handle and waited for the athletes to look his way.

Each man leaned on one leg, thigh muscles flexed, poised to fire into action, sweat already pouring off their faces and down their chests.

There was a collective, indrawn breath and then the rope fell, the men shooting forward as if Cerberus himself were on their heels.

The crowd erupted as the runners' legs and arms pumped

as they sped along, to the far end of the stadium and turned to run back for the second half.

One man fell, his knees bloodied in the dirt, and a rush of booing followed an elbow from a Thessalian who pushed a man of Cyrene into the crowd, getting himself disqualified by the Hellenodikai.

In moments it was over, and the runners stood sweaty and panting, being pat on the back by supporters or hanging their heads in desperation at their initial failure to make a good showing, hounded by insults and catcalls from the embankments.

Stefanos thought he had never heard such raucous noise, not at any of the other games, nor even in battle. The crowd at Olympia wanted the Gods on the very heights of Olympus to hear them.

The next heat stepped up, and Stefanos spotted Kratos in the line.

"Go Kratos!" he yelled, deciding to set his previous anger aside. "Remember Pandaros!"

Kratos looked up and saw Stefanos. He nodded, and swung his arms trying to stay warm, jumping on the spot as if readying himself for a boxing match.

On either side of him were a lanky Arkadian with a head of hair like a lion's mane, and a Spartan whose build was more feline than human.

The judge stepped up to the starting mechanism again and raised his hand for silence among the runners.

"If you push or trip, you will be disqualified from the pentathlon, do you understand?"

The runners nodded and there was a moment or two as they settled into their stances.

The rope dropped and they shot off as if each were fired from Orion's bow.

Kratos powered out to the front right away with the other runners tearing after him as if he were a stag to take down. Beside him the cat-like Spartan came up and had drawn even by the time they reached the end of the first stade. When they sped for the finish, the Arkadian was pulling away, followed by two Thebans whose city roared approval as they passed the Arkadian and dashed across the finish line together.

Stefanos watched Kratos bend over and gulp air. "Good run, Kratos!" he yelled, but his friend did not turn this time, storming off to the side and vomiting.

"Too much wine for that one!" a Corinthian behind Stefanos said as he and his friend watched Kratos wiping his mouth. "I saw him last night with some Argives at the stoa, drunk out of his mind!"

"Before the Games?" said another.

"Yes. You'd think he knew better."

Stefanos didn't say anything, but looked from Kratos' hunched form to Ocnus and his friends on the other side opposite him, laughing and pointing at Kratos. He shook his head, and as the third heat of racers shot off, he was walking up to Kratos.

"You all right?" he asked, his voice barely audible.

Kratos looked up and shook his head, bile dripping from his lip. "Fucking wine!" he said.

"Come'on, you need some bread and water to soak that up. You're still in another heat."

"Forget it!" Kratos said.

"Hey!" Stefanos slapped him. "What would Pandaros say?"

Kratos stood up, his bloodshot eyes looking at Stefanos.

"This is only the first event, right? You can salvage this and do better in the next ones, but if you bow out now, it's all over!"

"Fine! Yes!" Kratos said. "Where's the bread? I don't know if I have time."

"There are two more heats and then music before you're on again. Come!" Stefanos led him through the Krypte to the edge of the Altis where a few vendors were waiting in the shade. Stefanos paid for two buns and gave one to Kratos. "Eat."

"Why are you helping me, Stefanos?" Kratos asked pitifully.

"Don't be an idiot. We've been through a lot together, haven't we?"

Kratos looked up. "Yes. We have."

"I know you can do this!" he said through gritted teeth. "Do it!"

Kratos nodded. "I'm ready."

Together, they walked back to the stadium, the roar of the crowd and of music washing over them as they emerged from the Krypte again.

Kratos' second run was not much better than his first, and he did not advance any more that day.

When Stefanos approached him afterward, he did not wait to speak with his friend, but walked away, his naked form disappearing into the Altis, sliding his chiton over his head as he made his way back to the Argive camp.

Stefanos knew Kratos, knew that he needed to fall hard before he could work himself up enough to find the strength he needed. He knew that he always did find it, however, and so he left him to his solitude.

The rest of the afternoon, Stefanos trained in the Palaestra, his fists and arms pounding the korikoi as Axion watched him and the other competitors prepare for their events on day four of the Games.

Stefanos thought of Agesilaus with each punch, and got so worked up that at one point he had to sit down, he was breathing so heavily.

"What's wrong with you?" Axion said, sitting down beside him. "Get your head in the fucking Games, Argive," he growled.

"It is."

"No. It's not. I can see that you're distracted. Do you want to lose?"

"No."

"Then stop acting like it. Can't you see the men around here staring at you? You look like a piece of fresh meat for these jackals now. They can smell weakness, see how sloppy you are compared with a couple weeks ago."

Stefanos hung his head, and took long, deep breaths. "You're right," he said. "My mind's not in it."

"Olympia isn't a place for weakness or indulgence. It's a place for champions, a place where heroes and gods are made. Which one would you be?"

Stefanos looked up at the old man, the wrinkles of experience accusing him from his features. He knew that Pandaros would be saying the same things to him.

"Thank you."

"Now. Clear your head, and get back out there."

After a few minutes of watching the other fighters, Stefanos picked one whom he thought would be a good match.

The man was from Epirus, big and powerful. Stefanos walked up to him and asked if he wanted to spar.

The man turned to his friends who urged him to accept. He turned back to Stefanos. "Sure, Argive. You sure you're not feeling too stiff and tired? How old are you?"

Stefanos laughed. "No use, trying those old tricks on me. I've seen it all, my friend."

They stepped onto the skamma, one of the other athletes acting as judge. "Ready?" the man said, as the two raised their covered fists. "Go!"

The man attacked immediately with a flurry of fists and feints that almost caught Stefanos off balance, but the latter stayed light on his feet and jumped out of the way, blocking one blow as he did so and landing a follow-up on the side of the man's head.

"Nice," the Epirean said, bobbing and moving side to side

like a snake as he took in Stefanos' stance and tactics. Suddenly his fist shot up and caught Stefanos on the forehead as he pulled back, the himantes scratching his brow.

Stefanos spun away from the next swing, ducked under yet one more, and came up with a strong hit to the stomach that made his opponent stand straight and expose his face.

Stefanos did not miss the open target and his fist shot straight out, flattening the man's nose and sending him off the skamma into a group of onlookers.

The fallen man roared and wanted to step back in, but his friends told him it was not worth it for sparring.

"Save it for day four!" one of them yelled.

He spat in Stefanos' direction and walked away to tend to his nose.

Stefanos walked over to the bench and sat down, blood dripping from his forehead onto his bare thighs. "Better?" he said to Axion who stood before him, arms crossed.

"Sloppy. He almost knocked you out."

"But he didn't."

"On day four, if you move through to the final bout, you may have to fight up to four times. You take a hit like that in each bout, and your head will be spinning by your last fight. Be careful. Be fast. That's your advantage."

Stefanos nodded, as he dabbed his bleeding forehead, Axion walking away to check on the oiling room.

THE SANCTUARY WAS SILENT AT THE END OF THE FIRST DAY, men going back to their camps to discuss the first competitions, their favourites, and those who were worth putting money on.

Stefanos returned to the Spartan camp, carrying his armour, doru and weapons, over his shoulder, trying to avoid too many questions about his appearance.

Luckily, Pollux was on guard duty at the main gate and let him through.

"Just be careful," the Spartan whispered as Stefanos walked by. "You're being watched," he hissed.

Stefanos continued on through the torch-lit darkness, over the grass and beneath oak, olive, and sycamore trees to the open ground of Kyniska's camp.

He found her in the stables with her maids and Pirro.

They all turned when he entered, the enomotarch, Ajax, turning to go once Kyniska waved him away.

The princess looked at him standing there with all his belongings and frowned. "What's this?"

"I've had a disagreement with my host," Stefanos said.

Kyniska stared at him still, unmoving but for a slight twitch at the corner of her eye. She continued brushing Xanthus, leaving Stefanos standing there.

The four young girls stared at him too, as did Pirro who appeared as if he wanted to say something.

"Don't just stand there," Kyniska finally said. "Help brush them down."

Stefanos spotted the smile that barely touched her lips and felt an odd sort of relief wash over him. "Yes, my lady," he said, catching a brush which Pirro tossed to him and starting on Acheron.

Helle and Thais stood whispering to each other while Eunice and Euryleonis put fresh straw in the horses' stalls.

"If you two girls don't have anything else to do, go and put food out for us in my tent." Kyniska did not look up as she spoke.

The girls stopped whispering and Thais spoke. "For all of us, mistress?"

Kyniska looked up at Stefanos. "Yes, for all of us."

Helle and Thais smiled, bowed, and went from the stable to do as commanded.

Stefanos noticed Euryleonis staring at him, her mask of anger unveiled.

When Kyniska finished with Xanthus, they led the horses

to their stalls, while Pirro continued brushing down Zoe and Phaedra.

"What's wrong girl? Do I bother you?" Stefanos said to Euryleonis. She was pretty, and stubborn looking. Almost an adolescent version of Kyniska. "Speak your mind. What have you got against me?"

Euryleonis did not look to see if Kyniska was near, but spoke straight away.

"You are a distraction, Argive. My mistress is the greatest charioteer and horse trainer in all of Greece. She has the chance to show the Gods what a true woman can do."

"I know. She's glorious," Stefanos said, smiling as he watched Kyniska putting Xanthus away.

"Yes, but all her work will be thrown away for you, *because* of you. You should not be here." Euryleonis continued with her work and then went to Kyniska. "My lady, I'll go and help the others prepare the food."

"Thank you, my girl," Kyniska said, putting a hand on Euryleonis' face and watching her go.

"She doesn't like me much," Stefanos said as Kyniska came to help him lead Acheron to the stall.

"No. She's jealous of my attentions to you, and the distraction you are."

She spoke in sincerity.

"I'm really a distraction?"

"Of course you are."

Stefanos watched her with Acheron, how she checked his hocks and rump after the day's training.

"Why invite me here then?" he asked.

She looked up, frustrated, bemused. "Where would you go? Everyone here hates you besides me and Pirro."

Stefanos looked to Pirro who smiled back and nodded.

"I don't hate him!" protested Eunice from Zeta's stall.

"Of course you don't," Kyniska said, turning back to Stefanos. "You can stay, but we must honour the moment. This is the great Games, the Olympiad!"

"You don't need to tell me that. I'm aware of what it is. Would you like me to stay in the stables?" he said, hurt entering into his voice unwanted.

"Don't be ridiculous!" she said. "Some stallions are meant to stay indoors."

He looked at her and she smiled, gripped his hand as she stepped around Acheron and led Stefanos into the middle of the stable.

"Pirro. Eunice."

"Yes, my lady?" they answered.

"Go and help the others. We'll be along shortly."

"Yes, my lady," Eunice said, pulling Pirro along with her.

When they were gone, Kyniska turned to Stefanos, her face serious. "What did you see in the Prytaneion? Pirro says you stumbled back from the flames, that you looked fearful."

"I tripped over the threshold, that's all."

"Don't lie to me. We must be honest. If the Gods have shown you something else, tell me." Kyniska was directly in front of him, her hands on his chest as he breathed in and out.

"I heard a neighing of horses as I looked at the sacred flame. I saw chariot wheels spinning...and..."

"What else?" she asked, her hand going to the raw red gouge on his forehead.

"I think I saw the woman crying again."

"The one you saw before? Hippodameia?"

"I don't know. I think so."

Kyniska turned away from him, walked a few paces and stood staring at the ground. She wondered what the Gods were trying to say, what it all meant. *Goddess Hera, reveal to us what this means...*

Kyniska knew that Pelops had saved Hippodameia from her cruel father, that she had saved him from the brutal death that so many men had endured for her hand. Hippodameia's statue stood above the hippodrome of Olympia, her husband buried in the mound beside the temple of Zeus in the sanctuary.

"What is it?" Stefanos said, behind her now, his hands gripping her shoulders, firmly, longingly.

Kyniska turned and kissed him there in the orange light. "Don't speak," she said as she led him to the empty stable that had belonged to Hippolytus. She turned, pulling him down onto her, and pushing all her own fears aside, willing herself to think only of that moment, to avoid all the uncertainty and mystery that waited for them outside of that stable.

Day two of the Games built on the excitement of the first day as the sanctuary was abuzz early.

Kyniska saw Stefanos off early as he had wanted to make an offering at the temple of Hera before the start of the first races. She was glad of the extra time to train, though she felt, surprisingly, that a part of her went with him.

Their meal the previous night, after their lovemaking, had been awkward at first, the girls unsure how to behave in front of the Argive. However, after some initial conversation, and Stefanos' easy way with people, even Euryleonis relaxed as he asked them about their lives in Sparta, their families, and about horses.

In turn, they asked him about about the wars he had been in, about Argos and the faraway cities he had seen. Kyniska noticed that it was often with a hint of regret that he spoke of his mercenary ways.

What is he thinking? she wondered as she watched him laugh and smile, taking the girls' chiding with a good nature. She had not seen him so relaxed before. It felt as if they were an odd sort of family then and, if she was honest with herself, she enjoyed it.

As the mist cleared from the practice field and the horses were brought out, Kyniska thought of Stefanos. As she stepped into the cab to warm the team up for Pirro, she found herself wanting to win, not just for herself anymore, but for him. *Of all people...an Argive.*

"Ha!" she yelled and the horses jumped to, the chariot wheels churning the dewy ground before darting forward.

THE STADIUM OF OLYMPIA WAS ALMOST FULL IN THE MORNING, but not as much as it had been previously. The second day was dedicated to the foot-races, and the second part of the pentathlon.

On the stadium ground, the runners of the dolichos and diaulos races ran hard, their naked bodies breathing rhythmically as they paced themselves in the first heats, saving some energy for later.

They had their fans along the banks, but most of the crowds would come for the stade race, and then the second part of the pentathlon which involved the long jump, discus, and javelin.

After visiting the temple of Hera, Stefanos decided to run along the river, sprinting intermittently in bursts; the hoplitodromos was the following day, and something inside told him he was not as prepared as he should have been. It had been weeks since they had crossed the Peloponnese in armour, and he had been focusing on the skamma rather than the stadium.

Meanwhile, the sanctuary of Olympia was bursting with life, like a lively agora filled with music, entertainment, sacrifice, and toil. Men from the entire Greek world mingled, bought souvenirs, traded news and more in the arcades of the stoa, at the baths, on the slopes of the stadium, and beneath the forest of victory bronzes set up by victors in years gone by.

Stefanos walked among them all, nodding to some he recognized, carefully watching those he knew to be wary of. It seemed that everywhere he went, he saw Ocnus and his gang of sycophants, or Polydamas of Thessaly holding court.

The setting was exhausting, chaotic and messy, the smells of grilling meat, incense, and the tang of never-ending sweat constantly in the nostrils.

After a few hours of training, Stefanos decided to sit on

the steps of the temple of Zeus, opposite the walls of the Pelopion. He looked to the walls that surrounded the mound of the hero and wondered about all he had seen and experienced to that point. He did not want to go back in there so close to his events, but he did wonder if the stories of Pelops and Hippodameia were true. Had he loved her and she him? Or had it been a play for sovereignty over the land in which he now found himself?

Stefanos knew the poets often exaggerated events in subsequent years, but there had to be some truth to the stories.

The cheers from the stadium reached his ears and the entire Altis was filled with the roar.

"Sounds like we have a winner in the dolichos," a man said, sitting down next to Stefanos.

Stefanos turned to see the Athenian philosopher, Plato, smiling at him through his beard.

"It's quite something to be here, isn't it? We are witness to the culmination of men's toil, all their years of work leading to this one decisive moment in time."

"Are you not competing?" Stefanos asked.

"Oh no!" Plato laughed. "Socrates was a warrior, but I have other pursuits. I see the merit in staying healthy, of course - we must treat our gifts from the Gods with great respect - but I know where my own strengths are."

"Hmm." Stefanos continued to stare at the Pelopion, and Plato bit into the cheese pastry he had been eating.

"I remember you from King Agesilaus' tent the other night."

"Yes. And I you."

"Quite a lively discussion, wouldn't you say?"

"Yes," Stefanos turned to Plato. "But I would think you are used to lively discussion, no?"

"Yes. Quite. But not with a woman such as the princess. She is..."

"Wondrous..." Stefanos almost breathed the word.

"Yes!" Plato's eyes were wide and knowing. "I could tell you were smitten, my friend."

"Could you?" Stefanos frowned.

"Yes." Plato leaned in closer. "And so could everyone else in that tent."

"What is your meaning, philosopher?"

It may have been the kindness in Plato's face that stayed Stefanos' hand from grabbing him, but he leaned in to him nonetheless.

"I've heard rumours, and even though such talk is the weapon of the weak-minded, it can still do damage to a man...or a woman. Tread carefully, would be my advice. I can see something between you and her, but remember who she is...and who her brother is."

Plato rose from his seat and stepped down onto the grass where he looked up at Stefanos.

"You are here for glory too, are you not?"

"Of course."

"Then claim it. For then, a whole world of possibilities can open up before you."

Stefanos watched the odd man turn and stroll slowly through the Altis, stopping to talk with others here and there, not rushing at all, but seeming to soak up the world about him.

"Philosophers..." Stefanos muttered as he climbed down from his perch and made his way to the stadium to cheer Kratos in the discus and other events of the second day of the pentathlon.

The stadium was filled now, men watching the final heat of the diaulos race, a sprint of two stades that required careful timing and pacing, yet a sustained burst of energy so that one did not fall behind.

As Stefanos came out of the krypte and was behind the runners at the starting line, an eerie silence settled over the entire mass of people on the banks. This was the moment, and men knew the Gods were watching them intently.

The rope dropped and the runners exploded off the line, their bare feet eating up the surface of the stadium, their limbs pumping, their hearts already near to bursting.

The crowd's voice rose as a tidal wave, the cries for various cities ringing out for their chosen champions - Athens, Sparta, Corinth, Argos, Thebes, Syracuse, Elis and others.

Stefanos felt the hair on the back of his neck stand on end, excitement coursing through his limbs as if he were running himself as the men made the turn at the far end and the strong began to pull away from the rest.

It happened in an oddly slow way, the men's faces charging directly for the finish line, their grimaces of effort, anticipation, or pain.

In a burst that seemed a gift from Olympus itself, the Elean pulled away from the others, his legs a blur, the roar of the local crowd rushing alongside him, pushing him along until he burst over the finish line and his countrymen cried his name to the sky as he smiled, gasping for breath.

"Polites! Polites! Polites!"

Stefanos was near to him before he was swarmed by admirers, he saw his face, the elation, the confusion. He had just run like it was his very last race, as if he were running to save his dearest loved ones.

In that moment, Polites of Elis was a hero among mortals, and the men of every city could not help but praise his effort, even as their own representatives lay panting in the dirt and Polites was hoisted above the crowd.

The man actually looked directly at Stefanos for a moment, and nodded, as if encouraging him, as if saying, *If I can do it, so can you!*

The Hellanodikai began to clear people off the stadium surface in preparation for the next part of the pentathlon, and Stefanos began to look around for Kratos.

He walked about, looking among the dense groups of Argives and spotted Kratos standing with Ocnus and the others, a couple of them stretching in preparation for their competition, weighing up the discoi that those competing had brought.

Stefanos remembered Pandaros saying that the discus that would be used was the heaviest one brought by one of the competitors.

This fact hit home when he saw a massive Syracusan walk by with a discus that must have been two times the diameter and thickness of the heavy one Kratos had been practicing with.

He saw Kratos stop talking as the man walked by, his head dropping a little as he took in the sight of the discus. Kratos looked up and saw Stefanos, then nodded in the direction of the big man.

Stefanos shrugged. It was all he could do. The rules were clearly stated. The only way the man would be disqualified was if his throw went into the crowd on the embankments and killed someone. The discoboloi of the pentathlon lined up, and the crowd settled onto the grass. There were several dozen competitors.

Stefanos stood to the side, once more near the edge of the starting line.

The Hellanodikai observed the heavy discus that had been brought and there was some discussion and arm waving before they nodded in agreement and the big Syracusan was allowed to step forward.

Stefanos did not remember how the man, big as he was, had done in the foot race, but he knew that this event was made for him.

The man took off his chiton and tossed it to the ground a few feet away where his trainer stood.

He stepped up to the line, then walked back a few paces, weighing the discus in his hand, feeling its weight, and bending his elbow back and forth. After a moment he paused, looking down the stadium, twisted his torso back and forth a couple of times before he unravelled like the torsion of a great siege machine and the discus shot smoothly out of his hand to soar for a great distance until it hit the ground at about one and three-quarter stades.

Most of the men there stood gape-mouthed, some laughing, others shaking their heads as if this contest were already a forgone conclusion as the Syracusan pumped his thick, solid arms into the air and yelled "Syracuse!"

Kratos was next, having stepped forward out of bravery or sheer stubbornness. He congratulated the Syracusan on his throw and accepted the discus when it was brought back to him.

Stefanos watched as he made an effort not to drop the discus, but the strain in his forearm muscles told him that it was heavy.

Kratos stood ready, his long hair tied back so as to not fly into his face. The talk and laughter in the crowd simmered down a little and he turned slowly, flexing, relaxing, finding his balance before turning back one final time and letting the discus fly.

There were cheers as the discus gobbled up distance, farther and farther until it came down just under a stade. Then there were hoots of disappointment, for when everyone looked, including Kratos, he was a foot past the starting line.

"Kratos of Argos is disqualified from the discus!" one of the Hellanodikai declared.

"Ahhh!" Kratos yelled to the sky, storming away from the field. "It's a ridiculous weight to throw!" he said to the judges who shrugged and called for the next competitor.

Stefanos had seen enough and ran after Kratos who was once more, storming out of the stadium. When he came into the Altis however, he could not see him, the crowd thicker than it had been before.

Let him be, Stefanos thought. *He needs to be alone.*

He found himself thinking once more of the runner, Polites, and the look of glory upon his stubbly face, the joy, the sense of ultimate achievement.

That's what I want, Stefanos thought. *Gods, grant it to me...*

His eyes fell upon the temple of Hera then, and he remembered that that was where the shields of the hoplitodromos were kept.

Tomorrow...I run tomorrow... he reminded himself. At that moment, he decided no longer to watch others compete until he was finished, and burst into a run directly for the Kladeos.

A couple of hours later, after he had run and trained in the palaestra, and visited the baths to ease his muscles and mind, Stefanos found himself back before the doors to the temple of Hera.

In his hand, he gripped the bunch of herbs, rosemary and thyme, which he had purchased from one of the sellers near the palaestra. He walked up the steps and entered the temple again.

The familiar smell filled his nostrils as he picked his way through a few scattered worshippers praying before some of the smaller statues of the goddess, as well as before the large, central depiction of the queen of the Gods, where she stood before the cella of the temple.

As he waited to approach the main altar of the goddess, he stood still in the middle of the main aisle, his eyes going up to the cedar roof top, the painted panels depicting gods and goddesses, the exploits of Hippodameia prominently displayed among others.

A chill stole through Stefanos' body as he stood there; it felt as if some invisible force was constantly trying to chase him away from Olympia.

Just then, one of the men at prayer to the left turned to leave and Stefanos recognized Biton, one of Ocnus' friends. The man walked casually down the aisle toward Stefanos.

"No amount of praying will help you, you know," he said, his smirk mimicking the one that rested permanently upon Ocnus' face. "You and your whore don't stand a chance."

He slowed almost to a stand-still beside Stefanos. The priestess behind the great altar, looked up from where she was placing one of the newly polished hoplons against a column.

Stefanos had a sudden urge to crush the man's face but stayed his hand, allowed his muscles to ease, though not his alertness.

"You sure you can lift the sacred hoplon, little man?" Stefanos said, keeping his arms crossed.

Biton began to move toward Stefanos, but stopped himself, as multiple heads turned toward them in the centre of the temple. "You have no idea," he whispered, and began to laugh as he walked away.

Stefanos watched him go and disappear into the gathering dusk. He turned back toward the altar and approached, letting the looks from the others present fall away like dead leaves from the branches of a mighty oak.

The altar was filled with offerings, a dove, a chicken, their blood spattered about the surface of white marble, flowers and jewellery, votive offerings in the shape of a runner, a fist, and several round shields similar to the ones used in the race.

Stefanos placed his herbs down on the front edge of the altar and looked at the twenty gleaming bronze shields that had been set out by the priestesses of Hera. He wondered how heavy they really were and glanced to the far right to see his own shield which he had offered, leaning against the trunk of one of the Doric columns. His own looked larger, but the sacred shields appeared thicker. He looked up.

Oh Goddess Hera...commend me to my mother, wherever she is. Watch over me, Goddess, as my own mother did. Make me fast that I may honour you and my family in the race tomorrow.

His eyes were closed as he prayed, his head bowed above the offerings that others had left, the detritus of faith laid out before him.

When he opened his eyes, he half expected to see the apparition staring at him, Hippodameia, she who had established the Heraia at Olympia. Part of Stefanos felt that she would be there, leaning on the other side of the altar, staring at him, accusing him, weeping tears of blood from sorrowful eyes.

But there was only quiet, the soft footfalls of the priestess' slippers in the cella, and the flicker of flame. He turned and saw that the temple was empty now, that darkness had blanketed the world outside.

Stefanos looked up at the statue of Hera, her large eyes gazing down at him with mingled pity and daring. She was mother to him now, and she watched him as he backed away toward the Altis outside.

It was a clear out, cooler than the previous nights at Olympia. The stars were brighter, their torches flickering to their full heights in the blanket of the heavens.

Stefanos expected the Altis to be full of people, victors crowing among their friends, groups of would-be winners bolstering themselves with wine and sycophantic praise. During the day, the Altis was always humming but now, it was empty, as if the Gods had gone home for the night, back to Olympus.

But there was something strange in the air, something Stefanos, son of Talos could not quite discern, though it felt familiar. He wanted to run back to Kyniska, to take her in his arms and make love to her, but something held him back, though his thoughts pooled around images of her.

He walked, he knew not why, directly for the Pelopion. His steps took him around the pentagonal enclosure, the burial mound reaching up from within. At the entrance he stopped, his eyes searching for the woman again, but it was empty.

The sound of crickets replaced that of cicadas, and the Altis took on a misty glow, dotted as it was with torches and braziers placed around the monuments and among the forest of victory bronzes.

Stefanos walked a bit farther until he was among the sacred olive trees on the west end of the temple of Zeus. He paused there, breathing deeply, his ears straining in the half-darkness where the temple loomed over him. He stepped back to get a better view of the west pediment, of the scene of the battle between the Centaurs and Lapiths with Apollo in the centre, a calm amidst the storm, flanked by Theseus with his axe, and Peirithous with his sword, ready to kill one of the Centaurs.

The set was magnificent, and Stefanos stared up at it in awe, wondering for a moment if that battle had indeed happened as depicted. Had not Pelops raced Oinomaus across the land from Olympia to Argos?

A snapping twig made Stefanos whirl around quickly but not before something collided with the side of his head sending him barrelling into the olive tree and onto the grass and dirt below.

His vision blurred and his ears rang out as he stared up, grasping for the trunk, staring at the powerful form of Apollo with his arm outstretched, and then darkness.

WHEN STEFANOS SHIFTED ON THE GROUND WHERE HE LAY, HIS hair matted with blood, even the arcades of the stoa were silent, all in Olympia sleeping fitfully for the next day of the Games.

Stefanos pushed himself onto his hands and knees, and vomited. His head spun wildly and it took a few minutes to rally himself. Once the spinning slowed to a manageable speed, he gripped the trunk of the sacred olive tree and pulled himself up, his arms wrapped about a part of the broad, gnarled trunk.

The tree was warm against his face and chest, and he felt he could fall asleep against it, but he forced himself to stand up.

The torches of the Altis still burned, the braziers smoked. He stumbled to the bottom step of the temple of Zeus and held it as he walked along the southern edge. Once he passed the corner, he stopped.

There, in the dark space between braziers, a man in a long, white chlamys and chiton stood gazing up at the bronze statue set of the Diagorids. He stared so intently that Stefanos found himself trying to be quiet as he approached. The man whispered to himself, so low that Stefanos could not hear what he said, but there was something familiar about him, about the way he stood, the length and mass of his arms as they reached up to caress the bronzes.

"Did you..." Stefanos began to say, his head pounding. "Did you see anything? I was attacked."

The whispering stopped, but the man did not turn, and his arms remained raised.

Stefanos walked closer, going slowly so as not to fall. "I'm talking to you," he said, his voice a little stronger this time. "Did you see who attacked me?"

Still nothing.

"Old man," Stefanos said, his anger up. He was beside him now and grabbed the pale arm. "I said -"

Stefanos froze and fell backwards against the base of the one of the statues, his scream dying in his throat as he took in the face of his father, Talos, as it admired the statue of Diagoras directly above him.

Stefanos could not move even if he wanted to, his limbs heavier than bronze ingots. He looked upon the pale face of the father he had known, the eyes fixed in adulation or ecstasy upon the bronze hero from Rhodes standing over them.

The eyes were no longer the jaundiced tint of old age, as they had been not long ago, but were pale, still, and unblinking. The bronze called to his father's shade, and it was all Stefanos could do to keep from weeping.

"Fa...Father?" Stefanos croaked, urging his voice to be strong, but unable. "Is...is it you?"

For a long moment there was silence, Talos continuing to stare up, but then, as if the shade had only just heard Stefanos' voice, the features changed and the eyes fixed upon him.

It did not speak immediately, as if time did not matter.

Stefanos forced himself to stand up straight, though still against the statue base of Diagoras and his victorious kin. "Father?"

"I am," the shade said. "A part of Talos." The shade closed its eyes suddenly and inhaled deeply through the nose, relishing the scent. "The bronze...can you smell it? So pure...so perfect..."

"Why are you here?" Stefanos said, feeling his hands shaking as if he had no control over himself, his head throbbing where blood was now dry upon his scalp.

Those ghostly eyes again... "To remind you of your oath...my son..."

Stefanos hung his head, Kyniska bounding into his thoughts again.

"The woman... She distracts you..."

Talk of Kyniska gave Stefanos courage and he stood a bit taller. "She is magnificent. A hero in her own right."

"A Spartan."

For a moment, Stefanos wondered if the dead held onto their prejudices, and it seemed that bitter memory outlasted death.

"A champion," Stefanos countered, picturing her in her chariot as she raced about the track.

"As you should be," the shade chided, but then the features softened. "I know your lonely heart, son. I can see it." Talos made to reach out and touch Stefanos, the latter closing his eyes, but the strong, white hand stopped short and hovered above his head.

"I did not forget my ponos with your mother, all that I had worked for...my craft." The shade indicated the statues above them and became fixated once more upon the faces of Diagoras and his sons, Damagetos, Akousilaos, and Dorieus, and his grandson Eukles, all champions in the pankration or boxing.

"They are immortal now," the shade said, longing in his face. "Their monuments of bronze will remain for all time, pleasing and inspiring to gods and men..."

"I am ready for the Games, Father. I remember my oath to you."

"Do you know what it means to win in the Games? To have your image cast in bronze and set here among the victors, those crowned by Nike herself?"

"Yes," Stefanos answered, but the shade went on as if he had not spoken.

"It means that Eris Agathos has ruled you, heart and soul." It shuddered at the utterance of 'soul' and Stefanos stepped back a little. "If the Gods bless you with victory, because of the toils you have endured, it means that you and yours will be blessed, always, by the Gods, in life and memory."

"But, Father-"

"This is the ultimate agon, my son." The shade looked around, turning slowly to take in the forest of bronzes, pugilists, and wrestlers, heroes in battle, runners and equestrian statues, all set alongside the temples of the king and queen of the Gods, and the tomb of a hero. "I can see your image...there!" it pointed. "Yesss..." Talos closed his eyes, his outstretched arm still pointing to a spot near the sacred olive tree, at the end of the long row of which the Diagorids were the centre piece.

Stefanos heard a sound as of distant hammering upon an anvil, as he watched his father's shade in awe, its ghostly strength familiar. It was the sound he remembered from his workshop and forge, the very sound that had filled his ears to the day he had left for a life of war. There was also a smell of burning and heat, forge fire and molten bronze...so familiar, so full of memory.

"Father," Stefanos said, falling to his knees. "Forgive me..." There were so many questions that harangued his mind. Was he in a place of terror? What heroes did he meet? Did he see the Gods? Did he see Stefanos' mother again? - but forgiveness was what he craved as he swayed before the white visage of his father.

"Run like Achilles...fight like Herakles...and live on in bronze...bronze... It is here," it held its arms out, "that the Gods sort the heroes from the failures."

The hammering grew louder and louder in Stefanos' ears, so much so that he had to cover them, the sound so persistent, the rhythm his father's own as he remembered it - One, two, THREE. One, two, THREE.

Then it stopped and Stefanos looked up slowly to see the eyes gazing at him, the thick white hands on either side of his face.

"My...son..."

It tore at Stefanos' soul to see his father's shade full of desperate longing for its inability to shed tears which it seemed it would gladly have done.

"My...son..." The hands trembled. "Victory is yours..."

It was still dark when Stefanos rose from the damp ground at the feet of the Diagorids. His head whirled and he felt like vomiting, but more than that, tears poured from his eyes though he made not a sound.

His body was wracked by silent sobs, and his fist pounded the hollow earth. He pushed himself to his knees, then his feet.

"Ahhhh!" he yelled, releasing the anguish that seemed to sap all his strength in the darkness of the Altis where the torches and braziers had all burned away and the world was lit only by silver moonlight.

He was not sure how he managed it, but he stumbled, dizzy and sick, his limbs cold as if death had touched him, across the Kladeos and into the Spartan camp.

"Stefanos?" the voice of Pollux reached through the fog of his mind.

Stefanos searched the darkness and found his friend there on guard duty with a few other red-cloaked Spartan warriors.

He was at Stefanos' side immediately. "You shouldn't be here," he hissed.

"Take me to her, Pollux. Please." Stefanos gripped his

friend tighter than he realized, and Pollux shrugged off the hand quickly.

"I could get flogged for it or worse," he said.

"I'm her...her guest. Please take me there," Stefanos swayed.

"What happened to you?" Pollux asked, only just then noticing the blood upon Stefanos's head and face, his tunic.

"I...I saw... I was attacked from behind in the Altis. Someone...clubbed me."

"All right. Come." He turned to his fellow guards. "I'm taking him to the princess. You stay here and keep a watch."

The guards nodded and watched as Pollux took Stefanos to Kyniska's camp. It was quiet as they picked their way through the main camp to the heavily-guarded enclosure of the princess and her stables.

"Ajax," Pollux greeted the enomotarch.

"What's this?" Ajax answered, staring down at both of them. "The Argive? She's been asking after him."

"Take me to her," Stefanos said again, walking away from Pollux. He felt Ajax's big hand on his shoulder.

"Not so fast, little man. How'd you get like this?"

"Some coward attacked me from behind in the Altis. Clubbed me." Stefanos wished they would all just stop asking him questions and let him go. He felt suddenly very exhausted, his body needing to lie down.

"What's happening?"

Kyniska's voice cut through the darkness as two torches approached, one held by Pirro, the other by Helle.

Stefanos looked at her and smiled. "Sorry I'm late."

"What happened?" she demanded, looking to Ajax and Pollux. Then she spotted the blood and went to Stefanos. "Who did this?"

"Don't know," he said. "Some coward. I need to sleep."

Kyniska nodded to Pirro to take one of Stefanos' arms. "Let's get him inside." She turned to Pollux and Ajax. "Keep a close watch. First I'm attacked, now this. I swear if I find out who did this, the Gods themselves won't be able to save them."

Stefanos made for the tent entrance and let the orange light of the interior wrap around him as he entered and was led by Pirro and Kyniska to her sleeping area where he collapsed on the bed.

"Helle, water," Kyniska said.

Helle left and came back with a bronze basin of water and a couple of linen cloths which she dipped into the water and handed to Kyniska.

She said nothing as she dabbed his face and head, rinsing the bloody cloth several times in the basin until the water ran deep red.

Her face hovered above Stefanos' and he focussed on her, smiling through his cloudy vision.

He reached up and touched the side of her face with his bloody hand.

She did not pull away.

"I've been thinking of you. I can't stop."

"You must. You need to focus on the race tomorrow."

"Yes, but...you mean more to me than any race, Kyniska."

"Stop." Kyniska looked away then. "You dishonour the Gods with such talk. And your father."

"I saw my father," he gasped.

"What?"

"He came to me...in the Altis."

Kyniska's eyes widened and she looked up at Pirro and Helle. "Leave us now," she told them. When they were gone, Kyniska looked down at Stefanos, at his wide eyes, and the dried salt beneath his lids.

"I saw him," he repeated. "He spoke of bronze, of victory...of-"

"Shhh..." she soothed, her hand resting on his cheek, and one on his chest above his racing heart. "Tell me."

Chapter Nine

ARES AND APHRODITE

Ἄρης και Ἀφροδίτη

It was well-known among Greeks that the Spartans were orthodox in their faith, how they honoured and worshiped the Gods. All Greeks were, more or less, but the Spartans took faith with as much seriousness as they did battle. It was all or nothing.

However, as Kyniska lay awake in the dark hours of morning, watching Stefanos mumble in this sleep by the light of the lamp, she found what he said to be quite unbelievable. How many times had she prayed to the Gods that Archidamus, her father, should return to speak words of comfort to her, to give her strength?

It was something she had wished for, but never been given. It seemed only Odysseus had been able to venture into the halls of Hades to speak with the dead. And yet, the man laying before her, his head bandaged, had insisted to her that his own father had spoken to him in the Altis of Olympia that very night.

A rational Athenian might put such a thing down to the injury done to Stefanos' head, but Kyniska knew better than to question the Gods and their ways. Besides, Stefanos, from the moment she met him, never seemed to be the believing type, despite a mother and sister who had been dedicated to the work of the goddess.

How will he race today? she thought as her fingers touched his bandaged head. She knew he was a strong man - as she looked upon his sleeping form, the words *eumorphia*, *aner agathos*, and *promachoi* came immediately to her mind. And yet there was something about him which she had never seen in a man, something she had always been seeking but never found. Until then.

As Kyniska stared upon Stefanos, son of Talos, she felt a stirring in her heart that took her breath away. Her will had always been well-fortified against men's attentions, even those she had wanted, but in that instant, as he slept, something about the Argive lying before her darted through her defences with such speed and ease that, as she held a trembling hand to her lips, she was suddenly afraid for what it all meant.

As if hearing her thoughts, Stefanos moaned and opened his eyes to look up at her. Instead of groaning in pain, he smiled and reached for her hand.

"Do I look that bad" he asked, a frown upon his brow.

Kyniska shook her head and squeezed his hand tightly. "No. Well, you've looked better."

"Do you think I'm crazy?"

Slowly, she shook her head again. It might have been easier if it was the injury. "By the Gods, no. I don't think you're crazy."

"Ever since coming to this place...since I decided to compete...I've been seeing things that I never did before. Maybe it's a warning?"

"Or maybe you were meant to come to this place and win victory so that the Gods could take notice of Stefanos, son of Talos? A gift for your family's years of honour to the Gods?"

"Maybe." Stefanos tried pushing himself up to a sitting position and the tent lurched for a moment as he gripped Kyniska's arm, strong and supple like the branch of a willow tree by the river.

"Can you race today?" she asked.

"I have to race," he answered right away.

"When does it start?"

"After the pentathlon finishes. After midday, I think."

"Then you have time to rest."

"No. I need to move, to eat, to run," he said, swinging his legs over the side of the bed. "I'm sorry if I scared you last night."

"Scared me?" she said, looking a little upset. "How could you scare me? Do you forget who I am?"

"Never. In fact, you're in my thoughts always," he said, and Kyniska's head jerked. "I can't get you out of my mind, Kyniska."

"Aphrodite has cast a spell upon you," she laughed, but felt herself tense up, knowing the truth of it for both of them. "The Games, Stefanos... We need to see the contest through. The Gods expect it."

"As do the dead..." he muttered, remembering with a shudder the details of the previous night. "I'll win. I must, for my family, for my father. I have to..."

Kyniska stood up and held out her hands to him. "Then let's prepare you for battle!" she said, her arms straining as he let her help him up, his body swaying for a few moments before he stood still. "I'll have the girls prepare breakfast for us," she said, kissing him on the mouth before leaving to speak with them.

Stefanos watched her go, listening to the muffled voices on the other side of the tent before turning to his thorax, helmet and greaves where they lay on the floor at the foot of Kyniska's bed. He picked up the thorax and held it out before him, looked upon the brown and green leather, bronze, and linen he had cleaned of blood and gore countless times. The gorgon head in the centre seemed to roar at him.

It had been some weeks since he had worn it, but it felt as familiar as ever. He had marched, sometimes run, across a large swathe of Persia in that armour; he knew every dent and nick in its surface, where it had come from, what he had done to the men who had inflicted them.

He thought of the coward who had clubbed him the previous night, and asked the Gods for the chance to be avenged upon him if ever he found out who it was, but he pushed the thought away for the moment. He had a race to win.

Pandaros had always said *Focus on the race, event, or battle you're involved in on the day, and nothing else. If your mind strays, the Gods will abandon you as you have abandoned your philonikia.*

When Kyniska came back, her face worried for a moment, he turned to her holding the armour.

"Will you help me arm myself?" he asked.

The worry left her face and her eyes filled with intensity. "Yes."

Gods...what are you doing to me?

They ate in relative silence, Stefanos only speaking when Euryleonis plied him with angry questions about what happened the previous night, and how anyone could so disrespect the Gods in Zeus' own sanctuary.

Kyniska was quiet throughout the light meal. Her eyes observed Stefanos closely to see if his movements were sloppy, his balance unsettled. She found herself wishing him victory almost as much as she did for herself.

But can he win now? she wondered as she looked at him in his thorax and greaves, wearing them as if they were a part of his person.

He caught her eye for a moment and she thought she spied worry there, but he smiled through it. The Taraxippos of the hippodrome was, it seemed, not the only place in Olympia's sanctuary that was harassed by shades of the dead.

"Right," Stefanos said, clapping his hands and getting up slower than Kyniska would have liked. "I need to run, and you," he turned to Kyniska and Pirro who sat beside her, "both of you need to take care of those magnificent animals. Your race is in two days!"

"We're ready," Pirro assured, bowing his head to Kyniska.

"A little more work on the turns, and we're there," Kyniska said. "You should go, you don't want to be late for the sacrifices to Zeus."

"I've already seen them," Stefanos said.

"Not those!" Pirro piped up. "Today they offer a hecatomb at the great altar of Zeus, beside the Pelopion."

Stefanos shook his head. "A hecatomb? One hundred bulls! That will take all day."

"No it won't. Besides," Kyniska got up and put her hands on his shoulders. "Their meat will be the food of your victory feast this evening!"

Her dark eyes were close to his face and he felt the power she was lending him, the strength.

She kissed him then, slowly. "Go now, and run with the Gods."

"I will," Stefanos said. "I'll run like the wind."

Kyniska made a last check of the buckles and laces of his thorax, ensuring nothing was loose, then handed him his helmet which he tucked under his left arm.

They did not say anything else. Stefanos turned and walked barefoot toward the daylight.

Pirro turned to Kyniska. "I'll be back right after the sacrifices, my lady."

"Yes. But I will want you to watch his race and come back to tell me how he has fared."

"Yes, my lady." Pirro bowed, turned, and followed after Stefanos.

Kyniska went with the girls to the tent opening and

watched as Pirro caught up to Stefanos, the latter waiting for him.

"Do you think he'll win, my lady?" Thais asked.

"I pray he does."

Before Stefanos and Pirro came to the banks of the Kladeos and the crossing point, they could hear a deep lowing that seemed to rumble in the ground, as if an angry mob had gathered in the centre of an agora.

"What is that?" Pirro stopped before crossing the river.

"What do you suppose a hundred bulls sounds like? That's a hecatomb of meat."

"Zeus will be pleased then," Pirro said, his head low.

"Let's hope so." Stefanos began to cross and immediately the tang of fresh manure filled his nostrils. "Smells like a hundred bulls too," he laughed as they crossed the foot bridge and approached the baths and the Heroon of the sanctuary.

There was a massive crowd blocking the way to the Altis, every man turned to the North to watch the procession of the animals being led to the slaughter at the tall, conical altar of Zeus where smoke was already rising into the sky.

"They're starting!" Pirro said, trying to push his way through to get a better look.

Stefanos peered over the heads of the crowd and could see the long line of brown and black animals being herded into the Altis by hundreds of handlers. Most were donations from the people of Elis who were eager to offer their livestock in honour of Zeus during the sacred Games.

Pirro waved. "Stefanos, come! We can get through here!" he mimed, pointing to a gap in the crowd, between the Altis wall and the altar of Zeus Orkios next to the Bouleuterion.

They pushed on, Stefanos' armour providing a bit of extra incentive for others to let them through. Most of the athletes stood before the steps of the temple of Zeus and filled the grassy area between it and the great altar.

The chief theokolos stood in the middle of an area that had been blocked off, a huge black bull standing in front of him, a rope tied to each of its muscular handlers.

"Looks like this is the first one," Pirro whispered as they approached.

Stefanos' eyes scanned the crowd, looking for anyone who glanced suspiciously in his direction. There were too many faces for him to tell, and they all looked at the high priest who was about to make the first sacrifice. It was, however, easy for him to recognize his fellow competitors in the hoplitodromos, for they were the only ones wearing armour and carrying helmets.

The armoured warriors stood like sentries among the crowd of men dressed only in chitons or wearing nothing at all - there was a Spartan, a few Thebans, Athenians, Thessalians, Corinthians and others, all of them men who fought and could afford the equipment they needed to compete in the race.

Used to assessing their enemies at a glance, the competing hoplites in the crowd assessed each other casually, but with intent. Then Stefanos saw Biton, Ocnus' friend, and the man smirked at him, leaned over and whispered to another man who, when Stefanos caught a glance, was Kratos.

Kratos looked nervous, for his final events of the pentathlon would follow the sacrifices.

All their heads turned when the theokolos spoke.

"Competitors! You have toiled this far. Some of you have tasted victory, most defeat. But you have all worked toward the agon of this sacred sanctuary. Father Zeus! Hear us, King of the Gods! Bless these games, and honour the most worthy with victory! We offer you this hecatomb of bulls, the thigh bones and fat of which we shall place upon your altar, Great Father! Bless this third day of the Games, and let us honour you and all the Gods with the acts we perform here in your sanctuary!"

The priest lowered his arms and his blade slashed the

throat of the bull so quickly and deeply that blood soaked the priest's robes in one great gush as the beast moaned and fell to its knees, the handlers straining at the ropes to keep it from tossing its head.

Another bull was led out then, directly beside the body of the first, and the priest did the same, the bull's white coat turning crimson as it soaked up the blood like a horrible sea sponge.

The meat cutters of the theokoloi set to work quickly and efficiently, cutting up and sectioning off the corpses, setting aside the Gods' portions.

Stefanos wondered if he and Kratos would wear the ribbons of victory together that day as winners of the hoplitodromos and pentathlon.

Smoke began to curl up into the sky as the first of the thighbones were laid upon the altar of Zeus, the theokoloi climbing up the steep stairs to the top where the fire burned and the fat sizzled.

Beneath their breath, men muttered their prayers to Zeus, their wishes for victory, and promises of deeds to be done if they should be granted victory in the Games. It was a place of oaths and adrenaline, where the love of competing was in every man, and every man was ruled by his love of victory.

Stefanos could see in every athlete's eyes how much they wanted victory. They all wanted it, no matter what, but few of them would achieve it.

Then the sound of slaughtered bulls grew louder and louder and the air smelled of blood. Stefanos thought of how many times he had run in the armour he wore - into battle, and sometimes away from it, in order to fight another day.

This battle would be one of his greatest, he told himself as he watched the grass and dirt of the Altis run red.

KYNISKA WAS ALONE IN HER CAMP BUT FOR HALF OF HER bodyguard, including Ajax, who stood by her at all times, watching the trees, his doru in his thick hand, flexing and unflexing.

She liked the big warrior enough, but he was over-attentive now, where Typhon had been lax.

"Just guard the courtyard outside the stables, Ajax," she said as she went in to prepare the horses for their training that day.

"But, my lady, if one of the assassins is lurking inside?"

"You've had your men keeping a watch all night. No one will have got through, I am confident."

"Call, and I'll be there," he answered, backing away respectfully.

Kyniska nodded and went inside with the girls following. At first she thought that Ajax would become too familiar with her, his bulk and arrogant demeanour toward his fellows sometimes a problem, but it was quite the opposite.

His eyes avoided raking over her body, unlike Typhon's had often done, due, she knew, to her own indiscretion. She had noticed that Ajax actually watched Eunice closely and shied awkwardly when she approached him.

She went to Xanthus in his stall. "Good morning, my boy. How are you?" she said, pulling aside the rope that blocked the entrance and letting the stallion come close to her. His great neck rested across her left shoulder as her arms reached up and she hugged him, a child beside a giant.

There was a loud neighing as the other horses called to their mistress for her attention and Kyniska went to each of them in turn, finally stopping at Acheron. "You are all my favourites, don't worry so," she said as a mother to her children.

"My lady, quickly!" Euryleonis yelled on the other side of the stable where she stood in Hippolytus' stall.

Kyniska rushed over and gasped when she found the surviving stallion of her whites lying on the ground. His breathing was hard and fast, and his eyes shot wide in shock.

Her eyes were drawn immediately to the awkwardly-bent front fetlock.

"He seems to have broken it again, my lady," Euryleonis said, kneeling beside the animal, her hands feeling the broken area. The girl looked up at their mistress' face and she saw a mask of rage that she had never seen there.

Of course, Kyniska had been angry before, but never like this. It was as if the night of the attack were flooding back into her thoughts again, the pain, the blood, the howling of her beloved Adonis as his body was broken.

Kyniska struggled not to yell, for fear of alarming the other horses. They needed peace and calm for their race to glory, not death and alarm.

"Take the others outside," she said. "All of them. They can't be in here when I do this."

"Yes, my lady!" the four girls said in symphony, each one going to a stall and walking a horse out. Euryleonis came back for the last two horses.

"Tell Ajax to come here," Kyniska said.

"Yes, my lady." Euryleonis paused. "Would you...like me to do it? I'm not afraid, and you have already had to once."

Kyniska turned to the girl, standing now. "No. It must be me. They are my children, and I must care for them to the end."

The girl nodded, and led the white mare out of the stable. Ajax came inside quickly and stopped at the stall where Kyniska stood.

"Another assassin?" he asked.

"No," she answered, noticing the relief on his face when she said so. "His leg has broken again and it will not mend. It is his time."

"I can do it," Ajax said, drawing his xiphos from his side.

"No. Give me your sword," the princess demanded.

Ajax turned the handle toward her and held it out.

"Leave me," she said. "Take some of the men and begin

building a pyre on the opposite side of the camp, away from the training ground. We will burn him later."

"Princess," Ajax bowed and made his way out, ducking low to exit the stable tent.

Light angled through a crack in the leather roof of the tent, lighting the brilliant white coat of the stallion as he lay, his belly rising and falling rapidly. Kyniska laid a hand upon his great head, a spot where she had always pat and kissed him. His eyes closed briefly at one final touch.

"I am sorry. I tried to help you," she said, her voice unusually shaky. Part of her wanted to say she wished she had never come to Olympia, but she knew that that was not true. The guilt of this thought rushed through her as she considered what she was about to do. "I'm sorry," she repeated.

Kyniska took the handle of the sword and raised it above her head as she knelt beside Hippolytus' head. The blade caught the sunlight and the stallion flinched for a moment before settling back down.

"Forgive me..."

Kyniska brought down the blade into the soft area on the side of the stallion's head, and the beast's legs kicked out violently, knocking the stable wall over before a last great breath heaved out of the body and the teeth and tongue stuck out with a sort of equine grimace of pain.

Her hands shook as she continued to grip the xiphos' handle, the blade still embedded in the horse's head. With her eyes shut tight, she said the words to send him on his way.

"Poseidon, Lord of Horses...take this stallion into your care that he may ride free in the Elysian Fields. He has served well, and been a good friend to me and his brethren. Watch over him, my lord Poseidon..."

"You've lost another one?"

Kyniska registered the voice after a few moments and looked up to see her brother, King Agesilaus, looking down on her, his arms crossed, his eyes cold and grey in the growing light. "How many more must die for your obsession?"

"Leave me alone," she said through clenched teeth, as if a tiger protecting her cubs, the low rumble in her body threatening to lash out at any moment.

Agesilaus looked at the xiphos protruding from the horse's body. "You'll end up with no more at this rate."

"What do you want?"

"To see if you are ready for your races. By the looks of things, you are not. Get up." he demanded.

Slowly, Kyniska rose to her full height, taller than her brother by several inches.

"If you're about to embarrass Sparta, and me, with this ridiculous race, I'm pulling you out of it. My intention was to discredit the race in general, not to lay shame upon Sparta and our house."

"We will race," Kyniska said. "We will win."

"You'd better," he answered, turning to leave, but then stopping. "Oh, by the way, sister. I'm thinking of marrying you off."

Kyniska froze, her eyes levelled like spears at Agesilaus. "I've no need of a husband. I...don't want one."

"You sound unsure," he said, smiling. "In fact, there are a couple of options. Typhon has actually expressed an interest."

"By Hades, no!" she said.

"Careful. He is lowly, sure, but his family has served well in the past in the king's guard."

"Never." She rushed him and Agesilaus stood firm and unflinching. "There is also Aeson of Thessaly - he came to me yesterday with the idea. Apparently he was impressed with your vigour, despite your age. He also promised you herds of horses in Thessaly. I hear they love their horses there."

"You would marry me to a Thessalian?" she said indignantly. "He's an animal."

"He also holds the lands to the Thebans' backs, and that would make him a good ally."

"Power has clouded your mind, Brother. Father would never have allowed or forced-"

"Father is dead!" Agesilaus rubbed his sparse beard, as if frustrated by flies. "You would do well to remember that. By Spartan law, you must obey me in these matters, no matter how many other freedoms you enjoy."

"I don't want to marry either of those men. You are not my lord and master, no matter how great you think you have become!"

Agesilaus' hand shot out and caught Kyniska on the side of the face, causing her to take a step back, but she did not fall.

Kyniska's rage boiled inside of her, and she felt the pull of the xiphos in the corpse on the ground behind her.

"You've no right to strike me, Agesilaus," she said her fingers feeling the trickle of blood on her burning cheek.

"I have every right. I'm the king."

"You're a child, playing at king and war. Father would be ashamed of you."

Agesilaus rounded on her again, but stopped short when she did not flinch, her eyes steady upon him.

"You're a real Spartan woman then, are you?" he said, his posture easing, a familiar smirk on his lips. "So, you bed whom you wish. That's fine with me. I don't care what goes between your legs. But if you think I would let you marry some lowly, Argive mercenary, you have another thing coming, sister."

Kyniska's eyes betrayed her sudden thoughts and Agesilaus caught it.

"He can fight, true enough, and he respects our ways, but he is *not* a Spartan. He's not even Argive. His own people hate him!"

"He is more a man than you will ever be," she growled, her voice low and angry, and full of sincerity.

"Now who is the fool?" Agesilaus turned and began to walk away. "You will be permitted to race in the Olympiad, but be prepared to bend the knee to your new husband, whomever he may be."

Kyniska watched her brother limp out of the stable and

spat at his back as he went outside. Then she went over to Hippolytus' body and pulled the sword out, her hands shaking once more as she did so.

How can such a kind, loyal creature be made to die, when such a despicable one can be allowed to live? Tell me, Gods.

The thoughts were weak, and she chided herself, yet she could not stop them, for if anything, her horses had taught her that kindness sows loyalty.

"Stefanos..." she said to herself, thinking of him getting ready to race.

"My lady?" Pirro's voice came from outside the tent.

"I'm coming!" she called. Kyniska walked with the bloody blade hanging loosely in her hand and stepped into the sunlight. When she was outside, she covered her eyes briefly until they adjusted, and then lowered her hand only to hear the girls gasp and Ajax step closer.

"My lady?"

She looked sternly at him, willing him not to speak ill of his king, for it would mean his own death if Agesilaus' men found out, Typhon among them. It was enough that Ajax showed a momentary concern.

"I'm fine. Here." She handed him the sword. "Please see the corpse put upon the pyre. I will light it later."

"Yes, my lady," Ajax said, motioning for a few more men to come with him to carry out the order.

"Did he hit you?" Pirro said, coming up close to Kyniska, his face red with anger.

"Yes," she dismissed it with a wave of her hand.

"I'll get water!" Thais said.

"No!" Kyniska said loudly. "The team is ready, and we are only two days to the race." She turned to Pirro. "We train now. Only training, and caring for them. I want them ready and we need to help them be so. Understand?" Kyniska put her hands on Pirro's shoulders and she felt him calm, his shoulders relaxed as he saw that she was not hurt but for the spiteful scratch upon her beauty.

"Yes, my princess," he said lowly. "Do you want to warm them up first?"

"No. It will be you who leads them in the race. You should do it now. And let them lead you too."

Pirro nodded and stepped up into the chariot's cab.

"Ajax has had guards set around the practice track, my lady," Euryleonis said. "He checked the ground personally for any more dangers."

"Good. Let's go then, and you will see how beauty and perfection can be melded into one."

Kyniska and the four girls followed Pirro and the team as the chariot passed out of the circle of tents and out onto the track which was surrounded by trusted men of Kyniska's bodyguard.

Pirro stopped the chariot on the track and waited as Kyniska inspected each of the horses, talking to them, humming, stroking them. When she had finished, and was satisfied, she stepped back off the track and nodded.

Pirro flicked the reins and the four blacks began to walk around the track, once, twice, before going into a trot, their thick muscles flexing under the sheen of their jet coats.

As their speed picked up, their manes and tails flew in the breeze and the sound of their hooves upon the soft ground became as music. They ran together, no jostling in the corners. Even as Pirro drove them in fast and urged them out of the turns, they charged in unison, and Kyniska could feel a tingle of delight and relief running the length of her spine and up her neck.

She did not care about Agesilaus now, nor his threats of marrying her off. She cared only for the perfection before her, the fruition of her years of ponos.

"Gods, grant us victory," she said to the sky where the sun shone down upon the sanctuary on the other side of the river Kladeos. As she said it, she realized she spoke also of Stefanos, that she wanted victory for him as much as for herself.

It was an odd feeling.

. . .

Stefanos was still sweaty from his run along the river when the horns sounded from the temple of Hera to indicate the procession of the sacred shields.

The pentathlon finished just a few hours past midday, but he had been unable to find Kratos.

Stefanos had watched some of the events and caught Kratos take his turn in the wrestling. At first he had bested his opponent, using his longer limbs to lever some good moves and throws, but his shorter, stalkier opponent, an Euboean, had been unstoppable and Kratos had found himself pinned as the crowd roared like a wave washing over a drowned man on a beach. That had been the last event, and Stefanos had not seen him since, guessed that the points Kratos had accumulated over the days of the pentathlon had not been enough to hand him victory.

Stefanos felt badly for not watching all of Kratos' events that day, but he fancied it a bad idea to be standing still in the crowd of onlookers when he needed to keep his body limber. Now the horns blew loudly over the Altis as he joined the other hoplites for the procession into the stadium.

There were sixty of them standing there, three heats of twenty men who would be whittled down to a final twenty. Stefanos looked at each of the men around him as they waited for the priestess of Hera to finish speaking on the steps of the temple. His opponents were hard men, he could tell, some with well-used armour, like his own, others with richly ornamented thoraxes that cried wealth and favour.

Biton was there, whom he had seen in the temple of Hera the night before. The man glowered at him, as if assessing every inch of him.

Stefanos ignored him and looked upon the priestess as she raised her hands to the sky and called on the goddess to bless the sacred hoplons the men would carry in the running of the race.

The heat was getting to Stefanos and he felt his head throbbing as he stood there, not relishing putting his helmet back on his head. The sun beat down, and as the procession came out of the temple, its light glinted on the polished surfaces of the round shields, blinding some of the crowd.

A song was sung, and the words of the ode spread through the crowd of onlookers.

O mother of gold-crowned contests, Olympia, queen of truth; where men that are diviners observing burnt-offerings make trial of Zeus the wielder of white lightnings, whether he hath any word concerning men who seek in their hearts to attain unto great prowess and a breathing-space from toil; for it is given in answer to the reverent prayers of men - do thou, O tree-clad precint of Pisa by Alpheos, receive this triumph and the carrying of the crown. Great is his glory ever on whom the splendour of thy honour waiteth. Yet this good cometh to one, that to another, and many are the roads to happy life by the grace of gods.

As the last of the shields passed, Stefanos fell in behind them, along with all the other hoplites, to process through the krypte and into the vast stadium.

Until that moment, Stefanos had avoided thinking about the details of competition such as crowds, cheering, and the rank smell of the men next to him - one of sweat, garlic and oil. In war, he never thought of the blood of the men before him, their faces, their lives. He only focussed on his task, of fighting and surviving when the moment came.

However, as he walked into the stadium at Olympia, his first time at the Games, he felt a thrill of nervousness run through his body, like a stallion waiting to charge at the starting line of the hippodrome, champing at its bit in anticipation. It was not a pleasant or unpleasant feeling, but rather an intense one, so concentrated that it was overwhelming.

See the race. Focus! he could hear Pandaros telling him.

Even as he thought that, he saw Axion just below the marble box where the priestess of Demeter Chamayne sat by herself, the only woman permitted in this sea of men. She sat opposite the Hellanodikai, all of them on the south side, wearing their white chitons and purple cloaks. Men formed a sort of wall around the priestess, though none of them paid her any heed.

The last verse of the processional song died down and the final notes of the flute faded as the crowd settled. Two of the theokoloi led a goat onto the stadium floor, followed by their attendants. One of them held a bough of silvery olive leaves, and the other a shining bronze dagger.

"Hear us, oh Mighty Zeus, and Queenly Hera!" the priest began. "Favour this most sacred race and grant the victor everlasting glory among the Greeks."

Stefanos felt a chill, and took a deep breath as he watched the Alpha heat step up to the long, stone starting line, their bare feet finding the groove in the marble from which they would launch themselves. To Stefanos, the distance seemed long to the end, and they needed to run two stades, once there, and then back.

I've run across half of Persia in this armour, Stefanos thought. *Beloved Hera, guide me in this... Father, this is for you and our family... Kyniska...*

Before he knew it, the priests had finished their sacrifice and all that was left on the ground was a red patch of blood which was soaking into the sand and dirt of the stadium floor.

The priests stood before each of the runners holding one of the sacred shields, large round hoplons made of bronze decorated with meander patterns and a peacock in the centre, similar to Stefanos' own shield. The priests handed the runners each a hoplon and the men strapped them onto their left arms.

Stefanos looked down the line to see the muscular, greaved legs bent for the explosive start, the bristling horsehair crests of several of the runners. The leather of their thoraxes creaked, and there were several deep breaths as the priest cleared the way and the starting rope for the mechanism was raised to waist height.

The stadium was silent as the Spartans, an Argive, Athenians, Corinthians, Syracusans and others lined up, waiting to run, sweat already running down their backs, faces and legs.

Down the edges of the stadium, several Hellanodikai were lined up to observe the competitors and make sure there was no cheating to insult the Gods. A wave of anticipation seemed to radiate from those men on the starting line, infecting the crowd along the embankments of the vast space.

Stefanos felt his guts in a knot as he waited, watching, somehow detached from the racers on the line, but fully immersed in his own nervous energy shooting through him.

Then the rope dropped, and the world erupted all around him.

The hoplites shot off the line, their bare feet covering the distance of the first stade quickly, some of them jostling each other, a thump of shield here, a nicked greave there, but all twenty kept on, and the crowd roared approval.

Stefanos felt the hairs on the back of his neck stand on end, as if he were back in the battle line of the phalanx. He flexed his right hand open and closed, feeling the distinct lack of his doru. He and the other runners stepped forward to watch the running hoplites approach the finish when three of them went down in a cloud of dust.

The crowd was on its feet to get a better look, and when the dust settled everyone could see three of the judges pulling apart a Spartan, a Theban, and an unfortunate Cyrenaean who must have got caught up between the two others.

The victor, it seemed, was the Syracusan, followed by two Athenians and another Spartan, then the others. The winner raised his muscular arms aloft holding the sacred shield in one hand, before removing it from his arm and kissing the goddess' emblem.

"Beta group!" one of the Hellanodikai yelled.

Stefanos realized that his heat was up and looked about to see the competitors getting ready, lunging, stretching limbs, jumping up and down. Their eyes peered out of the eye holes of their bronze helmets, making some look like beasts, others like gods. Stefanos was used to this intimidation - how often had he stared into his enemies' eyes in the front line?

He put his helmet on, and took up his position on the starting line, third from the right side, and waited as the judges set up the starting mechanism again, raising the rope and attaching it to the wooden lever at the end.

The first heat of runners stopped along the sides of the stadium to drink water from the marble basins that were a part of the conduit network that supplied the spectators and athletes with fresh water.

Run like the wind. I run into battle, first to the enemy, Stefanos told himself, popping up and down on the spot, firing his muscles and readying himself.

"You'll lose, you know," said a voice beside him.

Stefanos turned to see Biton, his fellow Argive standing there.

"You don't have a chance. You're too old, son of Talos," he said, glancing at Ocnus and the others where they sat watching. He nodded, his blue crest of the Argive Thousand swaying, and laughed. "Just give up now."

Stefanos felt like driving his fist into the man's face, but thought better of it as the judges began to settle in for the race, their eyes already upon the next set of runners.

"Take positions!" one of the judges said.

"Try not to choke on the dirt in my wake," Stefanos said to Biton.

"Ready!" the judge called.

Stefanos glanced at the priestess of Demeter for a moment and saw that she was staring directly at him. He tore his eyes away from her unnerving gaze and stared down the stadium line. His head throbbed within his helmet but he focussed on the run, saw himself pulling ahead of all the others.

The crowd was quiet and then...the rope dropped.

Stefanos shot out, ahead of all twenty from the start, his legs striding longer and faster than all the others, his arms pumping of their own volition as he sped away.

He could hear the crowd crying out, calls of Argos, and of other cities. He could hear the rush of the other hoplites behind him and down the line, a few drawing even with him out of the corner of his left eye, but he was still pulling ahead. The voices of the spectators reached a titanic crescendo before there was a yell from behind him and two runners went down, and Biton pulled even with Stefanos.

The other Argive's arm slammed Stefanos' hoplon, once, twice, three times, but Stefanos stayed up, only just aware of the yelling of the judges.

The man at his side was maddening him and as he saw the finish line come rushing toward him, felt the anticipation of a victory, he was slammed again and instinctively, his shield flew out sideways to swat his harasser and Biton yelled as he crashed forward, his arm reaching out, his hand grabbing hold of Stefanos' ankle, and pulling him down with him.

The hard earth came up into Stefanos' face and chest as he crashed, feeling his arms and thighs scratching on the packed dirt.

"Boooooo!" some of the crowd yelled, while others laughed at the collision.

"Those two are disqualified!" Stefanos heard one of the Hellanodikai yell.

Stefanos looked around confused and dazed. His head pounded as he looked toward the finish line to see the winner and runners up raising their arms to the sky, joyful that they had moved to the final heat.

"You fucking idiot!" Biton cursed from behind him, grabbing Stefanos by the edges of his thorax and shaking him.

"Nice one, Argives!" someone in the crowd yelled.

"Now's not the time to roll around together!" said another to a chorus of raucous laughter.

Men were pointing at the two of them, hurling insults, and as Stefanos felt the tremendous shame that descended upon him then, he grabbed Biton by the hair and was about to pommel him when he felt the intense and stinging thwack of the Hellanodikai's rods upon his arms and legs.

"Do not disgrace the Gods in this place!" one of the judges yelled a them. "You are both out of the competition. Leave the stadium at once!"

The man was intense, spittle running down his mouth as he raged at them.

"All right!" Stefanos said angrily, handing the judge the sacred shield and turning to Biton. "You'll regret this, you piece of shit!"

"No! You will!" Biton said spitting at him before tearing off out of the stadium.

It was a shameful walk out of the stadium, the eyes of forty-five thousand of his fellow Greeks on him, harassing him, laughing at him, mocking him.

Stefanos felt sick, foolish, and weak. He also felt like killing them all, wishing at that moment that he had his own hoplon and doru in his hands.

Maybe that is all I am...a killer! he raged at himself as he went down the tunnel of the krypte, the jeers echoing around him, flushing him out of the stadium as the gamma heat prepared to run. *Kakochartos!* he could hear his father saying.

Still dressed in his armour, his face hidden by his crested helmet, Stefanos plodded through the Altis in fury. He searched for Biton, but he was nowhere to be seen.

His head pounded more than ever with his quickened pulse, and a part of him thought that it was good he could not find Biton at that moment, for he would surely have killed him without hesitation, right there in front of the temple of Zeus.

The temple.

Stefanos stopped at the triangular base of the statue of

Nike, Goddess of Victory, and had to turn his head away from her, ashamed. He looked up the steps to the massive doric columns of the temple, at the scene in the pediment depicting Zeus standing between the wicked Oinomaus on his right, and Pelops and Hippodameia on his left, their chariots ready for that fateful race from Olympia to Argos.

The statues seemed to move before him, from where they stood high above the sacred ground of the Altis - Oinomaus checking the tip of his spear which he had used to kill his daughter's suitors, Pelops leaning on his, calm, confident, and knowing.

Stefanos removed his helmet and rubbed his eyes to look up again. The horses of the two chariot teams stomped and rolled their chariots back and forth. Then Hippodameia turned to look down at Stefanos, her eyes full of dread and sadness, but also hidden depths of courage and of love. She did not weep this time as she looked upon Stefanos, but shook her head and raised an arm to pat the four horses standing behind her.

Stefanos tore his eyes away to look at Zeus, King of the Gods, great and powerful, majestic, every muscle of his torso writhing, with fire in his veins. The bearded head turned toward Stefanos then and he felt his knees buckle as he gripped Nike's pedestal.

The mortal man vomited on the spot, flashes of sacrifice and blood spilling over his thoughts, clouding the world around him. He felt like he was falling again, prostrate in the dirt, trampled by a hundred warriors, unable to see or feel, to lift his head.

The great bronze doors to the temple opened then and one of the priests came walking down the stairs. He was robed all in white, the fringes of his himation stained red. He walked toward Stefanos, his face a mixture of disdain and concern.

"Do you wish to make an offering to Olympian Zeus?" the priest asked, bending over a little so that Stefanos could see him from his crouched position.

Stefanos looked up, his brow sweaty, a string of spittle hanging from his mouth.

"Did the Gods not favour you with victory?" the man asked, not unkindly.

"I was pushed in the race and disqualified," Stefanos said.

"Then you were not meant to win."

"What?"

"Listen to me, Argive." The old man extended his arm and offered it to Stefanos, pulling him to his feet. "I've been priest here for several Olympiads. I've seen men win, and then come to nothing for the rest of their lives."

"Is that supposed to be of comfort, old man?"

The priest ignored the jibe, smiling. "I've also seen men lose...shamed...unable to return to their homes...unwelcome because of their loss. I've seen these men fall to the greatest depths of despair, and then be lifted up by the Gods themselves." He looked up at the statue of Nike above them, her marble wings radiant against the blue, summer sky. He then looked back at Stefanos.

"But these fallen men must take the first step and lift themselves out of the dirt. Only then will the Gods care."

Stefanos backed away from the priest, shaking his head, looking from the old man to the open temple doors and back.

Then, he turned and ran southeast across the Altis, passed the sanctuary of Hestia, and along the banks of the Alpheios river until he hit the outside embankment of the hippodrome and reached the top.

There he stopped, and fell to his knees, his fists pounding the ground several times before he lay on his back to stare at the sky above.

Gods, what have I done? How can I be worthy of her now?

He did not even realize he had thought it, but once he did, it made sense to him that Kyniska popped into his mind, like the first spring flower breaking through the winter-beaten earth. He focused on that, and began to breathe more calmly, until he fell asleep.

. . .

SLEEP ALWAYS AIDED IN THE ACT OF FORGETTING, BUT NOT FOR long. The solution was temporary, Stefanos knew. However many men he had killed and tried to forget, no amount of sleep ever banished them from his mind. He had never fully wanted to forget.

It was the sound of hoof beats that roused him.

At first he thought it was another vision or dream coming upon him, and he jumped up, looking for the ghostly apparition that seemed to haunt his dreams. However it was no shade that came at him. He turned to look down the other side of the embankment and before him, spread out like a titanic plaything for the Gods, was the great hippodrome of Olympia.

The track stretched from west to east, over four stades long, dwarfing the stadium to the north of it. Great embankments swept up from the raked dirt expanse of the track, just as the land rises from a still sea, where over one-hundred thousand spectators would sit to watch the equine competitions of the Games, including the four-horse chariot race.

Stefanos leaned on the low retaining wall at the top and watched two teams speeding around the track, tiny on the ground, as if they were the marbles of a colossus. Dust clouds whipped around them in the heat of the day, and Stefanos wondered at the thought of young Pirro racing with nineteen other chariot teams there, before thousands of Greeks.

He also thought of the pressure upon Kyniska, that if she lost before so many, her humiliation would be absolute. What was his loss compared to that possibility?

The words of his father's ghost wracked his spirit, and he felt a world of weight pressing down upon him, threatening to buckle his body and soul.

What if I fail?

What if Kyniska fails?

He knew that if he lost, he would simply return to the

battlefield on some far-flung soil, perhaps in the employ of one of the Black Sea lords. If Kyniska lost, where would she go? Where could a Spartan princess disappear to?

For so long, Stefanos had thought himself invincible, but as he stared at the circuit of the hippodrome, the central spine, and the statue of Hippodameia looking down on the starting gates from her lofty pedestal, a woman to be honoured and revered, he felt as though he were weak and inconsequential.

Kakochartos began to creep back into his veins and it felt like a poison to him, for all his father's talk of Eris Agathos and Philotimo. Stefanos, son of Talos, shook with rage at the person he had become, he, his mother's son. He was the only member of a family that honoured the Gods with their actions, who had done the exact opposite.

Stefanos turned away from the Hippodrome and walked back down the embankment to the Alpheios where he placed his helmet on the stony ground and splashed water on his face.

He knew he could not face walking back through the sanctuary, especially now that he heard the echo of victory celebrations ringing in the Altis and around the Bouleuterion.

Still wearing his armour, he crossed the river and began making a large circle south and west to approach the Spartan camp from the south side, draped as he was in shame and guilt.

Nightfall came, and the Spartan camp was quiet as those competing in the wrestling, boxing, and pankration the following day rested for competition. In other camps, the mood was jovial, prematurely celebratory, but in the Spartan camp, there was an air of silent preparation, both mental and physical. The mood was solemn.

Kyniska paced the floor of her tent by herself, the flames from the oil lamps flickering violently each time she passed them. She did not notice, but her hands were braced together in worry and rage.

She had heard what happened. Many, including her brother, had been sure to tell her of the Argive's disgrace in the stadium, how he had run out, a mockery of andreia. There was talk that he had been tripped by one of his fellow Argives, but also that he had tired toward the end of the race and dropped from exhaustion, swaying on his feet for a few steps before crashing to the ground.

"Goddess Hera," Kyniska said, stopping in the middle of the tent and holding her palms up, eyes closed. "May his honour be intact. Help him to overcome this disaster."

Even as the words left her mouth, Euryleonis came running in.

"My lady," she whispered.

Kyniska turned to see Stefanos walking slowly into the tent.

"Leave us, Euryleonis."

"Yes, my lady."

Kyniska looked upon the man who had left her that morning, his sad, soiled armour, the limp crest of his helmet which hid his hanging head.

She hardly recognized him. When she had seen the Argive hoplite in his armour the first time, he had seemed so proud, unbeatable, and confident.

But isn't that just when the Gods knock us down? she thought as he stood before her, a dejected shadow of the man she could not shake from her mind.

She tried to stanch the anger she was feeling, and not a little revulsion at his indulgence in weakness.

"Stand up, Stefanos, son of Talos," Kyniska commanded. "Stand tall, as you should!"

His shoulders went back and his head went up, but his eyes would not meet hers. There was shame there, oh yes, frustration and the knowing that he was being weak, and all the self-loathing that that brought with it.

"I'm sorry," he said, still not looking at her.

"For what?"

"For shaming you."

"It's not me who is shamed so much as you, and your city."

"Damn Argos to Hades for all I care," he growled.

"And you?"

Stefanos looked at her then, no words, just a look, and Kyniska stepped forward.

"I would not have you damned to Hades for the idiocy of one of your fellow Argives."

"I should have killed him on the spot, salvaged some of my honour and not shamed you."

"What then?" She stepped closer again. "Then you would be executed for breaking the Gods' laws at Olympia. You cannot kill during the Sacred Truce, let alone within the hallowed grounds of the sanctuary."

Kyniska saw the ignition of a spark in his posture, and knew he was starting to pick himself up out of the muck into which he had thrown himself.

She took his hand and led him to one of the couches where she sat him down and began to undo his armour. He did not try to touch her, or assume he should have her affection, and she knew that if he had tried, she would have throttled him. She was heartened to see that he was not such a man as that, but she also knew he needed words, as all men do when they have fallen hard.

"You remember the tales of the heroes, of Perseus and Herakles, Jason, Achilles and others?"

"Of course. All do."

"Yes, but not all of them fully understand."

He said nothing, but Kyniska continued.

"All of these heroes that men revere, reached great heights of achievement. When you think on them, they are what you all strive to be." Kyniska succeeded in undoing the straps of his thorax and removed it from his torso, laying it on the ground beside his helmet. As she continued speaking, she removed his sweaty chiton and greaves, and then dipped a sponge in water and began to wipe his shoulders, torso, arms and legs.

"You don't need to do that," he said, trying to stop her.

"I'll do as I like," she answered curtly. "All these heroes...do you think they succeeded from the outset - in their training, in war, in politics, in life - or did they fail, have false starts, like an eager stallion at the starting gate?"

Stefanos shrugged, but she could tell he was listening.

"You know as well as I, my despondent Argive, that they all fell at one time or another before the Gods crowned them with glory and everlasting renown. It is the same in Sparta, in the Agoge. Do you think every Spartan warrior came out of the womb perfect for battle, fearless, blessed by the fates with strength, and skill, and courage?"

"Of course not," Stefanos said.

"No. In the Agoge, they all fell at one time or another, they all lost, they were all beaten and scourged." She stood straight up, great pride in her demeanour. "But they got up, again and again, out of the mud and blood pouring from their many wounds. They were forced to get up, for they knew they would not be men if they didn't."

She tossed the sponge into the bronze basin on the nearby tripod and knelt before Stefanos.

"This life we live, it is one big Agoge. We will fall, we will be beaten and," she nodded, "and we will bleed. Oh yes. But by the Gods, Stefanos," she grabbed hold of his face with her wet hands. "We must get up and fight on! That is what the heroes did that few other precious men can do or have done."

Kyniska stared into his eyes and he saw passion and fire there, felt warmth flowing once more through his entire body and soul.

She saw his chest begin to heave again, slowly, strongly, his jaw set, his eyes not flinching from hers this time.

"Get up, Stefanos, and fight!"

Stefanos stood up and walked over the brazier where he stared at the flames without speaking.

Kyniska stood too, disappointment settling in painfully as she began to believe that he was giving way to his despair again as his head bent. She did not know how he must have felt, for he had had a long road to this point, meeting death and the ghosts of heroes, enough to drive any man mad. As she began to prepare to eject him from her presence as a drain upon her strength, she did not know that he was fanning the flame she had started, into a blaze to burn the entire world about them.

Kyniska thought she would try one last time as he stood there with his back to her.

"If you will not think of yourself, go back to thinking of me and my honour. I'm a descendant of Helen of Sparta! Would you give up after being rebuffed once upon the high walls of Troy? Or would you lay siege to those god-built walls of your own ego and self-pity for me, for us? Would you rather break yourself upon them? Tell me now, for my brother has planned to marry me off, and by the Gods, I will have none of it!"

Stefanos whipped around and strode toward her. "You think I would not burn down the world for you? That my own self-pity is so powerful as to make me forget you, or the threats of the shades that have haunted me?"

"Then what?"

He was about to say that he cared for her. Tender words were about to spill from his mouth, clumsy and childish, but he bit them back.

"Tomorrow, I'm going to fight, Kyniska. I'm going to step onto the skamma and meet every man who comes against me with all the strength I can muster. By the Gods, I swear it!"

Stefanos did not know it, but he was shaking, his fervour showing in his body, every muscle and tendon, the piercing gaze of his eyes as he looked upon the woman before him.

Without a word, Kyniska grabbed him and kissed him,

lifted up in his arms immediately to banish all thoughts of loss and despair.

As they made love, she thanked the Gods that she had been able to pull him out of the darkness, and she prayed that he would not plunge back into it.

Chapter Ten

TRUE STRENGTH

Αληθινή Δύναμη

The fourth day of the Olympiad dawned with grey clouds in the summer sky, unusual for the time of year, an ill-omen, and so a source of worry.

In her tent, Kyniska sat up in her bed, alone, staring at the newly-polished thorax, helmet, and greaves which Stefanos had left behind. The first rays of light had just emerged to pierce the clouds with their shafts, but Stefanos had gone long before.

Of course she had known he was awake in the night, and had respected his need to be alone with his thoughts on the eve of battle. It would be a long day, and she had her own work to do in preparing her team for the chariot race on day five. She needed to keep busy, to focus on them, her children, those who had ever been loyal to her.

However, Kyniska, no matter how much she may have wished to keep her thoughts fully focussed on her own race, could not help sparing a thought for Stefanos who would spend the day on the skamma before his mocking countrymen and men of all the other Greek city-states. His toils would increase ten-fold that day, and at her altar, she prayed to the Gods that he would be victorious.

Once dressed, she went to the entrance of her tent and stared at the smoky sky above the Altis and temple of Olympian Zeus. She knew Stefanos was there, at that moment, praying for the strength that he knew he needed.

HE WALKED BAREFOOT, WEARING ONLY HIS BRACAE AND chiton, carrying the satchel which contained his himantes, oil, and the dagger which he had worn across the world, marching from Greece, to Persia, and back.

Stefanos stood before the temple of Zeus in the dim, early morning light, looking up at the home of the god. He ignored the spot behind him where he had fallen in a pathetic heap the previous day, that man feeling so foreign to him at the moment that he was someone else entirely.

When the first rays of light spread across the roof top and the faces of the lions at the corners of the temple, the theokoloi opened the great bronze doors of Zeus' temple.

Stefanos walked up the steps.

One of the priests stood on the top step, looking out at the Altis, smiling, before his eyes fell on Stefanos. "Back again?"

Stefanos saw that it was the man who had tried to help him the previous day.

"I was not myself yesterday," he said.

"We never are when despair hammers on our souls," the man said. "I see strength in you today, however. Do you wish to make an offering to Olympian Zeus?"

"Yes."

"Enter now, then. For you have the god's ear all to yourself." The man then turned and walked around the side of the temple, leaving Stefanos alone to go inside.

He walked forward, over the threshold of the monstrous doors that could have guarded the heights of Olympus for all he knew. It was dark inside, and as he allowed his eyes to adjust, Stefanos saw the firelight rise to illuminate the cedar roof from where Zeus' lofty head stared down at him. He froze. The world was so still, in sound and sight, but for the rustle of the god's golden robes and the flutter of Nike's wings where she stood on the right palm of Zeus.

The chryselephantine statue of Zeus, created by the artist Pheidias within the sanctuary, was titanic, mesmerizing and terrifying at once. Stefanos walked forward until he came to the main altar, a table of pure white marble with reliefs of the Gigantomachy, that famous battle between the Gods and Giants. Beyond the altar, a pool of pure olive oil flanked by burning braziers lit the entire statue of Zeus so that he appeared to live and breathe before his suppliants.

Zeus' broad chest rose and fell, calm, powerful. His muscular arms flexed, the one holding Nike, Goddess of Victory, the other his great staff on which perched his eagle.

The throne on which Zeus sat also sprang to life. The lions at the base roared and snarled at Stefanos as he stood before them, the Muses danced around its golden legs, and the sphinxes upon the armrests shifted their wings, their breasts flexing, proud, the faces questioning of the mortal man.

Stefanos fell to his knees, only his strong arms holding him to the edge of the great altar, clinging as if he hung from a precipice to which he pulled himself up with supreme effort and will.

In the shadows, some of the theokoloi hovered, like white wraiths, but they did not disturb this man who came to lay an offering upon the altar of Zeus. They knew the meaning of such things, the need for men to make them, the need for the Gods to receive them.

"Great Father Zeus..." Stefanos began, steadying his breathing, then calming his shaking limbs until he was perfectly still and at peace. "I have marched across this world of yours, blind and weakened by Kakochartos." He shook his head. "It was never my intent to come to

Olympia." Stefanos looked down from Zeus's stern gaze to see the marble of the altar, polished of blood, oiled and shining like the god himself. He could hear lions roaring and the flutter of victory high above, but he dared not look up. Not yet.

"I am but a mortal man, Great Zeus, and I have made many mistakes in my life. My toils may not have been pleasing, but that has changed. My own father, please see that he is well wherever he wanders, he spoke to me of philotimo, and of Eris Agathos... I did not understand these things before, but I do now, and a part of me feels that by his death, my father Talos sought to save me from myself."

Stefanos felt his eyes burning then as he remembered his father's face in life...in ghostly death... He then reached into his satchel and pulled out the dagger that had saved his life in the battle line many a time, and laid it upon the altar of Zeus so that the sound echoed up to the cedar rafters of the temple as he raised his palms and his eyes to the ivory and gold visage of Zeus.

"Grant me the strength to create something of beauty this day, Great Zeus. I honour you, and I shall seek the victory that I've been told lays before me, with all of my strength, body and spirit. Grant me victory this day, for myself, for my father and family...and for her. I am ready."

WHEN STEFANOS STEPPED OUT OF THE TEMPLE, IT WAS WITH A mixture of awe and anticipation that he looked out from the top of the steps toward the stadium where he would compete later that day.

It was a day of battles, the fourth day of the Olympiad, when men would meet on the skamma in the wrestling, boxing, and pankration.

Stefanos went to the temple of Hera, as he did before every battle, to pray to the goddess with a little hope that his mother would hear him wherever she was. He did not stay long, and made a simple offering of a bunch of wild herbs which he picked near the Prytaneion.

"Today is the day, oh goddess. You have always been with me. Do not desert me now, I pray. Mother Hera...whisper to my own mother that she is ever in my thoughts, over all these long years of battle, that she has kept me from the brink."

As he knelt with his eyes closed, Stefanos felt a chill on the air, and something touch his shoulder, light, gentle. He dared not open his eyes this time for fear that it would sap his strength. When the touch left his shoulder, he stood, bowed to the statue of the goddess and turned. As he went, he passed the faces of the women who had been victorious in the Heraia, and prayed that Kyniska would be victorious once again, this time in the Olympiad.

HE WAS THE FIRST ONE AT THE PALAESTRA, AND AXION WAS waiting for him.

"Any advice?" Stefanos asked the gymnasiarchos.

The old, muscled man smiled and shook his head. "You have the skill, Argive. Don't waste it, your last chance at glory."

Stefanos smiled, removed his tunic, and stuffed it inside his satchel.

"When does the boxing take place?"

"The wrestling, boxing, and pankration will take place simultaneously throughout the day. There are many competitors in each event, so they need to keep things moving."

"Short bouts then."

"Not necessarily. I've seen a boxing match go on for almost an entire day. It ends only when a man is knocked out, when the hellanodikai think he is no longer fit to fight, or when one of the fighters submits."

"How many bouts do you think I'll have to fight?"

"Based on the numbers I've seen, if you go all the way, I would say about three. There are always instances where a man passes a round without having to fight too, because of odd numbers. We'll see." Axion smiled and looked Stefanos up and down. "I think you should stop asking me questions now and warm yourself up. Gently mind you!" He held up his hand. "You don't want to tire yourself. After that, get yourself oiled in the elaiothesion, and then strap on your himantes. If you end up going first, you want to be ready."

Stefanos nodded, slapped Axion on the shoulder, and set off at a light jog around the outer edge of the palaestra sand.

Time for battle... he told himself, going over his own ritual. *I won't die today. I am fast!* He punched out quickly, one-two. *I am strong!* he waved his arms back and forth, up and down. *I can win!*

With every stride, punch, feint, and parry, he began to see victory, to feel his opponents crumple beneath his fists. As he leaned into the korikoi, from lightest to heaviest, and back, he felt stronger and stronger, his body telling him that it was time, that he was ready to win, or else to die trying. For men did die on the skamma, often enough.

But Stefanos, son of Talos, was not afraid of death. He and death had come to terms a long time ago on that first battlefield outside of Hysiae. Where Phobos haunted him was in his wish to fulfill his promise to his father, and in his growing feelings for Kyniska.

As he finished his last sprint on the sand, the hot sun burning down on him, the clouds gone, Stefanos pictured twin blazing bronzes of himself and Kyniska in the sacred grounds of the Altis for all to see. Phobos could not keep him from attaining that. Fear was not so powerful as that.

Kyniska...I'm ready.

THE ALTIS WAS SILENT AS THE THEOKOLOI MADE THE DAY'S sacrifices to honour Zeus at the great altar north of the temple. The muted breathing of hundreds of men could be heard, as all bowed their heads toward the altar where the black ram was sacrificed, his blood running down the sides of the high altar, smoke from the thigh bones whirling about the competitors heads like ghostly laurels, a possibility of glory.

Stefanos stood among them, his body bare but for the himantes about his fists and forearms, and the fresh oil that covered every inch of him.

He had tied his hands and wrists tightly, methodically, wrapping the first layer of linen neatly between each of his fingers and around his knuckles, before placing the rawhide strips in their exact positions around his fists so as not to break any finger bones upon impact. He had done this a hundred times before, and yet it felt like the first time. The solid hide was now wrapped again by another layer of linen that would be changed the bloodier and more torn it got.

When he had tested the fit on the korikoi back in the palaestra, they felt solid, perfectly weighted. He looked around and knew that some of his opponents might be using lead instead of rawhide, but the latter made him faster, and speed was his ally.

The theokoloi concluded the sacrifices and the horns and flutes blasted throughout the Altis, readying the assembled for the procession into the stadium where the embankments were already lined with thousands of spectators from far and wide.

Now that the Gods had been honoured, men's arrogance and bluster began to spill out around him. Some flexed and grunted as they waved their arms to warm up. Others told their competitors that they would not last one bout, that they had no right to be there.

Stefanos hated the head games men played, and hoped that he would not be bothered by such things, that people would not recognize him without his armour from the previous day. However, one of the Athenians spotted Stefanos and laughed out loud!

"There's that Argive! Don't trip and hurt yourself before you reach the stadium old man!"

Stefanos ignored the comment, and tried very hard to do

the same with the rising chorus that echoed the mockery of the first. Men began to turn toward him and chuckle, others shrugged and got on with their own business.

As they stepped into the krypte, Stefanos could see the stadium stretch out ahead of them, just above the heads of the men before him.

The sound that greeted the athletes as they emerged from the krypte was like an angry wave upon a harbour wall in winter. It was deafening and the sound of the instruments at their head was immediately drowned out by thousands of Greeks screaming for blood and victory and the honour of their cities.

Stefanos gripped his satchel and followed the boxers to the space at the middle of the stadium. The wrestlers took their positions near the krypte, whilst the pankrationists, including a few dressed as Herakles in his lion skin, continued on to the far end of the stadium.

Hellanodikai stood everywhere, watchful, dressed in their white and purple chitons and carrying the rods with which they administered the Games' justice. Two of them stood at each of the six circular skammata that had been laid out, two for each event. The rest of the Hellanodikai sat in the stands, opposite the boxing area and the seat of the priestess of Demeter Chamayne.

Food vendors went along the embankments flogging their wares to the waiting crowd, and a steady flow of people came down and back up the embankment to get water from the small reservoirs along the edges of the stadium.

Stefanos could see Pollux in the distance, at the pankration area, waiting for his bout. The Spartan looked calm enough.

"Stefanos!" someone yelled.

He turned to see Xenophon waving at him from near the priestess of Demeter. Seated with him, toward the front row were Plato and Isocrates, while a little further along were Thrasybulos and his group of followers. Stefanos walked over and saw that some of the Athenians were laughing at him.

"Stefanos!" Xenophon waved him over.

"What is it?" Stefanos said, not fully pleased to see him, until he saw the kind look in his old friend's eyes.

"Take'em to Hades, my friend," he said, nodding grimly.

Stefanos nodded and turned back. He could not help noticing that on the other side of the stadium, above the Hellanodikai was a group of red cloaks, King Agesilaus among them. Beside them, where the Thessalians.

Focus! he told himself as one of the Hellanodikai stepped forward to address the boxers, just as cheers erupted from where the first wrestling match had begun.

"Boxers! May Zeus be with you in this sacred event!" the judge called out as a clay amphora was brought out and another judge reached into it to pull out a shard of pottery with a letter on it. "Kappa!" he yelled and two men stepped forward with their own shards, handing them to the judge.

Stefanos and all the other boxers moved to the edges of the stadium to give the men room and allow the crowds a good look of the Macedonian and the Elean who had stepped forward.

"Fight for Elis!" someone yelled and the crowd took up the chant.

The young fighter waved to his supporters and began to hop from one leg to the other until the judge came to inspect both his, and the Macedonian's himantes for anything illegal, maiming edges or harder materials besides hide or lead.

"Step onto the skamma!" the judge said and they did. The Macedonian looked as if he could wrestle a bear, and he had the fists to match. He seemed unphased by the Elean before him, and even as the music rose and the rod dropped, he did not move right away. Instead, he let the Elean dance about, this way and that, each move garnering cheers from the crowd.

Finally, the Elean moved in with a feint and three punch combination that roused the Macedonian and caught the big man on the shoulder. When he came back, it was fast, and for a moment Stefanos thought he could see where he was headed, that is until the Macedonian's bear-fist shot out and caught the Elean on the side of the head, sending him flying right out of the skamma, unconscious.

Men jeered and laughed, others stood still and shocked at the quickness of the bout. For Stefanos, he thought that the day would hold many surprises, and hoped that he would not end up like the Elean.

As the boxers made their way off the sand, Stefanos saw Typhon several feet away. The Spartan was staring at him with such hate that it made the hairs on his neck stand on end, but he rallied himself and stared back, nodding to Typhon. He had seen the look men have in their eyes when they are intent on killing. He could clearly see that look in the Spartan's eyes.

"Looks like you've made a few enemies, Stefanos."

That voice! Stefanos looked to his right to see Ocnus standing beside him, his lean, muscled arms crossed casually over his chest, his himantes of lead glinting dully in the sunlight where they peeked out between the top layers of linen.

"So, the Gods might just see fit to pit us against each other. "

"Then you can start counting your time to humiliation, Ocnus. You already smell of fear."

Ocnus, rather than get angry, smiled and chuckled. "That's the boy I had last night. Nothing like taking someone before a fight."

"You've never had a real fight in your life, Ocnus." Stefanos turned to him now, disdain in his eyes, even as the sound of the next bout shook the air. "You've always hidden yourself behind the walls of Argos when you should have been outside of them, defending them rather than terrorizing your fellow citizens."

"You have no idea. I've killed men on the skamma, you

arrogant piece of shit. And today, I'm going kill you once and for all."

"Get away from me before you get hurt. Tripping people in there," he pointed to the sand where another fighter fell in the dust, blood pouring from his brow, "won't help you today."

"I know you more than you think I do. I've learned things about you from your idiot friend, Kratos. Did you know he talks about anything when he's drunk? About your family, about your journey east...about how you fight?"

Stefanos tried to hide his shock, but Ocnus sniffed his discomfort.

"Yes. You have no tricks left which I do not know. Your father's shade will be disappointed today."

Ocnus laughed and went back to where he had been sitting with his fellow competitors.

Focus, Stefanos repeated to himself. *Eris Agathos...Philotimo... Focus.*

Three more bouts finished, two of them taking twenty minutes, and one of those ending with the death of a fighter, his head cracked open from a heavy double-punch to the same spot.

Blood dotted the sand then and the body was taken from the skamma, a solemn procession out of the stadium.

Stefanos had seen the man getting tired, knew that if he did not surrender, he would leave himself open to an attack. When Typhon walked off the skamma, he looked coldly at Stefanos, and pounded his bloody fists that had just taken a fighter's life.

He had begun to grow stiff as he watched the other fighters, so he began to jump up and down, stretch his limbs, and shadow box, just enough to stay limber and ready without tiring.

"Psi!" called the Hellanodikai all of a sudden. "Who has Psi?"

A broad Cyrenaean stepped forward and onto the skamma, but the Hellanodikai continued to look around.

"Who else has Psi?" he yelled above the din of the pankration bout that had just ended.

Stefanos picked up his satchel and looked inside for his shards and saw the letter.

"Psi!" he yelled. "I have it! That's me!"

Laughter washed over him as he crossed to the other skamma near to Xenophon on the north side.

"The Argive doesn't even know it's his turn!" someone yelled.

"Maybe he'll do a dance for us?" said another.

The Cyrenaean who was Stefanos' opponent began to laugh heartily as he eyed his competitor, indicating to his countrymen in the crowd that it would be an easy win.

"You ready, girly?" he said to Stefanos as he stepped onto the skamma and showed his fists to the hellanodikai.

"Oh, I'm ready, hairy. You're going to help me warm up," Stefanos said, moving his neck from side to side and bouncing from one leg to the other.

"He's dancing for us!" one of the Athenians said.

Father, Stefanos thought. *I'm ready. Focus, Stefanos! This is it!*

"Pygme!" the judge yelled and his rod came out from between the two fighters.

They circled each other slowly at first, Stefanos light on his feet, anticipating, judging. He feinted once, twice, three times to see how the Cyrenaean would react.

The tightly bound fists always pointed at Stefanos' head, no matter which way he went, and that told him he could hit him if he darted in, but was he fast?

Tired of waiting, the Cyrenaean lunged with a flurry of swings, and Stefanos dodged each, one-two-three, and then followed up with an upper-cut to the jaw that cracked the man's teeth. The impact felt good, and Stefanos began to relax, as he did after the first spear thrust in the shield wall.

"Stop dancing and fight!" the Cyrenaean said, spitting two teeth and a gob of his own blood.

Stefanos smiled and nodded. "Come, let's see what you've learned in the fighting pits of Cyrene!"

"Ahh!" the man swung in a wide arc, trying to force Stefanos into his other, oncoming fist, but before he knew it, the Argive was behind him dealing a blow to the back of his head.

The Cyrenaean wheeled around and was met by another punch to his nose. He swung, missing as he howled, missing again, unable to catch the fighter before him, and received another two punches to either side of his face, and then a third to his forehead that landed him on his back, groaning in the clotted sand.

Stefanos stood over his opponent, the crowd roaring wild, urging the Cyrenaean to get up, but the man, try as he might, could not gain his feet.

Finally he raised his finger in surrender, and Stefanos nodded as the judge pointed to him as the winner of the bout.

The shouts of approval were few and far between for Stefanos. Most had wanted to jeer, but found themselves unable to do so.

"Well done, Stefanos!" Xenophon yelled.

Stefanos waved to him and walked back to his spot along the water channel, his eyes meeting Agesilaus' for a brief moment, the Spartan king seemingly silent and severe as a statue.

Thank you, Gods... Stefanos said as he prepared for his next bout.

THE SUN WAS HIGH, AND THE SOUNDS OF VICTORY AND DEFEAT echoed across the stadium of Olympia into the hottest time of day. The sun beat down on the entire mass of writhing spectators and grunting, bleeding competitors.

The crowd had shifted along the embankments as the noise from either the wrestling or pankration reached a crescendo. With the excitement of a particular match, the spectators moved back to their original positions to catch bouts as they continued.

Stefanos felt as though he were waiting on the battlefield for a mass engagement to take place, biding his time in tortured anticipation of the conflicts to come. He knelt, stood, stretched, and jogged on the spot, drinking and eating sparingly in case he was called up next.

The men around him did the same, but he did not talk with any of them. His mind was focussed on the fights-to-come, and so he ignored those whom he recognized, Ocnus among them. He also noticed Typhon destroying men on the boxing skamma, and wondered if the Gods would pit him against the Spartan.

"Omega!" the Hellanodikai yelled at the end of the second round, and Stefanos stood up to walk over to the skamma to skattered heckling from the crowd.

"It's the dancing man from Argos!" someone yelled.

"Let's see him against this one!" said another, and the crowd turned to see Stefanos' opponent.

"Stefanos of Argos versus Antipater of Macedon!" the judge yelled as a tall, thick man walked onto the sand opposite him.

Antipater was not overly muscled, but solid-looking. His ears were permanently swollen, and his face puffy and bruised. He had huge fists.

Stefanos looked across at his opponent and noticed that he did not move very lightly on his feet. However, despite the obvious hits his head had taken, he saw that Antipater's eyes were supremely alert, that he was aware of everything his body did. It was obvious that the Macedonian could take many hits without his senses being dulled to uselessness.

"Take the Argive to Hades!" someone yelled, and out of the corner of his eye, Stefanos could see it was Aeson of Thessaly who had yelled it from the centre of his group.

Stefanos walked out to the centre of the skamma, rocking

his neck from one side to the other, loosening his limbs, arms and legs, flexing his wrapped fists.

"Before the Gods," the judge said, "I charge you to fight fairly and honourably. Pygme!"

The judge jumped back and watched as they circled each other like wolves, reluctant to jump into the fight.

Stefanos moved slowly at first, trying to tempt the Macedonian into an attack, but the man did not take the bait.

The crowd cried for action, for blood, but neither man dared make the first move.

Stefanos darted in and out, feinting, jabbing, but Antipater stayed where he was, walking slowly around, his arms down by his waist, leaving his face wide open.

Only one way to get this one to do something, Stefanos thought, before weaving in to take a right jab at the Macedonian's head.

The punch that came up from below nearly knocked Stefanos' teeth out, grazing the side of his cheek, as he got out of the way just in time. He could feel a little blood trickling from below his eye.

Now, I've got you, he laughed, the cries from the crowd only serving to spur him on. He made the same move again, but this time was ready for the counter punch and got out of the way even as his left hand smashed into Antipater's head on the right side. His follow-up missed, but the Macedonian was now angered.

Stefanos continued to move quickly in and out, landing a hit every fourth attempt, narrowly missing getting hit with one of those lead-covered fists.

The fight dragged on and on, and Stefanos struggled to see how he could win this bout without taking a serious injury, until the Macedonian rushed in with a speed he had not hitherto revealed, knocking Stefanos to the very edge of the skamma so that he teetered on the edge and had to jump out of the way of a punch that would have sent him into the crowd.

There was a roar of approval and laughter, and now Stefanos, conscious of the energy he was wasting, crouched low to the attack, searching for a gap in the Macedonian's defences.

Antipater's swings became wider and more arcing as Stefanos tempted him into further attacks, darting in and out, revealing the sides of his torso.

Then Antipater swung so quickly, seeking the knock-out the crowd cried for, that Stefanos was able to drop beneath the arm and bring his fist up into the Macedonian's jaw so hard that the sound of cracking teeth was audible. Antipater swayed and before the judge could come in, Stefanos followed up with a right to the left side of the man's head, driving his face into the dirt for good measure.

The judge checked the Macedonian and then rose to point at Stefanos, declaring him the winner.

Stefanos breathed rapidly, his lungs filling and exhaling the dusty, sweat-tanged air.

He made his way back to his spot and drank deeply of the water that ran in the channels along the stadium's edges.

"Come now, Argive!" someone yelled from above. "Give us a good match! No more dancing!"

Stefanos looked up to see a group of Athenian youths laughing in his direction and wondered what that sort of man would do for the great city. They were all bluster, hobby fighters. However, not far down the line, closer to the wrestling, he saw the tall form of Ajax looking his way, nodding to himself before turning to leave the stadium.

"Alpha!" the Hellanodikai yelled again.

Stefanos continued to drink, dabbing his face to see the blood upon his hand.

"Stefanos of Argos!" the call came. "We're waiting for you!"

Already? Stefanos wondered, turning to see dozens of eyes upon him.

"You're up again, Argive!" said one of the Syracusans. "Go on!"

Stefanos rose, a little slowly, and stared at the far skamma. He walked over.

"You ready?" the judge asked.

"Yes," Stefanos said, gazing across the skamma at Ocnus' friend, Ampyx.

The blond Argive stared with relish at Stefanos, his longer hair tied back, his muscles flexing, arms waving. He was shorter, but powerful, and well-proportioned.

A group of the Argive Thousand chanted Ampyx's name from the slopes, led by Ocnus and others.

"You're finished, son of Talos," Ampyx said, rolling his shoulders.

"Fight honourably, for your city!" the judge said, staring at the two men who obviously hated each other. "Pygme!"

Ampyx charged in immediately, a heavy fist aimed directly at Stefanos' nose, but Stefanos had been ready for it, had seen Ampyx practice that attack in the palaestra, and side-stepped to the right, bringing his fist hard into the side of Ampyx's head so that the Argive crashed into the dirt and did not move.

Now, we're even! Stefanos thought as he stood over the limp body of Ocnus' friend, a few more cheers from the crowd washing over them, directed this time at him.

"The dancer is invincible!" someone yelled to scattered applause and good-humoured laughter.

"One hit!" called others. "The Gods have not turned on him fully!"

None of the cheers came from his fellow Argives, and Stefanos did not care. When the Hellanodikai pointed to him as victor of the bout, he raised his bloody fists into the air.

IN THE NEXT HOUR, A VICTOR EMERGED IN THE WRESTLING, A small, lightning-quick Arkadian, named Hermios, who threw five men out of the skamma, and disabled two others with holds that were tighter than a vice in Hephaestus' workshop. As the stadium erupted in approval for the Arkadian's skill, the red linen band of victory was tied about his brow, marking him as the Gods' favourite in the wrestling until he received his sacred olive crown.

Amid all the noise and distraction, Stefanos began to stretch his limbs and rub his legs again. He saw a mass of people flow toward the pankration where one of the men of Croton was proving worthy of his ancestry.

It gave him time to rest, to strategize for the next bout which he expected to come at any time. He had not been ready to go so soon the last time, and did not want to be taken unawares again.

The crowds were restless and impatient - they had seen much blood and tasted victory. They had even witnessed death.

Groups of men, young and old, stood about, bare chested, or wearing chitons and himations, philosophers mingled with peasants and warlords, hardened warriors with boys upon whose faces the down of youth had not yet begun to show.

Olympia was the place where they came together as Greeks, to witness the best of men, the most skilled crowned by Nike when she swept down from the heights of Olympus.

The crowd ate bread and meat from the vendors who wended their way about the embankments, they drank water from the cisterns, they sweated, and yelled, and slapped each other on the backs as they commented on the performance of others, how they would have done something differently.

Stefanos heard a group of old men talking about how the games were more challenging in the time of their grandfathers, when all men were bred to war, not shaped in the gymnasium and palaestra.

Gods help me if I ever become such an old fool, Stefanos thought to himself.

A great cry went up from the pankration area and everyone stood to look.

A man lay unmoving in the dirt of the skamma, blood pooling out slowly from his cracked skull as the man of Croton stood over him, breathing heavily, his fists balled tightly, a look of shock upon his bruised, sweaty face.

"No! My son! NO!!!!" an old man yelled, throwing himself onto the skamma and the body of the fallen fighter.

A blanket of silence muffled the elation and joy that had rent the air only moments before, like shockwaves in the sea when Poseidon shakes the earth.

All that could be heard was the old man's wailing as he refused to let himself be moved from his son's side.

Seven of the Hellanodikai had to step forward to remove the man, and another few of their servants to take the body of the dead fighter out of the stadium.

The boxing matches that were going on stopped, as did any talk among the athletes. When one of their own died, it was an affront to the dead to disturb the Gods who took notice of a man's passing in that sacred place.

The man of Croton who advanced to the pankration final did not gloat or punch the air with his massive fist, but rather went to sit alone for a while, oddly disturbed by the way his match had ended. Men around him attempted to cheer him, but he would have none of it. The two pankrationists who were about to fight for the chance to meet the man of Croton in the final, looked at each other, nodded, and stepped onto the skamma when the judges told them to do so.

The sacred Games had to go on.

"Omega!" the Hellanodikai at the boxing skamma yelled after the previous bouts had finished.

Stefanos stood at once.

The judge looked down at his tablet and read the names of the fighters who were to compete next.

"Stefanos, son of Talos of Argos!"

Stefanos stepped forward to a few more cheers than he

had received previously, limbering his arms, legs and shoulders as he moved, trying not to think of what had just happened. He saw Ajax again, near to Agesilaus, the man watching him keenly.

Kyniska came into his mind like a refreshing wind and he felt revitalized, like he could do no wrong.

"The opponent..." the judge continued. "Ocnus, son of Nemos of Argos!"

From within a group of onlookers on the far side of the stadium, Ocnus emerged, smirking, his eyes like daggers seeking Stefanos' blood as he walked toward him.

Gods, you do play with me, Stefanos laughed inwardly. *Let me finish this, I beg you. For my sister.*

Both men stepped into the ring of the skamma, Ocnus' companions making the most noise behind him, baying for Stefanos' blood.

"Now is the time, Ocnus! Avenge your disgrace!" they urged him on.

Stefanos watched the man before him, his long, cat-like limbs, the methodical way in which he moved, his muscles shaped to perfect symmetry at the palaestra.

"I see you've not got your shiny new uniform on, Ocnus!" Stefanos said, his face unsmiling.

"And neither have you, Stefanos," Ocnus said. "Be careful you don't trip again, dancer!"

The crowd seemed to enclose them even more and the Hellanodikai had to push people back to keep them from disturbing the fighters in both the boxing skammae. The sound of heavy hits and grunts came from the other boxing match and Ocnus looked back over his shoulder in that direction, smiling as he turned back to Stefanos.

"You won't be grunting when I hit you. You'll be crying out for mercy."

"You're the one who'll be crying, little one," Stefanos said as he flexed his wrapped hands, the himantes stained with blood.

"Are you ready, men of Argos?" The judge for the bout stepped forward with his rod raised between them.

"Ready," they both said.

The rod stood raised between them, like a gate separating a bull leaper from the bull, shaking with the will to clash, and suddenly, it was withdrawn.

"Pygme!"

Ocnus attacked first, faster than Stefanos ever thought he could have done, two jabs, a feint, and then a right hook that nearly met his cheek.

Stefanos dodged every hit, but narrowly, and almost lost his balance at the edge of the skamma's circle.

"Look!" Glaucus yelled. "The dancer's lost his feet!" he laughed and several joined him as Ocnus laid attack upon attack on Stefanos who took the hits on his arms if he could not get out of the way quickly enough.

"Come'on old man!" Ocnus teased as he unleashed another attack. "What's the matter? Am I too much for -"

Stefanos' heavily wrapped fist struck out, shoving the taunt back down Ocnus' throat, and sending the younger man reeling backward.

"You talk too much, whelp!"

That was it, Stefanos had had his chance to watch Ocnus' movements, ascertained his technique which he had not seen to that point on any palaestra. He then began to bob, his feet light, his fists still, searching for the opening they needed to weaken his opponent's defences. He began to dance.

The crowd delighted in the display, and this enraged Ocnus who rushed in again, his fists faster than ever as they attacked Stefanos' head, chest, and stomach. He came close, almost every time, but it was never close enough, for Stefanos weaved, and dodged, and spun, and then attacked. He hit Ocnus on the ear, gave him a glancing blow to the jaw, and his fist swiped across Ocnus' sternum.

Then he felt himself knocked hard to the ground, a ringing in his head, his vision blurred.

The crowd was on its feet then, howling.

Stefanos shook his head, instinctively dodging another downward hit that gave him a glimpse of Ocnus' enraged and bleeding face. His own fist shot up blindly and connected sloppily with Ocnus' forehead sending him back.

Without thinking of where he was, Stefanos scrambled over to the prostrate enemy and straddled him, his left hand holding Ocnus as his right arm raised to come down.

He felt a sharp stinging on his back and threw himself aside to roll to his feet.

"No pinning!" the judge with the cane yelled, pointing at Stefanos.

Ocnus got to his feet and composed himself, wiped the blood and sweat from his face so that he could see.

Stefanos crouched, his legs finding their strength and light stance. He had no idea how long they had been fighting, but it seemed that the sun was falling in the West.

"Pygme!" the judge yelled again.

Ocnus charged and, missing his swing, spun himself around so that he ploughed into Stefanos back first, the latter pinning his arms behind his head and pulling him out of the skamma with him.

The two men rolled in the dirt outside of the circle and the Hellanodikai rushed toward them to separate them. In the confusion, Ocnus whipped his head back and hit Stefanos in the eye.

As they walked back to take their fighting positions, Stefanos felt the swelling start below his left eye, blood trickling.

Both men faced each other, their breathing rapid and intense, and Stefanos was reminded of how he might feel after an hour in the front line of the phalanx.

Keep going.. he told himself. *You have him.*

"You're the same as your father!" Ocnus said as he raised his fists. "A failure. And your sister, a whore in a priestess' disguise!" he laughed.

Stefanos stared directly at the man before him and pushed away the raging emotions that he knew could make him lose. He was back in his armour, his doru in hand, his hoplon on his arm, gazing out from beneath the dented bronze of his crested helmet.

Ocnus laughed, when Stefanos did not say anything, and then he attacked.

The first punch was wild and full of anger, and before Ocnus connected, Stefanos had quickly stepped aside and jabbed him in the side of his sweaty head, jarring his neck. Another swinging punch followed, the lead wrapped fist coming around in a deadly arc to just barely touch Stefanos' chin.

"You have him, Stefanos!" yelled Xenophon from the embankment, on his feet as he yelled. "You have him!"

"He's tiring, Ocnus!" Biton and Ocnus' other friends countered.

Zeus and Herakles, Stefanos thought as he dodged another two, then three blows. *Guide my fists!*

With a sudden burst of energy, Ocnus closed the gap and jabbed at Stefanos' face, but the latter ducked and punched, winding Ocnus.

Stefanos spun, dodged, ducked, and punched again, with such speed that Ocnus only realized he had missed when Stefanos' fist connected with his head one, two, then three times.

The crowd roared as Ocnus spun on his feet with the last blow and landed face down in the dirt, struggling to get up.

"Get up, coward!" Stefanos yelled down at the fallen man who had caused his family so much grief. "Get up!"

"Do you submit?" the Hellanodikai said, standing over Ocnus, blocking Stefanos' way with his rod. "Submit, or enter the fight again!"

Ocnus shook his head, blood running down his left side from where Stefanos' right fist had hammered him.

"Look!" someone yelled from among the Spartans. "The downed Argive is crying!"

There was laughter all along the embankment.

"So much for the Argive Thousand!" yelled one of the Theban contingent.

Ocnus pushed himself up, and for a moment Stefanos believed he would fight more, but then he collapsed back onto his stomach, his eyes wet with either sweat or tears, and raised his finger for mercy. He had submitted.

Stefanos spat at him and turned his back to walk to the centre of the skamma.

"Stefanos, son of Talos of Argos!" the Hellanodikai called to the crowd.

Stefanos looked around then and saw Xenophon cheering and clapping, but none other he might call friend.

Kyniska...I'm almost there... he dared to think, even as Agesilaus looked directly at him and nodded cold approval.

Stefanos did not return the nod to the Spartan king, but went to the cistern to drink cool mountain water and wash the blood from his face and torso.

"The final bout will take place after the pankration final!" the Hellanodikai cried the length of the stadium. "The finalists are Stefanos of Argos!" There were scattered cheers. "And Typhon of Sparta!"

The Spartans roared like lions then as Typhon emerged from the centre of them, his body seemingly unbloodied except for the himantes covering his fists.

Typhon's eyes bored into Stefanos from across the stadium, and it was as if there were no other people there present but for them. Stefanos saw hatred there, but a cold, calm demeanour that he knew would take him to the limits of his skill and endurance.

"Fighters! Be back here following the pankration!" the Hellanodikai said before the crowd began to flow toward the skamma where the man of Croton faced his Ionian opponent.

"Good fight, Stefanos!" one man said as he slapped Stefanos on the back on his way past.

"Well done!" said another.

Several of the other competitors from the boxing and other events congratulated Stefanos as they passed, but he simply nodded to them.

Where had these men been before, these same men who had mocked him the previous day?

Let it go, he told himself as he left for the palaestra to re-apply oil and rest his body and mind prior to the final fight.

THE SPARTAN CAMP HAD BEEN UNUSUALLY QUIET THE WHOLE of the fourth day of the Games with most of the men, including the king, at the stadium watching the fights.

Only the neighing of horses could be heard above the whirr of the cicadas, as well as the cries of Kyniska as she coached Pirro and her team through their toils.

The Spartan princess' eyes blazed as she ran along the sides of the track, calling out, watching the movement of her horses' bodies as they strode faster and faster down the long stretches, slowed into the corners, and burst out of them with explosive speed, just enough not to tip the chariot.

"Yes, Pirro! They have it! Let them go out of the turns!" Kyniska jumped into the air, her body and hair wet with sweat as she stood beneath the blazing sun, watching them, daring only now to think of the victory that was within their grasp.

"Give them rest and water, Pirro! They've earned it!" Kyniska said as the team came to a halt before her and she stroked each of them, their black coats frothy with sweat. She turned to Eunice, Helle, Thais, and Euryleonis who were standing back with some of the guards. "I want each of them washed with cool water from the river, brushed, and fed the best of the hay and barley tonight."

"Yes, my lady," they said, smiling at their mistress.

Kyniska's smile, however, departed when she saw Ajax

striding across the field toward her, his head down atop his mighty trunk. The hot wind whipped at his red cloak as he came toward her.

She felt a tightening in her breast and fear began to grip her. Even though she had been focussed on her team the whole of the day, thoughts of Stefanos had been constant in her heart. It had frustrated her, to be so distracted, but it had also been a comfort, and she had prayed to the Gods for his victory.

"What news, Ajax? Is it finished?"

"The competition is not yet over. However," he looked up at his princess. "The Argive is in the final bout. He has fought extremely well."

Kyniska's heart soared then and she nodded. "Thank you for this news, Ajax. The Gods smile on my prayers."

Ajax looked at the ground, at his mistress' feet then, and did not meet her eyes for a moment. When his head raised, his lips were pursed.

"What is it? Something more?"

"His opponent in the final..."

"Who is it?"

"It is Typhon, my lady."

Kyniska stared at Ajax for a few, stretched out moments. She had seen Typhon fight, knew how good he was. Certainly best among the Spartans. She had even seen him kill men on the skamma prior to the Games.

"Typhon," she said.

"Yes, my lady," Ajax said, looking from Kyniska to the four young girls and Pirro, then back. "He is but barely injured from his previous bouts."

"And Stefanos?" she asked. "Is he hurt?"

"A little. He was bleeding from a blow to his cheek, but he is well enough."

Kyniska hoped Stefanos had not been hit in the side of his head where the assailant had attacked him two nights past. *Gods give him strength*, she thought, her fists balled tightly.

Kyniska took a deep breath and looked up at Ajax, distancing her outward appearance from the rushing emotion inside of her.

"If it is the Gods' will that he win, Stefanos will come through this."

"But Typhon hates him!" Eunice said suddenly.

"Don't underestimate the Argive!" Euryleonis said. "He's strong, my lady," she reassured.

"And fast!" Pirro said.

"But so is Typhon!" Thais added.

They were silent a moment, all guessing at what their mistress must be thinking, but Kyniska put up her hands.

"It is in the hands of the Gods now to show us whom they favour. Stop this!" she said a little too loudly. "Our task is to care for the horses and prepare for the race tomorrow. Do you understand me?"

"Yes, my lady," they murmured.

"Good. Now get to work and I'll join you shortly." Kyniska strode away from them, across the track toward the river while Pirro and the girls led the horses back to the stable.

Ajax stood where he was, waiting for his mistress to return, watching her as she stood alone in the middle of the small hippodrome, looking up at the sun as it dipped red toward the western horizon.

"Gods of victory and strength..." she prayed. "Stand by the Argive in this fight. Grant him victory." She shut her eyes tightly. "Grant *me* victory tomorrow."

When she finished, Kyniska turned to Ajax. "Go, Ajax! Watch the fight and bring me news of victory or defeat as soon as it is over!"

The big Spartan bowed deeply to the princess, turned, and walked back toward the sanctuary as Kyniska made her way to the stables and her team.

. . .

STEFANOS SAT ALONE IN THE ELAIOTHESION, SMOOTHING HIS body with fresh oil that Axion had put out for him. His skin glistened as he ran his hands along his arms, torso, and legs, the oil soothing the cuts he had received in his previous bouts.

The blood had stopped flowing from his face, but he knew that one hit would set it to bleeding again. He was feeling limber though, able to keep the exhaustion at bay for the moment. He felt his head where he had been attacked, and it was tender, but the dizziness had long since vanished.

When he was finished oiling his body, Stefanos sat on the stone bench gazing at the outline of the doorway that led out into the late sunshine. He listened to the dripping of water from the nearby basin, the sound echoing off the walls of the oiling room.

Gods...this is it. Guide me in this battle... He held up his hands to see his calloused knuckles and thick fingers. He looked at the muscles of his shoulders, chest, and thighs, his body's armaments on the skamma. He felt the blood pulsing through himself, his heartbeat calm, steady, as he sought peace before the fight.

The water continued to drip and he took up the straps of his himantes, winding the first layer of linen tightly around his wrists, hands, and then each of his fingers. That done, he placed the rawhide braces over his hands and knuckles, before strapping them on tightly with the other set of linen straps. When he was finished, Stefanos stood and flexed his hands, pounded one fist into the palm of the other, ensuring the himantes were secure, not to come loose and leave him vulnerable to breaks.

"You ready?" Axion appeared in the doorway, his bulk outlined by the orange light outside.

Stefanos looked up and nodded, sweat dripping from his short hair down his back.

"I'm ready."

"It's time," Axion said. "They've just finished the proclamation ceremony for the pankration, naming the Crotonese as victor."

"Did he look any better than before his bout?"

"No. That death will haunt him for a long while, but he overcame his demons and won."

Stefanos looked down at the oily floor, his skin golden with oil.

"Are you ready to do the same?" Axion asked.

Stefanos looked up. "Yes," he said, thinking of his father in that moment.

"Then go to victory, Argive. Show the Gods what you can do."

Stefanos emerged from the palaestra refreshed and rested, his mind calm, though how long that state would last, he did not know.

He walked through the Altis as if in a daze, the myriad bronzes staring down at him as he passed, their voices urging him to fight, willing him to victory, none of them mocking, but rather frozen in serene victory and elation, each having conquered his ponos.

The sound from the stadium grew louder and louder as Stefanos passed the Pelopion, and the great altar of Zeus where the day's offerings still smouldered. He walked over the blood-soaked ground where the hecatomb of ox had been sacrificed and came to the tunnel of the krypte.

There he stopped and looked through the darkness to the light of the stadium and the thousands of men covering that vast theatre of athleticism. He heard the chanting funnelled toward him, pushing him back as he went down the tunnel.

"Sparta! Sparta! Sparta!" came the battle cry of the Lacedaemonians in the audience.

Their chants rose to a fever pitch and Stefanos stood at the line of the krypte's shade where it gave onto the burning earth of the stadium.

"There he is!" someone yelled, pointing to Stefanos where

he stood at the entrance to the stadium. "He's here! The dancing Argive's here!"

A cheer rose up from the groups who had decided that Stefanos was their choice for the final, those men who hated the Spartans above all others.

Stefanos stepped forward into the angled sunshine and hot breeze that seemed to grab him and pull him toward the central skamma where the Hellanodikai and Typhon awaited him.

To his left, a long-haired man in a white chiton stepped out onto the stadium floor, his bearded face looking straight at Stefanos. It was Xenophon.

"Stefanos, son of Talos!" he yelled. "Warrior of the Ten Thousand!"

A rush like a tidal wave swept the ranks of spectators as Xenophon held his fist in the air, followed by hundreds of other men who had made that fateful march to Asia and back and who now found themselves at Olympia for the sacred Games, trying to forget the past.

"The Ten Thousand!" they all chanted and cheered for Stefanos as he walked the length or the stadium, nodding to Xenophon, his old friend.

Men of Athens, of Argos, of Thebes, and of Corinth, who had marched to Persia and back, cried support for their brother. Even a handful of Spartans did likewise though with less fervour.

The whole time, Typhon waited at the edge of the skamma, seemingly calm and ready, his body relaxed and still. He flexed his hands, the lead of his himantes glinting dully in the sunlight, his hair tied back tightly so as not to get in the way.

When Stefanos reached the skamma, he held out his hands to one of the Hellanodikai who inspected his himantes and nodded. Stefanos thrust his arms into the air, his muscles flexing and shining in the light of this last fight of the Games.

He swung his arms loosely, and swivelled his neck, rolled his shoulders, jumped up and down.

He could barely hear anything coherent from all around him, only the rush and wind of the crowd, excited beyond reason.

The bout's judge stepped to the middle of the skamma and motioned for both men to approach and stand still while they faced one of the priests who had come to the altar at the side of the stadium.

"Father Zeus," the priest said. "These men come to compete before you and all the Gods in the Olympic Games. May the most worthy and skilled emerge victorious from the fight. We honour you!"

The priest stepped back and the judge turned to both men who stood staring at each other and nothing else.

"No biting, or gouging. If one of you submits, the other must stop or be penalized. Understood?"

"No one will submit," Stefanos said, his eyes on Typhon.

"No one will stop," Typhon added.

The judge looked at both men closely for a moment, then, with his rod held up between them...

"One...two...pygme!"

The judge stepped back and the two fighters' fists went up.

The flute players at the sidelines piped up as loudly as they could in a vain attempt to accompany the action at the centre of the stadium, but the crowd was so loud as the fighters circled each other that none could hear them.

As for Stefanos, he saw only Typhon, and the lead-wrapped fists held out before him.

A few cursory punches and jabs were thrown, more flexing than attacks, a prelude.

Typhon threw three swings which Stefanos easily dodged, but then his first real attack was as quick as lightning with a back-hand hit that landed on Stefanos' neck.

The pain shot through Stefanos but was momentary and

he quickly countered with a feint and then a hard hammer blow that knocked Typhon back a step.

The crowd cheered as the fight well and truly got underway, the fighters wary now, circling each other. The cries in favour of each fighter were roughly equal, as all had seen both men fight before. All admired their skill.

But the Gods, all knew, could only crown one Olympic victor.

Suddenly, before anyone watching realized what was happening, Stefanos and Typhon fell into a brutal dance of rolling punches, jabs, and swings, taking the measure of each other with every exchange, allowing a light hit to inflict a heavier one.

Typhon's swift attacks were hap-hazard, but Stefanos was able to move quickly, as he had trained, so as not to get hit, to weave in and out as if dodging ten spear tips in the shield wall all at once.

But the Spartan was methodical and patient and kept his attacks consistent until Stefanos slapped his fists out of the way and landed a direct punch to Typhon's chest, sending him backward.

Stefanos followed up and lunged again, parrying the Spartan's hands, but slipping so that his arms straddled and slid along Typhon's oiled shoulders.

Typhon took advantage of the closeness to spit in Stefanos' face and then head butt him beneath the eye, reopening the existing cut.

The judge stepped in with his rod to separate the two men, giving them a breath or two, which allowed Stefanos to wipe at the blood that was flowing from the reopened cut.

"He's blooded him!" someone yelled and the crowd cheered, slavered like wild beasts at the hunt.

Typhon approached Stefanos again, confident, his fists out, fast, as if cutting the air to get at the Argive.

Stefanos began to swerve, dodge, and dance, to try and

find a rhythm to counter and confuse the Spartan, but the latter was well-trained.

Stefanos moved in for a quick attack, one way, then changing direction to the other with a massive swing, but Typhon ducked beneath and rolled, and came up to pound Stefanos in the ribs.

Even so, Stefanos' right arm lashed out and caught the Spartan on the right cheek, sending a tooth flying out of Typhon's mouth to the great amusement of the crowd.

"Keep dancing, Argive!" someone yelled. "You'll have a Spartan necklace by the end!"

"Ten Thousand!" someone else began, and others followed the chant. "Ten Thousand! Ten Thousand!"

Stefanos straightened and relaxed his body, dismissing the cramping in his side as Typhon spat blood from his mouth.

His brothers from the Persian anabasis continued their chant and the memories of battles won against insane odds filled Stefanos' mind, and rallied him like a great bellows fanning the flames of a bronze smith's forge.

The flutes reached a fever pitch for a moment as the Spartans on the embankments began to chant for Typhon, the latter's fists moving more quickly as he attacked and feinted. His fists were a blur and he had Stefanos on the defensive, avoiding those lead, blood-covered himantes.

For a time, Stefanos kept the Spartan's attacks at bay, but Typhon feinted again, spun unexpectedly, and landed a blow on the side of Stefanos' head, sending him bloody and dizzy into the dirt.

"Sparta! Sparta!" the men around Agesilaus chanted, their fists in the air.

Then Xenophon was at the edge of the stadium, with Kratos too.

"Come'on Stefanos! Get up!" Kratos yelled.

Stefanos heard him somewhere at the back of his mind, but he was focussed on his writhing body and whirling head, willing himself to steady as he pushed up from the ground as if escaping a deadly pit of Hades.

"Finish him!" the king of Sparta suddenly yelled from the embankment, his cold voice high above the others. "Finish the Argive, Typhon!"

The Hellanodikai were leaning in close now to watch for Stefanos' sign of submission as blood poured from the wounds on the side of his head and cheek, and his eyes swelled.

Typhon stood over Stefanos and laughed through his laboured breathing.

"You see, Argive. You're nothing! No match for a Spartan, man or woman!"

As Stefanos had almost pushed himself up again, Typhon landed a heavy blow on his shoulders sending him flat into the dirt again.

"You're finished, Argive. And Kyniska is mine!"

The mention of the name made Stefanos look around to see the smirking Spartan's bleeding face.

"Ha, ha. That's right. The king said I could marry her if I win today." He spat. "Seems I will." He punched again as Stefanos pushed up. "How could a Spartan ever marry a filthy, pathetic, son-of-an-Argive smith!" Another punch. "Your family is nothing - your mother, sister, your father, are nothing!"

Stefanos felt his limbs writhing as his mind battled with them, willed them to get up despite the pain that wracked them.

"I'll see you in Hades, Argive," Typhon said as he raised his right fist to bring it down.

Stefanos turned his neck to see the fist, the angling sunlight of late afternoon behind it.

Kyniska!

As Typhon's fist came down for a killing blow, Stefanos spun upward, parrying the blow with his right forearm as he rose, and followed through with a left hammer to the side of Typhon's head.

A sound louder than what was heard on the battlefield between Gods and Titans crashed over the stadium as the crowd jumped to its feet again.

Both men stumbled away from each other, shaking their heads and trying desperately to regain control and balance.

A chorus of drums joined the flutes on the sidelines, and chants rose up once more as Stefanos stood straight, his fists up and ready, the very image of a bleeding Herakles.

Typhon looked up at his king for a moment and then around the stadium at the Greeks laughing at him. He no longer heard his fellow Spartans calling out to give him strength. He only saw the Argive before him and felt hatred.

The Spartan charged with a running punch, fast and deadly, but Stefanos parried it with his left as Typhon was airborne, and struck the back of Typhon's head hard, somersaulting the Spartan onto his back.

"Get up, Spartan!" Agesilaus shouted from the jeering crowd.

Typhon rolled sloppily onto his hands and knees and stood quickly, swaying on his feet before launching into another attack.

Stefanos dodged left, then right, landed a jab at Typhon's chest and then slammed both his fists on either side of Typhon's head.

The Spartan's eyes rolled, but he found the strength for another attack with a right which Stefanos parried with his left, giving him just enough time to plunge his right fist directly into Typhon's forehead.

The Spartan stood still for a moment, and then crumpled like a sack of grain onto the blood-spattered dirt.

It took Stefanos a moment to register the unconscious man before him, lying in the dirt, or the fact that the sight meant he was the victor. On the battlefield, he had never waited after felling a man.

It was only when the Hellanodikai shouted and placed the

ribbon of victory around his head that he came to and heard the cries of the crowd about the entire stadium of Olympia.

"In boxing!" the judge yelled. "Stefanos, son of Talos, of Argos! Best among the Greeks!"

Xenophon, Kratos, Pollux and others rushed the skamma at that moment and hoisted Stefanos into the air, making the world spin in a deafening maelstrom of praise in the dying light of the evening.

The crowd groaned and clapped like an immense hybrid beast, part man, part animal.

From the tops of his friends' shoulders, Stefanos saw the king of Sparta leave the stadium with his men, but for Ajax who stood where he was on the embankment watching and nodding.

On the other side of the stadium, as things became clearer, Stefanos spotted the Athenians, Plato, Isocrates, and even Thrasybulos clapping and nodding their approval of his performance. The priestess of Demeter also clapped for him near the Athenians. Argives, Corinthians, Thebans, Arkadians and others, all of them raised a cry for Stefanos.

Men of all city states praised the display and the victory then, for they admired the skill of that contest, the philonikia that evidently flowed in the bleeding Argive held aloft in the shadow of the Hill of Cronos.

"Aner agathos," some said. A good man, a man who embraces Eris agathos.

No matter his origins, on that day, they admired him and knew that the Gods favoured Stefanos, son of Talos.

As Stefanos was put down and the muted congratulatory shouts flooded his ears, he turned to look in the direction of the end of the stadium, and there, beneath a lone pine tree, stood the shade of his father, Talos.

The old man smiled, ghostly tears upon his face, his hands clasped tightly together as he watched his victorious son from the other side of Death's black river.

· · ·

THE HOUR AFTER HIS VICTORY WAS A BLUR.

As Stefanos' eyes searched for another glimpse of his father, men clapped him on the back and reached out to touch the champion's limbs.

At one point, Kratos, Pollux, and Xenophon had cut through the crowd to congratulate him.

"You did it, Stefanos!" Kratos roared, tears in his eyes. "I'm sorry!" he said, though Stefanos had trouble hearing. "I'm sorry, my friend. Your father and Pandaros would be proud!" Kratos cried through the tears.

It was the first time he had emerged from his tent after his defeat in the pentathlon. Stefanos wanted to speak more with him, but Kratos disappeared into the enveloping crowd.

When Agesilaus was gone, Pollux and Xenophon added their battle cries to the praise erupting all around Stefanos too, men of the Ten Thousand coming up and inviting him to celebrate with them in the camp of every city state there.

At one point, Stefanos panicked that he was dreaming, tortured by another waking vision of the Gods' making, and felt for the red linen band about his head.

It was still there, and on the morrow, as indicated by the judges, he was to present himself at the temple of Zeus for the binding of the olive crown and the parade of Olympic victors. On the morrow, he would come as close to immortality as any mortal man could.

As Stefanos was about to pull away from grasping hands, two men approached him and the crowd parted for both.

Hermios of Arkadia, the champion in the wrestling, and Iphitos of Croton, the champion of the pankration, approached their fellow victor.

"Fantastic victory, son of Talos!" said the smaller wrestler. "The Gods were surely pleased!"

"And by both of your victories," Stefanos made sure to say.

"Gratitude to you, Argive," said Iphitos of Croton. "Fortune loves you this day. May the Gods favour us always."

Stefanos noticed the man still seemed withdrawn, regretful of the man he had killed on the skamma, but he said nothing, only nodded his thanks before the two men turned and left Stefanos to the adulation of his new admirers.

"Time to drink!" Pollux said, raising Stefanos' arm in the air to a wave of cheers.

"Let the man rest!" Axion said, cutting through the crowd. "He'll join you all later!" The old gymnasiarchos held Stefanos at arm's length, and checked his face and head. "You'll heal. You were so fast, he couldn't get a solid hit on you."

"The hits felt solid enough!" Stefanos said, garnering laughter all around.

"How do you feel, Argive?" a Syracusan nearby yelled.

"Blessed!" Stefanos answered, feeling a little dizzy.

"Pandaros would be proud, Argive," Axion said, starting to walk with Stefanos back toward the krypte, with a tail of followers in his wake.

It was getting dark now and torches were being lit all around the sanctuary as festivities in the camps of the winners began to get underway, with past winners throwing celebrations of their own.

When they came to the Altis, Stefanos spotted Ajax standing before the statues of the Zanes. Pirro stood beside him, smiling broadly.

"I'm fine, Axion," Stefanos said when he saw the two Spartans waiting for him.

"Be sure to rest. You've earned it," Axion said, smiling. "Praise Zeus, you've earned it!" the old man said, clapping his hands as he went back to the palaestra.

"Congratulations, Stefanos!" Pirro said, walking up, but stopping short once his bloody features came into view by the light of a nearby torch. "Are you badly hurt?"

"Trust me," Ajax said. "Not as badly as Typhon."

"Where is he anyway?" Stefanos asked.

"The doctors took him away," Ajax said. "I think the king

was quite disappointed." Ajax looked at Xenophon and Pollux who both looked at each other.

The king of Sparta was not a man to cross, or disappoint.

Stefanos was quiet, his eyes roving over the Altis as the other men chatted about the fight. In the shadows, along the wall of the Pelopion, he saw a movement.

Stefanos walked a short distance to get a closer look. His body felt tired and he peered into the darkness to see the form of a woman. It was her - Hippodameia.

He expected her to be smiling, show some sign of favour, but she yet tore at her clothes, and clawed at her own face as tears fell from her eyes. She shook her head and leaned on the wall of the Pelopion.

"Ready?"

Stefanos jumped and turned to see Xenophon beside him.

"Time to celebrate!" Pollux said.

Stefanos shook his head. "Not now."

His friends looked disappointed.

"You go ahead and drink my health and good fortune for me." He turned to Pirro and Ajax who were standing on his other side. "Take me to her."

Ajax nodded and led the way back to the Spartan camp and Kyniska.

Chapter Eleven

THE DEFIANT DREAM

Το Τολμηρό Όνειρο

Kyniska stood outside in the darkness of her camp, staring up at the sky, at the starry images of Andromeda, and of Perseus holding aloft the head of Medusa.

That legendary prince of Argos had conquered much to win the day and the Gods' favour. She knew the tales. She also knew and felt that, somehow, Stefanos had suffered much more, and though he was no son of Zeus, his struggle was great.

Pirro had left a long time before, once the horses were stabled, resting for the race the next day. She had stayed with them to feed them and sing, her voice ever calming to her team, but she had been distracted. Her longing to know the outcome of Stefanos' fight with Typhon pushed and pulled at her mind so that she was completely unfocussed.

When she finished singing to the horses, she left the stable and stood outside, her ears straining against the night to catch wind of the day's outcome. However, no whispers of victory came to her, and as the chill night air began to descend on Olympia, Kyniska began to despair.

I'll kill myself before I marry someone of by brother's choosing! she told herself.

She looked at the starry firmament and wondered which gods might be looking down on her at that moment. Did she deserve their attention? Though she was not driving the chariot, everything she had done in her life had been building toward that one race on the morrow when Helios' chariot would break out over the eastern horizon on the fifth and last day of the Games.

"Father Zeus...Mother Hera..." Kyniska prayed as she stood in the solitary darkness. "Goddess Artemis, who runs with animals... Be with me and my team tomorrow. Rouse their hearts and help them to stand firm in the face of possible death in the race. Let their spirits shine, unafraid and beautiful for all the world to see. Grant me victory in the Olympiad, and the offerings from my hands to your altars shall be never-ending."

Kyniska knelt on the still-hot earth, her hands on her lap. "My struggle has been no less than any other, and I would not let my brother conquer me and humiliate me, or our house." She lowered her head, and then looked as if to search the shadows. "Father...Archidamus... You always believed in me, though I was not a son. You believed in the strength of a Spartan girl who watched you every step of your life. Smile on me tomorrow from across the Styx. I will show you the true nature of ponos."

Kyniska remembered her father encouraging her in her horsemanship, the scoldings he had given Agesilaus when he had sought even then to pull her down. She also thought of Hippodameia, who defied her cruel father, and others, for a man she had loved.

"Would it be possible?" she wondered out loud, her thoughts drawn inexorably back to Stefanos. "Gods let him have victory this day so that-"

She stopped in her prayers, her eyes drawn to movement some distance into the Spartan camp.

Stefanos!

Kyniska stood and walked a few paces, but she could only see the massive form of Ajax walking slowly toward her, with Pirro beside.

No.

The big Spartan approached, his head down, but his eyes on her from beneath his heavy brows.

"What news, Ajax?" Her voice was low, uncertain.

Ajax stopped, and Pirro beside him.

"Pirro?"

The young charioteer looked to her, his eyes wide, his mouth a straight thin line. But then that thin line began to crack, and bow into a great smile as he and Ajax parted to reveal Stefanos walking slowly behind them.

For a moment she stared in his direction, wondered if he was real, or an apparition. Then she spotted the thick, linen band about his head.

"Victory?" she asked Ajax.

"Yes, Princess." Ajax smiled. "The Argive fought like a god."

"Victory, my lady!" Pirro said.

Kyniska's hand went to her mouth and she ran to Stefanos without another moment's delay, crashing into his arms like the waves of the sea onto a pebbled shore, the water filling every crack and crevice in its embrace.

She kissed him, tasting blood on her lips, but she did not care. His arms wrapped around her and held her tightly, lifting her tall form off the ground.

"Thank the Gods," she whispered.

"They were with me," Stefanos answered. "As were you." He stood back to look at her for a moment before taking her in his arms again. "You gave me strength, Kyniska. You and the Gods."

She reached up to touch the band about his head and

there she imagined the olive wreath that would be placed upon his brow in the morning.

"You did it."

He nodded, his eyes holding her, not wavering for a second.

Her hand went down his face from the band to touch the wound on his cheek, raw, and painful looking, a battle scar to mark triumph.

"Are you badly hurt?"

Stefanos smiled in that relaxed, dismissive way that had so annoyed her when she first met him, but which she now found endearing.

"I've had worse," he said,

"Will you go to your victory celebrations tonight?" she asked.

"I only want to be with you," he said, his voice tired, calm, at peace.

"Let us go inside," she said, taking him by the hand, and turning to Ajax. "Thank you, Ajax. Will you watch over Pirro and the team this night?"

There was worry in Kyniska's face, and her guard saw it.

"Worry not, Princess. My men and I will be up all night to keep you and your team safe."

"Good." She turned to Pirro. "Pirro, tomorrow is our fateful day. Are you ready?"

"My lady, I've been ready for this day since you began training me. The Gods are with us. I feel it." He bowed to her. "I shall rest now, and wake to a day that will be marked in the history of the Olympiad."

She had never heard her young driver sound so certain, so full confidence. It made her smile. Kyniska kissed the young man on the brow and turned to go with Stefanos to her tent.

STEFANOS WASHED, THEN KYNISKA TENDED HIS WOUNDS herself by the light of several oil lamps as Thais, and

Euryleonis slept soundly in their small room, while Helle and Eunice spent the night in the stables in case the horses needed anything.

As Stefanos sat back, eating dried meat, cheese, and bread, he watched Kyniska fidget and pace as she asked him about the day's fights.

He recounted all he could remember, though admittedly, much of it seemed like a blur, similar to the fury of a battle that is difficult to recollect in detail after the fact. However, he knew that it was not the fights that made her pace, and her eyes dart. Her own battle was yet to be fought, and the stakes were no less than her life's work and ambition.

"Zeus, Hera, and Poseidon will favour you tomorrow, Kyniska. Have faith in your team, in Pirro. I've quite grown to like him, you know."

She stopped, her fists balled for a few seconds before she sat herself down next to him.

"I'm so frustrated with myself. I've never been nervous before now. Why is that so?" she asked him. "Are the Gods toying with me? My mind is churning like Caribdis."

Stefanos handed her a cup of wine, wincing for the pain in his ribs.

As if to calm herself, Kyniska ran her fingers along the contours of his shoulders and arms, his chest and neck. Almost timidly, she pressed her lips to his and it was as if all worry melted away by magic, or some trick of Aphrodite's.

Stefanos felt the weight of the world lifted from his shoulders then.

"I thank the Gods for bringing me to you," he said.

She looked at him, the brilliant blue of her eyes pulled between worry and elation, but she darkened as his brow creased and he rubbed his chin.

"What is it?" she asked.

"Will your brother force you to marry?"

She pulled away. "Why do you say this now?"

"Because of what Typhon said."

"But you beat him. My brother will not marry me to one who has dishonoured Sparta. It would not be fitting."

"And what of Aeson of Thessaly?"

"I won't," she said, growling like a she wolf. "My team will grind his into the dust tomorrow, just as you did Typhon today." She stood, frustrated and angry, her pacing continuing. "Why must you talk about this now?"

"Why?" he stood. "Don't you know by now, Kyniska?" His hands reached out to still her, his bruised and bloody face staring into her. "By the Gods, woman...I love you."

Kyniska froze in his grip, her face and neck reddening, her breathing growing rapid, so much so that her own heart pounded in her ears making her dizzy.

"I would fight the whole world, and lay siege to Olympus itself if only to spend the rest of my life with you. By sweet Aphrodite...nothing can change that now."

Her mind raced, and she sought to make some excuse, find a reason to turn him away, to say that she had only used him for a thing of comfort in the lonely nights since she had arrived at Olympia. But all of that would have been a lie worse than any other, and a betrayal of herself.

She stared at him for several moments, the silence filled with the sound of their breathing, and the fire flickering from the lamps about them.

"I... I..." Words failed her. "Gods..." And then she was kissing him, her arms grasping him desperately, as if to prevent anyone from tearing them apart.

In all her life she had never expected such a thing. What she had always perceived as a thing of weakness in others was now the very thing that gave her strength beyond measure - Love.

Stefanos did not care about the physical pain he felt as she gripped him, dug her hands into his battered body.

Nor did Kyniska care that his blood ran over her, or that she seemed to be falling in a downward spiral into an unknown abyss.

They continued to kiss, to hold and grasp at each other as if nothing else mattered or existed except the two of them.

Stefanos picked her up and carried her through the curtain to her bed where they made love with a passion and urgency fired by the goddess' spell.

Kyniska kissed his wounds and grasped him to her so that he could not leave, her eyes closed, the harassment of her worries temporarily held at bay.

And as Stefanos held her, ran his hands over her neck, arms, and thighs, and gripped her buttocks so that she was flush against him, he thought that life was finally something worth living, worth fighting for.

He continued with this thought as they lay side-by-side a while later, as the moon waxed high over Olympia and the sounds of carousing died into the night, leaving the world to nymphs, nereids, dryads, fauns, centaurs, and all those children of Dionysos who danced beneath the heavens, including lovers.

While Kyniska stared at the ceiling of the tent, her mind on the race only hours away, Stefanos enjoyed the feel of her body against his, the twirl of her dark hair as he ran his fingers through it.

She had not spoken much since the words of love had escaped the walls of his lips, but her thoughts did indeed whirl beside his.

"I won't give you up, Kyniska," Stefanos began, turning onto his elbow to look at her. Her eyes turned toward him and they were wide, like those of a cornered lioness, staring at some threat beyond his muscular shoulder. "You're a Spartan woman. No one can command you. You've said as much to me."

"Yes," she agreed. "But...my horses...my girls...Pirro... What about them? They are my true family."

"And me? Would I ever be accepted in Sparta? I don't have the charm of Alcibiades," he chuckled, but she did not laugh in return.

"You are more a man than ever he was," she said, her eyes hard and full of certainty. "As you say, I'm Spartan. I won't go to Athens or Argos to be called a whore, to be spat at."

"I would take the life of any who dared," he said. "I want to marry you Kyniska. I've never been more certain. Since I've met you, my entire world has righted itself. I could not have won this day without you."

She placed her hand upon his chest and felt his heart beating beneath the muscle, tissue, and bone. For a moment she did indeed wonder if there was fire in his veins, but then she knew he was no god, but a mortal man, a man she knew with certainty that she loved.

"Where would we go?"

Stefanos sat up and held her hands in his.

"As two Olympic victors, no one would turn us away."

"I am not yet a victor," she said, though he could tell that the words stuck in her throat.

"You will be. I know it. You're meant to tear them all down and show them true strength!"

Kyniska raised an eyebrow, but nodded. She could not help but agree.

"We could go to Sicilia, Etruria, or even to the shores of the Black Sea - when we marched through there on the way back from Persia we met many Greeks who had settled there. Some became friends of mine. We could make a life there!"

Kyniska sat up now, her dreaming piqued, her naked body red and gold in the lamplight.

Stefanos continued, his hands upon her cheeks. "We could go north into Hyperborea where Apollo travels, where they revere women warriors and horses above all else."

"What? Go to live among the Amazons!" she laughed. It seemed absurd, but then again, a part of her dared to think that perhaps that was indeed the life she was destined for. She looked at Stefanos and tried to imagine him as a husband, something she had never considered in any man previously. She looked upon him and saw a flash of what could be and her head began to nod, her eyes scream yes, though her lips did not utter the words at that moment.

"Kyniska..." he said, his voice deep and soft. "I don't care where we go. Anywhere is fine, so long as I'm with you until the end of my days."

"I won't make a dutiful wife, you know. I never could."

"And I would never ask it of you. I will protect that fire that burns inside of you at all costs. But I swear to the Gods that if you will have me as your own, you will forever be able to count on me."

Kyniska was silent for several heartbeats, and for a moment, Stefanos believed she might shun his thinking, that he had made a fool of himself.

But he held his tongue as her mind worked.

Kyniska thought of the two of them in some far-flung land with a herd of horses, of the two of them riding over the grass-seas to the North. She thought of long winter nights, nestled in furs before a blazing fire, and of summer twilight sprawled upon the grass, making love beneath the stars.

Her eyes met his in that moment, and she smiled, though her heart raced within her breast.

"If I win tomorrow...if Pirro drives my team to victory..." She reached up to hold his face and kiss him. "Then...my love...the Gods will have shown us that we can indeed go anywhere, and do anything."

SHE WATCHED HIM SLEEP THROUGH THE NIGHT, THE ARGIVE who had rushed into her life and turned her world on end.

Oh Father Zeus...Goddess Nike... Let me be victorious. Let the name of Kyniska of Sparta be burned into the histories as strong and defiant, as blessed by you. As Hippodameia was permitted to marry Pelops, let nothing stop us from - she stopped the thought, not wanting to call evil to it.

Kyniska reached out to touch Stefanos' shoulder, the wound at his head.

He did not wake, so peaceful was his sleep, more peaceful, she suspected, than it had ever been. How she wished to see him crowned on the steps of the temple of Zeus. Even more, she wanted to watch her team destroy all others in the hippodrome... *But how?*

A cock crowed out in the world beyond the canvas and leather of her tent, though it was still dark out.

Kyniska wanted to lie beside him, but knew there would be time enough for that. If she won, there would be all the time in the world, far from Sparta, far from Greece. And she was at peace with the thought, her lips curling into a hesitant smile.

She slipped her long legs over the edge of the bed furs and slipped her long red chiton over her body. Before leaving, she bent over to kiss Stefanos on the forehead.

On the other side of the tent, Kyniska went in to wake Euryleonis.

"Wake, my girl."

Euryleonis rubbed her eyes and sat up quickly. "Is all well, my lady?"

"Today is the day of our destiny," Kyniska said. "Rouse the others, and come to help me prepare the team. Have Thais set out food for our Argive hero when he wakes."

"Yes, my lady," Euryleonis said, standing and hugging her mistress. "The Gods will favour you this day, I know it!"

Kyniska smiled and touched the girl's cheek. Then, she left, drinking a cup of water before lighting a chunk of incense in front of the statues of Poseidon and Artemis.

She said nothing. Her prayers, she felt, had been exhausted, heard by the Gods so many times now that all that remained was to honour them by staying strong and seeing them to victory.

As she walked outside into the cool morning mist, she thought of the offerings she would heap upon the Gods' altars if she won - a hundred rams, fifty bulls, and more...

"Princess," the deep voice came out of the shadows and Kyniska jumped back, ready to fly, until she saw it was Ajax.

"Ajax. Didn't you sleep?"

"My lady, no. I didn't want to take a chance that your enemies might attempt to harm you the night before the race."

"All is quiet in the stables?" she asked.

"Yes. My men have been awake all night as well. It has been quiet."

"Good." She began to leave, but Ajax spoke up.

"My lady... The Argive."

"What of him?"

"Is he to stay with you?"

"That is my affair."

"Yes, my lady. It's just that...well...last night I overheard the king raging against him to Xenophon as they drank. He also plans on punishing Typhon -"

"Do not tell me you're afraid of Typhon, Ajax!"

"No!" He seemed insulted by the suggestion. "I only mean to say that the Argive may be in danger if he remains with you, after the Sacred Truce is finished, that is."

Kyniska knew there was resentment among the Spartans at her taking an Argive as lover...as more. The blinding lustre of Stefanos' victory would dull soon enough, and men would seek to best him, or worse. If she lost, she knew, he would be in greater danger from her brother, for she would be unable to protect him.

"Do not fear, Ajax," she smiled. "The Gods are on our side in this. Thank you for your loyalty."

"My lady," he bowed his head.

"Get yourself something to eat. It's going to be a long day," she said as she continued toward the stables.

When she entered, she saw Pirro standing before all the horses - Xanthus, Zoe, Phaedra, and Acheron - each waiting for their feed, and a brush.

As soon as she was there, their heads all turned toward her, the animals watching Kyniska, she who had raised them.

"They've been waiting for you," Pirro said, still wearing only his chiton. "They woke me up, as if they were aware of what was to come this day."

Kyniska smiled and stroked their muzzles and manes, then turned to Pirro.

"Did you sleep?"

"Yes." He glanced at the straw-strewn stall where Helle still slept.

Kyniska laughed. "If you win this day, Pirro, I will grant you and Helle lands where you can live and raise your own horses if you like."

Pirro's eyes went wide and he bowed to his princess. "My lady, I have no words."

"None are needed. Just guide them first across that finish line."

"I will," Pirro said. "They are ready, and so am I."

Kyniska looked at the young man whom Sparta would have cast off the cliff or exposed to the elements on the side of mount Taygetos. *What a loss that would have been*, she thought. "I know you are ready, my dear Pirro. I know it!" She gripped him tightly by the arms and he met her gaze as he had never done before, as if her strength was flowing into him.

"You've always been there for me, my lady. You've taught me well, when others would have killed me." He looked at the horses and then back to her. "I won't let you down."

She nodded, biting her lip slightly as she strove with all her might to believe in that outcome, and what would follow.

Silently, after a moment, they began to brush down the horses and feed them, taking great pains in looking over each one's knees, hooves and fetlocks, picking out the mud from their shoes, and making sure their dark manes ran like smooth black rivers down the sides of their muscled necks.

As the sun came up over the horizon, each of the horses

was prepared, their harness of red and silver dazzling in the angling light.

Pirro had polished the small chariot and looked it over several times to ensure that the axle was secure and untampered with, that the paint and wood were newly-oiled and shining.

Eunice, Helle, Thais, and Euryleonis were all gathered at the far end of the stable now, watching Kyniska and Pirro go over the team and the chariot fastenings. They discussed the strategy, Pirro nodding his understanding, fully aware of every move, every possible outcome.

They both knew that men and horses often died in the great chariot race of Olympia, especially during the tethrippon race.

"You seem ready to take on the world!" Stefanos suddenly said from the entrance to the stables, the sunlight bright behind him.

The four girls stepped aside for him to approach, each of them smiling at the Argive wearing his linen headband of victory, the man who seemed to have transformed their mistress.

"Good morning," he said, walking directly to Kyniska and kissing her, before turning to Pirro and the horses. "I dreamed of your victory," he said, a wide grin upon his face.

Pirro smiled and nodded. "When we win, then perhaps we can share a krater of wine between us?"

"Yes!" Stefanos laughed, then turned back to Kyniska. "I need to leave soon, as does Pirro, I suspect."

"Yes," she answered. "All twenty teams are to present themselves at the hippodrome for inspection and the drawing of lots to determine starting positions." Kyniska stepped back to look at Stefanos, and felt her heart lighten. "You look like a hero today."

"A bruised one!" he laughed.

Stefanos had washed and oiled himself before putting on the clean white chiton he now wore. The red linen band stood out against his short dark hair, soon to be replaced by an olive crown.

Kyniska looked at him, a sad smile marring her face. "I wish I could see you mount the steps of the temple to be crowned."

"I'll tell you all about it, and Pirro's race." Stefanos reached out to slap the young man on the shoulder. "As soon as the crown-binding is over, I'll head for the hippodrome. I don't want to miss anything."

Kyniska was silent for a moment, uneasy as she turned a matter over in her mind.

Stefanos observed the change. "What is it?"

"I don't want to miss my team's victory," she said.

"I know it must be difficult, my Spartan princess!" he joked.

She did not laugh. "I should be there."

Stefanos saw something in her eyes then, and it made him nervous.

"Pirro," Kyniska said. "You should go and put on the new Ionic chiton I had made for you. You will need to leave soon."

"Yes, my lady," Pirro said.

"Girls, help him get ready," Kyniska said to Euryleonis and the others, causing a stir of giggles as they shooed Pirro out of the stables.

"What are you thinking?" Stefanos asked without preamble.

"I can't miss the race," she said. "If I win, if Pirro and my team cross that finish line first, I need to see it with my own eyes, not somebody else's, no matter how beautiful they are." She reached up to touch Stefanos' face, but he held her hands and brought them down.

"This makes me uneasy, Kyniska," he said. "The rules are clear. If a woman violates the rules of the sanctuary, she will be humiliated, banished for all time, and maybe even executed. The Eleans won't stand for it, and nor will your brother."

"I don't care about my brother!" she said, pulling away. "Their rules are ridiculous! Even Hippodameia was in the chariot with Pelops when he raced Oinomaus across the Peloponnesos."

"I know." Stefanos suppressed a shudder as he remembered his visions in the mountains and the Altis. "And what if all your dreams, all your years of hard work, come to nothing? What then?"

"I'll be in disguise. It won't be the first time a woman has snuck into the Games. Seven years ago, the woman Kallipateira of Rhodes disguised herself so that she could watch her son's boxing match."

"And she was her son's trainer, the daughter and sister of Olympic champions. You are Spartan, the sister of Agesilaus of Sparta, a man whom most of the Greek world hates right now." Stefanos walked swiftly to her and grasped her by the shoulders, his face in front of hers.

"I know you are right, and I know that you should be there. But I would not risk anything if it meant losing you, or harm coming to you. Please promise me you'll stay here and wait for the Gods' answer to your dreams."

Kyniska looked up at him, her blue eyes bright and lively, their fires in full force for all the emotions that raged inside of her at that moment.

She knew she loved him, like she had never done before. She would do anything for him...but to give up her dreams?

"I know I ask too much, and I know by now the wonderful, rebellious nature of the woman standing before me. But you must know that your dreams have also become my dreams, and I want nothing more than to see your team win, to see you get the glory you deserve. Not glory for Agesilaus, or for Sparta, but for Kyniska!"

She felt a swelling in her breast, of exhilaration, of anticipation, of fear, and of utmost belief in the Gods and her destiny. She also felt an unimaginable love for the man holding her at that moment.

"Promise me that you will remain here."

She said nothing for a moment, then stood up on her toes to kiss him on the mouth. "I promise...I'll remain here, with Ajax and the girls."

Stefanos relaxed. He knew he had already pushed her more than she would usually have been willing. Kyniska was not one to bend to anyone's will or wishes. The fact that she had accepted to do this thing gave him utter hope, and he promised himself he would make it up to her.

"So. Are you ready?" she asked him.

"Yes. Though I would go to the temple of Hera and give my thanks."

She nodded. "The Gods should always receive their dues."

He stood there, unwilling to leave. Something kept him fixed to the spot, there amidst the hay and oats, the smell of horse, the heavy breathing of those magnificent beasts behind them.

Stefanos leaned in and kissed her, slow and lingering, his hands holding her face gently to his. "I love you," he said.

"And I love you," she answered, her frustration with him dissipating in that moment. "Now go," she said. "Go to be crowned by Victory, and start to think on the beautiful bronze that you will erect in the Altis."

Stefanos kissed her again and then backed away, touching the horses as he went. He stopped one last time at the bright entrance to catch another glimpse of Kyniska and her children. "I'll see you crowned, Princess!" he said, before leaving.

"Yes," she said to her team, stroking Acheron's black muzzle. "You will."

KYNISKA SAT IN HER TENT A SHORT WHILE LATER, WATCHING the sun play through the walls in the still, summer heat.

There was no breeze through the land. Kyniska stared at the statues of Poseidon and Artemis, and at that of the magnificent horse before her.

"I should be there," she said, her voice low, her eyes gazing out from beneath the strands of her dark hair. "If I can't hold the reins of my team, I should at least be there as witness to their victory or defeat."

Pirro had left only a short while ago, and Kyniska had wanted to go with him, to be escorted by her Spartans into the Hippodrome where all would see she was the owner of that magnificent team of blacks.

When he had limped out into the sunlight, wearing the long Ionic chiton of a charioteer, Pirro seemed like a young Helios, ready to race across the heavens.

"I'm ready, my princess," he said, bowing his head to her.

She lifted his chin and said, "Today, Pirro, you bow to no one. Drive them to victory, and remember what we talked of - not until the seventh lap."

"Yes," he nodded. "The seventh."

"And beware of the Taraxippos..." she shuddered as she said it. "Other teams will baulk wildly there. Be ready."

"I am," he said, the morning light flashing copper and bronze in his red hair.

"May the Gods guide you, and grant you victory," she said as she kissed him on both cheeks.

Pirro turned red and smiled. "May they grant us all victory, my lady."

He then mounted up into the chariot's cab as Kyniska whispered to each of the horses she had raised since birth - Xanthus and Acheron, Zoe and Phaedra.

"Keep them steady, Acheron," she said, patting the big black stallion.

Kyniska played the parting over and over again in her head as she sat in the tent - Pirro and the team setting off through the Spartan camp surrounded by her men, while she, Kyniska, Princess of Sparta, remained behind. Over, and over, and over.

Euryleonis looked up from where she sat with the other three girls who had just come in from their exercises.

"It will be victory, my lady," Euryleonis said assuredly. "You have trained Pirro for years, and the horses love him as a brother. Trust in the Gods," she looked to the statues near Kyniska.

"I do," Kyniska said. "Of course I do!" She stood, frustrated, wishing that Stefanos had not made her promise.

"Do not be angry with the Argive, my lady," Thais said unexpectedly. "He seems to love you deeply. He is changed since we first met him, since he first met you."

"How do you know I am upset with him?" Kyniska demanded, making the younger girl bow her head.

"My lady," Eunice said. "We can all see it."

"Enough! All of you." Kyniska waved a hand and paced about the tent. "I can't just sit here."

"But the law, my lady?" Helle protested.

"The priestess of Demeter is there, and the Rhodian mother was forgiven for being present a few years ago."

"My lady, what are you saying?" Eunice asked.

"Helle. Go and bring Ajax here."

Helle rose from the couch she was sitting on and dashed out of the tent into the sunlight. A few moments later she returned with the Spartan enomotarch.

"Ajax," Kyniska said

"Yes, my princess," he replied, bowing with his hand on his chest.

"I'm going to the Hippodrome."

The Spartan camp was not as empty as it should have been that last day of the Games. Many of the Spartans who would have been at the victory ceremonies for their own had stayed behind, and the horse races were not a favourite among the warlike race of Lacedaemon.

Typhon emerged from his tent on the far edge of the camp, ostracized as he had been from the king's presence for his utter defeat the day before at the hands of the Argive.

As the iatros had worked on his head and chest wounds, stitching and stemming the bleeding, Typhon had raged and struggled, but had been too weak to do anything against the four men who held him down so that the iatros could work on him.

They had given him a tonic of herbs to help him sleep and heal, but it had knocked him out so much that he had not woken until mid-morning.

But he had dreamt that night, oh yes. In his fevered dreams, he had thought of Kyniska and how many times they had lain together. He thought on how she had used him...replaced him...humiliated him.

When Agesilaus promised Typhon marriage to Kyniska if he won the olive crown, he had begun to think of all the ways he could avenge himself on her.

He had not accounted for the Argive, Stefanos, son of Talos, whose praises men were singing throughout Olympia. He hated the man, more than he had ever hated anyone, and longed to see him torn to pieces.

But he hated Kyniska even more, and as his eyes opened on that last day of the Games, he knew that he had to do something to rally some fraction of his honour.

No woman is going to humiliate me! he told himself when he awoke, and saw that he was alone.

Typhon slowly swung his legs over the edge of the cot in which he had been lain, and tested his feet. His long hair was oily and loose about his face, giving him the air of a wild animal rather than a Spartan warrior.

That bitch! he cursed. *She won't even know of her victory!*

He stood, slowly, wavering on his feet a little before he found his balance. He found his tunic on a stool nearby and slid it over his head. Slowly, he moved to the tent flaps, and peered outside. No one was around, and so he began to walk, making his way in a great circle, to avoid the king's tent, and come around to the far place where Kyniska's tent was located.

Every muscle and bone ached as he walked, but he ignored the pain and pressed on. He was Spartan, and pain was of no consequence. Pain was a teacher, and he had learned his lessons well.

"There's Sparta's champion!" someone laughed from the middle of a group of Spartan warriors.

Typhon continued to walk, throwing the men a hateful look.

"Watch out! He might try and box us!" laughed another.

The taunts continued as he passed them.

Typhon was not stupid though. He knew he could not fight then, not yet. He would remember their faces, and he looked directly at them to memorize their features, even as they spat at him and mocked him.

"Unbelievable, letting an Argive best him!"

Soon the taunts and jibes faded behind him, but Typhon had to stop, to control the rage that made his entire body shake, and his wounds begin to bleed again.

Just what I need, he thought as he came to a doru leaning against a tent. He grabbed it and continued on through the camp until he was on the grassy field before Kyniska's camp.

He could handle the princess and the girls, but he did not know how many of her guard were still there. He suspected Ajax might be, though he had left her to watch the boxing the previous day.

"The bastard. I'll gut him too," Typhon muttered.

No one was around as he snuck across the dried grass and dirt toward Kyniska's tent, where it baked in the growing heat of day. He stopped at the back of the tent and thought of cutting his way quietly in there, so as to take her by surprise before any guards could come running. He had a thought then that it would be sweet to kill her horses too.

The fucking animals! He hated them as well.

He stopped and crouched low behind a couple of bales of hay.

Voices. He listened, his ear pressed to the canvas of the tent.

"I'm going Ajax. You can't talk me out of it. I'm your mistress and you must obey!" Kyniska was saying.

"My lady, please. If you're caught, it will mean your death and the disgrace of Sparta."

"I don't care about Sparta!" she said loudly.

Ajax's deep voice was silenced for a moment before continuing.

"Don't say that. I beg you." The big man breathed deeply, trying to calm himself, for even he sounded flustered with the plan that was being presented to him.

"Listen to me," Kyniska said. "If the greatest battle on this earth were being fought, would you, as a Spartan, want to be waiting in some tent, left out of the action?"

"Of course not, I would want my spear, sword and shield to be hacking at the enemy in the front line," he answered.

"As I would."

He was silent again.

"I may be a woman," she said, "but I am also Spartan, and no more will I bow down and accept orders from any man, than would the sun decide not to rise on the day of battle."

Outside, Typhon lowered the spear and began to go over some wild plan in his mind as it began to take root. He hated Kyniska, and he hated the Argive. Surely there was a way to hurt them both, make them suffer. He continued listening.

"My princess," Ajax finally said. "Though it may mean both of our deaths, I will do this not because you order me to, but because I can see how the Gods have set a fire in your heart, and I for one will not be the one to stand in their way."

"Thank you," Kyniska said.

"You must have a good disguise. Take one of those wide-brimmed Thessalian hats that Pirro wears when he is in the field training the team. It will hide your face very well."

"Yes," she agreed. "Thais, Helle, Eunice?"

"Yes, my lady?" the three girls said.

"Get the long breast bands from my trunk and bring them

here. You need to bind me tightly so that I look like a man beneath the chiton. Get one for Euryleonis too."

"She is going also?" Ajax asked.

"I'm not leaving my mistress' side," the girl's young, strong voice said, cutting though the tension.

"Nor am I, girl," Ajax said. "Hurry now, and bind yourselves tightly. The two-horse races will almost be finished by now."

As the girls bound Kyniska and Euryleonis' breasts in the long linen bandages, Typhon listened intently outside the tent, lying flat to the ground behind the hay as two guards walked by.

"We'll take seats near the Taraxippos, at the top edge of the embankment where fewer people will be gathered," Kyniska's voice sounded excited, an edge of fear and thrill mixed together. "My victory will be the glory of Sparta." she said, her voice like that of a general.

"No, my lady!" Euryleonis said immediately. "It will be the glory of Kyniska!"

Typhon could hear Kyniska reach out to hug the little bitch he hated almost as much as her mistress. Who were they to shun the ideals of Sparta, of strength and manhood? *Mingling with Argives, fawning over beasts like they were better than men, as if horse racing were any more honourable than standing in the shield wall.*

How he wanted to tear into that tent and slaughter them!

Fool! he chided himself as he felt the pain shudder in his body. *Think!*

He wanted to make Kyniska suffer...wanted her dead. He also wanted the Argive to know his place, to be hurled down from the heights he had attained like the upstart he was...but how? With Ajax there, Typhon knew he couldn't just walk up and kill her. He would be dead before he said a word.

Unless... Yes! It came to him. Like a serpent strike. *If she were discovered in the hippodrome, she would be executed for breaking the sacred laws of Olympia, or humiliated at the very least, her team disqual-*

ified. But he knew he could not be the one to reveal her disguise. He would never be allowed to return to Sparta, and if Agesilaus discovered what he had done, he would simply kill him, discard him more easily than he had done for General Lysander. Death was preferable to that sort of humiliation.

No. Someone else needed to reveal Kyniska's treachery.

Typhon smiled as it came to him. *Of course!* He gripped the shaft of the doru tightly in his anger and excitement. *It's perfect, and Agesilaus will be humiliated as well, the ugly bastard!*

"Well, what do you think?" Kyniska's voice said in the tent. "How do we look?"

"Like two Thessalian peasants out for a stroll!" Thais said.

"That's the idea!" Kyniska said.

"You'll need to dirty your limbs a bit, my lady," Ajax said. "You're too clean."

"Easy enough," Euryleonis said.

"And you, Ajax, will need to change into a plain chiton," Kyniska said. "No one will believe a Spartan warrior is attending the games with two Thessalian peasants now, will they?"

Ajax sighed heavily. "I suppose not, lady."

"Quickly now, or we'll miss the start!" Kyniska said, her voice drawing nearer to the tent wall where Typhon was hiding. "I'm sorry Stefanos," she said in a low voice. "After this, we'll have a lifetime together..."

Typhon stepped back, checked that no more guards were coming, and slunk back across the field until he reached the trees on the banks of the Alpheios.

Through the shadows cast by the tree trunks, he could see the river glistening in the morning light, and just beyond the place he was searching for.

The Argive camp lay just on the other side.

Chapter Twelve

HEART OF FIRE

Καρδιά από Φωτιά

Day five of the Olympic Games was dedicated to the equestrian events, the tethrippon being the greatest and final event, the one which most present looked forward to.

Though the synoris, the two-horse chariot race, was still to take place, men had come early to get the best seats in the hippodrome so as not to miss out on the marquee event. The population of the sanctuary seemed to have tripled overnight as wave upon wave poured out of the Altis and the surrounding camps to the southeast corner of the sanctuary where the hippodrome lay along the banks of the Alpheios.

Musicians and poets stood in various places playing or reciting for the crowds, working them into a frenzy of celebration, and of devotion to the sanctity of the Games and the chariot races which had been run there for hundreds of years in honour of Pelops and Hippodameia's fateful race against Oinomaus across the Peloponnese.

The sound of flute, tambourine, cymbal, drum, and kythera snaked its way among the crowds, tying them all together like an invisible rope of the Gods' making while one poet's voice overarched it all as he recited the ode.

And he came and stood upon the margin of the hoary sea, alone in the darkness of the night, and called aloud on the deep-voiced Wielder of the Trident; and he appeared unto him nigh at his foot.

Then he said unto him: 'Lo now, O Poseidon, if the kind gifts of the Cyprian goddess are anywise pleasant in thine eyes, restrain Oinomaus' bronze spear, and send me unto Elis upon a chariot exceeding swift, and give the victory to my hands. Thirteen lovers already hath Oinomaus slain, and still delayeth to give his daughter in marriage. Now a great peril alloweth not a coward: and forasmuch as men must die, wherefore should one sit vainly in the dark through a dull and nameless age, and without lot in noble deeds? Not so, but I will dare this strife...'

THE HORSE TEAMS HAD GATHERED AT THE ENTRANCE TO THE hippodrome, packed wheel to wheel, and flank to flank, surrounded by admiring spectators, and their rich team owners who found themselves surrounded by sycophants and favour-seekers.

Among them all, Pirro stood in the cab of his red chariot, ignoring the crowd around him, more concerned with his team who were beginning to chafe at the noise and proximity of all the other teams.

He was sweating beneath the long xystis which he wore, but the Ionic chiton was the official garb of a charioteer, and every driver was bound to wear one. It hid his bad leg, and protected him against debris in the race, but while standing there, it was stifling, sticking to him where the leather straps crossed over on his chest to keep the fabric from ballooning out during the race.

He took a deep breath and was relaxed by the strong smell of horse surrounding him, tried to block out the raucous calls from those surrounding them, the politicians' lackeys who had come to scare opponent cities' teams.

A few scuffles broke out in the press of flesh as it flowed

into the hippodrome, but the Hellanodikai ejected all those who broke the peace, or rather, their muscular helpers did.

Pirro stepped down from the chariot and around to the front of his team.

"Ignore all of this," he told them, stroking and soothing each one, giving them some water from one of the many buckets that had been passed around. "It's all bluster. You are the fastest, my friends. We need to win this for our lady."

Just then Xanthus tossed his great head, the black mane waving about and fanning the others as he did so.

"Ha, ha," Pirro laughed. "That's right. We can do this. I know we can." He looked up and saw the delegation of Spartans cut to the front of the crowd.

Agesilaus was at the front, flanked by his men. His eyes met Pirro's and bore into the younger man, but Pirro bowed to his lord, earning him a curt nod from the king, who immediately made his way into the hippodrome to take his seat.

Pirro did not really know who the great men of Greece were. He did not much care, but he could see which men others were deferring too, and it seemed that most of the latter were those who owned the chariot teams that were waiting to race.

Thrasybulos was there, as well as Aeson of Thessaly, among other men of means and power.

He felt bitter that Kyniska was not permitted to be there, but then he grew angry at the thought of the things they would say to her, the disrespect they would show her, and he was glad of her absence. He knew he would not let her down.

The Hellanodikai were moving through the crowd to look at each chariot and team then, their purple cloaks cutting among the press of man and horseflesh to check wheel hubs, chariot cabs, and the condition of horse and driver.

After some time, the racers in the synoris moved into the hippodrome, and the crowds beyond the tall gatehouse of the track raised a cry to match the shrill music that floated aloft to the Gods' ears.

That gave the four-horse teams of the tethrippon more room to move around, and let their animals walk a little until the Hellanodikai inspected them.

Pirro could see the teams he would be facing much more clearly now - three from Athens, all owned by Thrasybulos, four from Thessaly, owned of course by Aeson, two from Thebes, three from Corinth, one from Cyrenaica, one from Ephesus, one from Halicarnassus, one from Syracuse, one from Massilia, one from Thrace, and one from Euboea.

The horses were magnificent, and Pirro found something to admire in each and every one. Were he not racing, he would have walked about the gathering in admiration of each team.

But he *was* racing, and he knew he needed to focus. Any of those other men would gladly ram him into the embolon of the track, or take a quick swing at his head to see that he lost his footing in the cab.

They are not my friends, he told himself.

"Look at that little one!" one of the Athenian drivers said to his comrades. "He's the driver for the Spartan princess we've heard about!"

There was a chorus of laughter all around Pirro which he did his best to ignore.

"You sure you can handle those blacks?" asked the Syracusan driver next to Pirro.

"As well as any other man," Pirro answered confidently, as he stroked Zoe's neck and held Xanthus' bridle to stop him from nipping at one of the man's horses.

"Watch your horses, boy!" the Syracusan shouted.

"Looks like the Spartans want a fight!" one of Aeson's Thessalian drivers called out from Pirro's other side. The man leaned over to his fellow driver and said in a lower voice, "Remember, if we win, Lord Aeson gets a princess."

The two men chuckled together and looked at Pirro and the black team.

The Spartan team was the only team of blacks out of the

twenty. Most were white, or dapple grey, others varying shades of brown. Their cabs and harness were all elaborately wrought beside the simple trappings of the Spartan chariot and horse harness. The other teams had gold, silver and bronze decorations upon the slim frames of their fast chariot cars, and the straps of their teams' harness.

Pirro did not care for any of it. Simple was better, more Spartan. He thought of what the Thessalians had just said and did not know if they meant for him to hear or not, but he knew what losing meant for him, and for Kyniska. He did not rise to their taunts, for he had always been used to ignoring such idiocy. As the taunts and jibes continued to fly his way from the other drivers, as well as from the owners, especially Aeson and Thrasybulos, Pirro whispered to his team, hummed the stable songs that he so often used to calm them before and after training.

The sound of the crowd was like a volcano building to a cataclysmic blast, indicating the final three laps of the race and some great event on the sand.

Pirro tried to ignore it, temper the fluttering nerves that made his hands shake ever-so-slightly. He thought of the olive groves outside of Sparta, the fields where he had grown up alongside the four horses before him.

Xanthus, Acheron, Phaedra, and Zoe were his brothers and sisters, as much as Kyniska was his mother. They had shared memories and experiences, the joy and pain of shared upbringing, the thrill of having met challenges together, of having overcome those challenges.

"Today is like one of those days," he told them. "Nobody has ever believed in us, or thought us worthy...except her."

The four black heads of the animals leaned in around Pirro's familiar voice and form, his lanky arms reaching up to touch each one of them.

Pirro closed his eyes for a moment, imagining himself back on the fertile green plains of home. He was in the cooling shadow of Mount Taygetos, with the river Eurotas running quickly by. Wheat chaff from the mills floated on the air while he drove his chariot past the walls of Sparta. It was a good memory, no matter what anyone said.

"Teams in the tethrippon!" one of the Hellanodikai stood on a pedestal to address the drivers and owners of the chariot teams. "Time for inspection! The judges will make their way to each chariot team and determine whether all is well, or if some rule of the Games has been broken. May the Gods punish the false and reward true victors. Praise Zeus!" the judges all said together.

WHEN STEFANOS LEFT KYNISKA EARLIER THAT MORNING, HE was surprised to find several Spartans greeting him with praise as he walked, and not just those who had known him from previous campaigns.

Oiled, and wearing only his plain tunic and the headband that marked him as a victor, he walked on with his large satchel slung over his shoulder, crossed the cool water of the Kladeos, and headed into the sanctuary.

It was as if he were in a dream, the world passing by him as if in some ethereal state. He stopped on the other side of the river and felt the breeze on his skin, the packed earth and grass beneath his bare feet. It seemed to him as if his pain had gone, that he was stronger than he had ever been, as if victory in the sacred Games had been a sort of apotheosis.

The activity around the palaestra was less than it had been in the weeks since he arrived at Olympia, and it was no wonder. The final day of the Games was for the great chariot races that commemorated Pelops' victory.

The thought came to him as he walked up to the pentagon of the Pelopion, the mound of the hero rising up from its midst. Stefanos stopped and looked around.

His eyes searched the Pelopion for any sign of the weeping woman whom he felt certain was the shade of Hippodameia. He fought back the chill that ran up his spine and turned to see a group of priests cutting branches from the sacred olive trees behind the temple of Zeus.

The priests were careful about their work, their clean bronze blades glinting in the morning light. Their helpers stood by with baskets in which they laid the silver-green boughs which they would weave into crowns within the temple itself.

Even in the shadow of the Pelopion, Stefanos could not help smiling to himself. He gazed around him at the fine bronzes erected over the centuries by the Olympic victors who had gone before him.

"Father..." he said in a low voice. "It will be a magnificent bronze... Something to be remembered for all time."

He continued on his way, cutting through the crowd, until he arrived at the temple of Hera.

It was, as ever, quiet within, the goddess ever willing to grant him peace in her sanctuary.

The only sound as he walked toward the main altar was the padding of his feet on the marble floor. When he reached the altar, Stefanos, son of Talos of Argos, put down the satchel and knelt before the queen of the Gods, his hands gripping the cold edge of her altar.

"Goddess Hera, I dedicate this victory to you who have watched over me...to my family, who has ever been faithful to you...and to Kyniska, who has been victorious in your own Heraia, and whose image hangs on one of the plaques here in your sanctuary." Stefanos paused in his words, his breathing slowing. "Grant Kyniska victory this day, oh Goddess. Let her show the world what she can do. Let us be happy together, from this day forward. I would give it all up for her to be victorious and live the free life she chooses. A life she wants to live with me by her side... For this, Goddess, I will build you a monument outside of the Heraion of Argos, something of beauty and honour."

Stefanos stood and looked at his hoplon which still lay at the foot of the goddess' statue, and then up at her motherly eyes which looked into him. He opened the satchel to reveal his thorax which he lifted slowly and placed upon the altar.

"Thank you, Queen Hera."

WHEN STEFANOS WAS OUTSIDE AGAIN, THE SOUND OF MUSIC filled his ears. The day's festivities were well underway and crowds were gathering around the temple of Zeus, with even more massing around the entrance to the hippodrome to the south-east.

"Congratulations on your victory, Stefanos of Argos!" a voice called from a shady spot near the temple.

Stefanos looked and there he spotted the Athenian philosopher, Plato. The man sat on a marble bench beneath an olive tree, alone, watching the people pass before him.

Not wanting to be rude, Stefanos approached. "Thank you, Plato."

"Think nothing of it. A champion deserves to be honoured, and from what I witnessed yesterday, you are truly a champion among the Greeks." He smiled broadly, his eyes observing Stefanos closely as he tugged thoughtfully at his beard. "How do you feel?"

"I'm not sure exactly, to tell you the truth," Stefanos said. "Grateful that the Gods saw fit to help me make my father's last wish a reality."

Plato nodded. "A most worthy cause."

"Blessed that I may now make a great change in the life I have led to this point." Stefanos looked absentmindedly at the crowds of people, the poets reciting over their heads, the musicians filling the air with their music.

"You speak of Eris Agathos, no?" Plato said.

"Yes... I...I do. My father, before he died, said that I had indulged in Kakochartos for too long." Stefanos was quiet again. "I fear he was right, and I hope to make it right, by the Gods."

"By the Gods, Stefanos of Argos, I do believe you have.

But," Plato stood and walked with Stefanos into the sunlight, toward the temple of Zeus. "Though you may embrace Eris Agathos, there will always be men, great and small, who embrace the darker side of Eris - Kakochartos."

"Believe me, I know it." Stefanos thought of all the wicked men he had met in his life, served, fought, saved and killed.

"Being here, in this sacred place," Plato continued, his chin up, his eyes closing as he smelled the smoke, sweat, and pine-scented air, "I have come to the realization that it is the duty of those who uphold Eris Agathos to help others, especially those who wield power or have a will to do so, to leave wickedness behind in favour of Eris Agathos." He looked back at Stefanos then and smiled. "Now, what would a world like that look like?"

Stefanos thought about it for a moment. It was a pleasant thought, to think that good deeds could inspire other good deeds so that they spread like summer wildfires. "It would be a true utopia. It would make Greece the greatest civilization this world has known."

Plato nodded emphatically. "Precisely." He began to walk away, his mind already working towards some wished-for end. "Wouldn't that be a world of wonders..."

Stefanos watched the philosopher disappear into the crowd and chuckled to himself. However, the weight of the words, the idea, that Plato had just spoken of, made Stefanos wonder at the possibilities of victory beyond an olive crown or a bronze statue.

"Stefanos! There you are!"

Stefanos recognized Axion's voice booming over the crowd of people.

"Good morning!" Stefanos said as the gymnasiarchos came striding towards him.

"You're supposed to be at the Bouleuterion for the sacrifice and then the parade of victors to the temple of Zeus for the binding of the crown. Where have you been?"

"Giving my thanks to Hera," Stefanos said.

"Well, that's good, of course, but now Zeus and Nike await you, and you shouldn't be late! Come-on!" Axion led the way, pushing aside some of the crowd as he went. "Make way, coming through. Stefanos of Argos coming through here!"

It was odd to Stefanos, but most of those who heard Axion's words immediately stood aside for him to get through.

THE AREA AROUND THE ALTAR WHICH STOOD BEFORE THE Bouleuterion was less crowded than it had been at the start of the Games. Three of the Hellanodikai stood nearby with three of the sanctuary's priests.

They were all gathered about the marble altar, two attendants holding a black ram for the offering. Standing there, before the altar, glistening with oil and dressed in pure white chitons, were the victors, Hermios of Arkadia, and Iphitos of Croton.

The two men nodded to Stefanos as he approached, each taking his hand and motioning that he should join them before the altar.

"Now that we are all assembled..." the head priest said, "the sacrifice may be carried out." The priest nodded to an attendant who held a skin drum. The latter began to beat a slow, steady rhythm as the priest raised his hands to the sky.

"Great Father, Olympian Zeus! We call on you to witness that these three men have proved themselves worthy of victory in your sacred Olympiad. Mark them as victors so that their example shines out as a beacon from this land between the Kladeos and Alpheios rivers, where you Gods held your first games ages ago."

The priest turned to the two other priests who took the black ram from the attendants and placed it on the altar.

"Accept this offering, Father Zeus. Look kindly on these men of victory as the sacred crowns are placed upon their heads by the goddess Nike."

In a flash, the priest's knife swept across the ram's neck

and blood ran thick and red onto the altar. After a few moments, the priest was poking and prodding the sacrificial guts, until he stopped, raised his bloody hands and spoke.

"Let them proceed to the temple and be crowned. The Gods ordain it should be so!" he said aloud, a smile spreading across his usually stern face. "To the temple!" the priest called as the flutes were struck up to accompany the drum and tambourine.

The three victors fell into step behind the three priests and the three Hellanodikai, and all together they, and those watching, began their slow walk to the steps of the temple of Zeus.

Cheers rose on either side of the procession as flowers, fruit, and greens were showered on the champions, the philobolia of adoration.

Stefanos and the others laughed and smiled as explosions of colour rained down on them, and hands reached out to touch their own hands, arms, shoulders and backs.

Every person in the crowd sought to touch those who had been set apart by the Gods.

As he walked, Stefanos thought that he had never felt so good, except in Kyniska's arms, or in the warm glow of her smile. For a moment, he hoped she was there to see him, but then realized that that was impossible.

I'll tell her all about it! he thought.

When they reached the white steps of the temple of Zeus, they stopped beneath the images of Zeus, Pelops, Oinomaus, and Hippodameia. The priests and Hellanodikai turned to face the crowd at the bottom of the steps, and the champions followed suit, their eyes taking in the view of hundreds of cheering faces, each man searching the crowd for those he recognized as a friend or comrade.

As they took in the sights, sounds, and delights of this penultimate experience, the priests within the temple were finishing the olive crowns that were to be placed upon the heads of the three men who stood outside in the sun's brilliance.

. . .

"CHARIOTEERS!" ONE OF THE HELLANODIKAI CALLED TO THE gathering of twenty teams from atop a marble platform in their midst. "You have all passed the inspection. The Gods have favoured you with a chance at eternal glory!"

Pirro watched as the men around him cheered and raised their arms to the sky, some of the horses becoming jittery. However, he remained quiet, his face looking to the sky, his eyes closed as he stepped back into the cab, his voice soothing the blacks.

Gods, I place myself in your care.

The Hellanodikai went on. "You have each chosen an ostracon with a letter upon it. That is your lane. When you enter the hippodrome -"

He had to stop talking for all the noise that swept out of the hippodrome as the victor of the synoris was proclaimed. When it died down to a manageable level, he continued.

"When you enter the hippodrome, you will line up before the Eagle Altar for the sacrifice. After the sacrifice is completed, you will then proceed to the hysplex marked with your letter. But this is not yet the start of the race."

The charioteers were more silent now, the tensity of the approaching moment full in their sweating faces.

"Before the ropes are raised along the hyspleges, you will parade around the hippodrome at a slow place so that your horses can be exercised, and so you can each be announced to the crowd. After the procession of all teams is finished, you will go back to your assigned hysplex and await the start of the race."

The Hellanodikai looked around at the charioteers and the gathered owners, glances shot this way and that, guesses as to who would come out in the lead, who would survive, and who would win.

"You will complete a total of twelve laps around the embolon, each lap indicated by the fall of one bronze dolphin."

The men nodded, as they had all seen the track, taken one

chance at practice upon it.

"Question!" one of the Thessalian charioteers said out loud.

"Yes?" the Hellanodikai said.

"What if every driver fails to catch up to me?" he laughed, as did his countrymen.

The judge was not amused. "You are the finest charioteers in the Greek world if you are here. I think it doubtful that you will be alone."

There was some laughter, but less than before.

"But, Nike can only crown one victor this day," the judge said. "And so, to the Gods' chosen, is granted the glory and the olive crown."

With that, the Hellanodikai dismounted the platform and went into the hippodrome.

As the large gates swung open to allow the chariots through, someone yelled and the two horse chariots came rushing out, their drivers sweaty and dirt-smattered, their horses foaming and wet.

Pirro counted out thirteen two-horse chariots. That meant the remaining seven more were not able to ride out of the hippodrome.

The last to come was an Athenian chariot, and a cry rose up from his fellows as he held the reins with one hand and waved with the other as he rode by.

When all of the two horse chariots had passed, the music was struck up again and the teams proceeded through the gatehouse and into the hippodrome of Olympia.

Several teams went before Pirro, mainly the Thessalians who had forced their way to the front, ahead of the Athenians. He fell in behind the driver from Massilia, a Celt by the looks of him, with long blond hair and an extremely muscular body covered in blue whorls. As the man reined in his big red-brown team, his muscles bulged beneath the ill-fitting chiton.

"Here we go, my friends," Pirro said as they passed out of

the shadows and into the light.

He had never seen anything like it. When he had had his practice run in the hippodrome, it had seemed vast, yes, but empty. Now, at its capacity, it was a living thing, a beast, and the charioteers mere game pieces upon a board of sand, wood, and stone.

The sound was deafening, as if one were standing on the edge of the sea during a winter storm, the waves crashing.

The horses' ears twitched nervously, and Pirro spoke to them as they walked forward to join the line before the Eagle Altar, a great white marble altar on which was an elaborately carved eagle with outspread wings in red, brown, and gold.

"It's just noise. They cheer for us, and our princess is with us, as ever," Pirro said to his team.

His eyes raked the embankments for signs of Spartan red, and he found it, as well as Argive blue, and Athenian white. He saw the grouping of purple where the Hellanodikai were seated, the priestess of Demeter Chamayne nearby, along with some of the priests of Olympia.

The factions of each city state were about to begin their chants, but the priest at the altar raised his hands, his white sleeves sliding down his arms to reveal the bronze blade he would use.

Pirro lined up with the other drivers before the altar, turning his head so that he could see properly.

"Great Father, Zeus!" the priest began, his words echoed by other priests down the line of the hippodrome. "On this last day of your sacred Olympiad, we ask for your blessing on this race. As the hero Pelops raced to glory across this land, so too let the best among the Greeks ride to glory here in your sanctuary!"

A pure white lamb was brought up then, and flutes piped up to lend song to the occasion. The animal had a wreath of wild olive about its neck, and the colourful blooms of summer flowers in its fleece. It bucked and kicked a couple of times, but the priests knew their work well, soothing it and feeding it washed grains.

"Accept our offering, Olympian Zeus, and know that each man here honours you."

The knife flashed in the bright light and Pirro saw blood shoot from the animal's neck, soaking the fleece about the wreath, and pouring out onto the marble of the altar.

Some of the horses jerked at the smell of the blood, but Kyniska's blacks were calm, their eyes staring directly ahead, down the track of the hippodrome, their ears pricking backwards to hear anything Pirro said.

After congregating about the altar, the priests declared that Zeus had accepted the sacrifice, and that the race could proceed.

A cheer ran along the embankments surrounding the vast track and some of the charioteers began to talk again.

As one, the row of twenty chariot teams moved forward, past the Eagle Altar, and into their assigned hyspleges.

Pirro was in the seventh lane, and on his right, one of the Athenian teams. On his left, the Massilian team driven by the Celt. The latter was stern-faced, his gaze directed in front, while the Athenian looked around, seemingly as relaxed as could be.

We'll give them a surprise! Pirro thought as the Athenian gazed down his nose at him.

A fanfare of music, of aulos, tambourine, and drums, rose into the air and the charioteers were ordered to begin the parade.

A few of the horses champed and stomped, others rearing, before they all started to move in unison, but soon they were moving, and for the first time, Pirro really began to look around.

The hippodrome was four stades long, and one stade, four plethera wide, so large two armies could have fought a pitched battle on its track and still had room to manoeuvre. To his left, the embolon began, the central spine of wood and stone that divided the two sides of the hippodrome, and around which they were to drive their teams. At the nearer end were twelve bronze dolphins, suspended along a bar, each with its nose pointing toward the sky.

These would count down the laps, one dolphin being tipped forward with the completion of each lap.

Above the dolphins rose a single marble column on top of which was a life-sized statue of Hippodameia, daughter of King Oinomaus, and Pelops' partner in that legendary race.

Pirro gazed up at her for a moment, and swore she looked like his mistress - the wild look, the wind-swept hair, the determination, strength and beauty, all of it. Again, he wished she could see him then.

Instead, as he passed King Agesilaus who sat with Xenophon and some of the other Spartans, Pirro bowed his head as the Hellanodikai announced his team to the masses lining the track.

Few cheers rang out for Sparta, but he did not care, even when the Athenians laughed at him.

Men clapped and chanted, heckled and cursed as the teams rounded the far end of the embolon.

Several horses jerked away from the Taraxippos, that dreaded corner of the hippodrome that was said to be haunted by a vengeful Oinomaus.

"Keep away!" Pirro yelled at the Athenian driver whose team kicked out, narrowly missing Xanthus.

"Easy, boy!" The Athenian said. "You'll be seeing my backside soon enough!"

"Stop it, Agron!" the Thessalian driver on the Celt's other side said to the Athenian. "You'll make the Spartan cripple cry!"

Pirro gripped the reins and tried to ignore them, thought only of his team, and what he had to do that day.

The pace was slow, and he wanted to warm the team up more, especially as they had been standing still for some time outside the hippodrome.

He flicked the reins and clicked his tongue, and the blacks shot forward for several feet before slowing again.

"Back in line!" the Hellanodikai yelled from where they sat on the west side of the north bank.

Pirro made other noises that he and Kyniska had trained the horses to, and they began to prance lightly, jump on the spot, loosen their limbs.

Many in the stands roared with laughter at this display, as did most of the charioteers, but he ignored them, backing his team up, and moving them slowly forward until the line of other chariots caught up with him.

"If you can't control those demons, Ginger, then stay away from the real charioteers!" the Athenian spat at Pirro.

"I guess the Spartan princess spread her legs to get into the race, just as they say!" laughed the Thessalian.

Pirro shot the man a murderous look, only to be laughed at again.

Back in the stands, Agesilaus sat sternly, his arms crossed, his face rigid.

"He's already making a mockery of Sparta," he said to Xenophon. "What a ridiculous display!"

Xenophon leaned in. "Actually, my friend, he is right to do it. The horses' muscles will have gotten cold with all the standing about. Young Pirro has just warmed them up a little before the race. Quite smart."

Agesilaus said nothing, but continued to watch the crowd, noting the eyes that met his, the looks his enemies and supposed allies gave him. Not everyone was there for the race, but the honour of Sparta was at stake, and that was always something to be reckoned with.

Eventually, the teams completed their circuit of the hippodrome, and took their positions back at the hyspleges.

Some of the drivers tossed jewellery and other ornaments they had been wearing for show to their attendants behind the starting gates, while others inspected their harness and chariot wheels.

By the feel of everything during the parade lap, Pirro knew his chariot was in right order, and that the team's harness was solid. He adjusted the crossed leather straps that ran over his chest to hold his chiton in place. He flexed and bent his knees, especially his damaged leg, ensuring that his footing was correct on the small platform of the cab.

"Ready my friends," he whispered to Acheron, Zoe, Phaedra, and Xanthus. "Whatever happens, it has always been my honour to ride with you."

He looked forward as the Hellanodikai raised the rope across the mechanism of the hyspleges.

The starting gates were arrayed in an arrowhead formation that would allow all teams to start without running into each other. The lots had been drawn, so there was no favouritism. The lead chariot was the Ephesian team, and Pirro was just a few to the left and back of him.

He could feel his heart beating then as the final moments elapsed and the crowd calmed, like the absolute quiet before a storm.

"Lord Poseidon, guide my team..." Pirro whispered.

The rope dropped, and the world was all thunder.

Twenty chariots shot out of the hyspleges, the arrowhead formation in which they started lasting for only a couple seconds before all chaos broke loose and the teams vied for the inside lane at the front of the pack.

Men cried out, and horses champed and pulled as their nostrils flared, their drivers slapping the reins upon their backs.

Pirro held his team back as planned, letting most of the others battle it out for the front before the first turn. From his vantage, with the wind blowing in his face and the black manes of his team dancing before his eyes, he thought he had never seen or heard anything so beautiful. As he planted his feet and urged his team to slow, his arms straining, Pirro thought that this must be what it was like at the first great making of the world, when the first horse herds were left loose upon oceans of grass to run free and fast without a care in the world as the ground shook and the Gods smiled.

The reverie was broken quickly enough as the first turn came rushing up and thousands of people cried out in terror.

As the teams pressed in upon each other for the turn, the Euboean team bolted from the far right, near the Taraxippos, and slammed into one of the Theban teams, sending one of the chariots into the air to land on the Ephesian driver's head. The Ephesian horses then ploughed into one of the Thessalian teams amid a chorus of shouts, screaming horses, and the cracking of bone and wood.

Pirro thought he spied something black at the Taraxippos but tried not to think of it as he bent his knees and urged his team toward the embolon, coming around the corner just ahead of the Massilian Celt.

Acheron held them firm to the turn with Zoe and Phaedra pulling them forward, and Xanthus deftly leaping a stray yoke that lay in the path before he followed the others around.

Once they were out of the corner, Pirro gave them the permission they needed and the Spartan team pulled away safely.

The race was on.

The crowd roared like some enraged beast out of Tartarus all around Kyniska, Euryleonis, and Ajax. As the teams passed the first turn, the track crews worked feverishly to clear the debris and bodies of the four fallen teams.

The race did not stop, even for that.

Kyniska loosened her grip on Euryleonis' hand when Pirro pulled through the first turn, the relief she felt like the water pulling out to sea before a tidal wave.

"He's through," Ajax said, peering over the heads before them. "Go, lad!"

They had found their spot at the very top of the embankment, just above the Taraxippos, where, as they had anticipated, there were several spots still available. From where Kyniska and Euryleonis stood, with their disguises hiding their gender, they could see the entire south side of the hippodrome in front, and the slope of the embankments behind, falling away to the Alpheios river.

They had had to take the long way to get to the hippodrome, avoiding the Altis, and missing a chance to see Stefanos crowned, because of the crowds milling about.

The intense smells of men's sweat, the screaming, curses, prayers, and praise that were thrown out over the track barely made her notice, for she watched every one of Pirro's commands, the motion of each of her team, anticipating everything as if she were one with each of them.

She could not speak, for she would have given herself away, even covered as she was in peasant's clothing and the broad sun hat.

When the first crash happened, Euryleonis gripped Kyniska's arms tightly, but the princess knew her charioteer's skill well, and they had discussed the possibility of collision at the first turn. She had not, however, expected it to be so violent and bloody, with five horses and two charioteers seemingly dead as they pulled them off the track just in time for the second lap.

The teams rushed on toward her, like an army racing to the battle front, but they went slower than before, except for the Thessalians and Athenians, both of whom weaved in and out of the fray, trying to get the better of the other.

When Pirro's red chariot came into view, Kyniska wanted to scream her encouragement to him, urge her children on, to listen, to wait, to be patient for that one moment when they should start to run, and when they would grasp their victory.

As the wind rushed in upon him, Pirro wiped the dirt from his face, his arms straining at the reins as he pulled the team into the turn to begin the third lap.

His ears rang with the sound of turning wheels, running horses, and shouting men, but he held his focus, even as he glanced up to see the third bronze dolphin tip forward to indicate the second lap was finished.

He was neck and neck with the Celt, whose muscled arms pulled, and steered, and strained. The Massilian driver was the only one who really seemed to pay him any heed, or to have a similar strategy.

Pirro knew he had to watch him, even as the other teams wreaked havoc at the front. For now, he and the blacks settled into a good, solid pace. They were warm now, their muscles firing with ease and rapidity that would come in useful when the time was right.

It was odd, to travel at such speeds, in such chaotic conditions, and yet feel as if the world was passing by slowly, at an observable rate.

Flashes of faces in the crowd of tens of thousands occurred to Pirro as he passed them, men pulling their hair, eating, spitting, making signs against evil. Some slapped the backs of their friends in excitement, others used the hysteria to rub up against elegant youths close by to them.

He noticed the horses most of all, each team, which ones were failing due to a fast start, which ones had the stamina to keep up the careening pace set by their drivers.

Like a battlefield general, Pirro knew everything that was happening on the hippodrome track at that time. He prided himself on it, used it. Was he not also a Spartan?

Like Kyniska, to whom he owed everything, he had been a misfit in their world far to the south east, and like her, he was determined to deliver the Greeks a blow such as they had never had before.

Half way through the fourth lap, just as they passed the Taraxippos, the three Thessalian chariots closed in on the Thracian driver who was making a sprint for the lead.

Like jackals around a lion, they closed in rapidly, bumping him lightly, trying to get him to panic and veer off course.

The crowd booed and cheered at the same time, and just as the Thracian seemed to be pulling away, one of the Thessalians came quickly in from the outside, surprising the Thracian team and sending them into the side of the embolon.

Pirro watched it happen from behind, heard the great splintering of wood as the Thracian chariot crashed, the cry of the horses, and the thump of the driver's body as he was flung into the column supporting the statue of Hippodameia.

The crowd was on its feet, many cursing the Thessalians who had brought ill omen to the race, the Thracian's limp body testament to that.

While two of the Thessalians untangled their spooked horses from the wreckage and debris, the Athenians, grabbed the lead which the Gods had set before them. Now, the three Athenian chariots spread across a large portion of the track, their mass like a moving barricade of wood, leather, and running flesh.

Down the straightaway they flew, Pirro passing one of the Thessalians, the Celt still keeping pace.

The far end of the hippodrome rushed up to them, and as they approached, Pirro spotted it, blinking his eyes in disbelief.

A shadow lunged out from the Taraxippos, a thing with claws and horns, and a gaping mouth to strike terror into the senses of beast and man alike. It burst forth from the embankment, seemingly hungry for discord and destruction.

The left was blocked by the Celt, whose horses' eyes bulged in terror, and so Pirro bent his knees, fear finally gripping him with icy hands.

"Run, my friends! Run!" he called to his team. "It's a trick of the Gods!"

The reins gripped in white knuckles, Pirro led his team directly into the shadow.

Poseidon, help us!

At that moment, Kyniska strained her neck to see what was happening far below, in what now appeared to be the dark pit of the hippodrome.

Hang on! she yelled inside, willing her team to hear her

words of encouragement. *Do not be afraid! Run! Run!* she thought, even as the crowd roared all around her.

The sounds from the hippodrome washed over the Altis, shattering the peace of the ceremonies taking place, giving pause to the priests of Olympian Zeus as they prepared to crown those chosen mortals who would wear the sacred olive crowns.

Smoke from the offerings burning on the great altar of Zeus drifted among the trees, weaved about the columns, and blurred the perfect lines of the bronze statues that ornamented the sacred precinct.

The bitter-sweet smell of burning flesh and incense from the altar reached Stefanos and his fellow victors, dizzying them with the ceremony of the moment. A flute, tambourine, and sistrum sounded gently at the back of their minds, a counter to the eruption of noise from the hippodrome.

"Father Zeus!" the head priest began from the top of the steps, just beside the three victors, each of them wearing only a loincloth now, in the smokey light of the sun. "On this fifth day of your sacred games, we crown these men victorious, and ask that they be recognized as best among the Greeks this day in their fighting sports.

Stefanos felt like he had seen all of it in a dream before, but knew he could not have. He turned his head slightly to see the athletes beside him, both dazed, and elated at the same time. Did they see something he did not?

"Oh Goddess Nike, this day we crown Hermios, son of Nesos of Arkadia, the victor in wrestling, best among the Greeks..."

The priest turned to take one of the olive crowns from another priest, and held it aloft, above the Arkadian's head.

The silver-green olive leaves twitched as the crown was held up, as if some god stood by unseen, blowing gently into the carefully-woven crown.

The Arkadian looked up, and Stefanos thought the younger man trembled as he stood there, muttering prayers perhaps?

As the crown came down, he leaned into it, his eyes closing and a tear running down his cheek as a sort of ecstasy washed over him.

No one in the crowd laughed at his tears, none dared such sacrilege, for they could only guess at the struggle that had led that young man from his remote mountain village to Olympia to be declared best among the Greek people of the world.

When his eyes opened, it was as if he had woken from a dream, for a startled look came over his face before he smiled and looked skyward into the great blue expanse.

Stefanos continued to watch the younger man, intrigued by what he had just experienced, wondering what the man of Croton would do next.

"Oh Goddess Nike," the priest continued as great plumes of smoke billowed past the temple steps like the unfurled sails of a ghostly ship. "This day...we crown Iphitos, son of Melinos of Croton, as best among the Greeks in the pankration."

The crown was brought, slowly and with great ceremony, the sacred bough fashioned into a circlet fit for a hero.

The man of Croton stared at the ground, no doubt, Stefanos thought, thinking of the life he had taken on the skamma, wondering if he would see that man in the Halls of Hades some day.

Then, Iphitos hearkened to the blue depths of the sky, as if perceiving something beautiful all of a sudden, for his eyes were wide and his mouth open in words of prayer that would not come forth audibly.

Stefanos looked away, unwilling to disturb the man's reverie, but he felt compelled to look, to try and understand the beauty of what he was seeing in his features. The pain of his toils seemed to leach away and be replaced by that same ecstasy he had seen in the face of Hermios of Arkadia.

Iphitos' massive shoulders shuddered and his head bowed at the last moment, just before the priest placed the olive crown upon his head.

When he opened his eyes again, Iphitos seemed to stand taller, to shine more brilliantly, his body an image of glistening perfection as one might have only expected of Herakles, the first pankrationist.

Stefanos felt his heart begin to beat rapidly as the priest went back into the temple to retrieve his own crown of victory from the altar before the great statue of Zeus. He spotted Kratos standing in the middle of the crowd of silent onlookers, men who had laughed at him, doubted him, shunned him for a mercenary, for an Argive, and for a man who had cared little for what they thought until that moment when their adulation was a thing to be appreciated.

Even the doubters had set aside their prejudices toward him, for if the Gods approved of Stefanos of Argos, then surely they should as well.

Kratos nodded to Stefanos as the priest came out of the temple, slowly, bearing a lush crown of olive which would be placed on top of his friend's head, over the red ribbon of victory.

Stefanos nodded back at Kratos. *This is it...*

His heart pounded heavily, but he felt light, powerful, blessed for all the toils that had led him to this one moment in time. He thought of the statue he would erect to appease his father's shade and honour his family's memory.

Stefanos knew Talos would receive a measure of joy in the Afterlife, something to match the beauty he had himself put into this life, this world, in the form of immortal bronze.

Father...for you...

The priest was walking directly up the stairs toward him now, and stopped to say the words.

"Olympian Zeus...King of the Gods... Bless this mortal who has trained, and fought, and excelled in this world. Stefanos, son of Talos, of Argos, has proved himself best among the Greeks in the noble art of boxing. We crown him now in your sacred sanctuary..."

The priest's words faded out of Stefanos' hearing as his attention was drawn to an opening of light in the pure blue of the sky above them. The world seemed to slow, to have its sound and movement muted for a few moments as the light grew more intense and filled Stefanos with a sensation he was not even capable of imagining.

Kyniska... She came into his mind. *I wish you could see this...*

He became aware of a fluttering of massive wings, and a flurry of white and blue robes out of the heavens, coming directly toward him out of the brilliance of that immortal light.

Goddess... he thought as he saw Nike swooping down, full of grace, and power, and radiance. In her lithe hand, she held aloft an olive crown that shivered and shook as it would have if it were still in the garden of the Gods.

Stefanos closed his eyes, ready for the touch of the crown upon his head, his heart beating faster and stronger with every second.

Until a scream rent the air.

His eyes shot wide, and the feeling of ecstasy that had begun to flow like godly fire through his veins, gave way to fear and terror.

Beyond the crowd, the woman stood, pointing and screaming, black tears running down her cheeks as she stared at Stefanos and pointed to a group of men nearby.

None seemed to see or hear her, but Stefanos knew her only too well.

Hippodameia?

He tried to focus on Nike, her descent to him out of the sky nearly complete, but the screaming of that sad shade racked Stefanos' body and soul with terror.

Then, he saw the men she pointed at.

They were staring at him as they walked past the Temple of Zeus, laughing. Ocnus and his four friends were going toward the hippodrome, that dread shade cursing after them as they went, screaming at Stefanos.

Ocnus looked directly at Stefanos and drew his hand across his throat before they disappeared into the crowd.

The shade of Hippodameia appeared a little farther off, pointing in the direction they had gone.

Nike was nearly upon Stefanos, her arm outstretched, the olive crown coming to rest upon his brow at any moment.

Kyniska!

Just as Stefanos felt the flutter of the goddess' wings upon his face, he bolted from the steps of the Temple of Zeus, pushing his way though the crowd in the direction of that dread shade, even as an overwhelming sense of loss invaded his psyche.

Once more the noise of the world erupted around the Altis, everyone wondering what happened to Stefanos, son of Talos.

It was almost impossible for Kyniska to remain silent where she stood on her eyrie overlooking the hippodrome, watching her blacks run, and slow, veer and jump, dodging destruction at every turn. She blessed Pirro for his skill and foresight in the heat of the battle. For a battle, it was.

She wondered if ever the Gods had seen such a race as this among mortal or immortal horses since Pelops and Hippodameia had sped across the land.

Pirro and her team seemed to have conquered their fear of the Taraxippos, even as it lunged for other teams, striking terror into even the fastest horses on the track.

On the sixth lap, the Syracusan team bolted from that dread corner, diagonally into the end of the embolon with a crack of wood, and splintered bone, and screaming.

Euryleonis turned and buried her head in Kyniska's chest for a fleeting moment, unable to bear the sight of savaged horses, writhing as they were in a pained and terror-stricken tangle, their driver a bloody, broken mass on the dirt before them.

Runners charged out as the other teams passed, their hurried actions lacking all pity and grace as they hacked at the tangle of reins, harness, and dead limbs to separate them before the other teams came around and slammed into the bloody mess.

The crowd, for a few moments, forgot the racers, their eyes on the fallen Syracusan team and the runners struggling to get them off the track just in time.

As they came into the seventh lap, the Athenians and Thessalians fought for the lead, dodging, edging, speeding up and slowing down, reckless, heedless of their teams' frothing mouths and bleeding nostrils as they kept the other teams gated behind them at breakneck speed.

The crowd roared so loudly that it seemed to shake the trees on the Hill of Kronos, like the wind in a summer fire storm.

Hold on Pirro... Kyniska thought as she watched, not taking her eyes from the track and her team as the eighth bronze dolphin turned over. *Almost time!*

Kyniska's blacks charged behind the three Corinthian teams who also seemed to be blocking the way to the leaders, harried by the remaining Theban driver who lashed his team cruelly with four laps to go.

Kyniska watched as Pirro picked up the pace, the blacks revelling in the speed she had taught them to love and cherish.

He moved to the outside, followed by the Massilian horses, the Celt shouting in his own tongue at his team.

They passed the Taraxippos and then sped away, passing the Corinthians on the outside and darting in beside the Thessalians who had given way to the Athenians in front.

The crowd cheered for the daring, but Kyniska knew of the danger posed by Aeson's teams.

Her fears were confirmed when, at the end of the eighth

lap she saw Pirro's head snap sideways as one of the Thessalians hemming him in reached out and punched him as they went into the turn.

"The Gods will punish you!" Ajax yelled out, unable to control his rage at what had happened.

Kyniska and Euryleonis lowered their heads quickly as a few of the people in front of them looked back at the big Spartan.

Kyniska gripped Ajax's hand and he looked at her for forgiveness, indicated with concern the chariot where Pirro was on his knees in the cab, far to the outside of the hippodrome track.

Keep on course, my children! Kyniska screamed inside, hoping they would hear her.

Pirro shook his head, and saw the flecks of blood staining his mud-spattered chiton. He still held the reins but was dazed.

"Slow!" he called to his team. "Left!"

Acheron's ears pricked up and the inside black began to pull them back toward the embolon, into the turn facing the Taraxippos.

As Pirro rose to his feet in the speeding chariot, the crowd cheered for his bravery, many booing the Thessalians as they passed, earning them audible threats from Aeson where he stood in the crowd.

Pirro spat blood onto the floor of the cab and flicked the reins quickly. He knew they needed to make up the lost ground.

He could see one of the Athenian teams tiring and falling behind, hemmed in by two of the Thessalians as they vied for a place behind the leaders.

He chanced a look up to see the bronze dolphins. *Not long now!* He flicked the reins, then with all his strength was forced to pull the team suddenly to the right as the Athenian and two Thessalians in front of him got their wheels tangled.

There was a loud crack, a scream, and in a moment, as if the hand of some god had come out of the sky to strike them, the Athenian chariot catapulted upward and turned sideways so that the horses slammed into the Thessalian on the right, and the chariot itself came down onto the head of the Thessalian on the left, sending all three sliding in a screaming dust cloud toward the hyspleges.

Pirro pulled hard to slow the blacks as the mass of wood, men, and horses careened before them, almost in a sickly slow vision, before the blacks jumped and his chariot wheels came off the ground as they ran over one of the flailing men.

Pirro peered through the dust ahead to see the remaining Athenian and Thessalian team fighting for the lead, the sound of their whips and the frenzied urging of their drivers over the cheering of the crowd. Peasant, priest, noble, and king alike, all were on their feet.

As they rounded the first turn of the ninth lap, Pirro bent his knees and slapped the reins on the sweating black flanks before him.

"Now! Run, my friends! RUN!"

The Spartan team shot forward, leaving the Massilian and others behind, as if they had only been waiting for this chance.

In the crowd, Xenophon and others were crying at the top of their lungs, tears upon their faces for the beauty of such creatures, uttering that they must surely be of the Gods' divine stock.

As the black manes waved wildly, freely in the wind, as surely as if they were soaring across the heavens, Pirro yelled at the top of his voice...

"Kyniska!!!"

. . .

Stefanos had never run so fast in all of his life, not into or from danger, not in his most gruelling days of blood when Kakochartos had its stranglehold upon his soul.

Never had his legs moved so swiftly, his heart beat so surely as they did in that moment when he sped from the Altis, his glory behind him, past the sanctuary of Hestia toward the river.

He ran without question, as if guided by some unknown force, the only word that rang over and over in his mind, Kyniska's name. He only saw her face before him, felt her touch, spoke her name as the sweat poured down his body, his muscled legs pumping, carrying him across the sanctuary until he was along the river, behind the south embankment of the hippodrome.

He stopped, his lungs burning, his mind awhirl.

Then he saw the shade, standing still, nearby, so close that he could see the strength and despair, the pity, and anger in her eyes, behind the fringe of her hair, wild as a horse's mane.

She stopped screaming and pointed up to the top of the hippodrome to where a tall man stood beside two with great sun hats.

For a moment, Stefanos was confused, anguished. He wanted to scream, to charge the apparition that had brought him to that spot, but then, he looked closer to where she pointed.

Kyniska, he thought.

The apparition nodded, its ghostly eyes piercing him, challenging him, and then looking past him.

Stefanos turned to see five men striding along the outside of the hippodrome embankment, the leader among them pointing up at the tall man and the two with sun hats.

"Gods, give me strength," Stefanos said as he ran to block their path in nothing but his loincloth and the red ribbon of victory.

The group stopped, the sun glinting off of the daggers they carried.

There was hate there, oh yes, such as Stefanos had never seen.

Ocnus and his gang - Krikor, Biton, Ampyx, and Glaucus - they all stood there battered, bruised, and filled with bitterness beyond reckoning, seething with hate and fury that Stefanos had seen little of in his days upon the fields of Ares.

"Seems you've lost your olive crown, Stefanos!" Ocnus spat.

Stefanos crossed his arms, feeling the heat of the sun upon his oiled body.

The sound from the hippodrome was such that a couple of the men looked for a crack in the sky.

"Kyniska!!!" they heard the cry from within the hippodrome, and Stefanos felt a thrill run through his body. He smiled.

"Your Spartan whore is in there, Stefanos, and we're going to expose her to the world. She'll be killed for her sacrilege!"

"You never learn, Ocnus," Stefanos said calmly, though his heart raced. He looked up at the broad-rimmed hat at the top of the embankment and then back at the men before him. "You're nothing!" he said loudly. "You've always been nothing. All of you. Go away, and crawl back into your holes. If you don't, I'll kill every one of you." He pointed at each of them, his hand steady as he did so, his eyes taking in the blades that faced him.

The group laughed, a couple of them spinning their daggers, longing for the chance to plunge their blades into his flesh.

"She's going to suffer," Ocnus said, spitting on the ground. "As you will."

"Ocnus! Stop this now!" came a voice behind the group.

Kratos! Stefanos saw his friend running full speed toward the Argives.

"What are you all doing? Leave him alone! Would you shed blood in the sanctuary?" Kratos stood facing Ocnus and the others, each of whom looked from him to Stefanos. "You've already gone too far!"

"What?" Stefanos said, moving slightly closer, until two of the blades were pointing at him again.

"Kratos," Ocnus said. "It's time for you to leave if you know what's good for you."

"Oh, I know what's good for me, Ocnus. It's standing right here beside my brother."

Ocnus turned quickly. "And dying beside him too!"

Before Kratos knew what had happened, Ocnus' blade had plunged into his bare chest, above the heart into the shoulder.

Kratos stumbled back, gasping and gripping his shoulder.

"Kratos!" Stefanos yelled.

"Go get her!" Ocnus said quickly.

Glaucus and Krikor made a dash for the embankment, but Stefanos intercepted them, moving faster than he ever had before.

He ducked under one sloppy swing of a blade and pounded Krikor in the jaw, sending him into the dirt. Glaucus, ran past them and was halfway up the embankment when Stefanos dove, grabbing his legs and pulling him down, the two of them rolling away.

Glaucus' blade caught Stefanos on the arm, and then on the leg, but Stefanos blocked the third thrust and slammed both his fists into Glaucus' ears so that his hands went to his head, cutting himself with his own blade in the process.

"Kill him!" Ocnus yelled, his voice barely heard above the roar of the crowd, just beyond the crest of the hippodrome's embankment.

"You won't touch her!" Stefanos said loudly, standing there bleeding from his two wounds facing the armed men with nothing but his fists.

He could see Kratos moaning on the ground, growing more and more still.

Glaucus and Krikor gained their feet again and stood to Stefanos' right.

At once, they began to close in on him, as a pack of hunters closes on a wounded lion.

Stefanos looked up to where Kyniska stood and then back at them. *They won't touch you...*

He felt the stab of pain in his left side first, then swung to break the face of Biton who fell backward. His fist swept sideways and broke the cheek bone of Ampyx then, before another slash of pain went deep into his right leg.

Stefanos stepped back and took stock of the men before him, most wounded but still deadly. Ocnus held back, walking toward Kratos, slowly, while keeping an eye on the four of his men surrounding Stefanos.

Sweat poured from Stefanos' face but he was still aware enough of what was happening.

A slash of pain ran down his back then, painful, deep, and it enraged him more than ever. He turned to see Krikor there, and rushed in, parrying the blow of his blade with his forearm and landing a direct hit on his windpipe, sending the man down, gasping.

Stefanos turned quickly, his arm flying out to take Biton on the side of the head, and his right following up with an elbow to the temple. Biton's blade fell, and Stefanos pounded his face five times, crushing it to an bloody pulp.

Kyniska! he thought as Glaucus' blade slashed his cheek, just below the right eye.

Stefanos dodged a second stab, and followed up with a kick to Glaucus' groin, kneeing the man's face hard when he doubled over in pain, then stomping on the back of his neck to snap it.

"Stefanos, look out!" Kratos cried as Ocnus held him up by the hair, his blade to his throat, but just as Stefanos turned, Ampyx's dagger plunged deep into his right pectoral.

Stefanos cried out and then gripped the dagger before Ampyx could pull it out, head-butting Ampyx who fell back.

Stefanos, like a fury, lunged at the fallen man and wrapped his hands about his neck, crushing with all his might.

Ampyx's flailing arm hit the protruding dagger and Stefanos let go, yelling out in pain.

With blood pouring from his gaping mouth, Stefanos pinned Ampyx by the neck with his left hand and pounded his skull with a hammer fist, over and over and over again until it cracked and the body convulsed beneath him.

The scene in the hippodrome seemed to reach a crescendo as the crowd boomed, voices raised in adulation or horror, triumph or despair.

The sound was muffled to Stefanos' ears, and his eyes were growing cloudy. He felt blood running over his oil and sweat-coated body, even as the thunder of hooves reached his ears.

"It's finished, Stefanos!" Ocnus said, standing closer now, having dragged Kratos toward him.

Stefanos caught his friend's teary eyes, the apology in them, the wish that things had gone differently for both of them. He nodded to Kratos, accepted.

At that moment, Kratos swung a fist up and pounded Ocnus on the face, but it was not enough with so little strength left in his body.

"To Hades with you, Kratos!" Ocnus said before drawing his blade across Kratos' neck, both men's eyes upon Stefanos' the entire time.

"No!" Stefanos yelled, lunging sloppily at Ocnus as he let Kratos' body fall to the ground and charged in for the kill.

Stefanos felt the blade puncture his gut, twist and writhe there in unimaginable pain, even as Ocnus' eyes locked onto his.

"You and your Spartan bitch will see each other in Tartarus. And no one will remember you or your pathetic family...ever...!"

Stefanos wanted to scream, to cry, to rage against the Gods that had brought him to this end...and yet, he knew that the remaining strength that flowed in his veins could do one last thing, despite the pain that tormented his body.

"You won't harm her while I live!" Stefanos hissed in Ocnus' face, then grabbed hold of Ocnus' collar bone with his left hand, puncturing the skin so as to have a good grip.

Ocnus cried out, but Stefanos would not let go, and with his already broken, bloody fist, and his elbow, he pommeled Ocnus' face, his neck, his ribs, anywhere he could hit, even as his lifeblood ran in rivers from his body.

It was over.

Ocnus' body, and those of his men, lay in a dead heap about Stefanos, son of Talos.

None saw what happened, for the crowd in the hippodrome raised their voices to the heights of Olympus then as the final lap of the race began.

Stefanos turned to look up at Kyniska and fell to his knees. He knew which one she was. *Just a little longer... You're safe now...*

WHEN THE FINAL DOLPHIN FELL FORWARD, KYNISKA WATCHED as Pirro let the team have their heads so that they charged to draw even with the remaining Athenian and Thessalian teams in front, the Massilian close behind.

Such beauty! Kyniska thought as she watched their black forms thunder down the length of the hippodrome. *Run!*

She clenched her fists as the Massilian team caught up to the Athenian and Thessalian teams, gaining the inside track while Pirro was still on the outside, just coming into the Taraxippos turn.

In that last turn, before that invisible terror of horses, the three teams in the lead bolted inward, bumping each other and slowing together in the turn, and it was then that Pirro made his move.

Kyniska watched as her blacks and Pirro, all fearless, blessed with strength, skill, and stamina, shot in a straight line from the Taraxippos, directly across the path of the lead chariots as they collided to get away from the turn.

Pirro's chariot skidded sideways, dirt churned up as water from a rapid mill wheel, and then they shot forward toward the finish.

Kyniska jumped up to see the finish line on the far side of the hippodrome as Pirro let go of the reins for that final stretch and raised his hands and blood-spattered face to the heavens as they crossed the line ahead of all the remaining teams.

Kyniska's soul screamed out in joy and elation. It was nothing like she had imagined, the sight of her blacks crossing that line, their beautiful forms, and the joyful face of her Pirro as he waved to the crowds of Olympia.

"Kyniska!" he yelled, his arms still held aloft in triumph. "Sparta!"

"Good lad!" Ajax said beside Kyniska, as Euryleonis hugged her tightly, tears in her eyes at the sight of her friend, their horses, trotting off on the track before them as the Hellanodikai came out to pronounce Kyniska of Sparta the winner.

It was a dream, a moment she had hoped for, almost all of her life.

Kyniska hoped her father was watching from that far side of the river, yes, but she could not wait to share the joy with the one man who had ever fully understood her.

Even as the crowd began to chant her name, to sing and praise her skills as a trainer, and those of her driver and her team, dread entered into Kyniska's heart, and she turned her back on the elation before her to peer over the wall and down the side of the embankment to a spot along the river.

Stefanos knelt alone among a half-dozen bloody, broken bodies, his own red with gore, his strength failing as he stared up at her.

He smiled briefly, a pained one that would forever be burned onto her soul, and then he mouthed the words she had hoped he would say forever after to her in their Hyperborean exile.

"I love you, Kyniska!"

She gripped the wall tightly, until her hands were bleeding as she watched him tumble over, blood pouring from his mouth and wounds.

He tried to get up again, but shook his head.

GODS WATCH OVER HER... STEFANOS THOUGHT AS HE FELL ONTO his side, reaching up to Kyniska where she stood, so far out of reach, her face receding from his sight and into darkness. *My love...*

Kyniska could not move, or cry, or say a word as she stared down at Stefanos' lifeless body. She gripped the wall, caught in the maelstrom of conflicting emotions that threatened to tear her apart.

"My lady?" Euryleonis said, stopping herself quickly as she saw the scene below.

"We have to go," Ajax whispered into her ear, his eyes scanning the slaughter behind them. "Come..." he said more softly. "Kyniska...before you are recognized. Come."

She let herself be led away, to disappear into the crowd and back to her camp on the other side of the river, even as Pirro had the red ribbon of victory tied around his sweaty brow, and as the men atop the embankment turned their attention to the grisly sacrilege beside the Alpheios.

EPILOGOS

The seasons changed, as is their wont. Summer gave way to autumn, and the light of the year died into winter.

The name of Kyniska of Sparta was known now across the Greek world, sometimes spoken with a sort of reverence, most often with a tone of mockery.

In the land of Lacedaemon, she was still the Eurypontid princess of Sparta, always the sister of King Agesilaus II.

The wars raged on among the city-states of Greece, the Sacred Truce now a thing of fading memory to all but the victors.

Now, Kyniska rode along the line of the Eurotas river which cradled the city of Sparta in the shadow of Mount Taygetos.

Armies of Helot slaves scythed through the stalks of golden winter wheat, sending chafe into the air, a soft echo of the snows now covering the mountain tops.

Kyniska went silently on Zeta's back, one of her remaining whites, while Euryleonis rode in silence behind her on Pasiphae. Both were cloaked against the wind with long, rough, grey wool wrapped tightly about them as they followed the river, across the bridge, south of the city, and toward the mountain trail that only Kyniska knew about.

She had been that way many times over the last weeks, but this time it was a special journey. They had left the villa where her stables were, early that morning as the sun lit the mountain's face.

As ever, Euryleonis had been the one to insist on accompanying her, and Kyniska loved her for her strength and spirit. Indeed the girl, her most promising protege, had not left her side since the final day of the Games.

That day...

Not a moment went by when she did not think on it, see it,

hear it, want to scream at the memory of it. But Kyniska had been silent, except for oaths of vengeance and victory.

Euryleonis was there, silent, ready only if needed, learning from her mistress' every action, from the silent strength that made her one of the greatest of Spartan women, a great height to aspire to.

Kyniska turned in her saddle to touch the basket that was tied behind her. Her eyes caught Euryleonis'.

"I will go up alone this time," she said, her voice sounding different.

"As you wish, my lady. I shall wait," Euryleonis said, bowing her head.

Kyniska smiled but a little, and turned to point Zeta up the rocky path. As they made a couple of sharp, upward turns, the low, tiled roofs of Sparta came into view where they clustered around the ancient acropolis.

After some time, the path became too narrow for the horses, and Kyniska and Euryleonis reined in. Kyniska jumped down and handed her reins to Euryleonis before untying the basket she had brought.

"Tie them up and give them some of the oats we brought. Build a fire for yourself too."

"Yes, my lady. Are you quite sure you don't want me to accompany you?" Euryleonis asked hesitantly.

Kyniska, her grey hood still covering her head, stepped forward and laid her hand on the girl's cheek.

"Quite sure. You have been...a great help to me these weeks, Euryleonis. I won't forget it."

The girl said nothing, but kissed Kyniska's hand before the latter picked up the basket and began to climb the narrow, rocky path.

More than once she slipped on slick rocks that were damp from the springs seeping out of the mountain, but Kyniska was swift and strong, and always caught herself.

She climbed for several minutes before reaching the gap in the path where she had to leap in order to reach her destination. A gust of wind whipped from atop the mountain, threatening to throw her off balance, but her hand shot out and grabbed hold of the branch of the olive tree on the other side.

For a moment she hung there, tempted, but then pulled herself to safety onto the open flat space.

There, overlooking the Eurotas valley, was an altar of black marble, waist-high and two feet wide. On the face of it was carved a laurel crown fastened with ribbons. The top edges were decorated with the simple curves of an Ionic column head.

Kyniska placed the basket on the ground and turned to face the altar.

She was silent for a few moments, her blue eyes scanning the world before her. Snow flakes drifted softly before her face where strands of her dark hair poked out from beneath her hood.

Kyniska breathed. In and out...in and out.

From her side, beneath her cloak, she pulled a dagger that bore traces of congealed blood and placed it upon the altar before raising her hands, palms upward.

"Goddess Nemesis, I offer you this dagger in thanks for the vengeance you have allowed me to wreak upon a traitor to Sparta. And I thank you for allowing me to be the one to take that cursed life."

Kyniska's jaw set then as she remembered the previous day, when finally she had taken the vengeance she had sworn to.

Argos had been fined for the extreme sacrilege of its seven citizens who had fought and died on the grounds of the sanctuary, outside of the competition. Murder there, and during the Sacred Truce, was a severe insult to the Gods.

It had never felt right to Kyniska, and when the shock had worn off, and reality set in, she set Ajax to making enquiries wherever he could. It took some weeks, an eternity to Kyniska, before her enomotarch obtained some useful information.

Some of the troops at Olympia, including Stefanos' friend

Pollux, remembered seeing the disgraced Spartan, Typhon, coming back from the direction of the Argive camp on the final day of the Games.

No one could explain the behaviour of Stefanos, son of Talos, in fleeing the temple of Zeus when he was about to be crowned victor, but the gymnasiarchos, Axion, remembered seeing the group of Argives taunting Stefanos in passing during the ceremony.

That was enough for Kyniska, when Ajax told her. She knew what had to be done.

"Let me kill him, my princess," Ajax said, fury in his eyes.

"No. I want to see him. Bring him here. Tell Typhon I want to speak with him, alone. Here, in my home which he used to visit."

"Is that wise?" Ajax asked.

"It is necessary, for I have something to say to him."

"If he harms you?"

"He won't. He can't. And you will be in the next room," she said. "Send for him to come tomorrow."

As the wind swept about Kyniska on the mountainside, she stared at the bloody dagger, her face grim as she remembered Typhon walking into her chambers as he always had, long ago, expectant and arrogant.

She let him approach, her eyes locked onto his, letting him think what he wanted.

"I'm glad you've come to your senses. You don't belong with that fool Aeson," Typhon said. "You belong to me, Kyniska. You always will." He reached for her then, his hard hands on her bare shoulders, and as he pulled her in, she plunged the dagger deep into his guts.

She did not look away from his eyes as she twisted the dagger in every direction, the blood pouring out of his abdomen like a hot waterfall onto her feet. She did not flinch.

"I know it was you," she said coldly, without a trace of emotion. "You were never worthy, to be a Spartan or my lover. But he was." She pulled the dagger out quickly, gripped him by the hair, and drove the blade up under Typhon's chin, letting him waver for a moment before his body fell in a pathetic heap at her feet.

When it was done, she only stood there, breathing, watching the play of sunlight through the window onto the blood pooling around the man who had taken almost everything from her.

"He didn't take everything..." Kyniska whispered to the winds where she stood before the altar now.

"Father Zeus...Great Goddess Hera..." Kyniska raised her arms to the sky. "Look favourably upon Stefanos, son of Talos. May he be treated as a victor, a man of courage who honoured you with his final act. I would not be here if not for him. I pray you, give him peace in Elysium."

Kyniska's hands began to shake as she held them out, listening for the Gods' reply.

High on a peak above, the cry of an eagle rang out, loud and clear, and she looked up to see its great wings set against the midday sun.

She then turned to the basket beside her, opened the latch, and reached in. Carefully, she removed something wrapped in red cloth, holding it before her in both hands.

Kyniska unfolded the cloth to reveal the olive crown of her victory at Olympia.

She still had her victory, and no one could take that away from her.

Sadness, however, could not be banished, despite the vengeance she had been granted, for not even a hundred-thousand deaths could make up for the loss of the one man she had ever loved, and all that they had been robbed of.

As Kyniska held the olive crown in her hands, the wind blew her hood back, her hair pouring out behind her.

"Stefanos...I hope you can hear me," she said. "This crown is as much yours as it is mine, and I would share it with you for all time for what you did for me...for all that you meant to me, and still do."

Kyniska laid the delicate olive wreath upon the altar, and fell to her knees, her hands gripping the black marble.

"You are the only one who ever understood me, who saw me. You believed in me like no other man." She could not control the emotion that poured forth then. For too long she had been strong, the pain barricaded inside her Spartan heart.

"I miss you, Stefanos," she wept. "I love you, and I will never love anyone like I love you."

The tears were hot and strange upon her face, the cheeks he had kissed and stroked with rough fingers. As they flowed from her blue eyes, she remembered his laughter, his touch, every part of him as if it were only yesterday that they lay together, and it all made her pain more acute, brought him that much closer.

Should a Spartan princess be weeping like that?

Kyniska's wet face looked up to see Stefanos on the other side of the altar, his arms crossed over his chest, the red ribbon of victory hovering about his short hair. He smiled at her and looked down at the olive crown.

I knew you could do it. I always did.

"I miss you, Stefanos," Kyniska said.

And I you. But I will always watch over you.

That smile again, the one she had teased him about, thought that it made him foolish at first, had become a warm memory to cling to in the dark of night as she remembered their time together.

"Why did you do it?"

The shade shook his head, still smiling. *You ask such questions, Princess.* He leaned forward, over the altar and the crown, his hands coming up to hover either side of her face as she closed her eyes. *Because I love you, Kyniska.*

"I swear, my love, that I will go back to Olympia and I will rip victory from their grasp and from their hearts, again, for you."

I know you will. He smiled. *And I will be watching, my love. Always... Thank you for loving me... Kyniska...*

There was silence again, but for the blowing of the wind and the rustle of the silver green leaves of the olive crown upon the altar.

Kyniska opened her eyes to see that he was gone.

"Goodbye, Stefanos."

She wiped her cheeks and the remnants of the only tears that she shed, there, alone on the side of that mountain with her agony and ecstasy.

There were no more tears after that, for she was Spartan, and she was victorious. The crown upon that lonely altar attested to that.

She gazed to the south where her horse pastures lay, her teams, her children awaiting her.

Kyniska smiled and breathed deeply of the high, free air.

"Gods, grant me another victory..."

THE END

Thank you for reading!

Did you enjoy *Heart of Fire*? Here is what you can do next.

If you enjoyed this journey through the world of the ancient Olympics, and if you have a minute to spare, please post a review on the web page where you purchased the book.

Reviews are the best way for new readers to find this book, and your help in spreading the word is greatly appreciated.

There are many more novels from Eagles and Dragons Publishing that are set in the ancient world, so be sure to sign-up for e-mail updates at:

https://eaglesanddragonspublishing.com/newsletter-join-the-legions/

Newsletter subscribers get a FREE BOOK, and first access to new releases, special offers, and much more!

AUTHOR'S NOTE

The world owes a lot to the ancient Greeks in the way of literature, art, architecture, education, philosophy, medicine, engineering and much more. We take much of this influence for granted, but if you look around, you will see the indicators of that ancient legacy everywhere.

Perhaps one of the greatest gifts that the ancient Greeks gave to us is organized sport, and athletic competition, and nothing represents that legacy more beautifully than the Olympic Games.

Historically, the most widely accepted date for the first ancient Olympic Games is 776 B.C. They ran for hundreds of years until about A.D. 393 when the Christian emperor, Theodosius I, banned all pagan cults and practices. This included the Olympic Games.

However, the Olympic Games found new life in the 19th century when Baron Pierre de Coubertin founded the International Olympic Committee (IOC) with Greek writer, Demetrius Vikelas, as the first IOC president.

The first modern Olympic Games under the auspices of the new IOC took place in 1896 in Athens, at the newly restored Panathinaiko stadium, near the ancient heart of the city. This was the foundation of the Olympic Games as we know them today.

However, the ancient Olympic Games were quite different from our modern games.

Today people talk about how it is a victory of sorts just to make it to the Olympics, to participate in the competition.

In ancient Greece however, it was about winning and nothing else. If someone came in second at the Olympiad, they went home by back streets in disgrace. On the other hand, if someone was victorious, they were lauded like a god until the end of their days. To be an Olympic victor was the closest any man could come to immortality. Winners were given free lodging and free meals in most Greek cities, especially their home town, and they were celebrated in epinikion sculpture and poetry. The Theban poet, Pindar, is probably the most famous epinikion poet of the ancient world.

The ancient Olympics were also not concerned with sportsmanship, though cheating was punished severely. The sports, especially the fighting sports and chariot racing, were brutal, and often resulted in death. But that was a price many were willing to risk for eternal glory.

It is important for us to remember also that the ancient Olympics were not simply a sporting event, they were also a deeply religious ritual intended to honour the gods and heroes of the Greek people. Whether or not one believes in the mythical foundation of the Games as related to Herakles, or Pelops' legendary chariot race, one cannot deny that they were religious at heart.

Every event of the ancient Games involved some religious ceremony or sacrifice to honour the Gods, and the heart of the Olympic sanctuary, the Altis, is a monument to this deep and abiding faith.

Olympic glory was something that, unlike today, only Greek men were permitted to reach for. In ancient Greek society, with the exception of Sparta, women were hidden away, took care of young children, and managed households. That's it. They had no place in public life, let alone sport. Ancient Olympia was a man's world, through and through.

It was fun for me as an historian and writer to imagine all of the historical personages who may have been at the Games of 396 B.C., including Xenophon, King Agesilaus, Plato, the Athenian general Thrasybulos, and others. Indeed, I used both Xenophon's work, *On Horsemanship*, and Plato's *Symposium*, as sources to inform *Heart of Fire*.

Xenophon was, of course, a horse expert, and a kind of ancient horse-whisperer, and because he was a good and favoured friend of King Agesilaus, his inclusion in this story was a forgone conclusion.

AUTHOR'S NOTE

As for Plato, he was younger at this time. It was shortly after the death of Socrates, but before his journey to Sicily where he experienced his ill-fated attempt to enlighten and civilize the tyrant Dionysus of Syracuse. There were a lot of power plays going on in the Greek world at this time between wars, so it seemed apt for Plato to be present, though writing about this philosophical titan was an intimidating task.

I have aimed for historical accuracy in as much as was possible, and as the extent of our knowledge allows when it comes to the people, places, rituals, and religious practices of this period and of the ancient Olympic Games. If you would like to read more about the ancient Olympics, Nigel Spivey's *The Ancient Olympics* is a supremely accessible book.

The structures of the Olympic sanctuary which I have included in the Olympiad of 396 B.C., as far as my research has shown, were all present at the time when *Heart of Fire* takes place. One exception to this is the *palaestra* which was built slightly later. It is not improbable, however, that such a building could have existed at ancient Olympia at this time, so I felt free to include it in this story, central as the *palaestra* was to Greek society. Another area in which I have taken a bit of license is in the order of the Olympic events. For a better fit with the flow and storyline of *Heart of Fire*, I have changed the order so that the chariot race was the final event of the Games. This added to the climactic scene in the last chapter. In truth, the chariot races and other equestrian events took place on day one of the Games. The pentathlon was on day two, and the foot races on day three. Wrestling, boxing, and the pankration were on day four, and the hoplite race took place on the fifth and final day of the Games.

As I have mentioned, ancient Olympia was a man's world. However, there was one way in which women could participate in the Olympic Games, and that was as the owners and trainers of chariot teams, just like Princess Kyniska of Sparta whom *Heart of Fire* is about.

Kyniska of Sparta...

AUTHOR'S NOTE

The first time I read about her, I knew I had to write this story. She was indeed a real person, a Spartan princess, and she did win at the Olympiad of 396 B.C.

She also won a second time in 392 B.C., as did her protégé, Euryleonis, in 368 B.C., whom I have also included in the story.

I don't think Kyniska's accomplishment in 396. B.C. can be overstated. She broke some serious ground in a man's world. It might be easy to dismiss Kyniska's achievement since she did not drive the chariot herself, but we cannot underestimate the strength of character and skill that were needed to train and raise horses, then to bring them to competition in this male-dominated society, even if she was a Spartan.

What very little we know of Kyniska of Sparta comes from very brief mentions of her in Plutarch and Pausanias, who were both writing about her brother, King Agesilaus. There is also the inscription on the statue base which Kyniska, as an Olympic victor, had the right to erect in the Altis of Olympia. It read:

> *Kings of Sparta are my father and brothers*
> *Kyniska, victorious with a chariot of swift-footed horses,*
> *has erected this statue. I declare myself the only woman*
> *in all Hellas to have won this crown.*
> *Apelleas son of Kallikles made it.*

Kyniska of Sparta shook the Greek world at a time when it was already torn apart by the Peloponnesian War, her brother Agesilaus being at the forefront of aggression.

The Olympic Games, sport, and politics of the time are, however, more of a backdrop to *Heart of Fire*.

At its core, this novel is a story about struggle and sacrifice.

The ancient idea of 'Ponos', or toil, was central to the ancient Greeks' psyche, and if the myths teach us anything, it is that there can truly be no victory without sacrifice.

Heart of Fire is also a love story.

AUTHOR'S NOTE

This is a story about love of one's family, and of the unlikely love between a man and a woman from two enemy city-states.

The story of Kyniska inspired me from the get-go, but there was so little written about her that I needed something more, someone to take us into the heart of the Olympic Games, someone to experience the struggle along with Kyniska.

I've always loved the tragic story of Romeo and Juliette, so when I was formulating the story for *Heart of Fire*, it came to me that Sparta and Argos were sort of like the Montagues and the Capulets. And so, our Argive mercenary came into being.

The lack of sources is often a gift to the historical novelist, for it allows one to let the imagination fill in the gaps in the historical record.

Stefanos, son of Talos, is a fictional character, but I suspect that his struggles and experiences during the years of the Peloponnesian War were not uncommon. He is, however, not young and idealistic like Romeo, but rather world-weary and uninspired, until the death of his father, and his meeting with Kyniska.

Argos was indeed famous for bronze smithing and art, as well as its Heraion, but war among the city-states would have drawn most young men to the fields of Ares, as it did Stefanos.

The battles in which Stefanos fought as a mercenary, including the March of the Ten Thousand led by Xenophon, and described in the latter's *Anabasis*, are all real battles.

The brutality of these conflicts cannot be exaggerated.

Kakochartos, that side of Strife that exults in wickedness, war, and bloodshed, was a very real thing to the Greeks, and after years of war, it would have been a great struggle to rise above it.

Stefanos and Kyniska, to me, represent aspects of all of us, our dreams, our sadness, our struggles to make things happen, to better ourselves in a world that seems to be trying very hard to grind us into the dirt.

For me, *Heart of Fire* was both a struggle and an inspiration to write, and I hope you have found something in it that, in turn, inspires you.

To read more about the world of *Heart of Fire*, and the ancient Olympic Games, visit http://eaglesanddragonspublishing.com/the-world-of-heart-of-fire/

Thank you very much for reading, and whatever your struggle and noble goals in life, may the Gods grant you victory!

Adam Alexander Haviaras
Toronto, June 2016

ACKNOWLEDGMENTS

Writing *Heart of Fire* has been an exceptional journey for me, and not one that I have gone through alone. As ever, many thanks are due to people for their knowledge, support, encouragement, and inspiration.

First of all, general thanks should go out to the countless scholars and academics who, over the years have contributed to our knowledge and understanding of ancient Greece. It is no mean feat to put the sparse puzzle pieces of the ancient world together enough to form a coherent picture of the past. People often rail against how boring academics can be, but everyone should know that without their dedication and diligence, their love of the past, we would know very little of the ancient world.

This story took root the very first time I set foot within the sanctuary of ancient Olympia, when I walked among the dry pines with the heat bearing down on me, and the cicadas whirring all around. That first trip, and my subsequent love of the place, was made possible by my parents who took me on my first magical trip to Greece. That was the trip of a lifetime, and it opened my eyes to a whole new world.

To my daughters, who both run as fast as Artemis herself, I am grateful for their example of determination and joy in their own daily challenges. Growing up in the world is no easy task, but I am in constant awe of their ability to rise to challenges in class, on track and field, or on stage.

As ever, the one constant in all of my writing is my wife, Angelina. Her help with the shape of the story, my use of ancient Greek, and her highly skilled and pointed editorial input were invaluable in bringing this book to life. All of my heart and soul go to her, and the gratitude I have for her support, and her belief in me and my abilities as a storyteller, cannot be measured.

Finally, *Heart of Fire* is dedicated to my late father, Stefanos

Policarpos Haviaras, for the combined strength, skill, and kindness he taught me in my youth. Through his example, I learned that, despite the great trials of life, beauty can still be found in it. His toil was never so great as it was toward the end, but he never gave up, and he left everything on life's battlefield. This book is his eulogy. *I love you, Dad…*

Adam Alexander Haviaras
Toronto, June 2016

GLOSSARY

acroterion – decorative element at the peak of a temple's pediment

agoge – the Spartan education system and regimen to turn Spartan boys into men from the age of seven

agon – a contest or competition

agora – a central market place and administrative center of a city

altis – the inner sanctuary of Olympia which contained the temple of Olympian Zeus, temple of Hera, other sacred sites, and epinikion statuary erected by victors

amphora – large clay container for storing and transporting goods such as olive oil and wine

anabasis – a march or expedition from the coast into the interior of a country

andreia – manliness; also courage, or fearlessness

aner agathos – a 'good man'

Anthesterion – ancient Greek month including February and March

apalaistroi – those without a palaestra (i.e. the poor or uneducated)

apodyterium – the change room of a palaestra or gymnasium

apotheosis – the process or experience of becoming divine or godlike

arete – the ancient Greek idea of 'human excellence'

aulos – an ancient wind instrument made up of two flutes

bouleuterion – an administrative center or building where leaders meet

braca – short trousers or leggings

caltrop – iron, star-shaped spikes used to lame horses in war

cella – the inner sanctum of a temple

centaur – a mythological creature that was half man, half horse
chiton – a standard piece of clothing resembling a long shirt with short sleeves, reaching to the mid-thigh or knees; usually worn with a belt of sorts
chlamys – a cloak worn by most Greek men
chryselephantine – a style of sculpture that used ivory and gold (ex. the statue of Olympian Zeus at Olympia)

daemon – a benevolent or benign spirit
deme – a district or neighbourhood of a city
diaulos – the 400 meter race; roughly two stades
discobolo – (plur. discoboloi) discus thrower
discoi – throwing discs (a discus) used in athletic competition
dolichos – the long distance race; usually 5000 meters (24 stades), or 2400 meters (12 stades)
doru – (plur. dorata) the cornel or ash-wood spear that was the primary weapon of a hoplite soldier; about three meters (ten feet) long
drachm – an ancient silver coin; based on Attic drachma

epeblema – a woman's shawl
elaiothesion – the room in a palaestra complex where athletes oiled themselves with olive oil
Elaphebolion – ancient Greek month spanning March and April; literally means 'deer hunting'
embolon – the central spine or divider in a horse racing track, or hippodrome
enomotarch – a Spartan officer who commanded an enomotia of hoplites which was made up of 36 men; this was the smallest unit in the Spartan army
enomotia – a unit of 36 hoplite soldiers led by an enomotarch
ephebes – adolescent young men
epinikion – a genre of poetry and sculpture dedicated to victories

erastai – the older man in a mentorship, or other, relationship between two men

eris agathos – 'Good Strife'; the useful, creative side of strife, that which fuels creative industry and is productive; applies to any trade or pursuit

eumorphia – to be 'in good shape'

Gamelion – the ancient Greek month spanning January and February

gigantomachy – refers to the war between the Gods and the Giants

gymnasiarchos – the head administrator and overseer of a gymnasium or palaestra

hecatomb – a sacrifice to the Gods of 100 cattle

hellanodikai – the ancient Olympic judges; marked by their purple cloaks

helot – the slave class of Sparta

Heraia – women's athletic competition in honour of the goddess Hera; begun by Hippodameia

heraion – a temple or sanctuary dedicated to the goddess Hera

herm – a protective statue made up of a male head on a pedestal, sometimes with carved genitals

heroon – a shrine dedicated to an ancient hero, or heroes

himantes – leather straps with rawhide or lead pieces used to cover ancient boxers' hands for fights

himation – a long cloak worn as a sole garment by men, or over a peplos by women

hippodrome – a chariot racing track; literally means 'horse road'

hoplite – an ancient Greek heavy infantry soldier; named after the 'hoplon', the large round shield used by these soldiers

hoplitodromos – the hoplite race in athletic competitions in which twenty men ran in full armour for two stades

hoplon – the large, round wood and bronze shields used by heavy infantry hoplites
hubris – excessive pride and self-confidence believed to be frowned upon by the Gods
hysplex – (plur. hyspleges); the starting gate in a hippodrome

iatros – an ancient doctor

kakochartos – 'Bad Strife'; that which exults in bad things like war, dissent, and a lust for battle and bloodshed
kalos – beautiful
kinaidoi – boy whores; literally 'little buggers'
kleros – the 'Sorting'; when competitors chose tokens from a pot to determine which heat they were in, or whom they would compete against in athletic competition
konisterion – room in which athletes applied dusting powder ('konis') prior to competing
korikoi – punching bags filled with seed or sand
krater – a large clay bowl used for mixing water and wine prior to serving
krypte – the barrel-vaulted tunnel leading from the Altis of Olympia to the stadium
kylix – a wide, shallow cup with a short pedestal, usually of clay, used for drinking wine
kythera – an ancient Greek lyre

larnax – a coffin used for inhumation/burials
linothorax – an ancient Greek breastplate made of glued layers of linen with leather; used from Mycenaean to Hellenistic times
lochagos – the commander of a Spartan 'lochos' which was made up of up to 600 hoplites
lochos – the basic unit of an ancient phalanx; contained up to 600 men
lyra – an ancient Greek string instrument or harp

GLOSSARY

maeander – also 'meander'; the 'Greek Key' pattern in ancient art
maenad – female followers or consorts of the god Dionysus
mastigophoroi – the whip-bearing police of ancient Olympia who kept the peace

naiskoi – little temples along the Terrace of Treasuries at ancient Olympia
Nike – Goddess of Victory

obol – a silver coin; 6 obols = 1 drachma
oikoi – little houses along the Terrace of Treasuries at ancient Olympia that served as treasuries or club houses for various city-states
ostracon – shard of pottery on which names or symbols were scratched

paiderast – a man who desires boys
paiderastia – a strong desire for boys
palaestra – a wrestling school; also where other fighting sports were practiced
pelopion – the burial mound, or barrow, of the hero Pelops within the Altis of ancient Olympia
pentathlon – ancient competition involving running, jumping, discus, javelin, and wrestling
pentekonter – the commander of a pentekostys, a unit of about fifty hoplites
pentekostys – a unit of about fifty hoplite warriors
peplos – a long tunic without sleeves worn by women
phaidryntai – the descendants of the sculptor Phidias who lived at Olympia and cared for the monumental chryselephantine statue of Zeus in the god's temple
phalanx – a rectangular, heavy infantry formation composted of hoplites with shields and spears; originally used by Sparta, followed by Argos, and then others; sizes varied

philobolia – flowers, fruit, and greens showered on Olympic victors during parade; literally 'love shower'
philoneikia – the love of competing
philonikia – the love of winning
phobos – fear
plethera – a unit of measurement equivalent to about one hundred feet
polis – a city
ponos – toil or struggle
promachoi – first in the battle line of a military confrontation or fight
propylon – a monumental entrance or gate
prytaneion – official hall of Olympia where banquets were held

satyr – a mythological creature that was part goat, part man, sometimes with horse features; also a follower of Dionysus
skamma – the sand where fighting took place in athletic competition, or in the gymnasium or palaestra
skiamachein – shadow-skirmishing; shadow-boxing
Skirophorion – ancient Greek month spanning June and July
stade – a measurement of about two-hundred meters; the sprint was the stade race
stadium – where athletic competitions took place, usually dirt, with embankments for spectators on either side
stater – ancient Greek silver or gold coin; 1 stater = 2-3 drachmas
stele – an upright grave marker or monument
stoa – a covered walkway or portico for public use; usually contained shops and other establishments, as well as space to congregate
strigil – a curved, bronze hook for cleaning oil and dirt from one's body when visiting the baths
strophion – a cloth or short undergarment women wore to support the breasts; could also be a very short tunic that left one breast visible

stylus – a wood or bronze pen for writing on papyrus or wax tablets
synoris – the two-horse chariot race

taraxippos – literally means 'horse frightener';
tethrippon – the four-horse chariot race
Thargelion – ancient Greek month spanning May and June
theokoleion – the home of the theokoloi at Olympia
theokolos – (plur. theokoloi); the priests of Zeus at ancient Olympia
thorax – a breastplate; body armour covering the torso
Tyche – the goddess of luck and good fortune

xenia – ancient Greek concept of hospitality; can also refer to foreigners (*xenos*, or *xenoi*)
xyphos – the leaf-shaped sword of a Greek hoplite
xystis – the long, ankle-length chiton worn by charioteers; also known as an Ionic chiton

zanes – bronze statues at Olympia made from fines levied upon those who violated the sacred rules of the Olympic Games and the sanctuary of Olympia

Become a Patron of Eagles and Dragons Publishing!

If you enjoy the books that Eagles and Dragons Publishing puts out, our blogs about history, mythology, and archaeology, our video tours of historic sites and more, then you should consider becoming an official patron.

We love our regular visitors to the website, and of course our wonderful newsletter subscribers, but we want to offer more to our 'super fans', those readers and history-lovers who enjoy everything we do and create.

You can become a patron for as little as $1 per month. For your support, you can also get fantastic rewards as tokens of our appreciation.

If you are interested, visit the website below to go to the Eagles and Dragons Publishing Patreon page to watch the introductory video and check out the patronage levels and exciting rewards.

https://www.patreon.com/EaglesandDragonsPublishing

Join us for an exciting future as we bring the past to life!

ABOUT THE AUTHOR

Adam Alexander Haviaras is a best-selling and award-winning author and historian who has studied ancient and medieval history and archaeology in Canada and the United Kingdom. He currently resides in Stratford, Ontario with his wife and children where he is continuing his research and writing other works of historical fantasy.

Historical Fiction/Fantasy Titles

The Eagles and Dragons Series
The Dragon: Genesis (Prequel)
A Dragon among the Eagles (Prequel)
Children of Apollo (Book I)
Killing the Hydra (Book II)
Warriors of Epona (Book III)
Isle of the Blessed (Book IV)
The Stolen Throne (Book V)
The Blood Road (Book VI)
The Eagles and Dragons Legionary Box Set (Books 0-I-II)
The Eagles and Dragons Tribune Box Set (Books III-IV-V)

The Carpathian Interlude Series
The Carpathian Interlude - Complete Trilogy Box Set
Immortui (Part I)
Lykoi (Part II)
Thanatos (Part III)

The Mythologia Series
Chariot of the Son: The Story of Phaethon
Wheels of Fate: The Story of Pelops and Hippodameia

A Song for the Underworld: The Story of Orpheus and Eurydice
The Reluctant Hero: The Story of Bellerophon and the Chimera
Mythologia: First Omnibus Edition

Heart of Fire: A Novel of the Ancient Olympics

Saturnalia: A Tale of Wickedness and Redemption in Ancient Rome

The Etrurian Players
Sincerity is a Goddess (Book I)
An Altar of Indignities (Book II)

Titles in the Historia Non-fiction Series
Historia I: Celtic Literary Archetypes in *The Mabinogion*: A Study of the Ancient Tale of *Pwyll, Lord of Dyved*
Historia II: Arthurian Romance and the Knightly Ideal: A study of Medieval Romantic Literature and its Effect upon Warrior Culture in Europe
Historia III: *Y Gododdin*: The Last Stand of Three Hundred Britons - Understanding People and Events during Britain's Heroic Age
Historia IV: Camelot: The Historical, Archaeological and Toponymic Considerations for South Cadbury Castle as King Arthur's Capital

Eagles and Dragons Publishing Guides
Writing the Past: The Eagles and Dragons Publishing Guide to Researching, Writing, Publishing and Marketing Historical Fiction and Historical Fantasy

Stay Connected

To connect with Adam and learn more about the ancient world visit www.eaglesanddragonspublishing.com

Sign up for the Eagles and Dragons Publishing Newsletter at www.eaglesanddragonspublishing.com/newsletter-join-the-legions/ to receive a **FREE BOOK,** first access to new releases and posts on ancient history, special offers, and much more!

Readers can also connect with Adam on Twitter @Adam-Haviaras and Instagram @ adam_haviaras

On Facebook you can 'Like' the Eagles and Dragons page to get regular updates on new historical fiction and non-fiction from Eagles and Dragons Publishing.

To watch Eagles and Dragons Publishing's mini documentaries and other fun videos, be sure to follow us on TikTok and subscribe to our channels on YouTube or Rumble.

More from

EAGLES AND DRAGONS PUBLISHING

Step into the world of Ancient Rome with the Etrurian Players!

Sincerity is a Goddess is a heartwarming story of friendship and love that takes you on a bawdy and hilarious journey through the world of ancient Rome.

If you like dramatic and romantic stories about second chances, misunderstandings, and a bit with a dog, then you will love *Sincerity is a Goddess*!

Read this book today for a theatrical adventure that will have you cringing, laughing, crying, and realizing that there is indeed hope for everyone. Well, almost everyone…

The Etrurian Players are coming! Brace yourselves!

Available from all major retailers and public libraries in e-book, paperback, and hardcover editions, or direct from Eagles and Dragons Publishing at:

www.eaglesanddragonspublishing.com

DISCOVER THE *MYTHOLOGIA* SERIES TODAY!

Long ago, when gods and heroes walked the earth in triumph and tragedy, true love and epic deeds were set among the stars...

Do you love Greek and Roman Mythology?

If so, then you will love Eagles and Dragons Publishing's newest series!

In this unique, ground-breaking fantasy series suitable for all ages, you will discover a world of Titans, Gods and Heroes.

Start the series the First Omnibus Edition of the *Mythologia* series and escape into unique retellings of the poignant and epic myths of Phaethon, Pelops and Hippodameia, and of Orpheus and Eurydice.

New books are being added all the time, so you will never run out of adventures!

Begin the *Mythologia* series today and embark on an epic adventure with the Gods and Heroes of ancient Greece!

Available from all major retailers and public libraries in e-book, paperback, and hardcover editions, or direct from Eagles and Dragons Publishing at:

www.eaglesanddragonspublishing.com

START A NEW ADVENTURE TODAY!

Do you enjoy stories set in Ancient Rome?

If so, then you will love our marquee *Eagles and Dragons* historical fantasy series!

Start your journey today with the #1 bestselling prequel title, *A Dragon among the Eagles* and experience the world of the Roman Empire like never before.

A Dragon among the Eagles is the first novel in Adam Alexander Haviaras' ground-breaking Eagles and Dragons series. If you like books set in the ancient world, then you will love this historical series that combines adventure, romance, and the supernatural.

Available in e-book, paperback, and hardcover editions from all major book retailers and public libraries.

Step into the world of the Roman Empire today!

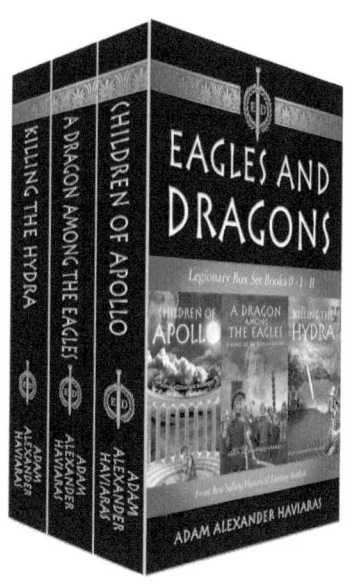

EAGLES AND DRAGONS LEGIONARY BOX SET

BOOKS O - I - II

Begin your adventure in the Roman Empire with a great deal!

Get the Eagles and Dragons series Legionary Box Set today.

This digital box set includes the #1 Best Selling prequel novel, *A Dragon among the Eagles*, as well as Book I, *Children of Apollo*, and Book II, *Killing the Hydra*.

The Eagles and Dragons Legionary Box Set is available from all major on-line e-book retailers, public libraries, or direct from Eagles and Dragons Publishing at:

www.eaglesanddragonspublishing.com

EAGLES AND DRAGONS TRIBUNE BOX SET

BOOKS III - IV - V

Continue your adventure in the Roman Empire with another great deal!

Get the Eagles and Dragons series Tribune Box Set today.

This digital box set includes the reader-acclaimed novels *Warriors of Epona*, *Isle of the Blessed*, and *The Stolen Throne*.

The Eagles and Dragons Tribune Box Set is available from all major on-line e-book retailers, public libraries, or direct from Eagles and Dragons Publishing at:

www.eaglesanddragonspublishing.com

THE CARPATHIAN INTERLUDE COMPLETE TRILOGY

BOOKS I - II - III

Do you love historical horror and books set in the Roman Empire?

Begin a new and chilling adventure in the Roman Empire with #1 Best Selling author and historian Adam Alexander Haviaras' ground-breaking *Carpathian Interlude* trilogy.

This digital box set includes Book I, *Immortui*, Book II, *Lykoi*, and Book III *Thanatos*, as well as a glossary of Latin words, and a new, alternate ending, not available anywhere else!

The *Carpathian Interlude Complete Trilogy* is available in e-book, paperback, and hardcover editions from all major book retailers, public libraries, or direct from Eagles and Dragons Publishing.

HISTORIA

A Gateway to Ancient and Medieval History and Archaeology!

Do you find ancient and medieval history and archaeology fascinating?

If so, then you will love Eagles and Dragons Publishing's *Historia* non-fiction series of books!

In this series, author and historian, Adam Haviaras will take you through such topics as Celtic mythology, medieval knighthood, and the search for the historical King Arthur and Camelot.

If you are interested in ancient and medieval history, and Arthurian studies, then you will want to check out the *Historia* non-fiction series.

Available from all major on-line e-book retailers or direct from Eagles and Dragons Publishing at:

www.eaglesanddragonspublishing.com

Do you love ancient and medieval history and mythology?

Visit 'EDPublishingAgora' on Etsy today to check out our array of vintage, used, new and handmade items including clothing, prints and stationary, jewelry, various collectibles, ceramics and, of course, new and used books, including signed and/or inscribed copies of our own titles.

Check out Eagles and Dragons Publishing's AGORA on Etsy at the following link:

> https://www.etsy.com/ca/shop/EDPublishingAgora

See you in the AGORA, the marketplace for history-themed gifts and books!

Planning a vacation in Europe or the British Isles?

Visit Ancient World Travel for a wide range or helpful articles, travel tips, travel resources, and amazing deals on everything from airfare and accommodation, to car rentals, museum passes, and behind-the-scenes tours of the world's greatest historical sites.

Check out Ancient World Travel today at:

https://www.ancientworldtravel.net/

*Ancient World Travel© is a subsidiary of Eagles and Dragons Publishing©.